ESSAYS ON MEDIEVAL AGRICULTURE AND GENERAL PROBLEMS OF THE MEDIEVAL ECONOMY

ESSAYS ON MEDIEVAL AGRICULTURE AND GENERAL PROBLEMS OF THE MEDIEVAL ECONOMY

M. M. POSTAN

CAMBRIDGE
AT THE UNIVERSITY PRESS
1973

Published by the Syndics of the Cambridge University Press
Bentley House, 200 Euston Road, London NW1 2DB
American Branch: 32 East 57th Street, New York, N.Y.10022

Library of Congress Catalogue Card Number: 72-93135

ISBN: 0 521 08744 9

Printed in Great Britain by
Western Printing Services Ltd,
Bristol

PREFACE

The present volume brings together a number of my papers and articles on various topics of medieval economic and social history, mainly devoted to the problems of English agriculture and rural society. The purpose of this collection, like that of most other collections of the kind, is not only to salvage from oblivion some treasured monuments of one's past endeavours, but to bring together in a convenient form essays and articles which I believe are still being read or should be read by scholars and students. The immodest assumption that these essays in fact deserve to be read and are in fact read led me to exclude from the collection a few articles, papers and reviews which have in my opinion lost (if they ever possessed) their usefulness to latter-day readers.

I hope the essays in this volume may still find their readers. This does not however imply that every fact and idea in the essays has stood the test of time. I believe that the main propositions which they have helped to establish and the historical argument behind them, still stand fully established; but on a number of detailed points I have changed my mind or improved my information and can no longer subscribe to their precise rendering in the original text. Thus the essay which has been cited and debated more than any other in this collection – that on the Chronology of Labour Services – contains statements on, for example, the relation between the size of demesne and the demand for labour services, or the extent and duration of the manorial boom of the thirteenth century, which I would have phrased differently had I been writing the essay now, and have in fact phrased differently in my more recent publications.

For this and other reasons I was sorely tempted to bring the essays up-to-date in both fact and opinion, but except in one instance I have resisted the temptation and chosen to present the essays in their original form. The only exception is my paper on the Economic Foundations of Medieval Society. This paper was read to the International Historical Congress in Paris in 1950, but was rewritten and expanded a year later for publication in the *Jahrbücher für Nationalökonomie*. The German version is the one I have chosen to reproduce here, but it was necessary for me to alter several important passages which, rendered literally from the German, would have been somewhat inaccessible to English readers.

Preface

The persons and institutions who in various ways helped me to assemble and to prepare for publication this collection of essays are too many to be listed here by name but I must single out for special thanks the various members of the editorial staff of the Cambridge University Press, more particularly Mrs Patricia Skinner, Mrs Christine Linehan and Miss Anne Boyd for the efficiency and patience with which they handled this collection and treated their author.

January 1973 M.P.

Acknowledgements

The author and the publisher are most grateful to publishers and learned societies for their co-operation while this volume was under preparation. They are further grateful to the Past and Present Society for permission to reproduce copyright material. Cambridge University Press has made every effort to trace copyright holders and it is regretted if any copyright has been unwittingly infringed.

CONTENTS

PART I
GENERAL

1

THE ECONOMIC FOUNDATIONS OF MEDIEVAL SOCIETY*

1

The subject is the economic base of medieval society. Thus entitled it carries with it a certain early-marxist implication. Yet its conventional meaning is fairly clear – population and land settlement, technique of production and the general trends of economic activity: in short, all those economic facts which can be discussed without concentrating on the working of legal and social institutions and upon relations of class to class.

These topics will be treated in what follows as a single theme. To have to separate them from other phenomena more obviously institutional and social, indeed to separate them from the whole flow of history, is bad enough. But to separate population from settlement, settlement from technique, and all the three from the general trend of prices and production would be a crippling act of mutilation. I therefore propose to deal with these topics more or less in combination.

What makes it necessary and possible to deal with this group of subjects together and yet apart from other topics of medieval history is that they have all been recently drawn into the discussion of general trends of economic activity, or, to use a more fashionable term, into the 'long-term movements' of social income. Historians need no reminding that the main debate in the last ten to twelve years has been concerned with the direction and speed of economic evolution in the Middle Ages. Did economic activity continue to expand through the centuries? Whether it expanded or contracted, what influenced the direction and the scale of the movement? Indeed the whole system of historical development has been questioned. For even if it can be shown that medieval development passed through distinct and even contrasting phases, it is still necessary to see whether the phases were all long enough to qualify as 'long-term trends'.

* This essay is a restatement of the author's paper to the IXe Congrès International des Sciences Historiques in Paris from 28 August to 3 September 1950, which was published in the *Rapports, Librarie Armand Colin* (Paris, 1950), Section III, Histoire économique, sub-section, moyen âge, pp. 225–41. An expanded and revised version was subsequently published in the *Jahrbücher für Nationalökonomie*, 161, 1951.

This last term is very new: indeed so fresh from the oven as to be almost half-baked. But the underlying issue, or at least an aspect of it, has been familiar to medievalists for some time. To Dopsch and Pirenne belongs the credit of having broached the subject, of thereby having broken with the *a priori* assumptions of nineteenth-century historians. The latter had taken it more or less for granted that things medieval started to grow from nothing or next to nothing at the end of the Roman empire and continued to grow without interruption until society reached its blossoming season in the nineteenth century. Both Dopsch and Pirenne set out to prove some sort of continuity between Rome and the Middle Ages; and thus, paradoxically enough, upset the simple continuity of medieval development. For they made the Dark Ages appear not as a starting point of a new and continuous line of evolution, but merely as a culminating stage of the declining trend of the late Roman era, soon to be succeeded by the rising trend of the early Middle Ages. Pirenne himself of course went further than that and introduced a break in the midst of the Carolingian epoch, thus somewhat complicating the symmetry of economic fall and rise.

Since those days, the focus of the controversy has somewhat shifted. It is not that the link between Rome and the Middle Ages has been explained to everybody's satisfaction. All that has happened is that interest has moved from the Romano-Barbarian link to links between later periods. Whether the ascent of medieval economy began in the fifth or the eighth century, did it continue indefinitely? And if it was broken, were the breaks sufficiently few and sufficiently profound to mark off entire epochs? And if whole epochs were marked off, is it possible to speak of periods of expansion succeeded by periods of contraction?

Here again Pirenne anticipated some of the later discussions. His famous study of the stages in the social development of capitalism for the first time formulated the hypothesis of commercial expansion and free trade in the earlier centuries of the Middle Ages followed in the later Middle Ages by commercial stagnation and regulated trade.[1] His thesis was, however, confined to trade, and trade, important as it may have been, was not the main economic activity of medieval men and women. But since his day several historians in various countries working and writing almost simultaneously – Abel in Germany, Schreiner in Norway, van Werverke in Belgium, Perroy in France, and several of us in England – have divided the story of medieval economy as a whole into at least

[1] H. Pirenne, 'Les phases sociales dans le développement du capitalisme médiéval', *Revue Belge de Philologie et d'Histoire*, vol. II (1914). In the history of towns and urban commerce the theme has been anticipated by German students of towns. H. Sieveking, 'Die Mittelälterliche Stadt. Ein Beitrag zur Theorie der Wirtschaftsgeschichte', *Vierteljahrschrift für Sozial und Wirtschaftsgeschichte*, vol. II (1904). For more recent discussions of the late medieval phase see E. Perroy, 'A l'origine d'une Economie contractée: les Crises du XIVe siècle', *Annales* (1949).

two corresponding phases: that of expansion culminating at the beginning of the fourteenth century and that of contraction covering the greater part of the fourteenth and fifteenth centuries.

Very few substantially new facts have been adduced in support of this division. Historians of different regions have always paid attention to the growing agriculture and trade of the eleventh, twelfth and thirteenth centuries. The local indications of an expansion of settlement and agriculture are so clear that the majority of historians have been prepared to accept them as facts.[2] On the other hand the problem of the decrease in settlement and agricultural production in the later Middle Ages has been much debated. Here too the facts have been known for a long time. Since the sixteenth century the Germans have known and written about their *Wüstungen*, the French historians have always known and written about the abandoned and devastated lands and about the reduced population in the later Middle Ages, and the Belgian historians have agreed to regard the late fourteenth and early fifteenth century as the *nadir* of Flemish urban development.[3] Until recently most of these studies were set against the restricted background of local events, by historians whose interests were

[2] In recent works, like that of Genicot on the district of Namur, an increase of settlement and population is in general assumed. L. Genicot, *L'économie rurale namuroise au Bas Moyen Âge* (Namur, 1943), vol. I, p. 66, note 1; also M. Bloch, *La Société Féodale* (Paris, 1939 and 1940), vols. I and II, p. 214; idem, *Les caractères originaux de l'histoire rurale française* (Oslo, 1931), p. 5; R. Doehard, *L'expansion économique belge au Moyen Âge* (Brussels, 1946); H. van Werverke, 'Essor et déclin de la Flandre', *Mélanges Luzzato* (1949). An indirect light on the increase of population and settlement will also be found in F. Ganshof, *Étude sur le développement des villes entre Loire et Rhin au Moyen Âge* (Paris-Brussels, 1943). Recently L. Genicot has directed attention to the indirect but cumulative nature of the evidence: 'Sur les témoignages d'accroissement de la population en occident du XIe au XIIIe siècle', in *Cahiers d'Histoire Mondiale* (1953).

[3] T. Sclafert, *Le Haut-Daphiné au Moyen Âge* (Paris, 1926); R. Boutruche, *La Crise d'une société* (Paris, 1947). The devastations caused by the 'Hundred Years' War in France as a whole have been summarized in H. S. Denifle's well-known *La désolation des églises, monastères et hôpitaux en France pendant la guerre de Cent Ans*, 2 vols. (Paris, 1897–9). The Scandinavian evidence has been dealt with in a number of works, e.g. S. Hasund, 'Den store Manndauden', *Det Norske Folks Liv og Historie*, vol. III (Oslo, 1934); A. Holmsen, 'Den gammelnorske Samfundsordiningen bryter sammen', *Norges Historie*, vol. I (Oslo, 1939); Aksel Christensen, 'Danmarks Befolkning o Bebyggelse i Oldriden', *Nordisk Kultur*, vol. II (Oslo, 1938). In England work has begun on the evidence relating to the 'lost villages'; see M. Beresford, *The Lost Villages of England* (1954), and the works cited therein. However, the 'lost villages' in England are unfortunately much less reliable as proof of the contraction of agriculture than are the *Wüstungen* in Germany. The disappearance of whole villages often results from the planned reorganization of his estates by a landlord, as perhaps was also the case at the time of the founding of the Cistercian abbeys or the enclosures by the wool producers in the late fifteenth and sixteenth centuries. Cf. op. cit. ch. 5. Much more important would be similar topographical evidence of expanding or contracting agriculture in villages which continued in existence; but these have as yet hardly been studied.

in local and regional affairs. Kowalewsky's important account[4] was perhaps the only older treatise on general history which properly emphasized the problems of shrinking economy of the whole of Europe. In recent years however economic historians have been increasingly tending to regard the many local examples of economic decline as symptoms of a single trend which affected most of western Europe and lasted throughout the second half of the fourteenth century and the first half or three-quarters of the fifteenth century.[5]

Dissentient voices have of course been raised. Very recently a very distinguished and much respected Soviet historian of the English medieval village – E. A. Kosminsky – has summarized in an article in *Voprosi Istorii* the results of recent English work in the agrarian history of the later Middle Ages, and, in doing so, has passed under critical (indeed very critical) review the interpretation of the fifteenth century as a period of economic stagnation and decline. Professor Kosminsky's argument is that the Cambridge historians responsible for this interpretation have been blinded by their manorial evidence. The feudal forms of economic organization were doubtless breaking down, but manorial documents, being feudal, were bound to exaggerate the extent of the decline and to neglect new growth outside the feudal villages. Had the Cambridge historians not been so blinded they would have seen that new growths – the cloth industry, the expanding towns, the rising numbers of free peasantry and proletariat – belied the theory of a falling or a stable economic trend. And if new growths were taken into account, the fifteenth century would fall into its place as a forward stage in the dialectical sequence of progressive evolution.[6]

To this point of view I shall have to return again. Other objections are not so radical and general. Most of the historians who raise them do not seem to doubt the agrarian depression or the decline in population in the majority of areas in western Europe. As a rule their doubts are confined to districts which in their opinion did not take part in this movement, and to certain branches of the European economy which in their opinion did not suffer from the agrarian depression but indeed benefited from it, for instance trade and industry.

But these deviations and disagreements apart, most of the current dis-

4 M. Kowalewsky, *Die ökonomische Entwicklung Europas bis zum Beginn der kapitalistischen Wirtschaftsform*, 7 vols. (Berlin, 1901–14).

5 The most recent contributions to this theme have been published in these *Jahrbücher*. F. Lütge, 'Das 14./15. Jahrhundert in der Sozial- und Wirtschaftsgeschichte', *Jahrbuch*, vol. 162, and the papers by Kelter and Abel, note 13 below.

6 E. A. Kosminsky, 'Problems of an English Agrarian History in the XVth century' (*Russian*), *Voprosi Istorii*, vol. 3 (1948). Recently this point of view has again been formulated with reference to the whole of Europe, by Marian Malowist in *Kwartalnik Istoriczny* (1953).

cussion has concentrated not so much on the facts of the fluctuation as on its probable explanations. And in trying to account for the later depressions as well as for the earlier growth, historians have incidentally brought to the surface the fundamental problems of medieval development inherent in the behaviour of prices, currency, technology and population.

2

It has of course always been known that prices rose in the earlier centuries and slumped in the later Middle Ages. True enough, the published price material for the Middle Ages is very exiguous. A few odd figures of local prices in Germany, a rather incoherent collection of figures of d'Avenel's, and certain local collections such as Pelc's for Cracow more or less exhaust all we know about prices on the Continent. But Thorold Rogers's and Beveridge's great work on the prices of England have been available to historians and have yielded invaluable information. That information brings out very clearly both the rise of agricultural prices before the mid-fourteenth century and the sagging tendencies of agriculture prices in the later Middle Ages.[7] In France and in many part of Germany the tendency is of course masked by even greater fall in the bullion content of money. But even where prices expressed in current coinage continued to rise or were at least fairly stable, they continued to fall in terms of silver. It can of course be argued that it would be wrong to calculate medieval prices in terms of bullion, and this argument is true of some commodities and of some classes of society; though it is not wholly true of wheat or rye. It is not, however, necessary to convert current prices into their equivalents in grains of silver to discern the decline of agricultural prices. For behind the apparent buoyancy of current prices it is easy to discover the signs of a fall, sometimes a headlong fall, of real values.[8]

[7] The data of Thorold Rogers's collection *A History of Agriculture and Prices in England 1259–1703*, 5 vols. (Oxford, 1866–87) have been used in several works, including Rogers's own *Six Centuries of Work and Wages* (1909), chaps. VI and VIII. For a somewhat more systematic tabulation of his data, see G. F. Steffen, *Geschichte der englischen Lohnarbeiter*, vol. I, Stuttgart, 1901. Both the data of Rogers's collection and the statistical argument based on it are due to be superseded by the price material assembled under the auspices of Lord Beveridge, and is at present being worked on by a group of English historians. Some anticipation of the data will be found in W. Beveridge, 'The Yield and Price of Corn in the Middle Ages', *Economic History*, a supplement to *The Economic Journal* (1927); idem, 'Wages in the Winchester Manors', *Econ. Hist. Rev.*, vol. VII (1936); M. Postan, 'Some Economic Evidence of Declining Population in the later Middle Ages', *Econ. Hist. Rev.*, vol. II, no. 3 (1950).

[8] There are Lamprecht's rather exiguous series for the Moselle region (*Deutsches Wirtschaftsleben in Mittelalter* (1866), vol. II, pp. 577, 613–14; for Lamprecht's own interpretation of his figures see his 'Die Wirtschaftsgeschichtliche Litteratur, etc.', *Jahrbuch für Nationalökonomie und Statistik*, N.F. XI (1885); and Hanauer's

Indeed the early rise and the later fall in prices have themselves been so generally accepted by historians that discussion has shifted yet another stage further back; to the causes underlying the movement of prices, and mainly to currency and population.

That currency or monetary conditions in general should have been responsible for the fluctuation in prices is an obvious enough conclusion for an economic historian to jump at, especially as it happens to be well supported by what is known about the supply of precious metals. It is now generally accepted that in the twelfth and thirteenth centuries, i.e. the period when prices were rising, European supplies of silver from the mines of Hungary, the Hartz mountains, Tyrol and elsewhere, grew very fast; and that the fourteenth and the first half of the fifteenth century, when prices were falling, coincided with a rapid decline of output in the older fields of silver mining. The conclusion that prices fell or rose through changes in the supply of newly mined bullion is therefore very difficult to resist and in fact has not been much resisted. It will be found in most books discussing the economic trends in the earlier and later centuries of the Middle Ages.[9]

Still more recently an additional currency hypothesis has raised a problem which faithfully echoes the experiences of our own day, i.e. that of European balances of payments. In his famous article on gold, Marc

for Alsace (*Etudes économiques sur l'Alsace ancienne et moderne*, I–II (Paris-Strasbourg, 1876–8). Some fifteenth-century series for Vienna will be found in A. F. Pribram, *Materialen zur Geschichte der Preise und Löhne in Österreich* (Vienna, 1938). Some figures for the very end of the Middle Ages are contained in M. J. Elsas, *Umriss einer Geschichte der Preise und Löhne in Deutschland* (Leiden, 1936). Disconnected price material abounds in local studies mostly in those dealing with the individual towns. For other countries the most useful and revealing has proved to be the study of prices in Cracow: Juljan Pelc, *Ceny w Krakowie w latach 1369–1600* (Lwow, 1935). In spite of D'Avenel's and Levasseur's pioneering efforts, the published evidence of rents, prices and wages in medieval France is more scanty than for most other parts of Europe. The published prices for medieval Netherlands also appear to be rather meagre; the only accessible collection of material is that assembled by H. van Houtte in his *Documents pour servir à l'Histoire des Prix de 1381 à 1794* (Brussels, 1902). Italian prices are available in local and rather disjointed selections, e.g. Magaldi and Faris, 'Notizie Storische e Statistiche sui Prezzi e Salari in Alcune Citta d'Italia', *Annali di Statistica* (1878), Series 2a, III — and L. Cibrario, *Della Economia Politica Del Medio Evo*, 2nd edn (1842). The latter contains the data of Piedmont, mainly Turin.

9 Cf. J. Schreiner, *Pest og Prisfall i Senmiddelaldern* (Oslo, 1948), pp. 50–4. The fluctuations of the silver mining industry have been well known since the early studies of Zycha, Neuburg and Jacob, and later studies have done little more than add detail to the accepted trend. Cf. J. V. Nef, *Cambridge Economic History of Europe*, vol. II, ch. VII, pp. 456–69; A. Zycha, *Des Rechts des deutschen Bergbaus* (1809), pp. 72 ff.; C. Neuburg, *Goslars Bergbau bis 1552* (Hannau, 1892); W. Jacob, *A Historical Inquiry into the Production and Consumption of Precious Metals*, I (1831). For a somewhat similar description of the effects of prices and precious metals on economic life, see M. M. Postan, *Cambridge Economic History of Europe*, vol. II, ch. IV, pp. 207–13.

Bloch tried to show how since the later centuries of the Roman empire Europe had been using up the gold which was its chief means of international payment. Working largely to his suggestion, Professor Lombard has greatly elaborated the theme.[10]

The theme is of course still no more than a mere *motif*; and not until M. Lombard has fortified it with all the necessary counterpoint and orchestration shall we be able to appreciate it and perhaps to criticize it as fully as it deserves. But even if Lombard's thesis were proved it could still apply only to international trade of the Italian cities or to those branches of domestic industry and trade which could be expected to feel the direct impact of Italian commerce. The bulk of medieval economy was not involved in international trade, and some of it was not involved in any trade at all. Fluctuations in foreign trade cannot directly account for new fields, new villages, more crops and more animals, indeed more men, in the thirteenth century, or for the decline in the area and output of medieval agriculture in the later Middle Ages. We are perhaps fortunate in having rid our textbooks of the exaggerated notion of natural economy, and we are prepared to credit the early Middle Ages with a greater amount of trade and, generally speaking, with greater economic sophistication than nineteenth-century historians were prepared to allow. Yet, it is possible to go too far in the opposite direction and to think of medieval peasants as if they were rubber planters of Malaya or cattle ranchers of the Argentine, sowing and reaping in obedience to the economic stimuli of international prices, and wholly dominated by the vagaries of the international balances. And yet nothing short of that would make gold supplies relevant to the main problem of the rise and fall in the general economic activity of the Middle Ages.

Silver coinage was the main medium of local trade. We are all now prepared to agree with Bloch and van Werverke that, whereas gold was used mainly as a means of international payment, silver was the everyday medium of exchange. Yet even silver cannot be easily made to account for the economic trend. If changes in the supply of silver were responsible for the rise in prices, we could expect the rise to be 'general', i.e. to affect more or less the entire range of medieval commodities entering into local trade. But most recent writers have pointed out that the movements of agricultural and industrial prices did not synchronize; that in the twelfth and thirteenth centuries industrial prices did not rise as high and as fast as the prices of wheat and did not fall or stagnate in the later Middle Ages. A closer attention to dates at which prices first rose and then fell in different parts of Europe would also reveal the difficulty of synchronizing

10 Marc Bloch, 'Le Problème de l'Or au Moyen Âge', *Les Annales d'Histoire Economique et Sociale* (1933); M. Lombard. 'L'Or Musulman du VIIe au XIe siècle', *Annales* (1947), no. 2).

the chronology of price movements with what we know about the dates at which the supplies of silver expanded or contracted. It will be equally difficult to relate the geographical spread of price movements with the location of mining activities.[11]

A still greater difficulty is that the stocks of silver, always large, became larger still by the end of the thirteenth century, so that newly mined metal made a relatively small and declining difference to the total supplies of mintable bullion. Much more important must have been the changing uses of existing stocks – above all the varying proportions of metal hoarded or 'de-hoarded' or employed as a base for credit. In fact, to use a more fashionable sentence, the changes in 'liquidity preferences' were bound to influence both the course of prices and economic activity much more than the annual increments of new metal.

As we know little about the changes in 'liquidity preferences' and the circulation of bullion, we must find it difficult to relate them to the long-term developments of the medieval economy as they are apt to be related in the discussion of our contemporary economy. During the twelfth and thirteenth centuries the techniques of credits and payments greatly improved and commercial turnover in general became much quicker. Some gold and silver may also have been tempted out of hiding and out of its various non-monetary uses. The volume of money must therefore have greatly increased, and in doing so helped to raise the level of prices. But can we be equally certain that in the fifteenth and fourteenth centuries the circulation contracted? The disturbed conditions of the time may have led to some hoarding, but royal and other taxation grew and thereby helped to put into circulation an even larger proportion of national incomes. Moreover, the financial technique of merchants and bankers did not deteriorate but may even have improved. It is thus by no means certain that the total volume of money in the later Middle Ages declined; and it is very doubtful whether the decline, if there was any, was sufficiently great to reverse the entire economic trend of the time.

3

Thus, on second thoughts, the connection between new bullion, on the one hand, and prices and economic activity on the other, loses much of its

[11] On the relative functions of silver and gold, see Marc Bloch, op. cit., and H. van Werwerke, 'Monnaie, Lingots ou Marchandises', *Les Annales d'Histoire Economique et Sociale* (1932). One of the most important features of Marc Bloch's and Lombard's articles is that they have for the first time in medieval historiography given full weight to the processes of 'thesaurisation' and 'de-thesaurisation'. Unfortunately the geographical and chronological landmarks in medieval price movements have so far escaped the attention of historians. The first steps should be a study of prices in the mining areas and in the regions with which their commercial relations were closest.

force. Indeed, second thoughts are bound to lead to another and perhaps a more fundamental factor than any so far discussed, i.e. population. On broad and largely theoretical grounds a rise and fall in population would be compatible with all the phenomena which our evidence exhibits and should raise none of the objections to which other general explanations are open. When population rose agriculture expanded under conditions which economists would recognize as those of steeply diminishing returns, and agricultural prices were bound to rise. On the other hand, when population fell supplies of agricultural products would be more plentiful, relative to the amount of resources engaged in their production and relative to the demand for food, and prices would be correspondingly lower. A rise and fall in population would also have a so-to-speak selective effect on prices in that they would produce a corresponding movement in the prices of agriculture products, but would have little effect on prices of commodities not greatly subject to diminishing returns, i.e. most industrial products.[12]

All this is theory and, like all theories, it may at first sight appear too simple to fit the infinite variety of medieval experiences; but it so happens that this particular argument also fits with what from independent evidence we have now learned about medieval population. One class of such evidence – that of occupation of the land – must be dealt with here in greater detail. It is perhaps too far removed from the conventional interest of demographers and sufficiently wide in its implications as to touch on almost all the aspects of economic history covered by this paper.

For the earlier centuries of the Middle Ages the facts of internal colonization, of new villages, and of new settlements provides our main evidence of rising population. In England, where the study of settlement is still in an embryonic condition, some light on the growth of population between the eleventh and the fourteenth century is thrown by manorial surveys. But in France and Germany, where the study of settlement has been more advanced and surveys are few, the evidence of internal colonization has been rightly used as proof of growing numbers of men and women. *Mutatis mutandis* evidence of falling numbers in the later Middle Ages has been found in the abandoned holdings and in the contracting areas under cultivation. In this way the story of expanding and contracting population merges into that of expanding and contracting agriculture: which is as

[12] This is not the place to cite the vast literature of *Siedlungsgeschichte*. R. Koebner's essay on the settlement and colonization in Europe in *Cambridge Economic History*, vol. I, with its bibliographies is still the best summary of the subject. Professor Koebner however differs from other historians in so far as he refuses to accept as proven the connection between expanding settlement and growing population in the early Middle Ages. The most recent statement of the position on the German dates for *Wüstungen* is to be found in H. Polendt, 'Die Verbreitung der mittelalterlichen Wüstungen in Deutschland', *Göttinger geographische Abhandlung*, Part 3 (1953).

it should be in a society where agriculture was so important and was so predominantly 'peasant'.[13]

Thus, prices, population and agricultural production reveal themselves as different aspects of the same process, going through more or less the same phases of development, combining and interacting in every important event of medieval economic history. But their very interaction makes it difficult to single any of them out as the prime mover of economic change. In some ways the movement of population was more fundamental than any of the other economic changes; yet it would be difficult to treat the population trends as the sole or final cause. The search for final causes, here as in other fields of history, will inevitably result in a circular argument. For if the fall and rise in population caused the general fluctuations of medieval economy, what caused the fall and rise in population? It is theoretically possible, but on historical grounds not very probable, that a biological factor was at work: some sudden mutation in the human capacity for procreation. The Black Death could perhaps be regarded as a biological catastrophe; yet it is doubtful whether the Black Death, even if taken in conjunction with other great epidemics of the fourteenth century, could by itself account for the population trend of the later Middle Ages. For one thing, signs of falling trends appear before the Black Death and do not disappear after the direct effects of the great pestilences should no longer have been felt. Of other more fundamental biological changes we know nothing, and I doubt whether anything about them worth knowing will ever be discovered.[14]

[13] M. M. Postan, *Cambridge Economic History*, vol. II, pp. 167–8 and 214–16; idem, 'Some Economic Evidence of Declining Population in the late Middle Ages', *Economic History Review* (1950); W. Abel, *Agrarkrisen und Agrarkonjunktur in Mitteleuropa vom 13. bis zum 19. Jahrhundert* (Jena, 1935), pp. 20–4 and 45–7; idem, *Die Wüstungen des ausgehenden Mittelalters* (Jena, 1943), pp. 53–71; idem, 'Wüstungen und Preisverfall im spätmittelalterlichen Europa', *Jahrbuch für Nat. Ökonomie und Statistik*, vol. 165 (1953), pp. 399 f., and F. Lütge, op. cit. See also A. Levett, *Black Death on the Estates of the Bishopric of Winchester*, Oxford Studies in Legal and Social History, vol. v (Oxford, 1916). An exact population analysis of the Middle Ages may be found in J. C. Russell, *British Medieval Population* (Albuquerque, 1948).

[14] This argument against the Black Death as the prime cause of declining population has been repeatedly advanced in recent discussion of the subject in England and in Norway: A. Levett, op. cit., cf. M. Postan, op. cit.; A. Holmsen, 'Den gammelnorske Samfundsordningen bryter sammen', *Norges Historie*, I (Oslo, 1939). The tendency to explain the decline in population only in terms of mortality and the epidemics of the fourteenth and fifteenth centuries, is clear in the latest German writings on the subject, especially in E. Kelter's work referred to above. Kelter presents a list of the great epidemics, which is unfortunately much longer than those previously available. He seems moreover to assume that famine and higher prices were always the results of a plague outbreak, that before 1349 and after 1500 there were hardly any epidemics and famines, and that the reduction in population began in 1349. If it had been possible to prove these assumptions, the population problem of the late Middle Ages would have been much easier to solve.

Could the change be accounted for by geographical, above all, climatic causes? There is every reason for thinking that the agricultural depression was ushered in during the second decade of the fourteenth century by a succession of disastrous harvests. In England a sequence of wet years and inundations spread ruin and famine over the countryside; in Germany and France the period between 1309 and 1323 was also punctuated by years of hard weather and low harvests. Some Scandinavian students have also blamed a climatic revolution for the permanent change in agriculture economics of West Norway and Iceland. Whereas both countries had been able to supply their own bread before the fourteenth century, they became greatly dependent on imports in the late Middle Ages, and to all intents and purposes ceased to grow their own corn.

The argument is plausible but inconclusive. As far as England goes, one or two decades of bad crops would not account for an economic trend lasting a century and a half. Even if it were proved that during that time the eastern coastline of England sank and a permanent change occurred in the hydrography of Britain, it still remains difficult to understand why climatic changes which were sufficiently 'permanent' to depress English agriculture until the last quarter of the fifteenth century, should yet have allowed an agricultural boom in the sixteenth century. It is just as hard to understand why the so-called wet cycle should have pushed agriculture into a depression not only in damp countries like England, where bad harvests indeed resulted mostly from excessive rainfall, but also in the drier areas of south and south-west Europe, where bad harvests were mostly caused by insufficient rain. As for West Norway and Iceland, it still remains to be proved that they had been able to support themselves out of their own food production in the earlier centuries, and that the decline of arable farming in the later centuries was not due to purely economic causes, such as the influx of cheap grain from the Baltic.[15]

4

We are thus inevitably thrown back upon the more conventional and more purely social explanations. By analogy with other and similar ages in European history or with other civilizations similarly conditioned, historians and economists will inevitably think of the inherent tendencies of

[15] A. Steensberg's lecture to the British Association in 1952 contains the most recent and best account of the climate theory. Cf. also W. Werenskiold, 'Klimavekslinger som historisk faktor', *Samtinden* (Oslo, 1924); O. A. Johnson, *Norwegische Wirtschaftsgeschichte* (Jena, 1939). In the thirteenth and perhaps twelfth centuries Norway was greatly dependent on imports of grain from England: see Hakon Hakonsen's speech in 'Köningsaga' cited by F. C. Dahlmann, *Dänemark* (Geschichte der Europäischen Staaten), vol. 1 (Hamburg, 1940). Cf. also H. Bächtold, *Der norddeutsche Handel im 12. und Beginn des 13. Jahrhunderts* (1910), pp. 165 ff.

populations on the Malthusian level of existence. Our knowledge of the demographic trends in the over-populated countries of the Far East, but above all recent studies of the Swedish population in the seventeenth and eighteenth centuries and of the Irish population on the eve of the potato famine, give us some insight as to what might happen to over-populated countries on a margin of subsistence. In Ireland the potato, which had borne well on newly reclaimed land, suddenly gave out in the late forties mainly through plant disease; and population, which had previously added to its potato crops as it married and bred, suddenly found itself faced with famine.[16] It will not be too fanciful to project a somewhat similar story into the facts of the Middle Ages and to see in the falling production of the later centuries a natural punishment for earlier over-expansion. As long as the colonization movement went forward and new lands were taken up, the crops from virgin lands encouraged men to establish new families and settlements. But after a time the marginal character of marginal lands was bound to assert itself, and the honeymoon of high yields was succeeded by long periods of reckoning, when the poorer lands, no longer new, punished the men who tilled them with failing crops and with murrain of sheep and cattle. In these conditions a fortuitous combination of adverse events, such as the succession of bad seasons in the second decade of the fourteenth century, was sufficient to reverse the entire trend of agricultural production and to send the population figures tumbling down.[17]

Once started this development may well have continued beyond the point at which, at least theoretically, a stable equilibrium between land and population had been reached, and as a result of epidemics, the lands unsuited to arable cultivation ceased to be taken up. Yet the reduction in area under the plough was so persistent, uninterrupted and cumulative that it might seem that in Europe at this time a period of 'secular decolonization' was starting. That such a secular process did indeed take place cannot as yet be proved with certainty. But in general the hypothesis

[16] E. Heckscher, 'Swedish Population in the Seventeenth and Eighteenth Centuries', *Economic History Review* (1950); K. H. Connell, *The Population of Ireland, 1750–1845* (Oxford, 1950); idem, 'The Colonization of Waste Land in Ireland', *Economic History Review* (1950).

[17] Some but not all of the aspects of this process are treated in the German literature under the heading of *Fehlsiedlung*. The role played by *Fehlsiedlung* in this narrower sense as cause of the subsequent *Wüstungen* has been worked out in a series of studies: e.g. in A. Grund's study of the Wienerwald in *Geographische Abhandlungen* (1901), or A. Dopsch, *Die ältere Wirtschafts- und Sozialgeschichte der Bauern und Alpenländer Österreichs* (Oslo, 1930). See also W. Abel, 'Wüstungen und Preisfall ...' in the *Conrad's Jahrbücher* (1953), pp. 405 ff., and the evidence cited there. The argument is however based on the assumption that *Wüstungen* could only occur on newly settled land or on poor soils. The concept of 'marginal land' is not a static one; soils could gradually become marginal in the course of centuries (see below).

of a decolonization is in complete harmony with the economic basis of medieval settlement and farming. Under the prevailing circumstances the pressure to give up marginal land in the fourteenth and fifteenth centuries could have been just as strong and as steady as was the need to bring new land under cultivation in earlier centuries.

This pressure might have been the consequence of *Fehlsiedlung* or of the exhaustion and working-out of the land. In time people found that they had reached the limits of the land's productivity; not only because they were reclaiming new, poor soils, but also because they had been cultivating old land for too long. Naturally historians are reluctant to subscribe to a theory of general impoverishment of the soil in the Middle Ages. Nevertheless it is important not to disregard the possibility that in the Middle Ages not enough was done to maintain the fertility of large areas of cultivable land, especially on the holdings of dependent peasants. In England the manorial smallholders were so weighed down with dues, and their grazing facilities were so restricted, that it must have been very difficult for them to keep their land in good heart.

As long as land was being subjected to excessive or improvident cultivation, a reduction in the area of older settlement and an exodus of population to virgin land was necessary, not only to support the growing population, but to replace the old land which had been exhausted. The fact that the settlement of fresh land ended in the fourteenth and fifteenth centuries, owing to the exhaustion of the reserves of virgin land, made it impossible to compensate for the deterioration of old land.[18]

If this is the case, the decline of settlement and of population in the age of the plagues must be attributed not only to the epidemics but also to more fundamental historical causes. The slow and unven way in which the population and agricultural production recovered from the plagues could be explained by the fact that the plague outbreaks occurred at a time when population and production were in any case on the decline.

[18] In England the question of medieval English harvest yields has been vigorously debated, but without result: W. Beveridge, 'The Yield and Price of Corn in the Middle Ages', *Economic History* (supplement to *Economic Journal*), 1929; M. K. Benett, 'British Wheat Yield per Acre for Seven Centuries', *loc. cit.* (1937). The result of the discussion seems to be that yields were indeed low, but that no noticeable decline took place in the course of the Middle Ages. This is not wholly convincing however; not only because no allowance has been made for difficulties with tithes, as R. Lennard, op. cit. 1936, has already stressed, but also because the conclusion is not certain. All the material which Beveridge has collected relates to harvest yields on the demesne of the bishop of Winchester. However, in the later Middle Ages the areas of directly cultivated demesne land declined because large areas of less productive land were rented out. Under these circumstances, constant yields must be taken as an indication of falling yields. The yields declined even though the demesne enjoyed advantages in manuring and cultivation, which the peasants' land did not as a rule receive. Cf. however R. Lennard. 'The Alleged Exhaustion of the Soil in Medieval England', *Economic Journal* (1922).

The persistent over-population may also have been corrected by this downward trend, as well as by the higher death rate in the year of the plague. According to the evidence from Italy it was only after the third, and apparently the last general outbreak of the plague in the last quarter of the fourteenth century that an equilibrium between population and production, or perhaps even the possibility of a renewed increase, would seem to have been re-established.

These hypotheses are tentative in the extreme; mere guesses which may well turn out to be untrue. They are suggested here not in order to account for the population trends but in order to underline the complexity of historical causation. The growth and decline of population was probably the most fundamental of all the processes behind the increasing and declining production; yet it may itself have been influenced by upward and downward trends in medieval agriculture. Further study may reveal other forces behind the population movement – above all forces springing from revolutionary and irreversible changes in the constitution of the family in time of agricultural expansion. Medievalists will remember the old-standing problem of the *Großhufe* and the *Kleinhufe* and the possibility that at one time the 'great family' broke into smaller families of a modern kind.[19] Recent archaeological research, especially in Denmark, has produced circumstantial evidence supporting the hypothesis of a radical change in size of the north German family some time in the early Middle Ages. But why should families have broken up? Many answers to this question are possible, but the most plausible appears to be that the movement of colonization opened possibilities for the establishment of new households and in general opened horizons which broke the cohesion of the patriarchial family of the *Großhufe*. Here again colonization, growth of production and a revolutionary change in the basic unit of population appear both as causes and as effects.[20]

19 The general tendency among historians is to treat the break-up of the great *Manse* or *Hufe* as a natural result of denser population, even though it ceased to be the typical '*terra unius familie*' long before the first signs of land scarcity appeared. C. E. Perrin, 'Observations sur le manse dans la région parisienne au début du IXe siècle', *Annales d'Histoire sociale* (1945). Marc Bloch, however, saw a connection between the great *Hufe* and the patriarchal 'great' family, and concluded that the occupation of European interior in the early centuries of the Germanic settlement must have been the work of the patriarchal family (*Cambridge Economic History*, vol. 1 (Cambridge, 1943), pp. 268–9). In his book on Burgundy, André Déléage also emphasizes the connection between the *Hufe*, the size of the ploughing team and the constitution of the family (*La Vie Rurale en Bourgogne jusqu'au début du onzième siècle* (Mâcon, 1941), pp. 300–60). Déléage's book also contains a useful summary of the literature on the subject and a fairly comprehensive bibliography. The only sociological study of medieval family, though unfortunately a static one, will be found in G. C. Homans, *English Villages of the Fifteenth Century* (Harvard, 1941).

20 The study on the ground plans of the family farmsteads is mainly that of the Danish archaeologists, Gudmund Hatt and Axel Steensberg. I am indebted to

5

The increases and decreases in production were related to changes in technique, especially changes in agricultural methods, although technical development remained remarkably static for the whole of the Middle Ages. Changes in agricultural technique in the early centuries were probably greater than they were to be in the later Middle Ages. Yet even then they were not quite so fundamental as it is sometimes assumed. We are sometimes told that men in the early Middle Ages harnessed draught animals by yoke from the shoulders instead of continuing the Roman method of harnessing animals from neck or horn. But such evidence as there is suggests that the medieval practice was neither consistent nor uniform, and that in some parts of Europe older practices not only survived, but were also apt to be revived. It is equally difficult to take *au pied de la lettre* the argument that Germanic settlers introduced into general use the heavy plough furnished with wheels, coulter and moulding board and drawn by a team of eight oxen. The evidence now available suggests that the transition from earlier and lighter types to the later and heavy ones was gradual and slow, and that the heavy plough was not in universal use in northern Europe for centuries after the German settlement. It also appears that on lands regularly cultivated, however wet and clayey, the lighter ploughs and the smaller teams were able to cut deep furrows and to turn them to one side no less effectively than the heavier wheeled plough. Where the latter was indispensable was not so much in routine ploughing of cultivated fields as in the breaking up of virgin clay. The use of the heavy plough and the large team was becoming essential and habitual as men in the early Middle Ages were extending their occupation of heavy soils. But if so, the operative factor was not the technical revolution represented by the new plough, but the great work of reclamation which men were called upon to carry out and, above all, the wholesale penetration of the lowland forests. At a risk of a quibble it is worth noting that what the early Middle Ages witnessed was not a major technical innovation which made new reclamations possible but a vast movement of reclamations which compelled men to use tools and techniques best suited for the purpose.[21]

Dr Steensberg for an opportunity to see the groundplans of the Jutland farms excavated by him. Cf. his preliminary studies, e.g. 'Middelalderens og Renaissancetidens Bondegoliger', *Naturens Verden* (Copenhagen, 1940), and 'To Gaardtomter og en Forsvarsvold paa Nördskov Hede', *Nationalmuseets Arbejdsmark* (Copenhagen, 1948), and 'Boligskik paa landet i Danmarks Middelalder', *Nordisk Kultur* (1953).

21 Lefebvre des Noettes, *L'attelage et le cheval de selle à travers les âges* (Paris, 1931); Axel Steensberg, 'North West European Plough-types of Prehistoric Times and the Middle Ages', *Acta Archaeologica*, vol. VII (Copenhagen, 1933), especi-

The invasion of plains and forests is the salient fact of European economy in the Dark Ages. Yet even this was neither as novel nor as wholesale an enterprise as historians had once upon a time believed. As a result of more recent work, archaeologists are now prepared to assume that deforestation by fire and the intermittent cultivation of forest lands began early in prehistoric times and had gone very far by the time the German settlers entered north-western Europe. We have also ceased to regard the shifting occupation and intermittent cultivation of soil as a prehistoric phase wholly replaced by superior field systems at the very dawn of the Middle Ages. Most historians of English agriculture are now prepared to find through the Middle Ages, indeed until the eighteenth century, signs of the system which is known in Britain as *Runrig*, or 'infield-outfield', with its small core of permanent fields surrounded by what Germans sometimes call *Außenland*, i.e. large areas intermittently cultivated.[22]

The older story of the evolving field systems has thus been 'concertinaed' out: made to spread over a greatly extended stretch of historical time. Yet, however extended, the story still places within the earlier centuries of the Middle Ages most of the medieval advances in land utilization. The permanent field system based on a two-field or three-field rotation became general; and, to judge from the English evidence, the period between the end of the twelfth century and the beginning of the fourteenth also saw further improvements in the field plans and, above all, the substitution of three-course rotation for the two-course. Elsewhere the period saw other great innovations in the man's use of natural resources. Men in the Netherlands perfected their technique of drainage and defence against the sea; the sheep-farming population of Britain bred the great flocks of high quality sheep which became such a marked feature of English agriculture in the twelfth century; millers all over Europe learned to build and to use overshot wheels; wine growers of Gascony created in the course of the twelfth and thirteenth centuries the largest region of specialized viticulture ever known in European history.[23]

ally pp. 279–80; G. F. Payne, 'The Plough in Ancient Britain', *The Archaeological Journal* (1947). Cf. Paul Leser, *Die Entstehung und Veibreitung des Pfluges* (Munster, 1931). Ch. Parrain, 'The evolution of Agriculture Technique', *Cambridge Economic History*, vol. I, pp. 138–41; also p. 166 (sheep).

22 M. W. Beresford, 'Lot Acres', *Economic History Review*, vol. XIII (1943); J. Saltmarsh and H. C. Darby, 'The Infield-Outfield System on a Norfolk Manor', *Economic History*, Supplement to *Economic Journal*, vol. III, p. 30 (1935). The survival or revival of *Feld-Graswirtschaft* or of the intermittent cultivation of outfields in eighteenth-century Germany is described in one of the oldest histories of North German agriculture: J. C. Koppe, *Mitteilungen über die Geschichte des Ackerbaues in Norddeutschland*, etc. (Berlin, 1860), ch. I; cf. W. Abel, *Die Wüstungen ...*, pp. 34–5; Ch. Parrain, ibid., pp. 127–8.

23 H. L. Gray, *English Field Systems* (1915); H. Pirenne, *Histoire de Belgique* (Brussels, 1929), vol. I, pp. 309–10, 313–14; A. Perrin, *La civilisation de la vigne*

It is thus more or less certain that technical improvements played their part, however modest, in the agricultural expansion of the earlier Middle Ages. Whether the improvements in the later Middle Ages were sufficient to compensate for the decline in production is more doubtful. From the end of the thirteenth century onwards improvement went forward more slowly and was less extensive. A little piecemeal enclosure, a few local departures from two-field rotation, and here and there an increase in the cultivation of legumes more or less exhaust the technical changes in fifteenth-century England. The cultivation of vine apparently spread all over Germany, mostly at the expense of arable farming. Technical crops – flax, woad, madder, hemp and hops – flourished in parts of Germany where rye and wheat used to be grown. Above all in Holland technical crops became one of the mainstays of national economy. Yet it is doubtful whether if measured in values and in areas the new crops were sufficient to compensate for the decline of arable farming in countries as hard hit by the depression as Germany. In Italy alone the revival of agricultural investment in the fifteenth century may have brought with it a great rise in agricultural output as a whole. Elsewhere investments and agriculture declined rather than grew and technical progress was insufficient to compensate for falling population and for adverse physical conditions.[24]

6

It would of course be too much to expect that the trends should be uniform all over Europe, and that in every branch of the economy they should have been equally strong. Our knowledge of the early Middle Ages is too slight for us to be able to discern the local conditions behind the apparently uniform façade of economic expansion.[25] Otherwise we would doubtless discover that certain areas were stagnating or were in decline, while other areas prospered. We know enough to be able to state that

(Paris, 1938); R. Dion, 'Grands traits d'une géographie viticole de la France', *Revue d'Histoire générale de la Philosophie et d'Histoire générale de la Civilisation* (1944); R. Boutruche, op. cit., pp. 142–3, 148–50; idem, 'Le peuplement de l'Entre-Deux-Mers', *Annales d'Histoire Econ. et Soc.* (1935); F. Bassermann-Jordan, *Geschichte des Weinbaues* (Frankfurt-am-Main, 1907) .

[24] C. M. Cipolla, 'Trends in Italian History in the later Middle Ages', *Econ. Hist. Rev.*, vol. II (1949); idem, *Studi di Storia della Moneta* (Pavia, 1948); W. Abel, *Die Wüstungen . . .*, pp. 30–3; J. Wimmer, *Geschichte des deutschens Bodens* Hule, 1905), pp. 263–7; H. Pirenne, op. cit., vol. II, p. 447; nevertheless the evidence which Pirenne quotes in these footnotes does not appear to be sufficient to justify his glowing account of abundant prosperity. The 1473 statement about the abundance of cattle does not reveal how recent the abundance was. J. F. Niermeyer, *De Wording van onze Volkshouding* (The Hague, 1946), chaps. V and VI and bibliographical references in Appendix; R. Häpke, *Die Entstehung der Holländischen Wirtschaft* (Verslag Hist. Genootschap, 1927); M. Postan, 'The Fifteenth Century', *Econ. Hist. Rev.*, vol. IX (1939).

[25] Cf. L. Genicot in *Journal of World History* (1953).

the trade of the Rhine delta did not participate in the great advances of the eleventh and twelfth centuries; that in the thirteenth century in Norway the economy and in particular trade contracted; and that the prosperity of French Flanders and Artois declined at the same time as Flanders was approaching its full glory.[26] We know just enough of both Sicilys and of Provence to recognize that their very promising developments of the early twelfth century were not carried into the thirteenth century, and that their economy was stagnating at the time when the rest of Italy and France were forging vigorously ahead. We are told that in Bavaria the settlement of the plains was complete and had clearly come to an end at the end of the twelfth century. For the greater part of the twelfth century whole areas of north and north-west England as well as parts of the west midlands may have passed through a period of decreasing settlement and falling land prices.[27]

Because of the relative abundance of sources it is easier to recognize the exceptions to the decline of the fourteenth and fifteenth centuries. Quattrocento Italy was an exception in more ways than one. Arguing from indirect evidence (and some of it is very indirect indeed), some Italian historians have recently shown north and central Italy forging ahead in the fifteenth century. The growth of agriculture may well have stimulated domestic trade. But other exceptions were also to be found. North Holland entered upon a period of great maritime commercial development in the fifteenth century, at the very time when English, French, Flemish and even Hanseatic trade was stagnating or even declining. It is also possible that the great Brabantine fairs and the towns of southern Germany may have begun at the same period to benefit from the tribulations of the Hansa. In England, London and perhaps also Southampton and Bristol flourished while most other towns experienced a decline. For a certain time the rise of cloth-working areas compensated to a limited extent for the decline in agriculture. The cloth industries of

[26] M. M. Postan, *Cambridge Economic History*, II, pp. 185 and 217; H. Bächtold, op. cit.; A. Bugge, 'Der Untergang der norwegischen Seeschiffahrt', *Vierteljahresschrift für Sozial- und Wirtschaftsgeschichte* (1906).

[27] R. Lopez, *Cambridge Economic History*, II, 301–2; Ph. Wolff, *Commerce et Marchands de Toulouse* (Paris, 1954), pp. 32–3; Regine Pernous, 'Le Moyen Âge jusqu'au 1291' in *Histoire du Commerce de Marseille* (Gaston Rambert), I, pp. 295 ff. For both Sicilys the rather exaggerated account of G. Yver, *Le Commerce et les Marchands dans l'Italie meridionale au XIIIe et au XIVe Siècle* shoild be compared with the more recent studies. Cf. R. Pontieri, 'Un capitano della guerra del Vespro' in his *Ricerche sulla crisi della monarchia meridionale nel secolo XIIIe* (Naples, 1942), pp. 158 ff. for the middle of the thirteenth century; and R. Caggese, *Roberto d'Anzio e i suoi tempi* (Florence, 1922–30), I, ch. v, and pp. 506, 536–7, for the general economic depression in agriculture and trade in the second half of the thirteenth and the beginning of the fourteenth centuries. For details on the Bavarian settlements see P. Dollinger, *L'évolution des classes rurales en Bavière* (1949), p. 79.

England, North Holland, Brabant and the smaller Flemish towns appear to have benefited from the decline of the great cloth exporting centres of Florence and the four great 'Leden' of Flanders. Some German historians have recently suggested that the late Middle Ages should be regarded as the high point in the prosperity of German towns, and that building activity in the towns should be seen as compensating for the *Wüstungen* in the countryside.[28]

Although this opinion has not yet been established, it is very probable that immediately after the great plague various European towns experienced a short, intoxicating period of prosperity under the stimulus of the relative superabundance of capital.[29]

Such anomalies are sufficiently numerous to upset the construction of a single line of development. They strengthen the historian's inborn scepticism of generalizations and trends. However, the comfortable luxury of any such scepticism is denied to the economic historian. In dealing with economic growth the historian must assume that there have been general, long-lasting economic trends in western European history, or otherwise the economic and social picture of Europe in 1950 would look exactly like that obtaining in 950. The contradictory nature of the late medieval sources may justify some doubts among economic historians as to whether, in the fourteenth and above all in the fifteenth centuries, the European economy did in fact experience a single and uniform reversal of its development trend.

If nevertheless I personally am inclined to play down these doubts and to accept the hypothesis of a general decline, this is mainly, though not entirely, because if properly weighed and tested, the evidence points in this direction.

The most important of the tests is that of historical consistency. Consistency is of course very difficult to test, as it demands the ability to identify the leading facts and situations from the outset. However, from time to time the sources give us clear indications. Thus we must try to set the local fortunes of trade and industry against the background of Flanders and the Hansa. By the same token favourable developments in local cloth industries must be related to the general decline of industry, which affected not only the older centres of the textile industry in Flanders and Florence, but also most branches of the mining industry.[30]

28 M. M. Postan, *Cambridge Economic History*, II, pp. 191 ff.; E. Carus-Wilson, idem, pp. 143 ff.; E. Kelter. op. cit., p. 343; F. Lütge, op. cit., *passim*. To put it mildly, it is very unrealistic to maintain that the fall in cloth production was compensated for by a growth of the silk or even the cotton industry, M. Malowist, op. cit.

29 R. Lopez, op. cit., p. 343.

30 M. M. Postan, op. cit., pp. 201 ff.; J. U. Nef, *Cambridge Economic History*, II, pp. 456 ff.

We can however take the test of historical consistency further. Thus we could argue that it would be difficult to reconcile the growth in trade and industry with the overall picture of economic life, especially the decline in agriculture. In the late Middle Ages, as in earlier centuries, agriculture was still by far the most important form of employment and the largest source of national income. On the basis of a rough *per capita* calculation, it must have accounted for 90 per cent of the entire income of western Europe. How can we reconcile a continued growth in trade and industry with more than a century of depressed income and production in agriculture?

It is of course possible to imagine an unusual interplay of circumstances which would allow trade and industry to expand while agricultural production and the income derived therefrom were shrinking. This might well have been the case if the demand for urban goods and services came mainly from the urban population itself. It could also have been caused by a restructuring of the income from land resulting from the plague. It has not in fact been argued that the money income of the rural population increased as a result of social and demographic changes brought about by the plague.

Some such changes may have taken place; yet even where they occurred, their general effect on urban trade could hardly have been as favourable as has recently been suggested by some historians. Much confusion on this point could have been avoided if a distinction had been drawn between national and individual incomes. The average real income of individual villagers may have risen, but this rise need not necessarily have led to higher aggregate cash outlays on urban products. These outlays must in the end be dependent on the sum total of money incomes of the rural producers and land-owners, and this was dependent on the total quantity of agricultural produce not consumed by the villagers themselves and available for sale. The volume of such produce cannot have risen very much, and may indeed have fallen. Certainly the number of rural consumers dropped, but so also did total production, while personal consumption by the individual consumers probably rose. On the other hand we know that agricultural prices had a general tendency to fall, so that even if here and there a small increase in marketable supplies did occur, its effect was in all probability counteracted by lower prices. One exception to this was perhaps those areas in which animal husbandry predominated and which benefited from higher prices for animal products. However relative price movement may have held back the effective demand for urban goods since urban prices were, as we know, rising relatively to corn prices.[31]

[31] M. M. Postan, *Some Economic Evidence*, etc., pp. 242 ff. The examination of this problem from the point of view of total money income has the advantage that it allows us to disregard changes in the costs of production and wages and

As conditions necessary for trade to flourish while agriculture languishes are very rarely present together, merchants and trade centres in all agricultural communities are apt to be badly affected by years of bad harvests and low agricultural income. For this reason alone we shall be justified in assuming that most urban communities were stagnating in the late Middle Ages. To be sure, the German towns have recently been presented as exceptions to this rule. Before one can accept this exception, it is necessary to subject the development of German towns to a more precise, purely economic analysis. Direct evidence of urban prosperity is very scant. Some such evidence is provided by the growing prosperity of the rising south German towns. But for the majority of German towns only indirect evidence is available, mainly that of the handsome buildings erected in the fifteenth century.[32] Unfortunately this evidence is not relevant to the problem of townsmen's consumption. Impressive buildings need not indicate increased wealth or greater economic activity in the towns. The periods at which the towns received their most distinguished buildings, were not always the times of greatest development in trade and industry. The erection of town buildings can be stimulated by a great number of social factors, of which a high average income of the inhabitants need not necessarily be one.

the differences between the various levels of agricultural society. For another method of estimating rural income, by reference to its sources, see Abel, *Wüstungen und Preisfall*, pp. 413 f.

32 E. Kelter, op. cit., pp. 198 ff. An additional argument is based on the large relative excess of capital as a result of the decrease in population. The new relationships between population, land and capital, which Lütge, op. cit., pp. 168 ff. has referred to, are naturally very significant for the changes in social structure and *per capita* wealth in the country. Whether these new relationships are of equal significance for the urban communities is not so certain. A redistribution of wealth resulting in larger individual holdings of capital might have caused an immediate acceleration of expenditure and a rise in apparent prosperity, but the upward movement must have been very transitory. If we leave out of account houses and land in the towns, the productive resources of urban industry consisted predominantly of working capital. The redistribution of circulating capital would lead to a rising *per capita* income only for as long as the sum total of resulting output also grew. If production and turnover in the main branches of industry and commerce declined, transactions *per capita* income could not have risen to the same extent as *per capita* capital. In these circumstances the returns on assets and rates of profit would have fallen (cf. R. Lopez, *Cambridge Economic History*, p. 344). If profits in fact declined as Professor Lopez believed they did, the same, or nearly the same, quantity of capital would be yielding a reduced quantity of disposable income. This is a special case of a reduction in the marginal productivity of capital so great as to reduce its average productivity as well. A remarkable variant of this argument is represented by the theory that when harvests failed, strangers took over the houses and properties of the dead citizens. This assertion is hard to follow. The facts themselves are as questionable as the reports of the chroniclers on which they are based. Town records from most Italian, French and English towns bear witness to the orderly transference of property in the years 1349 and 1350, and once again in all later plague outbreaks.

In comparison with these sociological considerations the bare facts of building in towns appear very simple; but they only seem to be so simple because they are not accompanied by the necessary dates and valuations. Treated with greater chronological and arithmetical precision the architectural evidence may sometimes equally well be cited as evidence of urban stagnation. Thus in England the widespread church building is cited as evidence for the prosperity of the fifteenth century; it is however apparent that many of the churches which are said to date from the fifteenth century, were in fact built in the fourteenth century or at the very end of the fifteenth century. Moreover it is by no means certain that the building activity in fact represented by fifteenth-century churches was greater or even as great as that of the twelfth and thirteenth centuries when the majority of the abbeys, cathedrals, parish churches, and royal and noble castles in England were built.[33]

Here as elsewhere the question of the general trend of development and of the significance of the exceptions can be a matter of quantities. Taken together, do the flourishing areas and branches of the economy represent as large or almost as large a part as the rest of the European economy? Most probably not. If we leave Italy to one side – and even in Italy there is no doubt about the economic depression in the fourteenth century – the prospering areas do not suffice to tilt the scales in their favour. If some historians think otherwise, this they in many cases do because they are dealing with areas which played an important role in the seventeenth and eighteenth centuries, and therefore view the fifteenth century record through the magnifying glass of later fortunes.

In this distorting perspective the colonial trade of the sixteenth century appears to be much more important than the latest studies show it to have been. The same shortening of perspective leads to the antedating of the high point of economic prosperity in the towns of northern Holland and south Germany. On closer examination it may transpire that the dominant position of Augsburg and Nürnberg in the sixteenth century was of relatively recent origin. Both towns had been important as trade centres for a long time, but it was only when the mining industry revived in the

[33] M. M. Postan, *The Fifteenth Century*, pp. 164 f.; W. G. Hoskins, *Midland England* (1949), pp. 25 f.; cf. however Hoskins' assertion that church building in the fifteenth century in Devonshire reflected a period of economic prosperity; W. G. Hoskins and H. P. R. Finberg, *Devonshire Studies* (1952), pp. 234 ff.; cf. also the accounts of the great building activity in eighteenth-century Antwerp in A. Thys, *Historique des rues et des places publiques de la ville d'Anvers* (1873). Has the lack of agreement between economic development and building activity in Florence not been noticed? The real significance of building activity is not that it is a result or a symptom of increasing wealth, but that it stimulates investment and employment. If great building activity could be proved for the towns of the fifteenth century, this would justify the conclusion that because of the building activity the depression was not as deep as it might otherwise have been.

last third of the fifteenth century, and when the conflict between the Hansa and Flanders in the same decades directed transcontinental trade into new channels, and trade over the Alpine passes shifted to the Brenner, that they grew rapidly to gain a position in the front rank of European commerce.[34]

In the north of Holland we can detect a slow and constant rise from the thirteenth century onwards; this does not, however, justify the conclusion that in the second half of the fourteenth century or even in the first half of the fifteenth century the north of Holland had even approximately reached the economic importance it was to acquire in the sixteenth and seventeenth centuries. Up to the end of the fifteenth century north European trade was carried on between the factories of the Hansa in foreign parts and the ports and fairs of Flanders and Brabant and the south and east coasts of England. The north of Holland still played a subordinate and provincial role in this powerful, but decreasingly significant, Hanseatic trade area. Of course the Dutch had already achieved their pre-eminent position in shipping, but in spite of this they did not establish their dominance in the shipping in the Baltic and North seas until the last quarter of the century.[35]

The quantitative arguments lead to similar results when applied to the study of new industrial developments. It is very doubtful whether the

[34] One must forgive the historian who, viewing the economy of medieval Europe from the point of view of conditions in Holland, south Germany or north Italy, understandably inclines to assume a continual upward trend; cf. H. Klompmaker's review of *Cambridge Economic History*, vol. II in *Die Ekonomist* (1954). As far as Italy is concerned, one must bear in mind that the upswing in the Quattrocentro was restricted to agriculture and internal trade, and for this reason cannot have had the same effect on the rest of Europe as the expansion of the Italian international money and capital market in earlier centuries.

[35] The unmistakeable increases in importance of Dutch trade begin in the second half or more precisely in the last decade of the fifteenth century. In the first quarter of the fifteenth century export trade remained almost static: F. Ketner, *Handel en Scheepvaart van Amsterdam in de vijftiende Eeuw* (Leiden, 1946), ch. I and pp. 137 f. The recurring disagreements with the Hansa repeatedly curbed Dutch trade up to 1474, and to judge by the few surviving figures, it increased rather slowly during this period, loc. cit., ch. IV. It is true that the earliest customs register for the Sound, dating from 1497, shows that of the 795 ships which passed the customs posts, 455 or almost 60% were Dutch. This was however obviously the result of a recent increase, and represents the significance of Dutch shipping in the Baltic, and not that of Dutch trade. The admittedly incomplete Prussian figures for the year 1476, the year in which Dutch trade had completely recovered from the setback of 1474, show that of 634 ships docking in Danzig, 156 came from Dutch ports of origin. One should bear in mind that these statistics are not completed; in 1474 the number recorded were 23 out of the total of 403. V. Lauffer. 'Danzigs Schiffs- und Warenverkehr am Ende des XV. Jahrhunderts', *Zeitschrift des Westpreussischen Geschichtsvereins* (1894). Cf. Ketner, op. cit., pp. 161 ff. These facts are not contradicted by the new book by N. W. Postumus, *De Oosterse handel te Amsterdam* (1953), even though the author displays a general inclination to exaggerate the commercial development of Amsterdam.

growth of the cloth industry in Holland, Brabant and the small Flemish towns was large enough to balance the decline of the Florentine and Flemish cloth industries. The supplies of raw materials reflect the shortfall in cloth production. The exports of English wool – and until the last quarter of the fifteenth century manufacturers of good quality cloths everywhere remained dependent on English wool – declined in the course of the late fourteenth and fifteenth centuries to a third of their quantity before 1350, and the total wool production of England no doubt dropped by a third.[36]

The test of consistency cannot however be purely quantitative. In the end our ability to distinguish the prevailing tendency from the local or exceptional cases is based on our finding general causes for the typical, while being unable to account for the untypical in other than local terms. One can logically and historically link the decline of trade and agriculture with the population problems of late-medieval Europe and perhaps also with state of currency and prices; on the other hand one cannot advance any similarly general reasons for the sudden prosperity of towns in south Germany and Brabant. We must accordingly regard the decline of trade as a 'typical' development: a distinctive feature of the period and a manifestation of its predominant trend of development.

[36] Although Spanish wool was already being used in small quantities in the smaller cloth-producing towns of Flanders and Brabant in the fifteenth century, it only began to play an important role in the cloth industry of the Netherlands at the beginning of the sixteenth century: A. Posthumus, *De Geschiedenis van de Leidsche lakenindustrie*, I (1908), p. 206. The total production of the Netherlands at the end of the fifteenth century amounted to approximately 56,000 'cloths'. If we assume that the town of Leiden always produced half of this – as was the case at the end of the century – the Netherlands' annual production in the middle of this century cannot have amounted to more than 30,000 'cloths' (ibid., p. 307). If we further assume that each 'cloth' contained approximately 30 Netherlands pounds of wool, then the total textile production of the Netherlands in the middle of the century can have contained no more than 900,000 Dutch pounds of wool, or not more than 2500 English sacks (according to the usual reckoning at Calais these were roughly 1100 to 1300 sacks). E. Power and M. M. Postan, *English Trade in the Fifteenth Century*, pp. 71 f. In fact Leiden was importing approximately 1500 sacks of English wool annually in the last quarter of the century. By comparison, in the thirteenth and the early fourteenth centuries the textile industry of the Low Countries required 20,000 to 30,000 sacks of English wool each year. The reduction of cloth production in Florence alone from more than 80,000 Florentine 'cloths' before 1338 to less than 24,000 by 1378 (Lopez, op. cit., pp. 321 and 342; Carus-Wilson, op. cit., p. 393) was probably greater than the whole of the cloth production of the Netherlands in 1450, and very much greater than the increase in production in the Netherlands between 1350 and 1450. Just how great the decline in production in Flanders may have been is shown by the estimates of J. Demey, 'Proeve tot raming van de Bevolking en de Weefgetouwen te Ieper van de XIIIe tot de XVIIe eeuw', *Revue Belge* (1950). The population of Ypres declined from 40,000 in 1260 to about 7600 in 1491, and cloth production went down from around 90,000 pieces in 1311 to about 500 pieces at the end of the century.

Our argument has thus ended in a circle. If the previously advanced explanations offered here, be they population movements or monetary changes were disproved, then the fact of the decline itself would be more questionable than it appears to be today. Until they have been disproved and the balance of the documentary evidence from the sources radically shifted, we must accept a downward trend as a working hypothesis.

Of course the significance, the range and the validity of this hypothesis should not be overrated. It should not be used to show that the depression was everywhere equally severe and persistent. Although signs of the depression can be found in most areas at all times between say 1325 and 1475, the decline began later and ended earlier in some places than in others. The hypothesis refers above all to the aggregate economic activity, not to personal wealth, and still less to the well-being of all or at least most of the individuals. In many parts of Europe the fall in agricultural production and in the volume of commerce and industry was accompanied by a new distribution and a levelling of personal wealth.[37] The hypothesis of a shrinking or stagnating economy cannot therefore lead to the conclusion that everybody was poorer than before. Nor does it mean that growing communities or institutions were not to be found. The instances of economic advances which have been cited here are examples of new growth and new starts from which great development was to come in later centuries. For a setback in economic development does not signify a break in the course of history. All it means is that for a time the new growths were insufficient to make up for the depressing effects of declining economies and shrinking communities.

Above all we are dealing here with working hypotheses which ought not to be considered conclusive. Their main purpose is to place the burden of proof on those who insist that all economic changes should be viewed as local incidents, as events which did not combine or interact, except accidentally, and did not continue for long enough to leave their mark permanently and irrevocably on the face of Europe.

[37] Cf. M. Malowist, op. cit. However much Malowist's argument diverges from mine in detail, it conforms with the most important of my conclusions. He concedes that there was a general decline in economic activity, but stresses new developments full of promise for the future. I am not aware that there are any scholars working on the fifteenth century who would deny this.

2
THE RISE OF A MONEY ECONOMY*

1

The 'rise of a money economy' is one of the residuary hypotheses of economic history: a *deus ex machina* to be called upon when no other explanation is available. The subject of economic history is sufficiently new to contain problems which economic historians have not yet had time to resolve, and problems which have not yet been resolved lend themselves only too easily to generalized assumptions. These stop-gap generalities have not so far been described or catalogued. But a critical reader would probably recognize them without the aid of a cautionary table. For most of them are little more than invocations of sociological theories underlying the Victorian idea of progress.

One such invocation is the so-called 'rise of the middle classes'. Eileen Power and others have already pointed out how frequently the middle-class formula has been used to bridge gaps in historical knowledge. The recipe has been to credit the rising middle classes with almost every revolutionary event of European culture to which a more specific cause has not yet been assigned. If towns grew in the eleventh and twelfth centuries, this was due to the rise of the middle classes; if lay culture and religious dissent flourished in the late twelfth and the early thirteenth centuries, this was also due to the rise of the middle classes. So, if we are to believe some writers, was the consolidation of national monarchies in England and France in the later Middle Ages, the dissolution of feudal power in the fifteenth century, the Reformation, the Tudor despotism, the Elizabethan renaissance, the scientific development of the seventeenth century, the Puritan revolution, the economic liberalism and the sentimental novel of the eighteenth century. In fact the martyrdom of Poland and the Russian revolution are very nearly the only historical phenomena which nobody has yet thought fit to lay at the door of the newly born bourgeoisie.

The very range of the occasions on which the formula has been employed is sufficient to warn us against its employment. Yet *au fond* its

* This paper first appeared in *Economic History Review*, XIV, 1944.

applications are not as absurd as they appear when strung together. Like most current sociological generalizations, the middle-class formula contains a modicum of truth without which it would not have found its way into otherwise creditable writings. At one time or another the middle classes must have risen; at some time or other they must have grown; and from their rise or their growth historical consequences were bound to follow. There is, therefore, nothing *a priori* wrong in an attempt to consider the rising middle classes as an important historical event. What is wrong is the frequent assumption that the middle classes rose suddenly at a clearly recognizable point in the past, and that, having risen, they went on growing in number and strength all through subsequent history. Equally erroneous is the notion that the most significant feature in the history of the middle classes was their increase. Eileen Power has shown that in the English Middle Ages the birthday of the bourgeoisie, the precise century or year when it first made its appearance, is impossible to discover. The English middle classes are as old as English history, and their record is not one of continuous and uninterrupted growth. Gauged by their power and wealth they were more prominent in the early fourteenth century than in the fifteenth, and were more 'capitalistic' in the freer conditions of the early Middle Ages than they were to become in the more rigidly regulated economy of the later Middle Ages.[1] Indeed, students will find that the changes in the structure, outlook and behaviour of the middle classes are much more significant than the mere swelling of their numbers or the inflation of their power through consecutive centuries of English history.

2

Another such formula is the 'rise of money economy'. Ever since the days of Cunningham and Thorold Rogers money economy has been repeatedly called in to help in dealing with recalcitrant problems of economic history – sometimes the same kind of problems as those which had elsewhere been palmed off on the middle classes.[2] Historians have frequently taken it for granted that a money economy, like the bourgeoisie, arose at a single point of English history, usually at a point best suited to their argument. They have thus been able to ascribe to the rising money economy an infinite variety of phenomena: the transform-

[1] Eileen Power, *The Wool Trade in English Medieval History* (Oxford, 1941), chap. VI.

[2] E.g. W. Cunningham, *The Growth of English Industry and Commerce*, I (5th ed. Cambridge, 1910), 22, 242, 458, 546, etc.; E. Lipson, *The Economic History of England*, I (7th ed. 1937), 94, 102, 105, 608. On the other hand, Ashley, when he wrote his famous text-book, refused to be drawn into the prejudices of his time, and did not even mention money economy by name.

ation of the Anglo-Saxon society in the tenth and the eleventh centuries, the rise of towns in the eleventh and twelfth, the development of royal taxation in the twelfth and thirteenth, the commutation of services in the thirteenth and fourteenth, and several features of the English renaissance in the sixteenth. All these and many other events, widely separated in time and space, have been explained as due to the rise of money economy.

Needless to say, in some contexts the formula is more convincing than in others. Its terms – the words money economy and more still the word rise – have been used in many different senses; but it is only in one of its many connotations that it has a meaning sufficiently clear, and some foundation in fact. In all its other senses it is more or less untrue, and from the point of view of European and English history more or less irrelevant.

It is least relevant when it happens to be used in its simplest and most direct sense. If the word rise is taken to mean the birth or the first appearance, and the term money economy is employed to point the contrast with economies in which trade is altogether absent or else is conducted without money, the formula cannot be of such importance. It could mean nothing to medieval historians, who have used it most often, even if it might mean something to archaeologists who have hardly used it at all.

I do not want to deny that a money economy in this sense must have appeared at one time or another on the continent of Europe, and that at some primitive stage in their development the European peoples were innocent of trade, or at least unfamiliar with the use of money. But this condition, if it ever existed, must have disappeared earlier than the earliest point at which European history can be said to begin. Have not the archaeologists traced interregional trade into neolithic days and was not at least one pre-historic civilization – the Bronze Age – dependent on international exchanges for the very metal from which it derived its name?[3] The use of money in trade may have been more recent than trade itself, but, however recent, it goes far beyond the beginnings of European civilization and is probably older than the oldest of the written records.

Money had apparently been current on this island long before the Romans came, and had been known to Angles, Saxons and Jutes before they invaded this country. Since then their institutions, their pattern of

[3] The only comprehensive account of prehistoric trade in all its aspects is that given by W. Stein in Ebert's *Reallexikon der Altertumskunde*. But since Stein wrote, very numerous studies of a prehistoric trade in different regions of northern Europe have appeared in various archaeological publications. In these studies the vital importance of long-distance trade in the Bronze Age has been brought out very clearly. On the part played in this trade by the British Isles see S. Pigott, 'The Early Bronze Age in Wessex', *Proc. Prehist. Soc.* (1938).

obligations and their economic life never ceased to reflect their familiarity with money. The oldest Anglo-Saxon laws, those of the sixth-century kings of Kent, fix murder fines in money terms, and so do the Anglo-Saxon laws of the subsequent centuries. And blood fines were not the only payments and obligations to be expressed in Anglo-Saxon documents in money terms. Professor Stenton has recently reminded us that one of the earliest payments to the Church, the plough-penny, may date back to as early as the seventh century.[4] The most important Anglo-Saxon payment to the church, that of churchscot, may have been paid in kind, for it was similar to the tithe of later centuries. But this was not a mark of natural economy, for failure to pay churchscot was apparently punished by a money fine. The principal agricultural imposts payable to the king were food rents from his estates and were, therefore, for a long time paid in kind. But long before the Conquest some of these rents had been paid in money.[5] Revenues, such as the gelds for specific purposes, and above all the Danegeld, were expressed in money units: so also were various payments between private persons. Men buying estates paid for them with lump sums of money. A payment of a thousand shillings for an estate has been recorded as early as Offa's reign.[6] The innumerable customary payments of ancient origin listed by Miss Neilson[7] appear for the first time in English records as 'pennies' of one kind or another, or in other words, as cash payments. There were numerous public payments, or to be more exact royal dues, which had become assimilated to feudal rent; the hidage, the cornage, the sheriff-silver, the wardpenny. And there were also payments in lieu of obligations more purely manorial; the heddornwerch, the woodpenny, the shernsilver, the hedgingsilver, the bedripsilver, the averpenny, and numerous other pennies and silvers in lieu of ancient labour services on land. Few of them are mentioned in documents before the twelfth century, but their character as well as their etymology are clearly Anglo-Saxon.

All this evidence of pre-medieval payments has been known to historians since the very beginnings of medieval scholarship: yet it has

4 F. M. Stenton, *Anglo-Saxon England* (Oxford, 1943), p. 152. Here, as elsewhere in his book, Professor Stenton has shown that it is possible to deal with the economic phenomena of the distant past without invoking the money economy in general.

5 The story of the commutation of the royal farms into money derives from the author of *Dialogus de Scaccario*, Bishop Richard, who himself got it from hearsay. But his dates, if not his other details, are somewhat doubtful. Cf. R. L. Poole, *Exchequer in the Twelfth Century* (Oxford, 1912), p. 27. In fact, as Professor Stenton points out, the traces of an organized financial system in England are 'unexpectedly remote'. There were rudiments of a national treasury in the ninth century (op. cit. p. 635). See also E. Lipson, op. cit. p. 602.

6 W. de G. Birch, *Cartularium Saxonicum*, I (1885), no. 271.

7 N. Neilson, *Customary Rents* (Oxford Studies in Social and Legal History, vol. II, 1910), pp. 50 seq. and 114 seq.

not prevented them from placing the rise of a money economy centuries later than the recorded dates of Anglo-Saxon money transactions. This inconsistency has sometimes been justified on theoretical grounds. In accordance with the terminological distinctions of modern economics, some historians have been inclined to explain away the early references to money on the ground that in the Anglo-Saxon period, as in the early centuries of the Middle Ages, money units were employed to measure obligations and not to make payments. In the jargon of the economist, money was a unit of account and not a medium of exchange.

For this distinction no historical proof has so far been adduced. What the facts tell us is that certain payments were reckoned in money, and unless the contrary is proved the conclusion must be that payments would not be thus reckoned unless they were also thus discharged. Other facts tell us that in this country gold was coined and circulated before the Roman conquest. Anglo-Saxon money was coined at least as early as the sixth century and was received, exported and hoarded by foreigners trading with England at least as early as the eighth century.[8] There can thus be no doubt that money was in fact employed in payment, and was not an abstract standard of value.

The whole argument that the use of money and coins for reckoning came sooner or easier to the primitive man than the handing over of coins in payment is not borne out by either archaeological or anthropological evidence, and is a pure piece of *a priori* reasoning. And until a better argument is found or better evidence is adduced, references in early documents to money payments must be understood in their literal sense. The onus of proof belongs to those who believe that obligations, though expressed in money, were discharged in other ways.

Thus, from the point of view of English history, and even from that of medieval and Anglo-Saxon history, the rise of a money economy in the sense of its first appearance has no historical meaning. Money was in use when documented history begins, and its rise cannot be adduced as an explanation of any later phenomenon.

3

The formula means more when used in its vaguer and more general sense. The expression 'money economy' can be taken to mean the relative frequency of money payments, while the word 'rise' can be used to

[8] Though in Professor Stenton's words 'the continuous history of English currency begins with Offa' (op. cit. p. 220), some Anglo-Saxon coins are much older. C. F. Keary, *A Catalogue of English Coins in the British Museum*, I (1887), p. vi. See also H. A. Grueber, *Handbook of the Coins of Great Britain and Ireland in the British Museum* (1889), pp. i–x.

denote not their birthday but their general expansion. In this sense the growth of a money economy means merely an increase in the relative volume of money payments and is something economists can understand and historians can test. For in this sense the process is historically not very different from what other historians prefer to describe as the rise of exchange economy and the decline of a natural economy.

Recently historians have cast some doubt and even a little aspersion upon the notion of a natural economy. It is now usual to argue that in all periods of recorded history men depended upon trade and markets, and that 'pure' natural economy was never known in Europe. Nevertheless, the fundamental principle underlying the distinction has not been wholly destroyed. Even if economies wholly natural never existed, economies largely natural did. The economic conditions of European societies at every stage of their existence was more or less natural and more or less self-sufficient; sometimes more and sometimes less. And it is in these changes towards or away from natural economy that the real meaning of the rise of a money economy will be found.

Indeed, the history of mankind, and still more the history of Europe, is marked by recurrent phases of active exchanges. No student of the thirteenth century will fail to notice not only an over-all increase in agricultural and industrial production, but also a greater emphasis on production for sale and the spread of more or less capitalistic agriculture on large estates, and the consequent growth of towns, markets and mercantile classes. Similar changes in the sixteenth or the eighteenth centuries are so familiar that some historians find them too trivial even to be worth mentioning. Used in this sense, the formula of the rise of money economy points to a real social process, easy to identify and dangerous to miss.

Yet even in this sense the formula is sometimes wrapped up in a great deal of theory and mysticism, or else hitched to irrelevant facts. The most irrelevant of facts with which it is sometimes identified is the so-called increase of money. How often are we told that the rise of money economy followed the influx of precious metals from this and that corner of the world? And yet how seldom are we told how and why this should have happened. The growth of money economy, if it is to mean anything at all, signifies an increase in payments, not an increase in bullion or paper money. Needless to say, a growing quantity of money can have and has had important consequences. Historians and economists will easily find instances of social transformations brought about by additions to the mere volume of the circulating medium. Situations of this kind recurred several times in the course of the eighteenth and nineteenth centuries. There was the well-known and much publicised increase in bullion in the sixteenth century, and a similar influx may also have occurred in the late twelfth and the thirteenth centuries. Yet by no means all these events necessarily led to any of the consequences with which the rise of money economy is commonly credited.

The influx of bullion could have different effects at different times. In periods and societies unaccustomed to money but otherwise fond of gold, an increase in the supply of precious metals would only make plate and gold buckles more abundant. In periods when gold and silver were mainly used as mediums of exchange, the chief effect of their increase would be to raise the levels of prices.[9] As prices rose and fell, social relations – and money economy with them – were bound to change. Yet at the cost of a little pedantry historians will do well to consider such changes as products of price revolutions, not as consequences of more abundant bullion.

To say, therefore, (as it is sometimes said) that in the thirteenth century commerce grew because the money economy was rising, and then to proceed to account for the latter by the influx of gold and bullion from the east, is to be wrong not only in fact (throughout the Middle Ages trade with the east set up bullion movements flowing from west to east, not from east to west) but also in logic. Prices were apparently buoyant all through that period, and as they rose some people may have felt inclined to use their money more frequently or else to produce for sale more than they would otherwise have done. But it is not at all certain that the rise in prices was due to an influx of precious metals, and it is certain that the expansion of trade was not solely due to the rise in prices. Peace, the growth of population, the expansion of settlement, the improvements in commercial and financial technique, all played their part in breaking up the self-sufficiency of local markets and in commercializing the economic activities of men.

What is true of the thirteenth century is also true of many other periods. Some of the best-known instances of commutation, i.e. of transition from payments in kind to payments in money, occurred at the time when prices were falling and the quantity of circulating medium presumably declined. In the fourteenth and fifteenth centuries substitution of money payments for labour services followed from the falling agricultural prices and from the general agricultural depression of the times. A still earlier wave of commutations, that of the early twelfth century, was not, apparently, preceded by any clearly defined movements of prices and possibly 'straddled' across two contrary cycles – a fall followed by a rise. Its explanation will probably be found in the general economic and political insecurity of the age, which made it difficult for landlords to control production in their outlying estates, to exact labour services and to move large quantities of agricultural produce across the country.

[9] Even that was by no means inevitable, for new bullion was sometimes absorbed without raising prices, and conversely, prices could rise independently of supplies of gold and silver.

In short, the rise of a money economy in the sense of greater preponderance of money payments is not identical with the greater abundance of money itself. More gold and silver could sometimes result in higher prices; higher prices could sometimes enlarge the relative volume of money transactions. But in general the volume of money transactions was an historical phenomenon of composite origin and reflecting an infinite variety of causes, social, economic and political.

4

Thus the rise of a money economy has a meaning wider and more general than that of mere currency inflation. Yet it is also possible to view it in too broad and too diffuse a light, or, as I have said elsewhere, to wrap it in too much sublimity and metaphysics. Now and again it has been interpreted as one of those inexorable tendencies of human progress of which the nineteenth century sociologists – Spencer, Buckle, Marx and Comte – were inordinately fond. In some writings, and especially in some German writings, the rise of money economy figures as a permanent tendency of historical development and as an ever-unfolding manifestation of the progressive destinies of humanity.

In reality it is none of these things. It is certainly not uninterrupted, and in that sense not progressive. Until the Industrial Revolution it was nothing more than a recurrent economic phenomenon unconnected with any elemental and mystical tendencies of human history, or with secular changes of human behaviour. The history of western Europe, and for that matter the history of the world, is not a continuous record of expanding exchanges. The unbroken growth of world trade between the beginning of the eighteenth century and the end of the nineteenth has misled historians into believing that the growth of world trade had been equally unbroken in the past. Medievalists and historians of the sixteenth and the seventeenth centuries should be guilty of no such delusion. In so far as growing money economy depended on growing production, it could not possibly be continuous, for the simple reason that world production itself did not grow progressively or continuously. In this country there was a protracted slump in the late fourteenth and the fifteenth centuries; possibly also a slump at the turn of the Anglo-Saxon and Norman periods. I do not know whether anything in the nature of an economic recession intervened in the middle decades of the seventeenth century, but there is no doubt that the rate of growth, if growth there was, was at that time much retarded. Abroad, the history of the last twelve hundred years was repeatedly punctuated by local falls in production and incomes. In short, cumulative increases in world production, now taken for granted by economists and politicians, are all too recent to be considered eternal, still less primeval.

It will, of course, be argued (and this also happens to be my view) that a money economy in the true sense of the term depended for its development, not so much on a general increase in production as on those subtler historical changes which led men away from domestic self-sufficiency and directed them towards shops and market places. But changes of this character were even less continuous and less progressive than the purely material record of world output. No historian will be unhistorical enough to lump together all the occasions when humanity forsook the habits of natural economy and showed a preference for buying and selling. This may have happened in the late twelfth and the early thirteenth centuries because peace reigned, because law was observed, and prices were buoyant, population was rising and more mouths had to be fed. This may have happened in the sixteenth century because prices were rising, but also because new riches were brought in by English merchants from abroad, and because new needs were following in the wake of the renaissance. Commercial production may have expanded in the eighteenth century because population was growing, because international trade was bringing in new wealth, while human ingenuity was finding new and profitable ways for employing capital in commercial production. American farmers may have gone over to cash crops in the second half of the nineteenth century because the very condition of their settlements in the middle west forced them to produce for sale; also because the virgin prairie made it possible for them to produce cheaply, while the new railways made it possible for the produce to be carried away; but chiefly because, for political and social reasons, the cash nexus had begun to penetrate the entire social fabric of the United States. The African natives may be producing for the market because of the incidence of colonial taxation; the Russian peasants because of the state policy of capital accumulation. From this point of view there was not one rise of money economy but several rises of several money economies. There was a series of independent peaks with a different road to each, and no peak except the last ever opened the prospect of continuous rises unbroken by descents.

For descents there doubtless were, and I have already mentioned some of them. In France at the end of the eighteenth century, in Germany during and after the Thirty Years War, all over the continent during the religious wars, during the troubles of the fifteenth century, during the conquests and migrations of the ninth and tenth centuries; at all these places and times economic activity declined or remained stagnant, and material life became more local and self-sufficient. These were times of a more or less general retreat from a money economy.

5

'More or less general': the reason why I am reluctant to commit myself to a more sweeping statement is that movements towards greater money economy, as well as movements away from it, were not only less continuous than people imagine but also less general. General recessions or general expansions of economic activity affecting every branch of agriculture, industry and trade were common enough, but general changes in the relative volume of money transactions were much less common. I doubt whether history could show a single example of the use of money expanding, so to speak, all along the line, unchecked and unbroken by local retreats. Let us look again at the English medieval examples which I have already mentioned. I have cited the fifteenth century as a period of declining trade, of growing self-sufficiency and, therefore, a good example of declining money economy. But while this generalisation holds good of most departments of fifteenth-century life and justifies my general verdict on the epoch, it does not apply to the labour market. For, as I have already pointed out, and as every schoolboy knows, the fifteenth century was also the time when labour services were being commuted and money payments were being substituted for labour dues. No wonder the economic historians who approached the period entirely from the point of view of agricultural labour jumped to the conclusion that the age was one of a rising money economy.[10] A clear contrast to the fifteenth century was presented by the thirteenth. At that time the general movement was towards bigger and better trade; more was produced and a greater share of what was produced went to the market. Yet in the employment of labour a contrary tendency prevailed. The lords endeavoured to enforce labour services to their legal maximum, to exact them in kind wherever their sales were optional, and to impose new services wherever the legal position was vague enough to permit it.[11] To an historian looking at the period from the point of view of labour it might well appear as one of a declining money economy.

Similar examples could be found in other periods and other countries. They all suggest that the changes in the so-called 'money economy' have been less uniform than the formula of money economy would suggest to the uninitiated. But nothing reveals the complexity of the process and the dangers of the formula better than the so-called 'farm'.

In present-day language the word 'farm' connotes the typical English

[10] E.g. A. E. Levett, *The Black Death on the Estates of the See of Winchester* (Oxford Studies in Social and Legal History, vol. v, 1916), *passim*, but esp. pp. 154–8.

[11] M. Postan, 'The Chronology of Labour Services', in *Trans. Royal Hist. Soc.* 4th ser. xx (1937), 169–93, and see Chapter 7 below.

unit of agricultural enterprise, but it derives from the more restricted term which was used in the later Middle Ages and in the early centuries of the modern era to denote a common type of contractual tenancy. It was a form of lease established on land (usually on the demesne) which had previously yielded to the lord a fluctuating income, in order to provide him with a stable, i.e. 'firm', annual income. In this sense a 'farm' was not a purely agricultural term, but applied to all transactions of 'farming out', i.e. letting out a fluctuating source of income for a fixed annual sum. There was a sheriff's farm, whereby a fixed annual sum was substituted for the hitherto variable revenues from royal vills and from other miscellaneous sources; the *firma burghi*, by which boroughs undertook to discharge their many and various payments to their overlord, usually the king, in a fixed annual sum; 'farms' of customs and so forth. Thus, on the whole, the creation of a 'farm' indicated a desire on the part of the owner to stabilise his income; a desire which would be most acutely felt at times when the revenues fluctuated unduly or else showed a tendency to fall. And this would, as a rule, suggest conditions of an economic slump and could be interpreted as a superficial symptom of an economic depression. But it cannot be safely used as a symptom of either a rising or a declining money economy.

On some manors of the late fourteenth and the early fifteenth centuries, farms were created on demesnes which had previously provided the lord's household with its provisions. These farms clearly meant a change towards a money economy and a further step towards the commercialisation of agriculture. But they meant nothing of the sort wherever and whenever they were introduced, as they were now and again throughout the Middle Ages, in outlying manors in substitution for fluctuating rents and money payments. And they may mean all sorts of things when they appear in the garb in which we meet them in the eleventh and the early twelfth centuries – that of manorial and monastic *feorms*.

In the earliest manorial surveys available to us, mostly those of the twelfth century, and in all other documents dealing with the financial organisation of large estates in the closing century of the Anglo-Saxon era and the first century of the Norman rule, we invariably find some if not most manors held by *firmarii* for a payment of a time-farm, i.e. a fixed payment representing the landlord's sustenance for a definite period – a month, a week, a day. This might be a *firma unius nocti* on royal manors or a week's *feorm* in a manor belonging to the canons of St Paul's or the monks of Christchurch, Canterbury. But in each case the arrangement would be roughly the same: a fixed payment, largely in kind, but often also in money, would be due from the manor at a fixed date.

This arrangement has been known to historians ever since the days of

Spelman and Dugdale; more recently it was described by E. H. Hale in his introduction to the Domesday of St Paul's; and more recently still by several students of early monasticism.[12] Yet I doubt whether the historical and economic meaning of the transaction has always been understood. Historians have sometimes been misled by the deliveries in kind which characterise the Benedictine method of estate management into believing that what they are dealing with is a primitive stage in manorial economy; a stage still characterised by direct payments in produce. The end of this stage is usually described as a 'commutation' of direct deliveries of produce, and as a substitution of a money economy for payments in kind.

This interpretation of the *feorm* is not wholly wrong, but it is certainly out of focus. The fact that some or most monastic *feorms* were fixed in kind is not the only element of the transaction. In fact many of them were paid in money, or at least in both produce and money. The Benedictine landlords always ran their 'headquarter estates' for the sake of their produce. But on all other estates the characteristic feature of the payments was not that they were made in kind but that they were fixed and firm. At the time when they were established they denoted not so much a choice between produce and money as a choice between fluctuating income and fixed income; and the historical situation they represented was not that of natural economy but that in which landlords happened to prefer fixed yield to fluctuating profits from rent and cultivation.

From this point of view the *feorm* of the eleventh century is not fundamentally different from the 'farm' of the fifteenth.[13] Neither can be represented as in any way primitive or in any way concerned with the general development of a money economy. Both are natural reactions of landlords to a combination of circumstances unfavourable to direct exploitation of estates: political unsettlement, difficulties of transport and commuications, falling prices. And both could be followed and preceded by periods of direct exploitation for fluctuating income. That in the twelfth and the thirteenth centuries direct exploitation as a rule followed the *feorms* of the eleventh century is now generally regarded as certain. Historians are not so certain about what condition preceded the *feorm*. But then, nothing is certain about the large estates in the Anglo-Saxon era, least of all their economic organisation. In the absence of proofs we are all thrown back on probabilities, and, to my mind, the probability of

[12] E.g. N. Neilson, *Economic Conditions on the Manors of Ramsey Abbey* (Philadelphia, 1899), and R. A. L. Smith, *Canterbury Cathedral Priory* (Cambridge, 1943). More synoptic accounts, both free from economic preconceptions, will be found in D. Knowles, *The Monastic Order in England* (Cambridge, 1940), pp. 441–4; and in F. M. Stenton, op. cit. pp. 476–8.

[13] Compare the early and the late references to farms in R. A. L. Smith, op. cit. pp. 128–33, 201–3.

an earlier agricultural boom – a time when estates were managed by speculative landlords in expectation of rising incomes – is very high indeed. Without an earlier phase of this kind most features of the eleventh- and twelfth-century manor would be impossible to explain. For how could we otherwise explain the juxtaposition on so many manors of 'old demesne' and 'new demesne', of new holdings with old, of ancient holdings and new ones; and how can we account for the innumerable signs of an earlier expansion and colonisation?

To conclude. The rise of a money economy does not mean the rise of money. It may mean an increase in the relative volume of money payments, as distinct from the increase in money itself. Yet even in this sense it is not a continuous process of human evolution. Increases in the relative volume of money transactions could reflect a whole variety of economic changes and were little more than passing, and sometimes recurrent historical phenomena, which combined with other phenomena to create unique and unrepeatable historical situations.

3

THE FIFTEENTH CENTURY*

Few periods of English economic history have been so much misunderstood by writers of general histories as the fifteenth century. The fault is partly the researcher's, who until very recently fought shy of the economic history of the period. Yet much more is now known to specialists than has penetrated the consciousness of the general historians. In text-books and political surveys the economic history of the fifteenth century is still made up of a few conventions for which recent research offers no justification.

The conventional notions die so hard, simply because they appear to fit into general preconceptions about the period. Coming as it does at the very end of what is regarded as the Middle Ages and just before the Tudor era, the century is easy to interpret as one of 'transition': as a time during which the so-called medieval development was completed and the great Tudor achievement prepared. And people who view the whole of English economic history as a continuous ascent from the barbaric primitivity of the pre-conquest days to the glorious efflorescence of the renaissance, find an easy explanation of the fifteenth century in its position between the fourteenth and the sixteenth. It is easy to assume, as most textbooks in fact do assume, that everything which the sixteenth century possessed – industrial and commercial expansion, mercantile capital, middle classes, agricultural progress, enclosures – was to be found in the fifteenth century in a degree somewhat smaller than in the sixteenth though somewhat greater than in the fourteenth.

This reading of the economic history of the age as one of 'transition' was at one time very nearly upset by the much advertised conflict of views between Denton and Thorold Rogers. While Denton brought out the deterioration of economic life during the Wars of the Roses, Thorold Rogers stressed the prosperity of the peasantry, and it fell to Kingsford to reconcile the conflict and to confuse the issue by arguing that the period being one of transition was bound to have a chequered record, and that its economic and political achievements were broken by intermittent light and shade, or as he preferred to describe it, 'prejudice and

* This paper first appeared in *Economic History Review*, IX, 1939.

promise'.[1] Yet had the hints contained in Denton and Rogers been followed up and the contradiction explored, a truer reading might have emerged. A further investigation of Denton's views would have revealed how little the economic development of the fifteenth century owed to its being sandwiched between the fourteenth and the sixteenth, and would have shown it not as a century of growth but as an age of recession, arrested economic development and declining national income. At the same time an investigation of Rogers's views would have shown that their contradiction to those of Denton was only an apparent one. For whereas Denton's pessimistic reading applied to the economic development of the country as a whole, Rogers's applied to the well-being of the lower ranks of rural society. That for a time a relative decline in the total volume of national wealth if fully compatible with the rising standard of life of the labouring classes is a proposition which students of post-war England will find it easy to understand. And that this is what in fact happened we shall presently see.

1

That the total national income and wealth was declining is shown by almost every statistical index available to historians. Most of these are indirect, but they are sufficiently unanimous to leave no room for doubt.

The most direct and the most important are the indices of agricultural production. That the cultivation of the demesne, the manorial home-farm, was declining throughout the century has always been known to historians, and the decline has always been accounted for by the changing organisation of the manor, i.e. the substitution of peasant leases for the direct cultivation of the demesne. But in the light of more recent study it appears that the reorganisation of agriculture was not the only cause of the drop in manorial production. The falling figures of manorial outputs reflect not only the letting out of the demesne but also a real decline in agriculture. On most of the estates for which the evidence is available, more land was withdrawn from the demesne than was let out to tenants. In other words there was a net contraction of the area under cultivation.

The impression of contraction is further supported by what we learn of the area actually occupied by peasant tenants. From the fifties and sixties of the fourteenth century right until the last quarter of the fifteenth ominous entries of vacant lands, '*terre in manu domini*', appear in manorial accounts; and the number of vacant holdings and lapsed rents

[1] C. L. Kingsford, *Prejudice and Promise in XVth Century England*, pp. 64–77; Thorold Rogers, *History of Agriculture and Prices*, vol. v, pp. 3–5, 23; W. Denton, *England in the Fifteenth Century*, pp. 115, 118, 119.

grow continually throughout the period. True enough, not all the lands which reverted to the lord after the pestilences of the fourteenth century or in the course of the fifteenth century remained permanently vacant, for some of them were re-let to new tenants, mostly on lease. But even if we make all the allowances for the new re-lettings there still remains a persisting deficiency both in the area of customary land in the hands of the tenants and in its total yield of rent. Of the 450-odd manors for which the fifteenth-century accounts have been studied, over four hundred show a contraction of land under cultivation, and a corresponding fall in rents.

The general impression is therefore one of a slack demand for land, and a relatively abundant supply of holdings. This impression is reinforced by what we learn of the petering out of reclamations – the assarts and purprestures. Although it would be wrong to think that the taking in of new land ceased altogether – in fact in some parts of the country, such as the weald of Sussex or the woodlands of Herts and Bucks, it was quite active throughout the fifteenth century – the great colonising effort of the earlier age is definitely over. At its most active the new reclamation is a matter of odd acres or perches here and there, carved out of the waste by individual peasant tenants. Nowhere do we find large tracts broken up and colonised on a scale comparable to the great colonising ventures of the late twelfth and thirteenth centuries.

It is therefore no wonder that the values of land, however measured, were falling off. The vacant customary holdings fetched lower rents when let out by the lords to leaseholders than they had done in the hands of the customary tenants. In many places both customary and leasehold rents had to be scaled down to suit the new situation. Entry fines which on some estates had soared up to unprecedented heights during the great land-hunger of the thirteenth century, now dropped again to their pre-thirteenth-century level or even lower. On most of the new leases, for which an economic rent was being charged, the fines disappeared altogether. So persistent was the fall of values that even the value of the demesne farm – and the demesne was frequently farmed with the express purpose of insuring against the fall of agricultural values – declined in the course of years.

Agriculture was thus obviously going through a secular slump, which began at some time in the fourteenth century – in some places before the Black Death – and continued with a slight halt in the first decade or two of the fifteenth century, until the late seventies and the eighties. An agricultural depression so general and continuous in a country as predominantly agricultural as fifteenth-century England would have affected all the other economic activities even if nothing had happened to produce an independent depression in industry and trade. But as it is, we know that independent depression of this kind was taking place in the urban economy as well.

Professor Gras has drawn our attention to the contraction of corn markets. Some such contraction would inevitably have resulted from the decline of agricultural production, but some of it must have resulted from the transformation of the manorial economy and the leasing of the demesne. The establishment of peasant leases on the lands once directly cultivated by the lords has frequently been represented as an 'economically progressive' change, the consequence and the cause of the 'growing money economy'. This conventional view will not stand scrutiny. The large estates of the great secular or episcopal landowners like the Duchy of Lancaster or the Bishop of Winchester used to produce very largely for the market. From the economic point of view large estates of this kind in the late thirteenth century were capitalist concerns: federated grain factories producing largely for cash. The growing of cash crops must have continued after the dissolution of the demesne, for food continued to be bought and sold. But in so far as the peasant holding represented a more self-sufficient type of economy the multiplication of peasant leases represented a tendency towards natural economy and a relative contraction of agricultural exchange.[2]

The diminution of buying and selling in the countryside was in part responsible for the decline of the corporate towns which is another familiar feature of the period. Not all the complaints of the towns at the bad times should be taken at their face value, especially when they were made in order to obtain remission of Royal taxation. Yet, many of the complaints had a foundation of fact. With the exception of London, which continued to grow, of Bristol, which benefited from the resilience of the Western and Southern trades, and possibly of Southampton, which occupied a special position by virtue of its connections with Italian imports and its function as one of the outports of the London region, the bulk of English trading centres, whether the ancient county towns or the old sea-ports, suffered a decline.

In a number of towns, like Norwich, Nottingham, Northampton and Leicester, the decline is shown in the sudden cessation of their territorial expansion. The decay of the older seaports is shown by the fall in their sea-borne trade. It is now well known that the lowest point of English foreign trade was reached at some time in the middle of the century. The ancient Scandinavian connections were repeatedly interrupted in the first half of the century and ceased to count with the definite establishment of the Hanseatic monopoly in Bergen in the second quarter of the century. The Prussian and Polish trade through Danzig was several times blocked in the first half of the century and finally destroyed during the great

2 N. S. B. Gras, *The Evolution of the English Corn Market*, pp. 12–44.

Anglo-Hanseatic conflict of the mid-century. The local trade of the south coast towns with Picardy, Normandy and Brittany had succumbed in the early phases of the Hundred Years War, and the ancient flourishing trade with Gascony was broken by the loss of Aquitaine in the concluding stages of the war. In short, most of the outlying branches of English foreign trade were lopped off, one after another, and by the third quarter of the century the Low Countries remained very nearly the only channel of trade open to the English, and London as the principal centre of that trade was nearly the only great seaport not impoverished by the crisis.[3]

Yet even the trade to the Low Countries, though more active than the other branches of English commerce, did not escape scot-free. In so far as it was concerned with wool it was bound to be affected by the decline in the wool trade which set in at the second half of the fourteenth century and continued without interruption until it dwindled to a vanishing point in the sixteenth century. We know of course that the dwindling of the wool trade was accompanied and in part compensated by the growth of cloth exports. But we also know now that the compensation was not as full as it was once imagined. The great rise in the English cloth exports occurred in the second half of the fourteenth century. But having grown rapidly and continually for about forty or fifty years the cloth exports and presumably the cloth production then remained stationary throughout most of the fifteenth century and, if anything, declined in the middle decades. And even at their topmost fifteenth-century level, the cloth exports were not large enough to account for the whole decline of the wool trade.

These facts about cloth must be borne in mind when the so-called development of the cloth industry is discussed. That the new industry largely made up for the declining income and production elsewhere is undeniable. If the old corporate towns declined, the new cloth-producing villages and towns in East Anglia, Yorkshire and the West Country were springing up, and if old sources of wealth were disappearing new ones were rising in their place. Yet even at its highest the compensation fell short of the deficiency; and over the greater part of the fifteenth century the compensating movements were well below their highest. The flourishing cloth towns did not flourish as abundantly in the fourteen fifties and fourteen sixties as they had done in the thirteen eighties and thirteen nineties. And it was not until the last fifteen or twenty years of the century that the fourteenth-century rate of progress was resumed.

The material recession was thus general. To deny its existence or to minimize its extent on the evidence of certain non-material signs is a sin which no economic historian should commit. Even if it were proved that

[3] E. Power and M. Postan, *English Trade in the Fifteenth Century*, *passim*, and esp. Professor Gray's essay on 'English Foreign Trade from 1446 to 1482.'

the period was rich in acts of private piety, graced by a flourishing religion, embellished by alabaster statues; better educated, more prettily coiffured and gowned, than any other period in the Middle Ages, the basic facts of material development would still be unaffected. One of the principal tenets of the home-made sociology, which the non-sociological historians commonly assume, is that ages of economic expansion are necessarily ages of intellectual and artistic achievement. As if the generations which make the money also know how to spend it best; and as if the abundance of material means leads inevitably and directly to a corresponding rise in the arts of life.

The pitfalls of this sociology must be remembered when the achievements of the so-called fifteenth-century perpendicular architecture are invoked as evidence of the century's material progress. What do the perpendicular churches prove? Their architectural excellence has nothing to do with either the growth or the decline of English industry, agriculture or trade. Their quantity, the sheer volume of stones and mortar, might be thought to be closely related to economic processes. But were the quantities of stones and mortar shaped in the perpendicular style larger, or even as large as, the stones and mortar that went into the building of the costly parish churches of the twelfth century, the abbeys and the cathedrals of the thirteenth and the fourteenth? And if we, in addition, remember that many of the so-called fifteenth-century buildings were in fact structures, which like King's College Chapel, were commenced at the beginning of the century but not resumed until the coming of the Tudors, or else structures built either before 1425 or after 1475, we shall perhaps be doubly careful in regarding either the cloth villages or their perpendicular churches as evidence of the great commercial efflorescence of the fifteenth century.

But however irrelevant to the period's intellectual and religious activity, the economic recession was certainly consistent with its political situation. The fifteenth century was the time of the last and the most disastrous phase of the Hundred Years War, of misgovernment and civil war at home. The political deterioration began in the closing years of Edward III's reign and was halted for a brief period under the early Lancastrians. But with Henry VI's accession, and especially after his attainment of seniority, the disruption of government led by rapid stages to civil war and military and diplomatic defeats abroad. In times like these a rising tide of production and trade could have been made possible only by a most unusual combination of favourable circumstances: a rapid accumulation of capital, a growth of population, a development of technical arts. The fact that none of these conditions were present makes the economy of the time all the easier to fit into its political background.

2

The redeeming features, such as there were, would be found not in the economic processes but in social relations: not so much on the side of production as on that of distribution. The economic recession was accompanied by social changes some of which may commend themselves to the moral judgment of our own day, even if they do not pass the test of the simple material measurements.

Perhaps the best known were the changes which occurred in the structure and position of the so-called middle classes. With the exception of the families involved in the outlying branches of foreign trade the mercantile elements of English society found themselves in a state of solid conservative prosperity devoid of both the prizes and the penalties of the more adventurous and speculative ages. The great breeding season of English capitalism was in the early phases of the Hundred Years War, the time when the exigencies of Royal finance, new experiments in taxation, speculative ventures with wool, the collapse of Italian finance and the beginning of the new cloth industry, all combined to bring into existence a new race of war financiers and commercial speculators, army purveyors and wool-monopolists. But the race was as short-lived as it was new. The great fortunes were lost as easily as they were made, and the period of reckless finance and gigantic fiscal experiments passed away with the first stage of the war. And while the heroic age of financial adventure was passing away, the speculator and the capitalist found themselves hemmed in by the contracting commercial markets and the slackening tempo of economic development. The Company of the Staple in its final form turned necessity into a policy and organised the wool trade in a way which prevented the development of large single fortunes. And what the Staple did on a national scale the innumerable municipalities and city companies did locally. The English merchant classes responded to the stability and recession of trade in the way of all merchants. They adopted the policy of regulation and restriction, impeding the entry of new recruits into commerce and attempting to share out the available trade. The view of medieval town-economy as one of restrictive and egalitarian monopoly, held and propagated by nineteenth-century historians, largely derives from the municipal and gild documents of the late fourteenth and the fifteenth centuries; and what is sometimes regarded as evidence of a typical medieval regulation is in fact nothing else than instances of fifteenth-century departure from the freer and more speculative conditions of the earlier centuries.

Still better known are the social changes in the villages. The real causes of the agricultural depression still await investigation. But if an anticipatory suggestion may be permitted here it should be pointed out that the most important cause will probably be found in movements of population. The prices of agricultural products, and above all wheat, were depressed, i.e. either stationary or gently falling, throughout the period, and the prices naturally affected production. But the action of prices was merely an outward manifestation of other and more fundamental processes. It was both caused and accompanied by a decline of the agricultural population of which there are innumerable signs.

The effect of a falling population and depressed prices on the condition of the peasants is easily imagined. It meant a greater supply of land and lower rents. The great overcrowding and land-hunger of the thirteenth century gave place to an oversupplied land market: there were fewer small-holders, and the full peasant holdings were on the whole held on more favourable conditions, sometimes at a lower rent, and nearly always free of labour services.

The improvement in the position of the landholder was accompanied by an improvement in the position of the hired labourer. With the decline in the numbers of the small-holding population the wages of agricultural labour rose. But while they were rising, prices remained either stationary or declined: hence the 'golden age of the English agricultural labourer' which Rogers discovered in the fifteenth century.

The real sufferers from the agricultural depression were therefore the landlords. The depression of prices and the rising costs of labour made the cultivation of the demesne unprofitable; the revenue from rents which at first grew with the letting out of the demesne was in the end affected by the 'vacancies' and the general fall of agricultural values. In short, in the countryside the main burden of economic change was borne by the upper ranks of society.

How far their dwindling revenue contributed to their restlessness and prompted them to seek additional income in political gangsterdom of the times we shall never know for certain. We can only surmise that in an age of dwindling agricultural profits seigneurial revenues derived from feudal rights and privileges were all the more valuable and all the more worth fighting for. And if attempts to defend and increase the feudal hold over local offices and revenues is to be discerned behind the personal struggles of baronial parties, then the agricultural depression can be said to have contributed, albeit indirectly, to that great reconstruction of the English landowning classes which prepared and maintained the rule of the Tudors. It is in this sense, more than in any other, that the roots of the sixteenth century will be found in the fifteenth.

4

SOME SOCIAL CONSEQUENCES OF THE HUNDRED YEARS WAR*

1

The Hundred Years War shares with the Reformation and the French Revolution the reputation of being a 'turning point' or a 'watershed'. It is commonly referred to as the culminating episode of the Middle Ages, marking the final failure of the feudal armies. Having destroyed the feudal order, the War also reared its successor. It has been generally accepted, even by Bernard Shaw, that out of the clash between the French and the English kings the national state and the nationalist conception of international policy emerged triumphant.

It is not our object here to quarrel with this generalization. As long as it is general enough and confined to notions as vague as those of the feudal order and the national state, it is both difficult and unnecessary to disprove. There is no denying that the hundred and fifty years which separated the beginning of the War from the final pacification of Western Europe under Louis XI were marked by many signs of popular nationalism. During the same period in one country at least, namely France, national monarchy and national unity were greatly strengthened. On the other hand, in countries other than France or Britain, national sentiment was no more in evidence in the fourteenth and fifteenth centuries than it had been in earlier times. Where it operated, in the Hussite War and at Tannenberg, it owed little or nothing to the issues which roused similar feelings at Crécy and Orléans. As for the national state, England of the twelfth and thirteenth centuries had nothing to learn from England of the fifteenth. If anything, the closing stages of the war, coinciding as they did with the civil war at home, stimulated centrifugal forces of every type and kind, and threatened to re-establish in England a feudal régime on the ruins of the Lancaster monarchy.

The generalization, so difficult to prove or disprove, had better be left alone. Our object here is to probe into the effects of the War at a level at which they are, by definition, more concrete, and therefore more amenable to proof. The War, like all historical events, must have had

* This paper first appeared in *Economic History Review*, XII, 1942.

immediate and apparent effects on economic life and social relations. According to some sociologists, notably Sombart, it is in the nature of war to revolutionize economic processes. This view has been tacitly endorsed by the hosts of writers, publicists, historians and sociologists, who have taken it for granted that since the First Great War the economic life of nations has never been the same, and that the Second World War is also bound to transform the entire economy of the world. Our object here is to find out whether this view holds good of the Hundred Years War.

2

The historian in search of tangible effects of the Hundred Years War will probably discover that the effects become less tangible as he penetrates the foundations of society. They are easiest of all to discover in the field in which they are probably most superficial, namely in the economic repercussions of the final territorial settlements.

In the second half of the fifteenth century the French kings extended their rule to all, or nearly all, the provinces which from then onwards have constituted the national territory of France, as we now know it. The economic and social consequences of this process have been much discussed but frequently misunderstood. Contrary to the common view, the territorial rearrangements in Western Europe were of more immediate economic consequence to England than they were to France. French territorial unity was not followed by an immediate economic and social merger. The re-establishment of French rule over Picardy and Normandy did little to establish closer economic and social links between those provinces and the rest of France than heretofore. The granaries of the lower Seine gave Paris and Île de France added security against famine, but in any case Île de France had not been greatly dependent on imported food, and the natural outlet of the vast grain surpluses of Abbéville continued to be not France but the Netherlands. Brittany remained what it had always been: a maritime province with an economic and social life intensely local and all its own. The time when the Bretons were to lead in the expansion of France overseas was at least a century off. Even Aquitaine, for all the spectacular part which in subsequent French history fell to the Gascons and to the Gasconade, was as yet alien to the economy and society of France as a whole. Generally speaking, France, for several centuries after the Hundred Years War, continued to function as a loose confederation of provinces, separated by customs barriers, local weights, measures and laws. It was not until the French Revolution that legal and administrative barriers to national unity were removed, and it was not until the coming of the railway that that unity was in fact established.

The effects on England, though less advertised, were much more immediate. For a time, England lost more than France gained. From a narrowly economic point of view, the Angevin empire was much less artificial than many empires before or since. Aquitaine and England were bound by economic links which, on the eve of the loss, were both old and strong. The two economies were mutually supplementary. Gascony produced little grain, had next to no wool or cloth, and specialized in the production of wine, certain technical crops (mostly dye-stuffs) and iron. On the other hand England was an unquenchable consumer of wines, a good customer for Gascon woad and Bayonne iron, and above all the principal supplier of cloth and food. England continued to export grain to Bordeaux long after she had ceased to export it to other countries, and on several occasions in the late fourteenth and the fifteenth centuries, when she had no grain of her own to send, she re-exported cereals of Baltic origin. Next to Germany, Aquitaine was England's principal market for finished cloth and, to some extent, for other industrial products.

This symbiosis was, for a time, severed by the loss of Aquitaine. England's loss of claret was neither tragic nor permanent. 'Thirst will find a way', and new ways, though expensive and restricted ones, were soon found, and by 1480 English merchants were again active in Bordeaux. But relatively brief as it was – a matter of some twenty-five years – the interruption was acutely felt and left an indelible mark. The markets of Gascony were lost at the time when other markets were also disappearing, and when outlets for the English cloth production were being steadily contracted. Students of English economic history will recall that by the middle of the fifteenth century the English cloth merchants had been excluded from all their more distant outposts. The Scandinavian market had been lost at the turn of the century. Connexions with Prussia, and, through that country, with the whole of central and eastern Europe were finally lopped off by the successive Anglo–Hanseatic conflicts in the thirties and fifties. The concentration of English trade in the Netherlands, the increasing specialization of the industry on unfinished cloth, the rise of the company and of the monopoly of the Merchant Adventures – all these familiar features of English trade at the close of the Middle Ages could be traced to the break-up of England's medieval empire at the end of the Hundred Years War.[1]

The territorial constriction of England's foreign trade had some obvious social repercussions. The expansive and speculative spirit which had dominated the activities of England's mercantile classes in the fourteenth century was bound to be damped by the loss of markets and opportunities,

[1] Cf. E. M. Carus-Wilson, *The Overseas Trade of Bristol, etc.* (Power and Postan, *English Trade in the Fifteenth Century*, 1933.) M. Postan, *Economic Relations between England and the Hanse* (ibid.), and reprinted in his *Medieval trade and finance*, 1973.

to say nothing of the loss of goods and cargoes in foreign lands. By the middle of the following century the narrowing horizons brought to the surface a new type of merchant and a new type of mercantile organization: sober, modest and disinclined to act alone. One of the paradoxes of English commercial history is that the merchants ceased to adventure at the very moment at which they arrogated to themselves the title of adventurer. Corporate monopoly, rigid definition of terms of trade, restriction of the volume of trade, were designed both to keep out the outsiders and to prevent a disproportionate aggrandisement of individual 'insiders'. Its effect was to secure the position of men of mediocre substance trading in a 'middle way'.

The effects of the changes in foreign trade were greatly enhanced by their domestic setting. They coincided and combined with similar changes in the structure of English industry and commerce at home, which had, strictly speaking, little to do either with the Hundred Years War or with foreign trade. It is now well understood that in the late fourteenth and in the fifteenth centuries the expansion of England's urban civilization was at an end. Not only were most of her ancient ports and corporate towns dwindling in size and population, but her town economy as a whole was congealed by the régime of corporate monopolies. Much of what has come to be regarded as evidence of the regulated and corporate spirit of medieval economy belongs not so much to the Middle Ages as to that phase of lost horizons which marks the English commerce of the late fourteenth and fifteenth centuries. The monopolies, the regulations, the rigid control of individual enterprise and the barriers to the entry of outsiders, and most of the other measures of restriction, were produced, rather suddenly, and rather recently, in response to the declining trade and falling prosperity.[2]

The changes in urban life were merely part of the general transformation of English society, and were in their turn due to the decline of population and to the contemporary reorganization of agriculture. The break in English commercial expansion abroad and the fall of England's medieval empire merely contributed their quota to the general movement of retrenchment. But for that general movement, the contribution of the War would probably have been less effective, even though it might then have stood out clearer in our documents and books.

3

The difficulty of defining the effects of the War grows as we recede from the political and territorial consequences of English defeat into the

[2] M. Postan, 'The Fifteenth Century', *Econ. Hist. Rev.* 1939 and see above Chapter 3.

economic and social processes of the War itself. Important social changes were bound to follow from a war effort extending over a century and a half. But the very fact that a chronic state of war continued for so long makes it very difficult to distinguish the action of war from the action of mere time. For it is only too easy to ascribe to the War what is, in fact, due to the hundred years.

A field in which the facts are easiest to distinguish is that in which national economy touched closest on the conduct of the War, i.e. war finance. Here certain causes and effects are so obvious as to require little proof. There has, undoubtedly, been much direct wastage of national wealth. With the outbreak of the War, Edward III's budgets probably rose three or fourfold, i.e. from somewhere between £40,000 and £70,000 in the first ten years of the fourteenth century to the average of about £200,000 in the twenties and the thirties. Much, though by no means most, of the wealth thus raised was sent abroad and wasted there to pay for alliances and to maintain garrisons and armies. As we shall see further, during the same period, national production and national income were not rising, but if anything falling, and this meant that the destruction of wealth by the War remained uncompensated and that England was getting poorer.

Some of the impoverishment, and even some of the decline in national production, could be traced directly to war finance. Edward's taxation and, even more, his levies in kind were bound to harm wool production. If we are to judge from the flood of complaints against purveyors, it appears that the requisition of foodstuffs in the countryside extended the depressing effects of war economy to agricultural production as a whole. It is also possible, though it still remains to be proved, that royal taxation, and still more royal seizures and confiscations, had something to do with the unmistakable decline of investment in agricultural improvements in dykes, drainage, and deforestation.

The main effects of war taxation, however, like the main effects of all taxation, would be found not in wealth destroyed but in wealth transferred. The signs of the transference were many and various, and at the very beginning of the War it looked as if the War would succeed in so redistributing the wealth of the country as to produce a major economic and social revolution. The readers of Miss Power's book on the wool trade will recall that the opening phases of the Hundred Years War saw the sudden emergence in English life of a small group of financial and commercial magnates. They were called into being by the King's need of loans and of assistance in handling the new taxation on wool and the great imposts in kind. Through their hands passed most of the money which Edward raised between 1322 and 1350: a sum not less than two million pounds and probably more. Edward's bankruptcy, which nearly ruined the Italian bankers, left the English financiers for a short time in sole possession of the field. But sooner or later their turn to be ruined came, and they disappeared from the English scene even quicker than they rose. Their function was taken over by the corporate body of the Staplers who shared out among a larger body of substantial men the monopoly of the English wool trade and the function of state banking.[3]

The establishment of the Staple helped to consolidate the middle-middle class, but it also nipped in the bud the first seedlings of England's 'high capitalism'. For a short time it had looked as if the War might raise in England the same class of financial capitalists which played so important a part in the genesis of early capitalism in the more advanced parts of Europe: the great commercial magnates of the Italian, South German and Provençal cities, the financiers of Arras in the thirteenth century, the Bardi and Peruzzi of the fourteenth, the Medici of the fifteenth, the Fuggers and Welsers of the seventeenth, the English nabobs and city bankers of the late seventeenth and eighteenth. National wealth was set moving out of the hands of the landed interests into those of men who might employ it in trade or commercial finance, or even in large-scale industry. In short, it seemed as if the social and financial prerequisites of an economic revolution, such as those which, in this country, appeared in the late seventeenth and in the eighteenth centuries, were being created in the fourteenth.

These hopes and dangers failed to come true. Not only were the great financiers in the end replaced by men of more modest substance, but what is more, neither the magnates nor their 'middling' successors were as yet ready to finance an economic revolution. In fact, the so-called transference of wealth was more apparent than real, for most of the wealth thus transferred did not stay in its new surroundings for long. As we have already seen, some of it was destroyed and wasted abroad. But even that part which was not pumped across the Channel failed to create great pools of urban wealth or to irrigate the fields of English industry and trade. Most of it, as a rule, went back to the land.

The repatriation of rural wealth proceeded by two channels. One of the channels had little or nothing to do with the War, but was an ancient current of English history. No student of English medieval society will fail to observe what modern sociologists would probably describe as its 'social mobility'. Not only were divisions between classes – between merchant and knight, serf and freeholder, freeholder and knight, knight and noble – so vague as to be indiscernible, but they were also crossed and recrossed, both up and down. It is now generally known that the upper ranks of the merchant classes were frequently recruited from land-owning

[3] Eileen Power, *The Wool Trade in English Medieval History* (Oxford, 1941), *passim*.

families. It is also known that successful merchants could, in their own urban societies, acquire the status of 'miles' or 'armiger'. But the process of social rise was not confined to elevation within urban society, for it usually ended in migration from the towns to the country. The Middle Ages were well familiar with the process so characteristic of the last two centuries, by which wealth amassed in industry and trade was, in the end, devoted to the acquisition of stately homes and of their social appurtenances. The ambition of the wealthy Londoner has always been to become a gentleman. It is very instructive to watch the stages by which the interests of the Cely family shifted from Mark Lane to their place in Essex. It is there that, in the end, we find the younger branches of the family all but merged into the county society, and all but absorbed in the pleasures of the hunt. It may be true that some city families took no more than three generations to pass from shirt sleeves to shirt sleeves, but it is equally true that some took no longer to pass from country house to country house. The true exception to the rule was not the family which succeeded in maintaining itself in wealth for more than seventy-five years, but the family which, having kept its wealth, was content to enjoy it in Town.

The attractions of the countryside and of the social prizes of rural society will account for many otherwise inexplicable gaps in the family histories of the fifteenth-century towns. Many, if not most, of the names of the great merchants who are known to have been enriched by the war expenditure of the twenties and thirties, sooner or later disappeared from the records of English towns, and even from those of English trade. Some of their bearers died out, others, we know, were irreparably ruined by subsequent royal depredations. But some of the best known war financiers, men like the De la Poles, the Poultneys, the Pickards, not only left an offspring, but also salvaged substantial portions of their war fortunes, and sooner or later established themselves in the country and founded there gentle and even noble families.[4]

This migration had an obvious effect on the economic processes of the Hundred Years War. Such success as royal taxation may have achieved in squeezing the landed interests and in enriching the financiers was largely nullified by the latter's investment in land. The fact that some merchants got rich quicker than they might have done in peace time meant merely that they themselves or their offspring were enabled to leave the towns sooner. As a result of the War, the interval between the Da la Poles who financed the War and the De la Poles who dominated

[4] The De la Poles began the purchases in Lincolnshire and Yorkshire, but eventually most of the family possessions were concentrated in East Anglia. Sir John Poultney's purchases were mostly in Kent. Henry Pickard bought land all over the country.

rural society in the eastern counties was cut down to one generation instead of the conventional three. Social mobility may thereby have been quickened, but the wheels of commerce showed no signs of revolving faster.

Another and even more important channel of repatriation was provided by the gentlemen of the sword and of the cloth. These men were probably the chief beneficiaries of the War, but conspicuous as they are in contemporary documents, they have been curiously neglected by historians. In spite of the central position which the army occupied in medieval life and of the voluminous records which its activities left in various royal offices, its administration and its social composition have, until recently, been little studied. Until more is known about the men who made up and ran the British expeditions abroad, all discussion of the subject is bound to be highly speculative and hypothetical.[5] But of all the hypotheses which the sources suggest, none is more fruitful and, therefore, worth exploring than that which stresses the rise and the importance of the soldier of fortune.

'The soldier of handsome fortune' would be a better and a more exact appellation of the type. It is now generally assumed that the organization and the composition of the army underwent an important change after the opening campaigns of the War. The national and feudal armies, which were raised by the mobilization of feudal levies and by Commissions of Array, and fought, or were supposed to have fought, on the fields of Crécy and Poitiers were, in the middle and the later stages of the War, largely superseded by units raised and maintained by professional military contractors. In the Hundred Years War, as in so many other English wars, it was the amateurs who were winning campaigns, and the professionals who were losing them. But whatever we may think of the military qualifications, the tactics and the strategy of the professional captains, it is impossible to gainsay the administrative and economic enterprise which went into the making and maintaining of their companies. The contractors, who appear to belong to every possible rung of the feudal ladder except, perhaps, the lowest, undertook to find, equip and feed bodies of fighting men for periods which often ran into months and years. The system had many obvious drawbacks. The professional companies attracted the débris of English society, the riff-raff of town and country, and the waste products of every occupation, including the Church, and spelt ruin to the countries in which they operated. But they opened great opportunities for enrichment to the men who ran them.

[5] Dr Lewis, in the University of Sheffield, has been engaged on the subject for some time. An unpublished thesis by Dr Rushton Coulborn, on the 'Crusade' of the Bishop of Norwich in 1383, contains a brief analysis of the composition of the expeditionary force.

A margin of profit was probably provided in the terms of the captains' contracts. But, in addition, there were countless openings for irregular gain. To begin with, the terms of the contract with the crown offered the captains every temptation to economize on the provisioning of their troops, and this temptation was often turned into necessity by the delays in royal remittances. The troops, left to their own devices, were often tempted and sometimes compelled to live on the country to an extent which, as the record of the English occupation of Normandy shows, could, even by medieval standards, be thought excessive. But the heavier the burden on the population, the greater were the captains' economies. And in addition to economies in purveyance, there were also prizes of war which were open to amateurs and professionals alike: ransoms and loot. Needless to say not every captain made a fortune, and certainly not every captain lived to enjoy one. But the royal grants and obligations to the military leaders are so numerous as to suggest that it is to them that a great proportion, if not the bulk, of the war expenditure went.

The only other group of the population whose opportunities for war profits or for war profiteering rivalled those of the military men were the gentlemen of the cloth: the royal clerks in charge of purveyance of the navy and the army and of the administration of the war treasuries. Their numbers were never very large, but the company, though small, was very choice. Richard De la Pole belonged to the profession, and William De la Pole was a royal purveyor and a merchant rolled into one. At least six of the men who figured prominently in the syndicates of the wool magnates, Wesenham, Chirton, Quedlinburg, the two brothers Melchebourn, and John Poultney himself, had, at one time or another, acted as officers in charge of purveyance. In addition, there were also clerks like William Burton, Mathew Torkesey, William Wenlock, Ralph Kesteven, William Rothwell and John Hatfield in the fourteenth century, or William Loveney, William Soper and John Feriby in the fifteenth, who operated on the frontiers of the exchequer and the army, and had every opportunity for enrichment.[6] Of these opportunities all of them freely availed themselves. Some of them, like the other magnates, were not allowed to enjoy their newly acquired wealth for any length of time and sooner or later fell victims to royal appetites, but many survived the royal depredations and saved at least some of their wealth.

6 Perhaps the best known of these is William Northwell whose fame was largely based on the Exchequer Proceedings which arose from spurious bills issued and circulated by him. Cf. *P.R.O. Chancery Miscellanea*, 68/1. But there were many other less notorious clerks among the King's principal creditors. Thomas Kent of the middle decades of the fifteenth century was one of the last of the race. Curiously enough, William Philipp, the official Treasurer of the War at the beginning of the fifteenth century, is least prominent among the beneficiaries of the War.

In the present state of our knowledge it is difficult to be precise either about the numbers or about the riches of the war captains and the clerks, but the employment to which the new riches were put is easy enough to discover. It is almost certain that very little went into industry or trade. It would be useless to search among the hundreds of names of the fifteenth-century wool merchants or clothiers for family associations with men who, in the previous generation or two, figured in the royal grants for services rendered in the War. Traces of indirect investment in trade are equally hard to find. England, unlike other European countries, did not develop the specialized legal forms of the 'Commenda' and the 'Societas' to serve the purposes of sleeping partnership and of other types of investment by non-merchants into mercantile or industrial enterprise. But the legal security of the Action of Account, in which the passive partner, or the investor, appeared in the fictitious guise of master or employer, performed the function of a partnership contract and produced a vast mass of evidence of medieval investment. In that mass, names of nobles and gentlemen occasionally occur, but they are no more frequent during or immediately after the Hundred Years War than they had been in the thirteenth or the early fourteenth centuries, or were to be in the late fifteenth. Most of the transactions are between merchants and merchants. Such 'non-professional investments' as are to be found belong mostly to widows, orphans and spinsters.

In so far as the employment of war profits by the military profiteers can be traced at all, it will be found to be identical with the use to which new riches were put by merchants. War wealth went the way of all new wealth: what was not wasted in riotous living or hoarded in plate and clothes was put into land. Some of the land was in the towns, but most of it was in the country. The captains and the clerks as well as the merchants preferred to invest in broad acres and social elevation. Indeed some of them were given no choice. The Crown was constantly in debt to its servants and to its war creditors, and more often than not paid its debts or rewarded its creditors' patience by grants of land or of reversions. The bulk of the vast land possessions of the De la Pole family, which later became part of the great Suffolk patrimony, was acquired in that way; so also were some of the lands of the famous war captains. Sir John Falstaff, who got much publicity as a result of the royal seizures in the late fifties of the fifteenth century, had received some of his lands from the King twenty or thirty years earlier. Documents also abound with grants to other famous soldiers: John Chandos, William Felton, Thomas Kyriel, Nigel Loring, Hugh Calverley, Thomas Ufford, Reginald Cobham, to say nothing of the feudal leaders, like John de Vere, Earl of Oxford. The fortunes of the Vere family, like those of the Beauchamps, the Berkeleys and the d'Umfrevilles, must have been greatly helped by the wartime enterprises of their members, and by the grants of land in payment of royal war debts.

But most of the new men also acquired land for hard cash. A student passing from the exchequer documents of the late fourteenth and the early fifteenth centuries to the study of the Ancient Deeds or of the recognisances which accompanied transactions in land finds himself among old acquaintances. The names of royal creditors on the Issue and Receipt Rolls occur so frequently in the records of land purchases and leases as to preclude mere coincidence. The identity of names obviously betrays the homecoming of the country's prodigal money. Wealth, wrung from the land in imposts and taxes, was now returning, much shrunk and depleted, to the place from which it came.

4

The circular tour of rural wealth had obvious social consquences. Even if the war finance did not revolutionize English industry and trade, it could and did affect the composition of rural society. It can be argued that class structure remained unaltered, for the War brought to the country new men rather than new classes, and affected the country's social metabolism without altering the layout of its social anatomy. Yet, the importance of the metabolic changes could be real and great enough, and their influence was all the greater in that it so often agreed and combined with other more purely structural changes.

What these changes were students of economic history well know. The closing hundred and fifty years of the Middle Ages were marked by a profound transformation of agriculture. The manorial system was breaking up all over the country. The capitalist or quasi-capitalist economy in demesnes or monastic granges was invaded and conquered by peasant units. By the end of the fifteenth century labour services, villeinage and cultivation by landlords or estate bailiffs were nearly everywhere replaced by copyholds, leaseholds and rent-collecting landownership.

It would be useless to attempt to explain the agricultural revolution by the effects of the War. What caused it we do not yet know, but all the indications point either to the falling prices, or to the declining population, or to both. Neither the prices nor the population were at the mercy of the War. The prices apparently broke before Edward decided to invade France. Their subsequent depression had very little to do with the war drain on the country's treasure, for it was also observed abroad. What caused the decline of population (if there was one) in the early fourteenth century it is impossible to say. But it is more or less certain that military expeditions did not absorb a substantial enough proportion of the population to have a lasting demographic effect. The Black Death and the pestilence of the sixties were infinitely more lethal, but neither could directly be ascribed to the War. The only direct bearing which the War may have had on the agricultural crisis was in discouraging and controlling investment in agricultural equipment and improvements. But even this was due more directly to the agricultural depression itself than to the action of war taxation.

Yet it would be wrong entirely to divorce the agricultural crisis from the War. Their causes may have been separate and independent, but their effects were not. In the upper ranks of society the impact of the War doubtless amplified and implemented the action of the manorial depression. As most students would now admit, the humbler ranks of rural society must have benefited from the agricultural changes. Wages rose, land became cheaper, average holdings larger. Not so the ruling classes. The decline of demesne agriculture was in itself a sign that circumstances were not favourable to large-scale agriculture. For the manorial lords the period was indeed one of profound crisis. It began with the break in prices in the opening decades of the fourteenth century, and was accentuated by shortage of labour and of tenants in the second half of the century. The falling profits of cultivation led to the leasing out of demesne and of customary holdings, and this produced a fall in land values, which even the demand from the *nouveaux riches* was unable to check.

The crisis was therefore bound to affect the fortunes of the landowning classes, though what effect it had upon their composition can, as yet, be only guessed. In spite of the abundant documentary evidence, the social condition of the ruling classes is the most conspicuous gap in our historical knowledge. The topics of economic history have been determined by the interest of its founders in social reform, with the result that more is now known about the Chartists and the trade unions than about the capitalists and manufacturers, and much more about the medieval labourer than about the medieval landlord. Guesses must take the place of knowledge, superficial impressions the place of proof.

The impression which is, perhaps, least superficial is that of a 'general post', a re-shuffle of ownership and of the effective occupation of landed estates. The magnates found it difficult to maintain themselves on their purely agricultural incomes. Some of them tried to supplement their incomes in other ways. Most of them must have found feudal revenues, profits of courts and of local influence relatively more important as agricultural revenues fell, and offices of state or shares in the spoils of political power must have become more tempting than ever. So also were the profits of the sword for those who could wield it.

It was at this point that the social consequences of the Hundred Years War impinged upon the social consequence of the agricultural crisis. The magnates, even men as great as the Duke of Lancaster, tried to stabilize their incomes by sub-letting their estates to men small enough to live on them, and substantial enough to afford them. Men of this type were rising to the surface all over the country. Some of them bought demesne farms or whole manors outright; others appeared merely as tenants ('farmers'), but all of them represented a new and rising class. Where they all came from cannot be said with certainty. We find among them local men of the humblest origin, the 'kulaks' of the English countryside, who had been assembling land piece by piece for many years, and also reeves, manorial officials or other officers of noble households. But many, possibly the majority, were merchants, clerks, or returned captains, in short, the *nouveaux riches* of the War. If the agricultural revolution created the demand for the 'gentry', the War and the war finance were there to provide the supply.

The distant repercussions of the re-shuffle must have reached far outside the confines of rural society and far beyond the span of the Hundred Years War. It does not require much ingenuity to follow them up through the Wars of the Roses to the political and constitutional developments which accompanied the establishment of the Tudors. The sub-letting of manors raised all over the country a wave of what looked suspiciously like subinfeudation. Even though the creation of new intermediate fiefs was all but illegal, the new 'farms' and beneficiary leases enabled many a great lord not only to stabilize his income, but also to consolidate his local influence and to augment his following. Some of the great northern families, like the Nevills or the Percys, may have found in the chronic wars with Scotland and in the disturbed conditions of the Border sufficient impetus and sufficient facilities for the recruitment of their great retinues. They may, therefore, not have needed the twofold upheaval of the War and of the agricultural revolution to stimulate either their demand for gentlemen tenants or their supply of suitable candidates. Elsewhere, and above all in East Anglia and the West Country, the decline of the great estates as agricultural enterprises was accompanied by the temporary resurgence of the great fiefs as a political force and by the formation of large, and mostly recent, quasi-feudal retinues. But the future belonged to the retainers and not to their masters. In the political struggle of the Wars of the Roses the 'great connexions' found their doom. As a result of that struggle the new men, who in the preceding two or three generations had succeeded to the commanding positions in rural economy, were also able to succeed to local power and political influence.

In this light the evolution of the landowning classes in the closing century and a half of the Middle Ages, like the evolution of the middle classes in the same period, appears as a joint product of a protracted war and of a deep-rooted economic change. Our main conclusions are therefore obvious to the point of being trivial. In the machinery of social change the War was not so much the mainspring as a make-weight. Wherever its action ran counter to the economic tendencies of the age, as in the development of financial capitalism or the movement of land values, it was on the whole ineffective. Only at points at which changes were taking place anyhow was its influence great and irrevocable enough to deserve the attention not only of the chronicler but also of the social historian.

5

THE COSTS OF THE HUNDRED YEARS WAR*

Nowadays most of us take it for granted that nations do not profit from wars; not even from victorious wars. Recently, however, we have been told that this assumption does not apply to the Hundred Years War.[1] The argument, if I understand it correctly, is that whereas France suffered war damage of every kind, England and Englishmen on balance profited from the military campaigns and from the occupation of French territory. I propose to inspect this balance somewhat more closely than has so far been done.

There are two ways of counting the costs and profits of war. One, the economic, is to reckon in real terms, i.e. in material resources and economic activities diverted to war or enlarged by it. The other, the financial or the bullionist one, is to confine the count to the disbursements and receipts of treasure. These two ways of reckoning overlap at certain points, but on the whole they deal with different sets of counters and must be considered separately.

1

The balance of the account in real terms is very simple and I am going to begin by declaring it. In real terms England's net balance of loss and gain in the Hundred Years War was bound to be in the red. The most obvious real cost was that of manpower diverted to war-making and in the first place that of soldiers in the field and in garrisons. This cost was to some extent discontinuous, for the demand for military manpower rose and fell as successive invading expeditions were mounted and wound up. The largest expedition was that of the Crécy–Calais campaign of 1346–7 in which the combatants numbered about 32,000. Others were smaller, though several, like the expedition of 1359 or that of Agincourt,

* *The Costs of the Hundred Years War*, The Past and Present Society, Corpus Christi College, Oxford, 1964. This article is reprinted with the permission of the Society from *Past and Present*, a Journal of Historical Studies, No. 27.

[1] K. B. McFarlane, 'England and the Hundred Years War', *Past and Present*, no. 22 (July 1962), pp. 3–13.

approached 15,000.[2] Taken alone these contingents may seem small, seldom larger than one modern division. But can they be taken alone? Most medieval expeditions carried with them some non-combatants or near-combatants, i.e. pages, grooms, courtiers and other attendants on the king and the magnates not included in the establishment of soldiers. In addition there were the various units making up the occupying army. In the intervals between expeditions as well as at the time of the expeditions themselves England kept garrisons all over the occupied territories, more especially in Calais and Gascony. During the fifteenth century the Calais garrison fluctuated around the thousand mark, exclusive of non-combatant auxiliaries; and there were garrisons in towns and castles all over the occupied territories.[3]

In sheer numbers even more important were the naval forces, both those engaged in warlike operations and those employed in the carriage of food and provisions. We are told that an armada of 1500 boats of twenty tons and above was mobilized to carry the army of Agincourt and its supplies and that the total number of mariners engaged in the operation was 20,000. Large as the numbers may appear at first sight, they are quite credible. To transport a king's court and a combatant army of 15,000 with their supplies, horses and arms this number of vessels would be required; and the average number of men needed to serve a medieval boat of twenty tons and above would not be far short of ten or fifteen. These computations can be cross-checked by the evidence of certain smaller contingents for which we have more detailed evidence. Thus, the personnel of the seventy-six boats which composed Sir Walter Manny's northern fleet in 1337 was about 2000 mariners for the 3000 or so fighting men it carried.[4]

To aggregate these various calls on the military manpower would of course be a hopeless statistical task, but I shall not go far wrong if I suggest that the total number engaged in various combatant and logistic tasks in the year of Crécy was somewhere between sixty and eighty

[2] The purely military establishment at Agincourt was probably about 12,000; the size of the Duke of Lancaster's raiding army in 1373 was about 10,000 not counting subsequent reinforcements. For the Crécy and other figures see A. E. Prince, 'The Strength of English Armies in the Reign of Edward III', *Eng. Hist. Rev.*, XLVI (1931); E. Perroy, *The Hundred Years' War* (London, 1961), pp. 118–19.

[3] J. Kirby, 'The Financing of Calais under Henry V', *Bull. Inst. Hist. Res.*, XXIII (1950). English garrisons in Aquitaine fluctuated very greatly, but often, especially in times of active warfare, ran into thousands. Under Henry V, Normandy was garrisoned by English troops who numbered some 4700 men: in addition 1400 to 2000 men had to be provided by the English recipients of Norman fiefs under the terms of their grants. Cf. J. H. Wylie and T. T. Waugh, *The Reign of Henry the Fifth*, vol. III (Cambridge, 1929), pp. 240–1.

[4] Cf. figures cited in T. F. Tout, *Chapters in the Administrative History of Medieval England*, vol. IV (Manchester, 1928), p. 101.

thousand and that the corresponding number in the year of Agincourt was somewhere between forty and fifty thousand. The total manpower requirements of other expeditions may have fallen short of these numbers, but on several occasions the totals could well have approached the Agincourt figure very closely.

These totals may at first sight appear to be paltry; but in viewing medieval figures it is necessary to adjust our sights to medieval scales. Considered in proportion to the population in the late fourteenth and fifteenth centuries the employment of 50,000 men might approach ten or even fifteen per cent of the total male population aged between eighteen and forty-five and be thus equivalent to the call-up of three quarters of a million men and more in England in the 1960s.

Yet even these figures do not give a full measure of what manpower budgets of nations at war would comprise nowadays. For relevant comparison with modern manpower budgets the medieval estimates would have to include men engaged in the making and growing of the supplies which the army consumed. Miss Carus-Wilson has shown how rapidly the numbers of cloth workers in Castle Combe increased in the first half of the fifteenth century.[5] It is probable that one of the reasons for this increase was that Castle Combe was making cloth for army uniforms; and it is more or less certain that many of the men who settled in Castle Combe in the fifteenth century were weavers and finishers diverted from other cloth-working places. But is it necessary for me to hazard the guess that Castle Combe was not the only cloth-working village making cloth for the army or that the supplies which the army drew from home were not confined to cloth? Men engaged in producing war stores must also be sought among iron workers, leather workers, armourers and shipwrights, to say nothing of the husbandmen who bred and reared the war horses or grew food and other provisions for the army. For, contrary to what is frequently assumed, English armies at war did not wholly live upon the country they occupied. Most expeditions carried some provisions with them, and the garrisons of Calais and Gascony were regularly supplied by imports.[6]

What all these categories of men involved in the war amounted to in the aggregate is a calculation no historian and no statistician would attempt with impunity. I shall not, however, be sticking out my neck too far if I suggest that at the time of the Crécy campaign the total manpower engaged in fighting, in transporting the army and its supplies, in

[5] E. M. Carus-Wilson, 'Evidences of Industrial Growth on Some Fifteenth-Century Manors', *Econ. Hist. Rev.*, 2nd ser., XII (1959), pp. 198 ff.; repr. in *Essays in Econ. Hist.*, ed. E. M. Carus-Wilson, vol. II (London, 1962), pp. 151 ff.

[6] S. J. Burley, 'The Victualling of Calais, 1347–1365', *Bull. Inst. Hist. Res.*, XXXI (1958). Grain was sometimes imported into Gascony from the Baltic by English shippers, but it was of course paid for by English cloth exports to those regions.

occupying the garrison of the country, and in producing supplies in England, should be reckoned not in tens but in scores of thousands. And even if it were as low as, say, 80,000 it would still be equivalent to a proportion of the 1340 population corresponding to at least a million Englishmen in 1960. Even this figure represents a burden very much lighter than the one this nation bore in the last war without being crushed by it; yet nobody in their senses would regard it as weightless or consider a war which imposed it as being costless.

The costs were in fact higher than they might have been owing to the economic conditions under which they were incurred. In the second half of the fourteenth and the first half of the fifteenth century England was suffering from an acute shortage of manpower resulting in high wages and rising costs of production. A diversion of as much as ten per cent of its adult male population to war uses might perhaps have been suffered easily and even gladly in the over-populated thirteenth century; but the country could ill afford it in the man-hungry generations following the fourteenth- and early fifteenth-century pestilences.

This simple demographic and economic fact cannot be argued away by contending that the men employed in war could be easily spared because they were not gainfully employable in peace. The make-up of the levies raised by Commissions of Array and the social position of the men 'elected' to serve abroad are problems which still await their final solution, but the knowledge we now possess does not justify the argument that the rank and file of the king's armies in France was entirely composed of men not wanted at home. The argument would not have cut much ice with the burgesses and knights in Parliament, the royal clerks and Justices who called forth, drafted and enforced the Statutes of Labourers. Nor would it have done so with the eleven Painswick widows whose husbands, Sir John Talbot's tenants, had been slain abroad in Sir John's battles; or with the forty members of the third Thomas Berkeley's household who, as archers, accompanied him to France; or with the villagers who probably provided most of the two hundred foot archers of his troupe; or with John of Gaunt's tenants who in 1372 and 1373 served in his force of 1000 men-at-arms and archers; or with the Bishop of Winchester's tenants raised in fifteenth-century arrays on his estates. References to peasant landholders elected to serve abroad, absent or missing or slain in their lord's or the king's service recur quite regularly in court rolls, peasant genealogies and inheritance cases.[7]

[7] S. Rudder, *A New History of Gloucestershire* (Cirencester, 1779), p. 594; Talbot took 16 men from his lordship of Painswick, of whom eleven were killed and left widows; J. Smyth, *Lives of the Berkeleys* (London, 1883–5), I, p. 320; *John of Gaunt's Register*, ed. Armitage-Smith (Camden Soc., 3rd ser., XX, XXI [1911]), nos. 49–53, 968–9 and *passim*. The ratio of men raised by local levies to those hired by contract could be as high as five to two, e.g. in the

No doubt medieval armies comprised large numbers of men not engaged in any useful occupation. Mr Coulborn's researches into the composition of the Bishop of Norwich's 'crusade' of 1383 have shown that a considerable proportion of the Bishop's force consisted of miscellaneous riff-raff.[8] Yet even if we knew nothing about the actual cases of village householders serving abroad, we should still have had no right to assume that the waste products of fourteenth-century society, which may have been sufficient to provide a sizeable part of the Bishop's band, would also have sufficed to meet the entire military, naval and logistic demands of major campaigns in the war. After all, some loafers and beggars must still have been left in England even in the years of Crécy and Agincourt.

Even with regard to the officer ranks, i.e. the men in the knightly and baronial classes, it would be rash to assume that their continued absence abroad was of no consequence. Most historians who have tried to distinguish the different types of land-ownership and estate management have taken it for granted that liability to military service and high incidence of absentee ownership were among the reasons why smaller lay estates so often appear to lack the continuity and the efficiency of estates under ecclesiastical or conciliar management. Agrarian historians have also argued that what distinguished the small knightly manors from others was that their owners themselves managed their demesnes and were directly dependent on their demesne produce; and that in this respect the smaller knightly properties had much in common with the larger peasant holdings.[9]

And what about public service? Have not constitutional historians been telling us how indispensable knights had become in the conduct of local government and how great was the burden of administration and service they bore in the shires? And yet if Professor Morris's, Mr Denholm-Young's and Professor Treharne's estimates of the numbers of knights in England are compared with the numbers of knights in the armies abroad, it would appear that a very large proportion of this class, perhaps its bulk, was repeatedly drained off for service in France.[10] The shortage of

Calais force of 1347, or even higher: Michael Powicke, ***Military Obligations in Medieval England*** (Oxford, 1962), p. 185.

8 Rushton Coulborn, 'The Bishop of Norwich's Expedition of 1383' (unpublished thesis in the University of London Library).

9 Cf. E. Kosminsky, *Studies in the Agrarian History of England in the Thirteenth Century* (Oxford, 1956), ch. v.

10 Mr Denholm-Young (*Collected Papers on Medieval Subjects* [Oxford, 1946], pp. 56–7) accepts Professor Morris's guess that there were in the thirteenth century about 3000 actual and potential knights. The expedition of 1340 contained about 1946 men-at-arms and 589 knights, the latter figure being about equal to the numbers of soldier-knights among the 1500 knights in the late thirteenth century: F. M. Powicke, *The Thirteenth Century* (Oxford, 1953), pp. 548–9; the numbers of men-at-arms and knights at Crécy may have been more than twice as great. Allowances must be made for the possibility that not

knights available for local service in the counties in the middle of the fourteenth century has been commented on by Mr F. Nichols and Miss Wood-Legh and may not have been wholly accidental. It certainly did not pass wholly unnoticed and unregretted by contemporaries.[11]

Thus, however great our allowances for the dispensability of soldiers, we must not conclude that most of the manpower in military and naval employment (and still less the manpower engaged in supplying the armies) was 'surplus' to the country's needs and could be diverted to foreign war without any real cost to the national economy and polity.

In counting the real costs some provision should also be made for economic disturbance. England may not have been fought over or occupied, but it did not stay wholly unruffled by the business of war. I reckon that on the average once in every four years shipping had to be mobilised for the transportation of troops and supplies. Commerce and navigation were repeatedly disturbed, especially in the narrow seas. In the initial stages of the war the English wool trade was thrown into confusion by loans and taxation on wool and on at least one occasion by the confiscation of the entire wool crop. In addition, there were the regular purveyances of grain and cattle for provisioning the armies and castles abroad. Mr Burley reckons that Calais alone received 26,000 quarters of grain and over 2800 head of cattle in the fourteen years between 1347 and 1361; and these were not necessarily the most voracious years in the history of Calais, and Calais was not the only garrison provisioned from England.[12] Parliament complained at the purveyance and prisage of victuals – we all know about the petition of the Commons in 1351 – and students who have had occasion to look into medieval purveyances and prises will sympathize with the resentment they caused in the fourteenth and fifteenth centuries.

In short it will not do to pitch our estimates of real costs too low. They may not have been as high as the simple arithmetic of military manpower might suggest; even at their highest they were very much lighter than the real burdens of total wars in our own time; they were nevertheless high enough to be taken account of. But what made them

all the men who figured as knights in lists and expense accounts of military expeditions would be identical with the knights counted by Denholm-Young or Sir F. M. Powicke. But in general it is impossible to disagree with Mr Michael Powicke that the classes which supplied the archers, the men-at-arms and presumably the fully armed and attended knights 'were also the backbone of local administration and justice'; op. cit. pp. 97–8.

11 Miss Wood-Legh believes that the ratio of belted knights to 'other ranks' returned to Edward III's parliament depended on the business to be transacted; however, she cites instances when sheriffs reported the scarcity of belted knights in their counties: K. Wood-Legh, 'Sheriffs, Lawyers and Belted Knights in the Parliament of Edward III', *Eng. Hist. Rev.*, XLVI (1931).

12 Above, note 6.

higher still is that they were borne for a century and a quarter and that for most of that time they remained almost wholly uncompensated. No material additions to manpower, or to capital assets in real terms, or to consumable commodities accrued as a result of military operations abroad or of the occupation of French territory. The only *quid pro quo* were the various payments received as profits of war from booty, fiefs and ransoms. These receipts however were mostly in the form of money and treasure and belong to the more purely financial account of the war to which I now propose to pass.

2

Financial expenses are somewhat easier to assess than real costs since their main stream flowed through the Exchequer and the king's Wardrobe and left behind them a deposit of financial records. They were, moreover, paid for by taxes, the yield of which can also be ascertained. Mr McFarlane estimates the total of taxes levied for war purposes during the one hundred and twenty years of the Hundred Years War at about eight and a quarter million pounds, of which four came from the taxation of wool; and as far as I can see his estimate is about right.

This estimate is, of course, subject to a number of adjustments of which I shall have to say more presently. I do not, however, think that it will be right to scale it down at all drastically, still less to brush it aside altogether, on the ground that half of it was levied on wool and that the entire burden of the wool taxes was borne by foreign customers. Such scaling down involves a number of misunderstandings, and in the first place a misunderstanding as to how the incidence of the tax is to be judged. Had the tax been as high, and only as high, as the foreigners were prepared or able to pay, the total exports of wool would have stayed at the same level as before the taxes were imposed. The fact that wool exports slumped sharply and eventually fell to less than one third of their pre-tax level means that the charges were higher than the traffic would bear; or, in other words, that foreigners were unable to buy wool in the old quantities at the new prices, while English buyers were getting it cheaper than they would have done had the foreigners been prepared to buy on the same scale as heretofore. We must therefore conclude that the growers were probably receiving less than they would have done had the tax not been levied. This conclusion is wholly consistent with the behaviour of wool prices. The lattter happen to be notoriously difficult to interpret since they reflect not only changes in demand for wool but also changes in supply. It is, however, of some significance that, with the exception of the post-pestilence and post-murrain years in the middle of the century and the short-lived flutter of wool prices at the turn of the fourteenth and the fifteenth centuries, the general trend was downward, and that prices of high-quality wool in the 1450s stood below their level of a century earlier.[13]

How much less the growers were in fact receiving cannot be estimated since we do not know what their receipts would have been had foreigners continued to take wool in the old quantities. But if the decline in foreign sales is any guide, it will justify the guess that the burden of the tax may have been shared between domestic growers and foreign buyers in the same ratio of two to one. Therefore, if we want to allow for the possibility that foreigners bore some of the weight of wool taxation, the deduction we would be entitled to make on this account from our estimate of gross fiscal costs should not exceed about one third of the yield of wool taxation, say one and a half million pounds.

There are of course other deductions to be made. For instance, we cannot assume that the entire proceeds from taxes levied ostensibly for the war were spent for purposes which would not have required some expenditure even in peace-time; some armed forces, some shipbuilding, some garrisons. On the other hand the residual estimates must be increased by certain simple additions. The war, especially in its early phases, was to some extent conducted on credit. Edward III owed vast sums of money and failed to repay debts in full to a large number of his creditors, foreign and English. In the first quarter of the fifteenth century the deficit and corresponding debts ran at the rate of about £15,000 per annum and exceeded £370,000 by 1449.[14] Some of these debts were sooner or later repaid out of current revenues, but others were repaid in other ways: out of extraordinary war profits or by an assignment of land and revenues from land. And every time the latter was done some of the financial burdens of the war were shifted from taxes to other assets and revenues. From the accounting point of view these disbursements must be reckoned as additional to the costs of war computed from the yields of war taxes.

Some further additions, especially in the early campaigns of Edward III, came from payments imposed on counties and towns for the direct maintenance (i.e. wages and supplies) of local levies.[15] There were also

13 Lord Beveridge, 'Westminster Wages in the Manorial Era', *Econ. Hist. Rev.*, 2nd ser., VIII (1955–6), p. 28. This trend will, I trust, be exhibited even more clearly in Mr T. H. Lloyd's chapter on prices in the projected third volume of the *Agrarian History of England*. Contrary to the impression formed by Mr McFarlane (op. cit., p. 8), nothing I have previously published on this subject either alleges or assumes that the burden of wool taxes in its entirety was borne by English wool growers.

14 E. B. Fryde, 'Materials for the Study of Edward III's Credit Operations 1327–1348', *Bull. Inst. Hist. Res.*, XXII and XXIII (1949–50).

15 Despite the provisions of the Statute of Winchester and the subsequent enactments against distraint of men to arm themselves at their own or communal costs (e.g. *Statutes of the Realm*, I, p. 225; II, p. 137) royal levies of men

other, smaller, extra-budgetary burdens, such as victuals taken as royal prisage free of payment. I would not of course dare even to guess what these various extra-budgetary costs of the war amounted to. All I can do is to emphasize that they must have added, and at times added greatly, to the total financial outlay.

All these were outlays by and for the king, made so to speak on national account. What about outlays on private account, i.e. those made by individuals in preparation for the war or in the course of it? Captains, knights, men at war, had to equip themselves with armour and weapons, to provide themselves with horses, perhaps to mobilize some reserves of cash. It is reckoned that in 1258 the equipment of a knight for military service in England could easily cost the entire annual revenue of a knight.[16] Under the usual agreements between the Crown and its military contractors and between the latter and their subordinates, wages, upkeep of men, and wastage of horses were repayable, and so too were some other costs; but some were not. The dazzling accoutrements, brocades, gold-encrusted armour and silver-tipped arrows, which Humphrey duke of Gloucester considered appropriate to his status, or the velvets on which were embroidered swans with ladies' heads and which were supplied to the Black Prince in the midst of his Gascony campaigns, were not military expenses recoverable under contracts with the king. The gorgeous white uniforms which gave Sir John Hawkwood's company its name were obviously paid for not by the king but by Hawkwood out of his earnings as a 'freebooter' and a mercenary. Other great captains may not have been as ostentatious as the Black Prince or Duke Humphrey, or as lavish in dressing up their troops as Hawkwood. But some conspicuous display was inseparable from late medieval warfare, and it would be absurd to pretend that all the private outlays on the pageant of war were, or could be, reimbursed. In fact we know that even the wages and upkeep of troops, which according to most military contracts had to be paid quarterly, often remained owing by the king for many years after they had been incurred, and some were never repaid.[17]

equipped and maintained (at least up to the moment of embarkation) continued throughout Edward III's reign and more sporadically in later periods, 'notwithstanding . . . the King's . . . liberal promises, there were issued from day to day commissions to array all over England men-at-arms, hobelours and archers: the weapons were charged to the commons': W. Stubbs, *Constitutional History of England*, 4th edn. (Oxford, 1906), II, p. 572. See also Michael Powicke, op. cit., pp. 198 ff.

16 R. F. Treharne, 'The Knights in the Period of Reform and Rebellion, 1258–67', *Bull. Inst. Hist. Res.*, XXI (1948).

17 We are told that Talbot 'served the Kynges fader too yere in his seide Reaume of France atte his oune costes withoute takyng of any wages': *Rot. Parl.*, IV, p. 338. If this assertion is true, Talbot must have gone out with a private company, and there were others who did likewise. But even those who served under a formal contract often failed to get reimbursed in full, if at all.

3

Needless to say, these financial costs, both national and private, did not go uncompensated. Military operations in the Middle Ages were expected to yield profits, and we know what these were. They were booty, indemnities (*rachâts*) paid by occupied fortresses and towns, issues of fiefs and offices abroad and above all ransoms. In certain periods, especially in years of active and successful campaigning, private profits of war could be large and enable fortunate individuals to enrich themselves; in all periods they figured very prominently as inducements to soldiers and as fuel for warlike sentiments. Yet none of the accounts and estimates so far made for the Hundred Years War would be sufficient to convince a sensible person that the balance of the various war profits made by English combatants would in the aggregate come to anything like the millions spent on the war. But as it has been argued that the balance of financial outlay was favourable to England, I propose to look into its constituent items.

Of the various war profits those of miscellaneous booty were most likely to produce a favourable balance since the war was always fought on foreign soil. But what difference these profits made to the cost of the war is difficult to say. It is even difficult to decide who benefited from them most. The sharing of booty was subject to ancient and elaborate rules which usually compelled the soldiers in the lower ranks to deliver to their immediate superiors one third of their gains; and the rules came to be standardized in military contracts of the fourteenth and fifteenth centuries.[18] I suspect that in spite of these rules most fruits of soldierly pillage stuck to the fingers of lesser folk, the men-at-arms and the common soldiers of every kind. But what they proceeded to do with their gains, how much they caroused away while abroad, how much they were able to save up and bring home to England, are questions nobody would be able to answer. In all probability some, but not very many, of the soldiers were lucky enough not only to survive, but to return home better

An appendix to Mr G. A. Holmes's Cambridge Ph.D. thesis on 'English Nobility in the Reign of Edward III' contains an interesting though incomplete list of the royal debts outstanding to some of Edward's captains as recorded in the Enrolled Foreign Accounts of the Exchequer 1372–7. Of the nineteen accounts listed only two smaller accounts, both in the name of the Earl of Warwick, were in balance, or to the king's credit; most of the others were still in debit in 1377. Hugh Calverley, Edward le Despenser, Ralph Ferrers, Hugh earl of Stafford and the Duke of Lancaster were still owed from 60 to 75 per cent of the acknowledged indebtedness. The Ferrers debt remained unpaid after eleven years. The 163 men listed in *Calendar of Close Rolls, Edward III, 1341–1343*, pp. 82–8, as the king's creditors for wages unpaid, are mostly of humbler status.

18 D. Hay, 'Division of the Spoils of War', *Trans. Roy. Hist. Soc.*, 5th ser., IV (1954).

off than they had been at the moment of enlisting. Taking the war as a whole there must have been many thousand, perhaps as many as twenty to forty thousand Welsh soldiers serving in various expeditions to France; but the social history of Wales in the fifteenth century (and surviving Welsh homesteads) bear very few traces of new wealth brought in by returning soldiers. Nor is the English evidence any more revealing. In the whole mass of fourteenth- and fifteenth-century documentation bearing on the village land market I have found no indication that any substantial proportion, indeed any proportion at all, of the various buyers of land, engrossers of holdings, or recruits to the new 'kulak' class, were returning soldiers. References to returning and disbanded soldiers are, of course, common in the sixteenth century but at that time they are supposed to have swollen the ranks of beggars and vagabonds.

We hear a little more about the booty accruing to the leaders. Contractual rules notwithstanding, it appears probable that the higher a leader stood in the chain of command and the further he happened to be from the actual business of house-to-house and church-to-church pillage, the less he benefited. We have lurid accounts of the pillaging exploits of a Hawkwood or a Dagworth, but these were leaders of bands, some of them freebooting bands. And such were apparently the expenses of maintaining a company and such were the uncertainties of campaigning that in spite of all the pillaging and ravaging of the European countryside, Hawkwood found himself at the end of his life in constant financial difficulties and dependent for his income on annual payments from the government of Florence.[19] Sir Thomas Felton, for all the ravaging by his troops, did not enrich himself very greatly. When he was taken prisoner in 1377, his ransom, admittedly a very large one, had to be paid by the king. Others – Hugh Calverley, Robert Knollys, James Pype, John Jowell – may have done better. Hugh Calverley died a wealthy man, and contemporaries tell us in some detail how he and his band of 2000 men pillaged the territories of the Earl of Armagnac; but we do not know how much of the Calverley wealth came from the Armagnac booty. There was surely not enough of it to enrich both Calverley and his 2000 freebooters. Sir Robert Knollys – one of the most successful war profiteers – is said to have received as his share of the booty taken in Normandy by his Great Company the sum of 100,000 crowns – say ten to fifteen thous-

[19] He apparently emerged much in debt from his service with Gian Galleazo Visconti in 1385 and remained in difficulties until his death in 1392. About a year before he died, the government of Florence increased his pension and the provision for his wife and daughters, but for at least five years before then he was busy selling his lands in different parts of Italy, partly in preparation for eventual return to England and partly in order to repay his debts. Cf. the full, if somewhat amateurish, account in J. Temple-Leader and G. Mareotti, *Sir John Hawkwood* (English translation), (London, 1889), pp. 205–8, 280–7.

and pounds. But this sum was somewhat counterbalanced by the 10,000 marks he had to pay the king a few years later for a pardon, and was overshadowed as a source of profit by what he got from the indemnities of Châlons-sur-Loire and Auxerre or from his share of the Guescelin ransoms or even by the profits of his French and Breton estates.[20]

We find ourselves on somewhat more certain ground when we come to reckon up the indemnities – the *rachâts* – of occupied castles and towns. With time and patience it should be possible to compile a fairly full list of payments made to Englishmen on this account. My own list is woefully incomplete, though I believe it contains most of the important and well-recorded indemnities. It shows the king receiving in the aggregate rather less than £250,000, including all he was entitled to (more, that is, than he may have actually received) from the wholesale indemnification in 1360 for all the occupied fortresses around Paris, in Touraine and Normandy. My corresponding tally of private receipts under this head is even less complete. Such as it is, it falls well short of the king's list and amounts at most to £200,000. These are very approximate and inexact figures, but they err on the generous side. However much one would wish to lean over backwards and to magnify, a credible total would not be much greater than £400,000 – an impressive amount but, of course, far short of the millions of English money disbursed on the war.

Another obvious source was the profit of offices and estates in occupied France. Of these, least important were the profits of offices. Indeed they were so uncertain as to be almost not worth counting. Some of the offices such as the Captaincy of Calais, the Lord Lieutenancy and the Seneschalship of Aquitaine, or the Governorship of Paris were as likely to be a source of loss as of gain. Sir John Talbot's multiple offices do not appear to have brought him a great fortune. Humphrey Stafford, first duke of Buckingham, was owed £19,000 by the king in 1449 for wages of soldiers during his Captaincy of Calais. His earlier office (1430) as Constable of France and Governor of Paris had not apparently been very profitable either. John Holand, earl of Huntingdon, the future duke of Exeter, must have failed to make his numerous offices remunerative, for he begged and received in 1438 an annuity of 500 marks from the king, presumably as compensation. In the following year he had to be offered £1000 to induce him to accept the Lieutenancy of Aquitaine. Ralph, first earl of Stafford, had been anxious to resign the Seneschalship of Aquitaine in 1346 but was induced to stay on in return for a grant of money. I daresay some other offices brought in a fair income, but I have yet to find convincing instances of many fortunes derived from them.

[20] Thomas Walsingham, *Historia Anglicana*, ed. H. T. Riley (Rolls Series, 1863), I, pp. 286, 311; Walsingham also mentions the withdrawal of previous royal gifts.

Almost equally uncertain were profits from estates. Sir Robert Knolly's possessions abroad – his 'forty castles' in the valley of the Loire, the lands of the Doreval and Rougé in Brittany with their reputed rental of 2000 *livres* – were probably the most profitable as well as the best advertised of the foreign estates acquired by English soldiers during the war. But Sir John Chandos's beloved estate in the Cotentin did not bring him a large fortune.[21] Nor did the lordship of Sparre in Aquitaine or of Ivry do much to redeem the shaky fortunes of John Holand, by then duke of Exeter.

The truth of the matter is that, as with most other war prizes, foreign estates were unequal and unstable in value. In war-ridden France, estates, especially when under absentee foreign grantees, were hard to run; and the policy of the English government overseas was not likely to make estate ownership any more profitable or the profits any easier to remit to England. The theory behind the land grants in Normandy was that their object was to maintain local defence. And even when and where conditions were so settled and the estates were so good that regular profits could be drawn from them, it is not at all certain that the profits were available to augment the English fortunes of their owners. For, in general, residence on the estates was an implied condition of most of the Norman grants.[22] We are thus left with a somewhat unclear picture – a few large fiefs which could be profitable and a large number of possessions whose rentability was doubtful and whose ability to yield remittable funds more doubtful still.

However, none of these profits ranked as high in people's expectations or figure as prominently in modern accounts of war-finance as ransoms. I suspect that the historian's sanguine view of ransoms is coloured by the vast sums – over £250,000 – which Edward III received in the 1360s as ransoms for King John of France and David Bruce, combined with the indemnity of Burgundy. So large was the sum and so eminent were the parties to the contracts that they have dazzled and confused even as well-informed and intelligent an historian as Edouard Perroy. In his view the remittance of King John's ransom to England sufficed not only to fill the gaps in Edward's war budgets but for a time to revive the entire economy of England: to raise the price level, to surmount agrarian crises and to stimulate industrial activity.[23]

In fact this vast ransom, like so many other war-time windfalls, washed

21 We are told that Sir John Chandos's heirs parted with his castle of St Sauveur in the Cotentin for an annuity of £40: note on John Chandos in *Dict. Nat. Biog.*

22 Most of the grants of land recorded in the *Rotuli Normanniae*, ed. T. D. Hardy, (London, 1835), imply or specify defence of castles or districts and personal military service: Wylie and Waugh, op. cit., III, pp. 74–5. Some grants of estates were paid for by the recipients. Knollys may have paid as much as 2000 florins for the temporary custody of castles in Brittany: *Foedera*, III, pp. 307, 312, 622.

23 E. Perroy, 'Les profits et rançons pendant la Guerre de Cent Ans', *Mélanges d'Histoire du Moyen Age à la Memoire de Louis Halphen* (Paris, 1951), p. 574.

over the economy of Britain without even wetting it. Such ransoms were almost invariably diverted to war purposes and sometimes did not even pass through the financial machinery of the Exchequer and Wardrobe. Tout has shown that a large portion, perhaps as much as a third, of King John's ransom was kept 'salted up' in the king's chamber for subsequent use in war disbursements abroad.[24] The king's and the Black Prince's shares in many other ransoms were often paid to them abroad and immediately spent or assigned by them, sometimes in payment of ransoms on behalf of men of the king captured by the French.[25] But to whatever use the king put these profits, they could in no case be set against the cost of the war as measured by war taxes or by military disbursements by the Exchequer. They were supplementary sources of military income and were usually devoted to the additional military liabilities which taxes and loans were insufficient to meet.

What about the ransoms received by individuals and the chance of personal enrichment they offered? Large sums undoubtedly were received, but large sums were also paid out. The Hundred Years War, in which victorious phases alternated with phases of defeat and retreat, would be most unlikely to set a stream of ransoms flowing in one direction only. Throughout the war Englishmen were taken prisoner; indeed there was hardly a military leader who was not at one time or another taken prisoner and compelled to pay ransom. William Montacute, first earl of Salisbury, was captured at Lille in 1340 and had to be ransomed by the king with money for which the king apparently designed a special levy on wool. Ralph, later first earl of Stafford, was made prisoner in 1342 and next year exchanged for a French prisoner. Sir John Talbot, later earl of Shrewsbury, was captured at Patay in 1429 and spent four years in prison, having been 'sette to unresonable and importable raunceon'. So great was it and so much in excess of Talbot's own resources that a public subscription was projected in England and the king himself offered to contribute.[26] John Holand, earl of Huntingdon, the future duke of Exeter, was taken prisoner at Baugé in 1421 and among the many other English prisoners taken at that battle were the earl of Somerset and

24 Tout, op. cit., III, pp. 243–8; M. Broome, 'The Ransom of John II King of France, 1360–70', *Camden Miscellany,* XIV (Camden Soc., 3rd ser., XXXVII [1926]). Miss Broome also makes it clear that a proportion of the ransom, about £15,000, was paid by the English clergy out of the proceeds of a clerical subsidy: ibid., pp. XVII–VIII.

25 Broome, op. cit.; Tout, op. cit., V, pp. 362–5. Direct assignments of profits of prisoners to king's creditors at home and abroad were not confined to Edward III's reign. Cf. the grant to Robert de Vere in 1386; Tout, op. cit., III, p. 421, n. 1.

26 *Rot. Parl.*, IV, p. 338. For a reference to the subscription by the mayor and the good men of Coventry see J. Hunter, *History of Hallamshire,* ed. Gatty (London, 1819), p. 63.

Lord Fitzwalter. Huntingdon himself stayed in prison for over four years until he was exchanged for the Count of Vendôme;[27] even then he had to pay a ransom for which he received financial compensation from the king. Sir Thomas Felton was taken prisoner in 1377 (and possibly also in 1367) and could not raise the necessary ransom until the king granted 30,000 francs for this purpose out of the ransoms of French prisoners. Robert Hungerford, Lord Boleyn, was taken prisoner in 1422 and stayed in prison for seven years. His mother, Lady Margaret Hungerford, had to sell jewels and pledge estates before she was able to raise £14,000 for his liberation. Walter Hungerford was taken prisoner in 1425 and was ransomed by his father for 3000 marks.

The list could be made very much longer.[28] It may well be that a complete tally of prisoners on both sides would show that more prisoners were taken by the English than by the French, though until that tally has been compiled we shall not know how much more numerous the French prisoners were. But before the comparison is even attempted and the balance of loss and profit is struck, it is necessary to allow for the possibility that in the business of ransoms both parties might lose, and that in the aggregate the English war leaders and captains would not emerge with net gains unless the promises of ransoms they wrung from French prisoners were several, in fact two or even three times as great as the promises they themselves had to make to French captors.

The reasons for this are that ransoms as a rule passed through many hands, were subject to deductions in favour of superiors including the king, were frequently and heavily discounted with merchants, and bore high charges for collection, for interest and for upkeep of hostages. In general the sums contracted were very much larger than the sums actually paid by the prisoners and their families, and the sums paid by the prisoners much larger than the sums cashed in by the captors. Even King John's ransom, for all the stupendous backing by illustrious hostages and guarantors, was not fully paid. According to Miss Broome's computation only three-fifths of the ransom originally contracted was received by Edward III.[29] Yet even this proportion was much higher than what English captors frequently got for their pains. In the next most famous English case of a ransom – that of the Count of Denia – the principal claimants, Robert Hawley and John Shekel, do not appear to have received more than one-eighth of the £32,000 due to them. Thirty years

[27] Walsingham, op. cit., II, p. 339; *The Complete Peerage*, V, pp. 206, 208.

[28] Knollys himself may have been made prisoner in the Combat of the Thirty: Froissart, *Chroniques*, ed. A. C. Buchon, vol. I (Paris, 1853), pp. 293–9. His other captivity in Spain in 1367 is more doubtful, though the note published by S. Luce in his edition of Froissart, vol. VII (Paris, 1869–99), p. 303, suggests that he was then taken together with Thomas Felton and others.

[29] Broome, op. cit.

after the capture some £24,000 was still outstanding, the original captors having received only some £3000 or £3500. In the instances of ransoms which came up before the French *Parlement* and have been studied by Professor Timbal's team, no more than one third of the sums contracted reached the captors. The average proportions are about the same in the cases cited by Hewitt, Bossuat, Richardson and others. If, therefore, we assume that English captors in general received the same proportion, that is one-third, of the amount stipulated in ransom agreements, the total value of ransoms claimed by English captors would need to have been three times as great as the amounts promised by French prisoners, before English gains from this source could even have begun to equal their losses.[30] The benefits accruing to the overall national balance of losses and gains on ransoms might however be somewhat more favourable, in so far as the intermediaries were English and the expenses of maintaining hostages were incurred in England.

4

These are the many and various reasons why I refuse to believe that the profits of war could have been sufficiently high to match the English outlay both public and private. However generous we may be in our estimates of net gains from offices, booty, estates and even ransoms, we should still find it very difficult to make them equal the five millions *plus* spent on national and private accounts.

It is of course arguable that the costs, as we have reckoned them here, both real and fiscal, are no measure of the true economic consequences of a war. A sophisticated economic historian, able to play with modern theoretical concepts, might contend that a country could benefit from war activities and war finance, even if its balance-sheet of real costs or financial outlays showed a visible loss. For in spite of the losses, war-time use of resources could be more efficient, that is capable of generating a much higher level of economic activity and of producing a higher level of income, than the same resources would generate in peace-time. In the special case of economies as static and traditional as was the English economy in the Middle Ages it can be argued – as Sombart and Schumpeter have argued – that war taxation helped to transfer command over resources from the hands of landowners and peasants who used them unproductively, into the hands of war contractors and profiteers, who

30 P. C. Timbal, *La Guerre de Cent Ans vu à travers les Registres du Parlement* (Paris, 1961); André Boussuat: 'Les prisonniers de guerre an XVe siècle', *Annales de Bourgogne*, XXIII (1951); H. G. Richardson, 'Illustrations of English History in the Medieval Registers of the Parlement of Paris', *Trans. Roy. Hist. Soc.*, 4th ser., x (1927); H. J. Hewitt, *The Black Prince's Expedition of 1355–1357* (London, 1958).

were likely to use them as wealth-producing capital. I myself for a time toyed with these possibilities, for, during the opening phase of the Hundred Years War, Edward III's financial dealings in fact called into existence a new breed of native capitalists which, had it survived, might have altered the entire complexion of the English economy. The reason why I eventually abandoned the idea is that over the one hundred and twenty years of the war taken as a whole, these transfers of wealth as between the country interests and the mercantile classes, were apt to cancel themselves out. Such was the structure of English society and such were the social values within it that the wealth acquired by merchants and war profiteers at one stage of their careers, or in one generation, was bound eventually to be employed in buying land and social position in the countryside. This is what I had in mind when, in an earlier essay, I spoke of the circular tour of wealth in war-time England – a tour in the course of which wealth wrung from the agricultural interest by war taxation was eventually brought back into the countryside by merchants, soldiers and officials investing in land. This reference to the circular tour of wealth has provoked a certain amount of very literal comment; yet I still believe it describes correctly the final result of the various transfers of wealth through war finance and war taxation.[31]

Must we therefore conclude that nothing changed in the one hundred and twenty years of war; that England in the 1450s, her economy and society, were very much as they had been in the 1330s? Certainly not. Time did not stand still, and there were bound to be social changes which the war may have speeded up. Some great fortunes were doubtless amassed; other fortunes were extinguished during that period. Some fortunes and families, and among them those of famous captains, may not have been ruined by the war but merely failed to benefit from it.[32] In 1434, after nearly a lifetime of campaigning in France and despite the high commands and offices he had held, the great Sir John Talbot, earl of Shrewsbury, could describe himself as living 'in great necessity', and had to obtain £1000 from the king in compensation for his many and various claims upon the crown.[33] Towards the end of his life the first duke of Exeter turned out to have done no better. On the other hand a number of men of relatively modest origins throve to great wealth and high status. The Hungerfords who rose in the service of the Lancaster

[31] For my earlier discussion of these and similar questions, see 'Some Social Consequences of the Hundred Years War', *Econ. Hist. Rev.*, XII (1942) reprinted as Chapter 4 above.

[32] 'If the wars went well, they paid handsomely; but with the turning of the tide, they might be a crippling drain on the fortunes of a noble house': so K. B. McFarlane, 'Bastard Feudalism', *Bull. Hist. Res.*, XX (1945), p. 178.

[33] 'La grande necessite en quele le dit Sire etc.': *Ordinances of the Privy Council*, ed. N. H. Nicolas (Record Commission, London, 1834–7), IV, p. 202.

family, or other men in royal service like Ralph Stafford third duke of Buckingham, profited during the period from their patron's largesse and from dynastic marriages. Others like Sir Robert Knollys or his reputed brother Hugh Calverley or Sir Thomas Felton, or indeed Sir John Fastolf himself rose from relatively inconspicuous positions to all but the highest ranks in the country.[34] But even in such careers (certainly in Kyriel's, Felton's, Audley's, Manny's or Brian's) an important, sometimes the chief, source of bounty was not ransoms or any of the other profits of war, but the largesse of the king, the Black Prince or the Breton Pretender. Very few of the windfalls of war could bring in anything like as much as the £400 annuity for life which the Black Prince gave to Audley for his good service at Poitiers.

Important changes were also taking place in the somewhat lower strata of society. Numerous knights and gentlemen, clerks connected with war administration, men-at-arms and county freeholders, were swelling the ranks of the gentry and adding to its aggregate wealth. And this movement may have been sufficiently general to have altered the relative balance of wealth and power as between magnates and gentry.

Yet most of these changes were occurring and would have occurred anyhow, war or no war. It was Mr McFarlane who, in a deservedly famous essay, pointed out how much the smaller landowners were enabled to benefit from the working of 'bastard feudalism' and from its system of retinues and retainers. In recounting the heavy expenses of retinues and the wealth lavished on them by great magnates, Mr McFarlane was led to conclude that 'no wonder lords were impoverished and the gentry flourished'.[35] With this most reasonable conclusion I can only concur, but in doing so I must point out that what made the fortunes of the smaller men was not the war or at least not the war alone, but the general configuration of social and political circumstances. A social historian, especially a Marxist one, may believe that the social changes of the fifteenth century were 'pregnant with promise', since they paved the way for the great 'leap forward' of the Elizabethan age. But whether true or not this belief has little to do with our assessment of the Hundred Years War, for we must not ascribe to the war what was due to the hundred years. To quote my earlier essay on this subject, the Hundred Years War was at best a makeweight, not the mainspring, of social change.[36]

34 'Robertus Knollis ex paupere mediocrique valleto mox factus ductor militum et divitias usque regales excrevit ibidem': Walsingham, op. cit., I, p. 286. He was of course no pauper, but a descendant of a family of small landowners. For Fastolf, see K. B. McFarlane, 'The Investment of Sir John Fastolf's Profits of War', *Trans. Roy. Hist. Soc.*, 5th ser., VII (1957).

35 McFarlane, 'Bastard Feudalism', p. 177.

36 'Some Social Consequences of the Hundred Years War', pp. 61–2 above.

6
WHY WAS SCIENCE BACKWARD IN THE MIDDLE AGES?*

It is generally agreed that the Middle Ages preserved for the use of later times the science of the ancients. Therein lies both the scientific achievement and the scientific failure of the medieval civilization. The achievement was all the greater for being indirect. Men in the Dark Ages did not find in the parts of the Western Empire which they occupied a scientific tradition as rich as that which the Arabs inherited in the eastern provinces. Scientific learning came to them later, mostly in the twelfth and thirteenth centuries, from the Arabs and the Jews. To have borrowed and absorbed a scientific culture from peoples which were at that time so distant and so alien was indeed a great achievement. It was all that great, but no greater. What the Middle Ages took over they did not very much enrich. Indeed so small was their own contribution that historians of science are apt to regard the Middle Ages as something of a pause.

Needless to say, the pause was not undisturbed or unbroken. In the course of centuries medieval men improved somewhat their practical arts and added a little to their understanding of nature: and in some periods, such as the turn of the twelfth and thirteenth centuries, their own advances were sufficiently great to make it possible for us to speak of the scientific renaissance, or revival, in the Middle Ages. As a result of the revival, scientific knowledge became much richer than it had once been. As late as the early eleventh century medieval mathematics were still confined to simple computations, to an elementary theory of simple numbers, to some rudimentary propositions of pre-Pythagorean geometry, the use of the counting frame (the abacus), and perhaps to decimal fractions. But by the end of the thirteenth century mathematicians were tackling advanced problems of the geometry of Pythagoras, approaching the solution of cubic equations by the intersection of cones, discussing spherical trigonometry, and indeed advancing to the very verge of differential calculus. In the same period the astrologists had not only

* From *The History of Science. A Symposium*, ed. J. Lindsay, Routledge & Kegan Paul, 1951.

absorbed the Ptolemaic astronomy of the ancients, but had also got to know the map of the skies and the courses of stars and planets and had thereby prepared the great Copernican revolution in astronomy. Similarly the medieval alchemists had stumbled across some new facts about the properties of metals and gases, while the compilers of medieval lapidaries or lists of magic stones, of medieval herbals and of the medieval bestiaries, paved the way for the great scientific classifications of the sixteenth and seventeenth centuries. Some curious and learned men went even further than that. We have all heard about Frederick II's dissection of animals, but he was apparently not alone in this kind of investigation, for by the end of the Middle Ages dissectors and surgeons had accumulated a certain amount of new anatomical knowledge as well as a few rudimentary facts of human physiology. Now and again we find men engaging in practical tests which look like primitive experiments.

On the more practical plane we find here and there instances of great technical progress. Thus at the beginning of the medieval epoch, in the Dark Ages, the tillers of the soil were sufficiently enterprising to invent, or at least to adopt, what was at that time a brand-new system of agricultural technique – the rotation of crops by a two- or three-field system, the use of the heavy wheeled plough, and above all the modern system of harnessing animals from the shoulder, none of which had been known to the Romans or, if known, used extensively by them. During the same period the large water-mill, sometimes equipped with the overshot wheel and geared transmission, replaced in many parts of Europe the small horizontal water-mill of the so-called Irish or Norse type. It is also probable that, during the period of active land reclamation in Flanders during the tenth and eleventh, and in eastern Germany in the twelfth and thirteenth centuries, peasants adopted a more efficient lay-out of villages, an improved method of drainage, and possibly even more intensive forms of agriculture. We also find great technical ingenuity in mining and in the construction and improvements of implements of war, especially of machines for siege. Above all there was continuous technical progress in the greatest of medieval practical arts, in that of building. In the interval between the tenth and thirteenth centuries the technique of building developed much faster and went much further than during those four or five centuries of renaissance architecture which were to come between medieval buildings and the ferro-concrete structures of our own day.

Thus some advance on planes both purely intellectual and technical there was; yet taken together and placed against the vast panorama of medieval life, or indeed against the achievements of Greek and Hellenistic science in the fourth century B.C., or with the scientific activity of the seventeenth century, all these achievements are bound to appear poor. Why then this poverty?

To this question many answers can be and have been given. But what most of them boil down to is the absence in medieval life of what I should be inclined to call scientific incentives. Students of science sometimes differ about the true inspiration of scentific progress. Some seek and find it in man's intellectual curiosity, in his desire to understand the workings of nature. Others believe that scientific knowledge grew and still grows out of man's attempts to improve his tools and his methods of production; that, in short, scientific truth is a by-product of technical progress. I do not want here to take sides in this particular controversy, what I want to suggest is that the Middle Ages were doubly unfortunate in that both the inspirations, the intellectual as well as the practical failed more or less.

The easiest to account for is the intellectual. The Middle Ages were the age of faith, and to that extent they were unfavourable to scientific speculation. It is not that scientists as such were proscribed. For on the whole the persecution of men for their scientific ideas was very rare: rare because men with dangerous ideas, or indeed with any scientific ideas at all, were themselves very rare; and it is indeed surprising that there were any at all. This does not mean that there were no intellectual giants. All it means is that in an age which was one of faith, men of intellect and spirit found the calls of faith itself – its elucidation, its controversies, and its conquests – a task sufficient to absorb them. To put it simply, they had no time for occupations like science.

In fact they had neither the time nor the inclination. For even if there had been enough men to engage in activities as mundane as science, there would still be very little reason for them to do so. In times when medieval religious dogma stood whole and unshaken the intellectual objects and the methods of science were, to say the least, superfluous. The purpose of scientific inquiry is to build up piecemeal a unified theory of the universe, of its origin and of its working. But in the Middle Ages was that process really necessary? Did not medieval man already possess in God, in the story of Creation and in the doctrine of Omnipotent Will, a complete explanation of how the world came about and of how, by what means and to what purpose, it was being conducted? Why build up in laborious and painstaking mosaic a design which was already there from the outset, clear and visible to all.

So much for intellectual incentive. The practical incentive was almost equally feeble. Greater understanding of nature could not come from technical improvements, chiefly because technical improvements were so few. Medieval occupations continued for centuries without appreciable change of method. After the great period of initial development, i.e. after the late eleventh century, the routine of medieval farming in the greater part of Europe became as fixed as the landscape itself. In the history of the smithies, the weaving shops, or the potteries, there were occasional periods of innovation, but taking the Middle Ages as a whole technical improvement was very rare and very slow.

For this medieval economic policy was largely to blame. In the course of centuries, economic activities got surrounded with a vast structure of bye-laws and regulations. In the villages regulations were necessary in order to guarantee to the landlords that their tenants would be able to pay or to work off their dues, but also in order to secure the rights and obligations of individual members of a village community. In most towns of the later Middle Ages there were regulations to secure fair prices, to maintain wages, to lay down standards of quality, and above all, to protect individual masters from competition. But, however necessary or commendable these objects may have been, they made technical improvement very difficult. For bye-laws were as a rule based on the technical methods in existence when they were framed; and once framed they were to stand in the way of all subsequent change.

What is more, so deeply ingrained was the spirit of protection that in every local trade the technical methods were treated as a secret. The medieval craft gild described itself as a 'mystery' and often was one. To take an example, the prosperity of the Bologna silk industry, famous all over Europe, was in its early stages due to many new processes and labour-saving devices. But it is characteristic of medieval technology that the machine for throwing silk which was invented in 1272 by Borghesano of Bologna (and was certainly employed in the Bolognese silk industry in the later Middle Ages) was not to be known outside Bologna until 1538, and was not effectively imitated until a travelling Englishman obtained its designs by ruse in the seventeenth century. Much of the specialized local skill of certain areas of medieval Europe was rooted in knowledge carefully guarded from outsiders. It is for that reason that industries with advanced techniques, e.g. mining or cloth finishing, seldom spread to new areas except by mass migration and resettlement of the men who practised them.

It is thus no wonder that knowledge painfully acquired in industrial practice so seldom percolated into the realm of science, while the scientific knowledge of the scholars so seldom influenced the industrial technique. Thus the main qualities of iron had been discovered and its resilience known at the very dawn of the Middle Ages and before, but we have no record of the leaf spring until the seventeenth century or of the spiral spring until the fifteenth. For several hundred years after the appearance in Europe of Arab numerals, and for at least a hundred and fifty years after the earlier western treatises explaining their use in computation, commercial and state accountancy still employed the awkward Roman numerals. On the other hand, for centuries after the pump, especially in its simpler syringe form, was employed in industry, the development of theoretical mechanics floundered in error through the failure to employ the concept of vacuum. None of the experience accumulated and utilized in the construction of appliances, mostly military, employing the pressure of water and air, or the expansion of heated air and steam, was capable of affecting the official theory of hydrostatics or of suggesting a theory of the expansion of gases or of atmospheric pressure. And although levers, both curved and straight, had been employed in construction since time immemorial, mechanics did not arrive at the concept of 'moment of force' until about the end of the thirteenth century. The practical knowledge of the medieval farmers and stockbreeders remained virtually without effect on biological theory, the experience of the dyers and the fullers remained without effect on the chemical theories. Medieval technology and medieval science each kept to their carefully circumscribed spheres.

Indeed, nothing exemplifies this general condition of technical stagnation better than the exceptions I have already mentioned. The great agricultural innovations of the early Middle Ages took place at the time when medieval population was still, so to speak, on the move, and when the medieval economic organization and its laws had not yet taken shape. Agricultural innovations of a later age, such as the Flemish and German of the twelfth and thirteenth centuries, were part and parcel of the colonization movement, i.e. were only possible because society was again on the move. The great technical discoveries in industrial occupations took place only when and where the industry happened to be beyond the reach of local authority. The technology of war was in the service of princes, and princes were not bound by the social aims or economic objectives of medieval gilds. The great technical changes in the English cloth industry in the fourteenth century were made possible only by the flight of the industry from the towns to the villages over which the authority of municipalities did not extend. Above all, medieval building was in the hands of masons who were 'free', free in the sense that they were migratory labourers seldom subject to supervision and technical control by town governments.

In spheres more purely intellectual, the quickening of scientific activity in the late twelfth and thirteenth centuries, the so-called medieval renaissance, was also in some respects exceptional. It will be a mistake to put it down solely to the influx of translations. The translations, far from explaining the scientific activity, themselves require an explanation. For at least three hundred years the Arabs had been there with their versions of ancient philosophy, while the contacts with them were not necessarily closer in 1250 than they had been, say, in 850. Yet neither in the early centuries of the Middle Ages nor in its closing centuries was there a comparable flow of translations.

How are we then to account for the spate in the thirteenth century? Certainly not by the Italian trade in the Levant or by the Crusades. Few of the translations came from the Levant; hardly any were the work of Crusaders or of the Italian merchants or of anybody in their service. A cause more fundamental and more directly intellectual was obviously at work. For, unless I am mistaken, the intellectual climate in the middle centuries of the Middle Ages had changed. It is even possible that, for the time being, faith itself did not wholly absorb the interests of men. Mundane and secular preoccupations, both literary and philosophical, suddenly appeared amidst a culture still mainly religious. Within religion itself minority movements of every kind, including those of the early friars, disturbed more than ever before the uniformity of ideas. Disagreements appeared at the very centres of medieval learning, philosophical controversies seemed to shake the very foundations of dogma, and behind some of the milder manifestations of dissent lurked the possibilities of the profoundest scepticism and doubt. No wonder a Frenchman, Taine, described the whole period as an epoch tormented by doubt. And from the doubts of the thirteenth century, as from similar doubts in later ages, there was bound to issue a current of intellectual curiosity, a willingness to re-open questions which hitherto appeared closed, and to seek answers from every source capable of giving them. Hence the revived interest in the philosophical and scientific doctrines of antiquity; hence the eagerness to learn from the Greeks and Arabs; hence also the translations.

In this way the very achievement of the late twelfth and thirteenth centuries merely underlines the verdict about the Middle Ages as a whole. The men of the Middle Ages were unable to do more than they did because they were lacking in scientific incentive. What they achieved in advancing the practical arts of humanity or in preserving and transmitting ancient learning, they did in so far and as long as they were not typically medieval.

PART II
AGRARIAN

7
THE CHRONOLOGY OF LABOUR SERVICES*

1

The chronology of labour services in the Middle Ages has been agitating agrarian historians for nearly a hundred years. In view of this, it is surprising to find how many of the dates are still a matter of assumption. On the whole, economic historians know much more about the final demise of labour dues than about their previous history. They may disagree as to the exact dates of the fourteenth-century commutation, or as to the extent to which England had been manorialized and was therefore likely to be affected by the dissolution of the manor. But, on the whole, they are agreed that commutation did take place in those parts of the country which were manorialized; and it would be generally accepted that commutation was rare in the first quarter of the fourteenth century, that labour services were exceptional in the last quarter of the fifteenth century, and that consequently the final substitution of money for labour dues took place some time between the first quarter of the fourteenth century and the last quarter of the fifteenth.

This may not be much to show for half a century of research, but little as it is, it is a great deal more than is known about labour services in the preceding periods. Were they rising, stationary, or falling, and if they fell or rose how are the ups and downs to be dated? None of these questions has been answered, and for England as a whole they have not even been asked. And in the absence of definite knowledge, economic and constitutional historians have been thrown back on a series of purely conventional assumptions.

Economic historians have been inclined to assume a gradual dissolution of the manorial structure, which extended over two or three centuries and was due to a gradually expanding money economy. This assumption usually enters their language and thoughts in the form of an adverbial figure. When students find money rents on thirteenth-century manors they regard labour services as 'already commuted'; when they find them

* A revised version of a paper in *Trans. Roy. Hist. Soc.*, 4th Series, xx, 1937, printed in W. E. Minchinton, ed., *Essays in Agrarian History*, vol. i, Newton Abbot, 1968.

still enforced in the fifteenth century, they say that commutation has not 'yet' begun. The adverbs are employed to register surprise, or to record what is thought to be a 'local peculiarity'.

On the other hand, the general assumption of the constitutional historians is that labour services in the twelfth and thirteenth centuries were growing, in consequence of the clarification of the feudal and manorial structure under the Normans and Angevins. Services, it is held, became generalized and intensified as the manorial organization crystallized and spread in the two or three centuries following the Conquest.

These two assumptions may appear to clash, though a useful chronological device for reconciling them can be, and has been, found. It is indeed possible to hold both, by assigning the extension and the increase of labour services to a period which terminates with the Hundred Rolls; and their disappearance to the end of the thirteenth and the fourteenth centuries, when economic forces began to play on the framework of the manor, gradually dissolving it.[1] But even if these two assumptions can be reconciled with each other, they are difficult to reconcile with the results of recent studies in other fields. The assumption of the increasing uniformity and rigidity of manorial forms in the twelfth and thirteenth centuries does not tally with what historians have recently told us about the active market in land in that period, the rapid process of subinfeudation, the morcellation of manors and vills, the traffic in land (especially in free land), amongst villeins and other tenants, and the traffic in manors, tenements and fees among the landlords. It is even more difficult to reconcile the recent studies with the assumption of the gradual disappearance of labour services under the pressure of an expanding money economy. If services were disappearing with the growth of money economy, how is it that in the more backward parts of the country, farthest from great markets, above all in the north-west, labour services were shed first, while the more progressive south-east retained them longest?

Indeed, the explanations underlying the assumed chronology of labour services are even more difficult to accept than the chronology itself, and the chief fault is not so much with the dates, as with the logic on which they are founded. That logic is simpler than is sometimes imagined; indeed, so simple as to be almost a truism. If labour services varied in quantity from manor to manor or from time to time, the causes of that variation were much more local and direct than the cosmic forces which historians have been in the habit of invoking. Given the social conditions

1 This seems to be Vinogradoff's view, though on occasions he appears to assume a constant tendency to commutation 'checked during the feudal period by the scarcity of money'. *Growth of the Manor*, 1920, p. 329. Cf. *Villeinage in England*, 1892, pp. 297–8, 307 and 181.

of medieval England, a legal and political organization dominated by feudal landlords and a working population largely composed of occupying landholders, labour services were a natural and easy way of meeting the landlord's demand for labour, more especially for seasonal tasks requiring simultaneous exertions of large numbers of men (regular day-to-day work was as a rule performed by permanent servants). Where these social conditions were present, and as long as they were maintained, the fluctuation of labour services requires no other explanation than that which is provided by the ordinary interplay of supply and demand – demand for villein service and supply of villein labour. And in so far as the cultivation of the demesne accounted for the demand, and the extent of villein settlement determined the supply, the differences between labour services exacted in different places should in the final resort have been influenced by the relative balance of villeinage and demesne.

For England as a whole and for the Middle Ages in their entirety this connection may be impossible to establish. Differences in social structure and economy, in soil and methods of cultivation, could produce local variations in services, which overshadowed and concealed their relation to the size of the demesne. The passage of time could have the same effect. Labour services could become fixed and conventionalized, and in this way survive later changes in the relative proportions of demesne and villeinage. The numerical relations between labour services and the needs of the demesne in the later centuries of manorial history – the thirteenth and the fourteenth – cannot therefore be observed and exhibited except in places marked by similar geographical and social conditions and on manors which had changed little in composition since the eleventh or the twelfth centuries.

Such places and manors were, however, sufficiently numerous for the underlying economic relations to remain perceptible in the manorial returns of later centuries, and more especially in the returns aggregated for England as a whole or for large areas within it. They are evident in Professor Kosminsky's analysis of the large and small estates in the *Hundred Rolls*, but would have stood out more clearly still, had he illustrated his arguments by the measurements of demesne lands in manors belonging to the same vills or the same lordships.[2] Take for instance the entry in the *Hundred Rolls* for Cottenham in Cambridgeshire. The village contained six manors, belonging respectively to the Abbot of Crowland, Gilbert of Cottenham, Robert de Insula, Simon le Waleys, Walter de Pelham and the village rector. On four of these roughly the same amount of money, rent and labour services is imposed on each unit of villein land.

[2] E. A. Kosminsky, *The English Village in the Thirteenth Century* (Moscow, 1935) (Russian); 'Services and money rents in the 13th century', *Econ. History Review*, v (1935), 22–45.

The rent may vary from 4*s* 6*d* on one manor to 5*s* 9*d* on another, the value of the services from 1*s* to 10½*d*, but roughly they are the same, especially if compared with those prevailing on the remaining two manors. These two manors stand in sharp contrast both to each other and to the rest of the village, for on one of them 1*s* 9*d* is paid in rent and 4*s* 9*d* is the value of labour services, while on the other only money rent is paid and no services are demanded or evaluated. The cause of the variation is not difficult to find: the proportion of villein to demesne land on the four similar manors is roughly the same, while the demesne is altogether absent from the manor which does not exact labour services and is proportionately larger than anywhere else on the one manor on which services are valued at the exceptionally high figure of 4*s* 9*d*.

The same is true of most vills on estates for which a similar comparison is possible, e.g. the Hertfordshire estates of St Paul's, the Fitz Hamme manors in Buckinghamshire, the Beauchamp estates in the South Midlands or the western group of the Peterborough estates. All these are groups of manors, each of which is situated within the same geographical and social area and belongs to the same lord; yet we find that within each group the labour services vary from manor to manor and that the variations reflect the differences in the relative sizes of the demesne.[3]

But if this is the true logic of the labour services it should account not only for differences between them, but also for their evolution. The changes from time to time, as well as the variations from place to place, were affected by the exigencies of demesne agriculture. When and where these exigencies changed more quickly or more slowly than the supply of villein labour, the labour services should have changed accordingly. And such evidence as we have suggests that they did.

2

The dimensions of both demesne and villein land fluctuated throughout the Middle Ages, but before the Black Death the fluctuations of the area under demesne cultivation were far more marked than those of villeinage. Much as the village population may have changed, the core of villein land, at least before the fourteenth century, remained relatively stable. Therefore of the two elements in the equation – demesne and villeinage – the demesne was bound to exercise the stronger influence upon the evolution of labour dues. When the demand of the demesnes declined, the lords could dispense with some of the services previously required and the manorial documents would either contain the rubric of 'services sold' or else record the progress of commutation. *Mutatis*

[3] P.R.O. Inq. Post Mort., *Hen. III* 7/3. Maxwell-Lyte, *Two Registers, etc.* Somerset Rec. Soc., vol. xxv, 1920.

mutandis, when and where the demand grew, the lord would be inclined not only to exact the services in full, but also to impose additional obligations. This connection is generally admitted for the fourteenth and fifteenth centuries; it is understood that the letting out of the demesne at the close of the Middle Ages, with a consequent curtailment of demesne cultivation, was accompanied by the commutation of labour services. What is not so well understood is that the connection could also be responsible for certain general movements in the earlier centuries.

Isolated and exceptional changes in labour services could occur at any time; a spendthrift heir, too long a vacancy, a slack and careless landlord, might lead to a decline of the demesne, and consequently to a relaxation of labour services. On the other hand, a new broom, a reforming landlord or a competent abbot, might in time lead to the intensification and improvement of demesne cultivation, and to an increase in the customary services performed by the villeins. But in addition to these exceptional and sporadic movements in both directions, there were, in the four centuries for which reliable evidence exists, movements which were so general and so widespread as to suggest the possibility of distinct phases in the history of labour services.

Of these phases the least known and most unexpected is that which is revealed by the earliest manorial surveys. Manorial documents of the twelfth century show, on the bulk of the manors which they cover, labour services declining and the cultivation of the demesne receding. Some ten or eleven surveys compiled in the twelfth century, and two or three later surveys reflecting twelfth-century conditions, have been investigated for the purposes of this inquiry, and nearly all of them exhibit the same trend.[4]

If historians of the last generation have failed to notice or to emphasize the direction of the twelfth-century changes, this has perhaps been due to the accident that the surveys best known to them happened to be those

[4] *Liber Niger Petroburgensis*, MS. 60 of the Soc. of Antiquaries. A photostat was placed at my disposal by the late Mr W. Mellows, whose generous assistance throughout my work on the Peterborough documents was invaluable. The Camden Society's printed version has not been used here. *An Inquisition of the Manors of Glastonbury Abbey of the year 1189*, Roxburgh Club, 1882. W. H. Hart and P. A. Lyons (ed.), *Cartularium Monasterii de Ramseia*, 3 vols, Rolls Series, 1884–93. W. Greenwell (ed.), *Boldon Buke*, Surtees Society, vol. xxv, 1852, and *Bishop Hatfield's Survey*, ibid. vol. xxvii, 1857. W. Hale (ed.), *The Domesday of St Paul's*, Camden Soc., 1857. B. Lees (ed.), *Records of the Templars in England in the Twelfth Century*, 1935. L. B. Larking (ed.), *The Knights Hospitallers in England*, Camden Soc., 1857. *The Red Book of Worcester*, MS. Eccl. Com., 2/121/43698, printed in M. Hollings (ed.), *The Red Book of Worcester*, Worc. Hist. Soc. *The Shaftesbury Cartulary*, B.M. MS. Harl. 61 (I am much indebted to the generosity of Prof. Stenton, who lent me his own transcripts of the MS). *The Cartulary of the Abbey of the Trinity of Caen*, Bib. Nationale MS. Lat. 5650; a photostat of this was procured, through the assistance of the Prof. M. Bloch and Prof. Eileen Power.

on which the trend is least noticeable. One of these is the twelfth-century survey of the estates of the Abbey of Peterborough, the so-called *Liber Niger Petroburgensis*, which was apparently compiled at some time in the third decade of the century. This document depicts manorial economy at its more robust.[5] With the sole exception of the sokemen on the Lincolnshire and on some of the Northamptonshire manors, and perhaps of the burgage tenants of Oundle and Kettering, the bulk of the Abbey's tenants were villeins discharging full labour services. But the fact that historians have been inclined to overlook the tendency towards commutation in the other well-known and most widely read twelfth-century survey, that of Glastonbury, is probably due more to the uncommunicative nature of the document than to the actual conditions on the manors. Unlike the Black Book of Peterborough, the survey of Glastonbury reveals the existence of very large bodies of rent-paying tenants holding wholly or chiefly for money rent, especially on the outlying manors of the Abbey in Wiltshire, Dorset and Berkshire. Unfortunately, the document, like most surveys, depicts a static condition, but unlike most of them contains very little evidence of recent changes. In the absence of these indications, to assume that the numerous money-paying tenants were a product of recent commutations would perhaps be to beg the question. Yet an observer with his eyes wide open, and his theories suspended, will find some indications even here; for the documents contain more than a score of references to land-grants and changes in tenurial conditions carried out during the rule of Abbot Henry of Blois (1126–71) and his successor, and with one or two exceptions all of these are grants of land to be held for money and commutations of villein tenures. Even more pointed are the references to the changes on the demesne. With the exception of two small additions to the demesne, most of the references concern leases to tenants. In the Wiltshire estate of Grittleton the whole manor is let out to the villagers, and there is hardly a manor on which portions of the demesne have not been leased, mostly by Abbot Henry.

It is somewhat more difficult to understand the insufficient attention which has been paid to the evidence of the long-available twelfth-century surveys of the estates of Ramsey Abbey (which are the very estates which Vinogradoff chose to cite as an example of the 'immutable' manorial custom) and to those of the Bishop of Durham. On the Ramsey estates the manors not only contain large bodies of tenants described as *censuarii*

[5] On some of the Peterborough manors, however (e.g. Irthlingborough), we find labour services partly or wholly commuted in 1308. The commutation apparently took place earlier, but how much earlier we shall not be able to tell until we know something about the Peterborough estates in the second half of the twelfth century: *Peterborough Account Rolls* for 1292 and 1308. Photostats of the Accounts were made available through the kind generosity of Mr Mellows and Miss Wake of the Northamptonshire Record Society.

and discharging the bulk of their obligations in money, but, what is still more important, they have undoubtedly been affected by a recent process of commutation. Not everywhere is the evidence as clear as on the manor of Holywell, about which we are told that in the time of King Henry I there were twenty-three virgates *omnes ad opus,* and *nunc autem quindecim tantum ex hiis operantur et cetere sunt al censum.* But even where the changes have been less wholesale, as in Cranfield or Shitlington and Pegsdon, they have all been in one direction – from labour services to rent.

More significant still is the evidence of the famous 'Boldon Book' of the Bishopric of Durham. The fifty-five manors, for which this survey (*c.* 1183) gives sufficient information to justify a verdict, fall into three distinct groups. One of these is made up of some twenty manors organized on the pattern of the manor of Boldon, on which manorial institutions function with undiminished vigour. Villeinage with heavy labour services characterizes their social structure and conditions of tenure, the demesne is either farmed out as a single unit or, as in at least eight manors, managed directly by the Bishop. Then there is an intermediate group of some eighteen manors, such as West Auckland or Stockton-on-Tees, on which the manorial organization is not so complete, and the labour services are not so heavy, as on the manors of the Boldon type. But the real contrast is provided by a third group, consisting of nineteen odd manors, Newton-juxta-Boldon, South Bidick, Warden-Law, Morton, Trillesden, Mainsforth, Carlton, Darlington, Blackwell, Cockerton, Redworth, Lanchester, Ryton, Crawcrook, Winlaton, Westow, Bedlington, Whickham, and Haughton Parva. In none of these do we find villeins burdened with week-work; on some of them the very name of villein has disappeared and the bulk of the population consists of money-paying *molmen,* or more commonly *firmarii.*

On nearly all of the manors in the last group the money-paying tenancies arose from what once upon a time had been ordinary villeinage. The twelve molmen of Newton-juxta-Boldon are described in a fourteenth-century survey as erstwhile villeins, the eighteen bovates held by *firmarii* of Wardon are described as *terre bondorum* in the fourteenth-century survey and so also are the lands of men who figure as *firmarii* in the 1183 survey of the manors of Morton and Carlton (Carleton). But the most significant indication of the change is to be found in what we can glean of the fate of the demesne. With the exception of Haughton Parva, the manors in this group do not contain any functioning demesnes, though they must have possessed them at some time. In Darlington, which is the only place where the holdings of the *firmarii* are differentiated from those of the other rent-paying tenants, the twelve bovates held by them in 1183 correspond exactly to the twelve bovates of the erstwhile demesne, as described in the later survey. More transparent still is the position on the Ryton group of manors. We are told in the 1183 document that the men of Ryton, Crawcrook, Winlaton and Westow hold their manors, demesnes and works at farm, while in the later survey each of the men is holding his customary tenement *cum parcellis dominicis* pertaining to it. The process is described best – for it has apparently taken place most recently – in the 1183 survey of the village of Whickham. The entry in the Boldon Book tells us that the '*dominium ... erat tunc in manu episcopi, nunc autem predictum manerium est ad firmam cum dominico*,' and then, as in Ryton, we find the later survey showing the demesne held in parcels attached to the customary holdings.

One other familiar survey, the so-called Domesday of St Paul's, though later in date, throws backward glances, which are numerous enough to give us an insight into twelfth-century conditions. What we learn does not differ much from what we have observed in the surveys already mentioned. Not only were rent-paying tenants of every sort and description predominant at the time of the principal survey of 1222, but many of them had obtained their holdings and established a purely monetary connection with the landlord in the course of the preceding century. Some of them appeared as a result of assarting, which on the St Paul's estates was continuous throughout the greater part of the Middle Ages. But in addition to holders of assarts, there are also numerous money-paying tenants, whose tenures bear witness to the transformation of either the land in villeinage, or the demesne, or both. In Kensworth the territory of the village is very largely made up of holdings of this kind. In Caddington nearly twenty virgates of demesne land are let out – 12 to rent-paying tenants and another 7½ to tenants owing labour services. Large portions of the demesne arable are also let out in Ardleigh, Sandon and Luffenhall, Beauchamp, and Heybridge.

Somewhat rarer are references to commutation of villein holdings and it would, indeed, be wrong to suppose that all the tenements *ad censum* need necessarily have arisen as a result of commutation. Yet occasional references show that some must have appeared in that way, and while there are also a few instances of money rents which have been turned into labour services only very recently (which, as we shall see further, was to be expected), there are in the manors of Kensworth, Ardleigh, Luffenhall, and Runwell clear traces of somewhat less recent changes in the direction of commutation.

That these changes must have taken place in the twelfth century is shown by a number of chronological indices. The evidence is clear in the case of the manor of Beauchamp in Essex, for which we possess a survey of 1181, revealing roughly the same proportion of land held for rent in the demesne, land let out and land assarted as we find in the survey of 1222.

Elsewhere indirect evidence is provided by the names of men responsible for the innovation. In 'Adulfsnasa', the men chiefly responsible for the letting of the demesne and of the 'assessed' hide were Richard Rufus and Hugh de Runwell, who were active in the second half of the twelfth century, and Allard who probably administered the manor at the turn of the century. In Runwell the additions to the rent-paying holdings on the lands of the *antiquum tenementum*, the wholesale letting out of lands described as 'East Strete' and the letting out of parcels of demesne elsewhere, are associated with the names of the same Richard Rufus and of Gilbert de Arches, another twelfth-century administrator. In Heybridge it is the predecessors of the 1222 farmer who are responsible for the letting of demesne land. In Ardleigh some of the demesne was let by Ralph de Diceto, who was active in the eighties of the twelfth century and Richard of Stapleford who, though alive in 1222, was no longer farming the estate at the time. In the list of tenants *ad censum* we are referred to the activities of Master Alberic and Nicholas the Archdeacon, both twelfth-century men. It would take too long to enumerate all the references of the same kind on the other estates of St Paul's, but the evidence of Navestock (Knavestock) is perhaps worth singling out. On that manor the 'new demesne' was largely let out by Richard Rufus and his successors, but the list of tenants also contains a large number of men holding portions of the 'old demesne', which must have been let out even earlier.

The significance of these familiar documents would perhaps have been realized more fully, had the earlier writers been able to study them in conjunction with other surviving surveys of twelfth-century estates, some of which have only come to light or become easily available quite recently. Of these the most important are the surveys of the estates of the Templars, the Bishops of Worcester, the nuns of Shaftesbury and the nuns of the Trinity of Caen. These, in conjunction with several smaller and more fragmentary surveys,[6] provide a great deal of new and important evidence supporting the impression made by the more familiar sources.

Some of this information merely adds supplementary instances of the same kind as those which have already been observed elsewhere. Thus the description of the estates of the Bishop of Worcester in the 'Red Book' of Worcester shows the manors of the Bishopric in Worcestershire and adjoining counties in 1182 containing both typical tenures *ad opus*, and large bodies of peasant, i.e. non-military, tenures for money. Anything in the nature of an exact enumeration of these is made difficult by the ambiguous term of *geld* which the compilers employ to denote money

[6] E.g. the Survey of Binham in Douglas, *The Social Structure of Medieval East Anglia*, 1922, app. ii, no. 3; or the Survey of the Lands of the *Camerarius* of the Abbey of Abingdon: T. Stevenson (ed.), *Chronicon Monasterii de Abingdon*, Rolls Series, 1858, vol. II, pp. 297 seq.

payments. Yet those instances in which the word unmistakably describes money payments to landlords account for some 225 virgates, as compared with 255 which may or may not have been held for labour services.

As elsewhere, the bulk of money tenures on the Bishop's estate may well have been older than the survey, possibly older than the bishopric itself; but, as elsewhere, many of the rents were undoubtedly a result of recent commutation. In Hartlebury, a manor on which money-paying tenants are relatively more predominant than on almost any of the other possessions of the bishop, we are told that they *deberent esse operarii*, that is, should be, but are not. We are told the same about Wodmancote, a hamlet of Bishop's Cleeve. In Tredington most of the money virgates are described as men *que solent operare*. About Newton, the hamlet of Ripple, we are told that 8½ virgates, listed in the survey, *novissime tenentur pro gabulo*. In most of the manors we are also given some indication as to the dates at which the lettings for money occurred. They are those of the mid-century bishops, John, Alverd and Simon.

Different in character, though similar in implication, is the evidence of the Templars' Inquest of 1190. The immense landed properties of the Order were distributed all over the country, covered every possible variation of geographical and social background, and included, side by side with well-rounded and perfectly articulated manors, a miscellaneous collection of fragmentary estates forming part of no clearly recognizable manorial units. Moreover, unlike most of the monastic estates surveyed in the twelfth century, those of the Order were administered primarily with a view to the money revenue which they yielded, rather than to the direct sustenance which could be derived from them. Hence it would be natural to expect the Inquest to reveal a development of rent far more extensive than elsewhere. Indeed, so marked is this feature of the document, that Vinogradoff, who saw it in manuscript, was impressed by its similarity with the rentals of a much later age.[7] And with the exception of a few estates, chiefly those in Gloucestershire and Oxfordshire for which the evidence of the document is not clear, the Survey has very little beyond rents and very light services to record.

Needless to say, many of the rent-paying tenures on the Templars' manors, especially on their non-manorialized properties in Lincolnshire and Yorkshire, are part of the inherited social order and require no explanation. Yet something in the nature of commutation will be required to account for the almost entire absence of tenures for full labour services in the manorialized areas of Warwickshire and Essex, and a process of commutation is in fact indicated by a few traces of recent changes which the document contains.

Thus in the Warwickshire manor of Balsall, we find, in addition to the

[7] *Villeinage in England*, p. 207.

main group of tenants who hold for rent and light occasional services, a group of tenants who pay a higher rent than the rest therefore *quieti sunt de omnibus consuetudinibus ville*. On a large number of manors rent-paying tenements have been carved out of the demesne lands. In Newton we are told that *una duarum hidarum qui erant in dominico est assisa* at 5*s* a virgate. In the Sherbourne group the demesnes of Newbold and Tysoe are let out, and so are portions of the demesne in Balsall and in most of the Essex manors.

Yet it is not the evidence of the Worcester survey or of the Templars' Inquest that historians of Seebohm's or Maitland's age would have found most revealing. Of the documents which have recently become available by far the most important are two or three surveys describing their respective manors at several successive points in the twelfth century, and thus giving an image less static and consequently more significant than that which historians have been able to derive from the better known documents. A typical document of this kind is the Cartulary of the Abbey of the Trinity at Caen.[8] The English estates of the nunnery are described in three successive twelfth-century surveys. The first, which apparently belongs to the early years of Henry I, shows in the Gloucestershire manor of Minchinhampton, 26 virgates *ad opus* and 9 *ad censum*. The second, belonging to the early years of Henry II, enumerates in the same manor, 9 virgates *ad opus*, 11 wholly commuted, and 11 with the option of performing the work or paying rent. The third survey, made some twenty years later, shows all the virgates of this manor commuted for a money rent. The same thing apparently happened at the Abbey's manors of Avening, near Minchinhampton, Felstead in Essex, Tilshead in Wilts, and probably also at Horstead in Norfolk.

A view at two successive points of the century is also available for a number of Dorset and Wiltshire estates belonging to the nuns of Shaftesbury. The manuscript in the British Museum contains copies of two surveys, of which one has apparently been drawn up in the late twenties or early thirties, and the other in the seventies.[9] The comparison between the two is made somewhat difficult by changes in the areas of some of the manors and by numerous mistakes in the medieval copy. Yet there is little doubt that the forty or fifty years which elapsed between the two versions, witnessed a considerable extension of money rents. Thus in the manor of Iwerne Minster, at the time of the first survey, there were 55 odd tenements, of which some 35 virgates and 60 acres were held for full labour services and about two virgates were held for money combined

[8] The dating of the manuscript will be discussed elsewhere. The dates adopted here are roughly those suggested by Miss T. Birdsall in her essay on the English manors of the Abbey in *Anniversary Essays in Medieval History by Students of C. H. Haskins* (Boston and New York, 1929), pp. 25–44.

[9] For the dating of the two texts I am indebted to Prof. Stenton.

with somewhat substantial autumn services. By the time of the second survey there were only nine virgates on full labour services, while the rest were held either for money only or for money and autumn services. The same process occurred in the interval between the surveys on the manors of Tisbury, Chiselborough, Fontmell and Handley (Sixpenny) and of all the Shaftesbury manors for which comparable evidence is available, the manor of Holt in Bradford-on-Avon, alone fails to provide clear evidence of the process.

Another eloquent sequence of surveys will be found in the Burton Cartulary, though its evidence is perhaps too eloquent to be dismissed with a passing mention and must be reserved for special consideration at the end of this essay. But even without that evidence the conclusions should be clear. The twelfth-century surveys available at present deal with more than three hundred manors differing in almost everything in which it is possible for manors to differ – geographical environment, density of settlement, methods of cultivation, type of land-ownership and system of management. Where the differences are so striking the similarity of local changes suggests a general transformation at work. The exact magnitude of the transformation cannot, and probably never will, be properly measured, for it would be wrong to assume that the bulk of the money-paying tenures enumerated in the surveys are of recent origin. But even if the magnitude of the change can be disputed, its direction cannot. To unprejudiced eyes every sign points to a movement towards the commutation of services and the dissolution of the demesne.[10]

3

If what the twelfth-century surveys demonstrate is true, and the period did in fact witness a general movement of commutation, does this not mean that the founders of economic history were right after all? Can we say that what now emerges is not fundamentally different from the old assumption of a slow and gradual commutation, which began almost as soon as the manor came into existence and continued as long as the manor functioned? Unfortunately this is not what we can say as a result of the foregoing discussion. A continuous and uninterrupted process is the one thing the available evidence does not exhibit, and the failure of the twelfth-century commutation to remain equally general and strong in the thirteenth is one of its most conspicuous features.

10 Vinogradoff could not help noticing that a process of commutation was at work on the estates of Glastonbury, St Paul's and Burton: *Villeinage in England*, pp. 307, 327, 330. He was however prevented from drawing the conclusion, which the texts suggest, by his general theories of the development of feudalism and the absence of money economy. More emphatic are the references to twelfth-century commutations in Prof. Douglas's book: op. cit., pp. 83, 123–9.

On some estates it may indeed have continued well into the thirteenth century, as it did on a few of the St Paul's manors. The Survey of the estates of St Mary's Priory, Worcester, compiled in the first half of the thirteenth century, describes a number of manors on which services had been commuted and the demesne leased. At least some of them (e.g. Tibritton) must have undergone the change much earlier, but it is quite possible that the lettings under the 'new assize' were very recent.[11] In the more backward parts of the country the movement may have gone on unchecked. Thus it is likely, though by no means certain, that the wholly commuted estates depicted in the fourteenth-century survey of the Bishopric of Durham stand in direct succession to the half-commuted estates of the twelfth century. But on most other manors for which we possess thirteenth-century documents, and above all on manors situated in the more progressive parts of England, in the heart of the arable and populous south, south-east and south-west, what the evidence reveals is not the signs of a combined general commutation, but the action of a diametrically opposite process. At some time or another during the 150 years following the commutation of the twelfth century and preceding the wholesale commutations of the fourteenth, many manors stabilized, or even increased, their labour services.

In the agrarian history of England these 150 years were a period of *Hochkonjunktur* – an age of rising production, expanding settlement, technical improvements and intensified cultivation (i.e. the application of greater amounts of labour to the same amount of land). On a number of the estates, for which we have evidence, demesne acreages also grew or at least ceased to contract for a time. But where and when the demesnes happened to grow or to expand, their employment of labour, the amount of land subject to villein labour seldom increased to match. Circumstances therefore favoured a fuller exaction, or even an augmentation, of the labour services borne by villein land.

The relevant facts have been known to historians for a long time, but, as most of them have been collected in the course of local studies, they have been commonly treated as local phenomena. Maitland noticed a tendency to increasing labour services on his Cambridgeshire manor, Miss Neilson pointed it out on the Ramsey estates, Mr Feiling discovered it on an Essex manor of Battle Abbey, Professor Douglas on some of the estates of Ely. A depression of a different kind has been described in Mr Bishop's study of the Cistercian granges in Yorkshire, while Professor Kosminsky and Professor Petrushevsky have drawn our attention to the general feudal reaction of the thirteenth century, and Vinogradoff found

[11] W. Hale Hale (ed.), *Registrum Prioratus Beate Marie Wigorniensis*, Camden Soc., vol. XCI, 1865.

instances of it in the *Hundred Rolls*.[12] There is thus nothing in the so-called 'manorial reaction' to surprise scholars who have studied rural conditions in detail, though it is only when the local evidence is brought together that the frequency and the ubiquity of the reaction becomes evident.

The ubiquity of the process may sometimes escape attention, owing to the variety of ways in which the increased demand for labour services could be met, and additional burdens imposed. One of the ways was to subdivide units of villein tenure without decreasing the services attaching to them. This was one of the methods by which Glastonbury Abbey raised the amount of labour available on a number of its manors. The commonest way, however, was by the addition of new services, as on the estates of the Bishopric of Winchester, where new *precaria* may have been introduced and enforced, or on the estates of Ramsey, for which Miss Neilson has tabulated the additions made to the customary services of the tenants during the century.[13]

A method equally common, though even more likely to escape the attention of students, was the 'definition' of services, formerly left undefined. It is a common assumption that this earlier indefiniteness was against the peasant's interest. But, as a matter of fact, that was not always so. Frequently, the translation of the undefined week work into a definite task to be done in a day was and was meant to be a far heavier burden on the villein than an undefined day's work. By way of definition a number of new burdens were imposed on some of the estates of Ely between 1222 and 1277, on some of the estates of Peterborough before 1308 and on the estates of the Bishop of Worcester.[14]

The method, however, which most merits the term 'reaction' was the attempt to abolish earlier commutation and to impose full labour dues on tenants who used to hold for money rent. Instances of this which are easiest to trace are those of destroyed 'options'. The earlier surveys of estates frequently provide the tenants with an option of either paying their rent in money or performing services. The choice was in most cases the lord's, but whenever the lord chose to take money the full labour

[12] F. W. Maitland, 'The History of a Cambridgeshire Manor', *Coll. Papers*, II, pp. 366 seq.; N. Neilson, *Economic Conditions of the Manors of Ramsey Abbey*, 1898, pp. 26, 45–52; K. Feiling, 'An Essex Manor in the Fourteenth Century', *Eng. Hist. Rev.*, 1911; Douglas, op. cit., p. 112; A. Bishop, 'Monastic Granges in Yorkshire', *Eng. Hist. Rev.*, 1935; P. Vinogradoff, *Villeinage in England*, p. 204; Kosminsky, op. cit., pp. 206 seq.

[13] E.g. the fardellers of East Pennard and East Brent, half-virgaters of High Ham: Elton and others (ed.), *Rentualia et Custumaria . . . abbatum . . . Glastonie*, Somerset Rec. Soc., vol. v, 1891; B.M. MS. Vesp. F. xi. H. Hall, *Pipe Roll of the Bishop of Winchester*, 1209, and MS. Eccl. Com. 2/159477: (e.g. Brightwell and Taunton). Neilson, op. cit., pp. 26, 45–52. Also Douglas, op. cit., app. ii, no. 3 and MS. B.M. Claud. D. xiii fo. 7 seq.

[14] Hollings, op. cit.; MS. Eccl. Com. 2/121/43698.

services were *eo ipso* foregone. In the thirteenth century however we find survey after survey destroying the option and both imposing a rent, as if the tenure were *ad censum*, and exacting labour services heavier than those which had accompanied rent tenures in the past – sometimes the full labour services. This indeed was the method adopted in the thirteenth century by Glastonbury, and a number of smaller estates.

Most significant of all, however, are instances of reaction in the narrowest sense of the word – the simple revocation of the earlier concessions and a return to the heavier terms of the dim and distant past. By a lucky accident, one of our documents has preserved obvious signs of some such reaction in preparation. The twelfth-century survey of Glastonbury bears on its margins notes in what appears to be a somewhat later hand, suggesting alterations in the conditions of tenure recorded in the text. In almost every case the note is against entries of parcels of demesne let out or of services commuted, and in almost every case the comment on the former is that they had better be drawn back into demesne (*utilius esset in dominicum*) and on the latter that they had better be let again for work (*utilius esset ad opus*). And even a cursory reading of Abbot Michael of Amesbury's survey in the thirties of the following century will show how closely the spirit of the instructions was followed, though it was left to the compilers of the survey of Abbot Roger Ford, a generation later, to record a yet further increase in the needs of the demesne and a yet further augmentation of services.

4

Thus the typical sequence is from labour services to partial or complete commutation, and then back again to partial or complete return of labour services. To say that this sequence was typical is also to insist on the fact that it was not universal. We have noted complete estates, such as those of Peterborough, or individual manors in other estates, which were not affected by the twelfth-century commutation; there were also estates, such as those of Durham, which may not have been affected by the reaction of the thirteenth century. Moreover, a number of manors which were not subject to the action of the early commutation, were nevertheless visited by the later urge to expansion and saw their labour services intensified. Above all special circumstances could produce local deviations. Professor Stenton has noted the creation of demesnes on some of the Lincolnshire sokes in the twelfth century. At Wargrave, one of the manors of the Bishopric of Winchester, services were commuted in the year 1252, when the bulk of the other Winchester estates were imposing them. At St Ives, a Ramsey manor, the proportion of holdings for labour service was falling in the thirteenth century, at the very time when the Abbey was imposing new labour dues on the bulk of its estate.[15] For the two latter manors the explanation is obvious; St Ives was a market town, Wargrave was engaged in a piece of large-scale colonization. But for the Lincolnshire case an explanation will be difficult to find, and a diligent search would doubtless reveal others equally difficult to explain. In short, exceptions there were, and it would be strange if there had been none, but numerous as they may be they do not obscure the general trend, which no statistical test, however simple, will fail to exhibit. Nor do they overshadow the typical instances of manors, or whole estates, going through the entire sequence of alternating stability and dissolution.

It is because a manor of Burton Priory in Staffordshire and Derbyshire provides one such typical instance that a consideration of it has been deferred until now. The condition of the Burton Priory manors in the twelfth century is portrayed in the two consecutive surveys: one probably belonging to the first quarter of the century, and the other a few decades, perhaps a generation, later. The interval between the two surveys was too short for any sweeping changes. In at least two of the manors, Burton and Stretton, the significant transformation – that of labour-burdened tenancies into rent-paying ones – must have occurred some time before the first survey. In both of them about half of tenanted land listed in the earlier survey was held by villeins *ad opus*, and about half *ad censum* or *ad malam*, i.e. for rent. Some further changes apparently occurred by the time of the second survey, but they were not great, and are sometimes difficult to assess. On one of the manors, however – that of Bromleigh – the intervening period saw some drastic changes. While in the earlier survey some 8 or 9 tenancies comprising 20 to 22 bovates were held for rent, 5 tenancies comprising 10 bovates were still held for full villein services. But in the later survey nearly all the 32 bovates of tenants' land were at rent. In this particular manor the transformation probably resulted from, or led to, a farming agreement between the Abbey and the villagers by which the latter took the manor on lease for thirty years. But on the other two manors the spread of rent-paying tenancies was probably linked with the contraction of the demesne. On both of them some tenancies had been carved out of the demesne (on these manors it still went under its ancient title of 'Inland'). On the manor of Stretton the survey records a corresponding contraction of the demesne from an area requiring three ploughs for its cultivation to an area cultivated by two ploughs. The same manor also comprised some 8 bovates of waste land (*terra vasta*), of which only two bovates were let for the low rent of two shillings.

15 Stenton, *Danelaw Charters*, p. cviii; idem, *Types of Manorial Structure, etc.*, p. 26. For Wargrave, see Eccl. Com. 2/159447. For St Ives, see the Ramsey Surveys referred to above.

This twelfth-century condition was not, however, to remain undisturbed. A third, thirteenth-century, document is a judicial record concerned with litigation between the Prior and his tenants, with the tenants complaining to the courts that the landlord is treating them as villeins and not as *censuarii* and is demanding from them villein service. The cycle is thus complete, though it is destined to be broken again in the late fourteenth and fifteenth centuries, when a new, and this time a final, wave of commutation lays for ever the ghost of manorial order on the lands of the Prior of Burton.[16]

In this Burton example the social relations implied in the reaction are as characteristic as the reaction itself. In many instances the re-imposition of the old labour services or the addition of new ones was brought about by something resembling a bargain and was accompanied by compensating concessions to the tenants. It has been tacitly assumed in this essay that rents and labour services stood in a complementary relation to each other, and that an increase in one would, in normal circumstances, be accompanied by a decrease in the other. This was certainly so whenever labour services were remitted, and it was occasionally so in cases when labour services were re-imposed. A very illuminating illustration of this is provided by the manorial accounts of the Crowland manors.[17] When, in the second half of the thirteenth century, the landlords required additional labour from their customary tenants, the accounts contain allowances of rent in compensation for the extra labour performed. The arrangement continues for years, until at last, at the beginning of the fourteenth century, the additional services are merged into the customary ones and the rent is permanently lowered. A similar procedure was adopted on the manor of Brightwell in Hampshire, belonging to the Bishop of Winchester. There are traces of similar transactions on some of the Hospitallers' manors in Oxfordshire, which had formerly belonged to the Templars, and on some of the Battle Abbey manors.[18]

Very often, however, the procedure was simpler, shorter and more like that of Burton. The lords imposed additional services without a *quid pro quo* of any kind, cancelled earlier commutations, reduced their tenants to

[16] Charles G. O. Bridgeman, *The Burton Abbey Twelfth Century Surveys*, The William Salt Archaeological Society, 1916 (London 1918), pp. 209–23; also *Staffordshire Plea Rolls*, Wm. Salt Soc., vol. VI, part I, pp. 60, 98, 109 and 116; for the dating of the Survey, see Horace Round, *Burton Abbey Surveys*, vol. IX, N.S., pp. 272–6. Round was unnecessarily puzzled by the differences in the amounts of farm in the two surveys.

[17] F. M. Page, *Estates of Crowland Abbey*, 1934. Cf. the rents on p. 284 with the table of services on p. 84, and the accounts of Cottenham and Oakington and Drayton, pp. 21 seq., 233 seq., 176–9. Also idem., *Wellingborough Manorial Accounts*, Northampton Rec. Soc., vol. VIII, p. xxvi and text.

[18] Cf. the terms of virgate tenures in Merton in the twelfth-century Templars' Inquest with those recorded in the Hundred Rolls. Also Scargill-Bird, *The Estates of Battle Abbey*, pp. 58–82.

simple villeinage, refused to recognize customary contracts. Thirteenth-century instances of complaints brought by tenants before the royal courts are frequent enough, but they are much less frequent than the cases of oppression which must actually have taken place, since the only ground on which royal interference could be claimed was the plea that the manor was on ancient demesne, and the estates on which the peasants had any reason at all to believe themselves to be on what was once King's land must have been very few. As in the very similar movement of the German *Bauernlegen* three hundred years later, the will of the lord could not be easily resisted.

The parallel with the East German *Bauernlegen* applies also to what is the most important feature of the process, as well as the most important omission in this paper. Nothing has so far been said here of the causes of the movements, of forces responsible for the expansion of the demesne, and for the rise and fall of services. The object of this essay has been to indicate the main chronological landmarks and only incidentally to question the assumption of a continuous evolution towards free tenure. If, as a mere by-product, a doubt has emerged as to the effects of the so-called rise of money economy, we shall do nothing here to remove it. For it is a salutary doubt. The rise of money economy has not always been the great emancipating force which the nineteenth-century historians believed it to have been. In the absence of a large reservoir of free landless labour and without the legal and political safeguards of the liberal state, the expansion of markets and the growth of production is as likely to lead to the increase of labour services as to their decline. Hence the paradox of their increase in Eastern Germany, at the time when the production of grain for foreign markets was expanding most rapidly, and hence also the paradox of their increase in England, too, at the time and in the places of the highest development of agricultural production for the market during the Middle Ages.

8
THE CHARTERS OF THE VILLEINS*

1

The document is highly unusual, and, as far I know, the only one of its kind as yet known to historians. The circumstances in which I came across it are in themselves evidence of its novelty and importance. In the spring of 1938 my wife and I were paying one of our recurrent calls on Mr W. T. Mellows of Peterborough. A couple of years previously he had introduced us to the great collection of documents in the archives of Peterborough Minster and in his own possession; since then both of us frequently visited Peterborough to work on the archives and to discuss them with our charming and enthusiastic friend. On this occasion the conversation turned on the misdeeds of the antiquaries of the seventeenth and eighteenth centuries. Sparke's credulous edition of a Peterborough survey started us off,[1] and as a further illustration of how careless the great antiquaries could be, Mr Mellows took down from his shelves a little volume in what appeared to be a parchment cover, bearing on its back the legend 'Carte Nativorum'. He hoped to look more carefully into its contents than he had so far been able to do, but he thought that the volume must have belonged to an eighteenth-century antiquary, who may or may not have assembled it, but who certainly gave it its title. And all three of us agreed that an antiquary should have known better than to perpetuate on the cover the title of *Carte Nativorum*. Was it not a commonplace of legal history that villeins could not acquire or transfer property by charter? For one thing, charters were sealed documents, and only a freeman could have a seal and was allowed to use it for authenticating documents.

This argument, so obviously in accord with legal doctrine, seemed

* First published as an introduction to C. N. L. Brooke and M. M. Postan, eds., '*Carta Nativorum*', *a Peterborough Abbey cartulary of the fourteenth century*, Northamptonshire Record Society, 1960 (referred to hereafter as *C.N.*). The diplomatic characteristics of the MS and its relation to certain other MSS are discussed in a separate introduction by C. N. L. Brooke, ibid.

[1] J. Sparke, *Historiae Coenobii Burgensis Scriptores Varii* (London, 1723), pp. 175 ff.

conclusive, and we passed to other subjects. But while the conversation continued I absent-mindedly turned over the pages of the document and equally absent-mindedly noticed that some of the names in the charters were familiar. At the time this did not strike me as unusual or specially interesting for I was then working on Peterborough sources and my head was full of local names. But in the evening of the same day, back in Cambridge, while counting the labour services of villeins in one of the abbot's surveys which I had transcribed during the day at Peterborough, I realized that some of the familiar names in Mr Mellows's volumes were those of villagers in the surveys, and that the title *Carte Nativorum* need not have been quite as wrong as a few hours previously we had judged it to be. Two days later I found myself again at Peterborough and was able to collate a number of entries in the volume with the evidence of the surveys, and finally to satisfy myself that in most of them villeins figured as parties.

My conclusion was that the volume was probably true to its title and was nothing else but a peasants' cartulary. For this is what the *Carte Nativorum* apparently is. This conjunction of a thirteenth-century date with inter-peasant charters is somewhat unusual and, to put it modestly, significant.[2] However, the date of the charters is not the only point of interest in them. What gives them their significance is the peasant status of most of the parties.[3] A few of the men in the charters are described as freemen and probably belong to the upper crust of village society. Thus, the family of Solomon of Werrington are listed in the thirteenth-century surveys as holders of at least 4 virgates, and are described in charters as freemen.[4] Similarly, William of Anstey, a seller of land in Cottingham, is described in the charters as a *liber homo* even though he owed the bishop rent, ploughing service, and *precaria*.[5] Among the sellers

[2] For the dating of the charters, see *C.N.* pp. xvi–xix.

[3] The majority of the parties seem to have been of peasant status; the following are the chief exceptions. The tenants of Walton appear in a number of charters (*C.N.*, pp. xiii–xiv); although one at least was of peasant origin (Richard of Crowland), they were tenants of one-quarter of a knight's fee (cf. P, pp. 142–3 and n.). Ralph of Carham, 'warden of the manor of Scotter', need not have been a peasant (*C.N.* 458, 474a); and one ought perhaps to include holders of abbey serjeanties (e.g. John the Almoner, *C.N.* 53, 108; cf. also 152). The grantor of no. 315 may have been a knight. The grantor of no. 339 was the son of a knight, but the family was impoverished by this date. Burgesses (of unknown status) are parties to nos. 398, 402; most of the persons described as merchants in nos. 64, 105, 369, 451, 455, 460–8 (a merchant's widow occurs in no. 40), could be assumed to have been town merchants and therefore free. But villagers described as 'merchants' could be villeins, and one or two of the parties to charters thus described were abbot's villeins (Robert son of Brand, nos. 460–8; and for Martin, nos. 451, 455, cf. p. lxii). The abbot himself is party to a certain number of charters, and the prioress of Stamford to no. 391.

[4] See *C.N.*, introduction by C. N. L. Brooke.

[5] *C.N.* 393 a–e.

of land in Glinton we find at least three men described as freemen.[6] In addition a large number of men – in fact the majority of men whose names could be identified by cross-reference to the thirteenth-century surveys – were sokemen or holders of soke land.

On the other hand, some of the sellers of land and most of the buyers were apparently unfree tenants. Now and again the charters expressly state that one of the parties, usually the buyer, is a bondman, or that the land he bought is held in bondage. Thus, in listing the various pieces of land acquired in Castor by Reginald son of Walter atte Lanesend, the cartulary notes that the land is held in villein tenure: *et tenetur in bondagio*.[7] The last two entries of leases in Irthlingborough are between villein and villein. John son of John Rose of Irthlingborough is described as *nativus* in an entry recording the abbot's seizure of his land. *Nativus abbatis* is also the description of William Gressop of Ingthorpe about whose purchases more will be said presently.[8] Now and again the servile status of the buyers can be surmised from the manner in which they are described in the charters. For if we are right in assuming that the man whom a Glinton charter describes as Robert son of Ralph *le Freman* or *Fraunchumme* was in fact a free man, we must on the same grounds be justified in assuming that Arnold *le Leif* to whom he sold his land was in fact a *lief* or a serf.[9]

Charters with explicit references to villeins are not of course very numerous, but this does not mean that villeins did not figure in most of them. The whole collection appears to be devoted first and foremost to villeins' business. The fourteenth-century compiler assembled the collection under the general title of *Carte Nativorum*, and in grouping his charters according to manors he has prefaced each group by a similar heading. And if negative evidence is not altogether to be spurned it would be worth noting that in the charters contemporaneous with the thirteenth-century surveys, only some of the names, mostly those of sellers, will be found among the sokemen and freemen listed in the surveys. Most of the other names, as a rule those of the buyers, will not be found in the surveys, and must have belonged to the category of tenants whom the surveys did not list by name, i.e. that of the abbot's villeins. And in keeping with the villein character of the main collection many of the other documents of the volume, which were presumably added at other dates and did not form part of the main cartulary, are also concerned with the affairs of villeins. We find among them an inquisition into the break-up of some villein virgates into free lettings, a list of holdings of the villagers in the meadows of Alkborough (Lincs.),

[6] Robert son of Ralph (*C.N.* 274, 277–80, 308, 322, 324, 326); William (292, 296) and John son of William (305, 317).

[7] *C.N.* 359 (gloss). [8] *C.N.* 390 cf. p. 119 below. [9] *C.N.* 308, 324; 274.

manumissions of two villein tenants of the abbot of Peterborough, and a survey of a gift of land whereby a very considerable number of villeins and their chattels were granted away to Thurgarton Priory. It is indeed very difficult to think of any reason why these documents were appended to the cartulary unless the compiler took it for granted that the cartulary was the proper repository for documents concerning villeins.[10]

We may thus be justified in accepting the document's terminology and in treating the collection as primarily concerned with land transactions of the unfree. But the probability that most of the men mentioned in the charters (certainly most of the buyers) were the abbot's bondmen does not signify that the land sold, bought, or let was necessarily or always bond land. On the contrary, as I have already indicated, the names of many of the sellers, the terms on which they sold the land, and the services which they owed for it to the abbot all suggest that the land was as often as not free land. My own impression is that many of the charters combine in the same transactions the free and the unfree elements of the village: villein and villein land, with freemen and free land.

In this combination lies the main business of the cartulary and much of its interest. Very frequently the apparent object of the transactions which initiated the series of charters relating to any single holding was to supplement the customary tenements of villeins or to carve new villein holdings out of land which may previously have been held by freemen or sokemen. It also appears that even where the seller happened to be a villein and the land was described as bondland, the buyer almost invariably held it for rent.[11] This did not, however, alter the nature of the transaction and did not affect the status of either the land or its holder. Economic historians now well understand that in the thirteenth century large portions of villein land (on some estates it was the whole of the land in the villeinage) were held wholly or mainly for rent. It was therefore possible for the land transferred by our charters to be held for rent and yet to form part of a villein holding and be held on customary or bond tenure.

However, the most significant feature of the charters is not the status of the land but the status of its buyers and sellers. The frequent occurrence of villeins among them bears witness to an active market in peasant property and to this extent belies more than one assumption commonly made about the English village in the twelfth and thirteenth centuries.

[10] *C.N.* 551, 550, 530, 540, 481.

[11] One or two entries say that the land was to be held in bondage without specifying the service (see gloss to *C.N.* 359 on Reginald son of Walter atte Lanesend of Castor); a few others mention boon works or ploughing services (e.g. Robert Fauvel's land in Cottingham, *C.N.* 393 e). However, both free and soke land could be liable to boon works; and it was also common practice to retain boon works and other light services from villein holdings put out to rent.

True enough, most of the charters in the *Carte Nativorum* date from the middle and the second half of the thirteenth century, and thus, at first sight, require from historians little more than a slight readjustment of conventional dates. It is now generally agreed among historians that during the closing century of the Middle Ages – the late fourteenth and the first half of the fifteenth – peasants bought and sold property in most parts of England. Both Miss Levett and Miss Page have described at length the sales and leases of land on the estates of St Albans and Crowland in the late thirteenth and fourteenth centuries. Professor Douglas has drawn our attention to the active sales and exchanges of property amongst peasant sokemen and freeholders of East Anglia in the same period. Vinogradoff, helped, as he doubtless was, by his knowledge of the contemporary Russian village, took it for granted that at the time of the Hundred Rolls, i.e. in the 1270s, informal sales and leases of land among peasants were common. More recently Kosminsky has tried to make full allowances for the increasing importance of leases and sales of peasant land in the late thirteenth century; and the same possibility has more recently still been suggested by Mr Hilton.[12] If so, all the *Carte Nativorum* may appear to do is to push the full development of the land market a little farther back; a decade or two earlier into the thirteenth century.

This view of the *Carte Nativorum* does not perhaps go far enough, or for that matter deep enough. It assumes that the land market made its first appearance in the late thirteenth century and that it may not have been important until well in the fourteenth century. In general it follows the distribution of documentary evidence too closely and perhaps too uncritically. For it appears to assume that if references to peasant alienations appear in our records in 1270, or thereabouts, and become frequent in the last decades of the century, the practice of alienation itself also began and developed at the same dates and at the same pace. Conclusions like this, identifying the history of the document with the history of its subject, may come naturally to medievalists; but a more careful attention to the available evidence might suggest that the suddenness with which documents like the *Carte Nativorum* appeared in the late thirteenth and the early fourteenth centuries does not necessarily mean that the economic and social relations in the village changed equally suddenly and at the same time. The turning-point which the documents signify

[12] A. E. Levett, *Studies in Manorial History* (ed. H. M. Cam, M. Coate, L. S. Sutherland, Oxford, 1938), pp. 187 ff.; F. M. Page, *Estates of Crowland Abbey* (Cambridge, 1934), pp. 112 ff.; D. C. Douglas, *Social Structure of Medieval East Anglia* (Oxford, 1927), pp. 61 ff.; P. Vinogradoff, *Villeinage in England* (Oxford, 1892), pp. 330–1; E. A. Kosminsky, *Studies in the Agrarian History of England in the Thirteenth Century* (Oxford, 1956), pp. 211–13, 224–226; R. H. Hilton, 'Gloucester Abbey Leases of the late Thirteenth Century', *Univ. of Birmingham Historical Journ.*, IV (1953–4), 12.

may well have been one of the manorial administration and diplomatic rather than one of village economy and society.

2

There are strong grounds for believing that the *Carte Nativorum* were merely a local instance of the new methods which some landlords of the thirteenth and the early fourteenth centuries began to use in regulating land transactions of their villein tenants. What apparently happened was that on a number of estates on which much land had been previously leased or even sold without the regular and organized participation of the lord, or at least without a settled routine, the administrators began to record and register all the land transactions of their tenants.

These changes in manorial attitudes and procedures left a clear mark in the records, but they have not so far been described and may therefore repay a closer inspection. Historians have generally and rightly taken it for granted that in medieval law the villein was not permitted to alienate or to exchange his land without his lord's permission. This attitude is echoed and re-echoed in countless cases before national and local courts, in repeated enactments of manorial officials, and in corresponding clauses in manorial ordinances, custumals and surveys and private charters.[13] A corresponding attitude to movable property does not figure equally prominently in our evidence; it can, however, be detected in some of our records without much difficulty. Now and again we find it expressed in injunctions against the sale of ploughing animals, such as the injunction promulgated in some Ramsey surveys of the mid-thirteenth century, or invoked on behalf of the lords in legal proceedings.[14]

This attitude was rooted in feudal land law as well as in the doctrine of villein status. In law the villein had no right to property. Both his land and his chattels belonged to the lord who could resume them at will and which in fact he resumed or pretended to resume at the end of each

[13] For the unsuccessful thirteenth-century attempts of Abbot Roger of St Albans see *Gesta Abbatum Monasterii S. Albani* (Rolls Series), I (1867), 453–5; also A. E. Levett, *Studies in Manorial History*, pp. 187–8. Cf. W. H. Hart (ed.), *Historia et Cartularium Monasterii Gloucestriae* (Rolls Series), III (1867), 217 and F. W. Maitland (ed.), *The Court Baron*, Selden Soc. 4 (1890), p. 102. For the legal doctrine see F. Pollock and F. W. Maitland, *History of English Law* (2nd ed., Cambridge, 1898), I. 329 ff. and esp. p. 382; prohibitions of subsequent alienations were sometimes incorporated in documents licensing sales, e.g. E. Toms (ed.), *Chertsey Abbey Court Rolls Abstract*, Surrey Rec. Soc. XXI (1954), p. 14, no. 142.

[14] E.g. on Ramsey estates: W. H. Hart and P. A. Lyons, *Cartularium Monasterii de Rameseia* (Rolls Series, 1884–93), I. 303, 304, 437. Also *Curia Regis Rolls* (1210–12), VI. 294; *Year Book, 18–19 Edw. III* (Rolls Series, 1905), pp. 502 ff. In this case the lord's authority is confined to his right to protect his villein's animals from distraint by third parties.

tenancy. If, in obedience to his own interests, the manorial lord in fact did not arbitrarily dispossess his villein tenants in the midst of their tenancies, or interfere with the day-to-day sales of stock and produce, this did not mean that his right to do so had lapsed or was not recognized in law. And though villeins in fact enjoyed full security of life-long tenure or even rights of inheritance in accordance with local custom, landlords could always be expected to oppose the alienation of villein holdings or even their transfer by lease.

In theory – and the emphasis is on theory – the lord's opposition to alienation could be justified by the needs of manorial economy. Where and when alienation was piecemeal and threatened the integrity of a customary holding – a virgate or a bovate – it could also be construed to threaten the efficient discharge of the tenant's duties and obligations to his lord. The argument behind the construction is not difficult to imagine. Money rent could perhaps be paid and collected *pro rata*, even from holdings broken into a number of small and irregular plots. But other dues, such as manual labour on the lord's demesne, ploughing services with the village plough teams, attendance at boon days or at court, were not easily divisible and could not be assigned in proportionate fractions to each acre or rood. Where such labour dues and personal obligations were still exacted, it was in the lord's interest to prevent the holding from sinking below a certain economic level and, above all, from being broken up into a multitude of petty parcels.[15]

On the same grounds it is possible to argue that from the lord's point of view the most dangerous sales were those of villein land to free tenants. For although in law villein land in the hands of a free man did not become free land, transactions of this kind threatened to take customary land out of the sway of the lord's unlimited rights and powers. It is very largely for these reasons that manorial injunctions against alienation of villein land frequently single out for special prohibition sales of villein land to freemen or sokemen. Even the king – the most liberal and indulgent of medieval landlords – was anxious that the 'sokemen of the ancient demesne' – a privileged group of villein tenants – should not alienate their holdings to other sokemen.[16]

The concern of the village community in preventing the alienation of villein holdings is perhaps less obvious and is less thoroughly documented.

15 The doctrine with special reference to partible inheritance is summarized in Pollock and Maitland, I. 381–2.

16 Sometimes the landlords' licences to alienate include a proviso against subsequent alienation to ecclesiastics and Jews to safeguard against danger of mortmain and forfeiture to the king; below, Additional Note 2 on *Land Transfers on the Estates of the Abbey of St Albans*. It is, however, strange to find the prohibition many years after the expulsion of the Jews, as in 1334 on the Chertsey estate: *Chertsey Abbey Court Rolls*, p. 56.

Professor Homans, in his book on the thirteenth-century village, discusses several cases from which it appears that the village custom was often inimical to the break-up of villein holdings or to their passing into the hands of non-villeins.[17] This attitude may have represented nothing more purposeful than the natural conservatism of peasant society and its vigilance on behalf of the inherited social relations and class structure (which is the view Professor Homans himself appears to favour); or else it may have reflected the villagers' reluctance to allow holdings to get into the hands of men who did not share the collective burdens of the village, such as tallages, ploughing dues, payments for the agistment of animals, or liability to manorial offices. It is also possible that communal attitudes merely echoed the wishes of the lords. But whatever the reason, there is no doubt that the bias of communal custom and of the lords' courts was to favour the maintenance of the traditional pattern of village holdings, and to discourage the unrestricted transfer of villein land.

How much this bias was in fact capable of deciding the lord's attitude is a matter on which I shall have more to say later. But in considering the effectiveness of the communal bias we must not think of it as the only influence at work. For in the twelfth and the thirteenth centuries the village was open to pressures and inducements which were bound to stimulate sales and leases of land. Some of the inducements were purely economic; they might even be described as commercial. For as good land was getting short, and rents and land values were rising, many a wealthy villager may have been tempted to cash in on the rising market and to offer his lands for sale in parcels. Such may have been the explanation of the numerous sales of land by the abbot of Peterborough's substantial freeholders and sokemen. Similarly, it is possible that some men bought land for speculative purposes, i.e. in order to re-sell or sub-let again at a profit. The abbots of Peterborough themselves engaged in such operations from time to time, and so may have done some of their tenants. Yet the balance of evidence suggests that the main stimulus for traffic in land was generated within the peasant community and owed more to certain abiding features of peasant life than to the higher land values of the thirteenth century and their attractions for speculators.

On general grounds, i.e. those of mere common sense and of comparable experience in other peasant cultures, we must assume that in societies in which the family is the unit of ownership and exploitation, the needs and the resources of individual families are too unequal and too unstable to allow family holdings to remain uniform or unaltered in use and size. Ideally the size of a family holding in peasant society is one which is large enough to fill the family's mouths and small enough to be worked

[17] G. C. Homans, *English Villagers of the Thirteenth Century* (Cambridge, Mass., 1940), ch. xiv.

with the family's hands. This ideal many families could approach; few could realize in full. In all peasant societies (certainly in Europe) there always have been holdings inadequate to the needs of large families or to the resources of rich ones, as well as holdings too large for the unaided labour of small, poor or aged holders.

Inequalities of this order were also to be found in medieval English villages at the very dawn of documented history. The presumption therefore is that in the English village, as in all peasant villages, the inequalities were remedied in ways open to most villagers. One of the remedies was that of the labour market. The smallholder could – and we know he did – hire himself out to the lord or to the more substantial villagers; the latter hired labour to supplement the labour resources of their households. But an equally obvious remedy was to be found in the land market. A family well provided with land, but deficient in labour or stock or tools – childless couples, widows and widowers, old men and invalids, or merely poor or improvident husbandmen – might find their larger holdings too much for them, and be compelled to sell or let what they could not work themselves. On the other hand, smallholders with large and strong helpers at home, or wealthy and energetic peasants capable of providing themselves with the necessary stock, or of finding outside labour, or anxious to build up a rent roll of their own, would buy or hire such additional land as there was to be had.

The existence of these 'natural' sellers and buyers has not escaped the notice of historians, especially of historians like Miss Levett and Miss Page, who had access to large collections of manorial court rolls. Miss Page found on the manors of Crowland Abbey groups of persons who habitually let or otherwise alienated portions of their holdings as well as groups of men who habitually acquired land from others. There were thus the Attetouneshends of Oakington, who in the second half of the thirteenth century held a tenement of 15 acres. William Attetouneshend the First let out parcels of the holding three times, and then through 'impotence' surrendered his holding to his son William, who in the twelve following years appeared in the Court Rolls thirty-four times as a lessor and finally gave up his land through inability to cultivate it himself. Other regular lessors on the Crowland Court Rolls were Geoffrey Kyng of Oakington and the Stirmys of Drayton. Geoffrey Kyng was apparently under the same compulsion of 'impotence'.[18]

Needless to say not in every village were the aged and the decrepit able to find relief in sub-letting their holdings. On manors, such as those of Glastonbury, on which traffic in land was effectively controlled, so

[18] F. M. Page, *Estates of Crowland Abbey* (1934), pp. 112–13; for accumulation of holdings, cf. A. E. Levett, *Studies*, p. 187 (Walter Wyggmore of Park) and p. 190 (Hugo Cok of Codicote).

many of the customary tenants are recorded as having surrendered their holdings to the Abbot *propter paupertatem*, *propter impotenciam*, or *propter senectutem* as to suggest that on these estates the acres of men who could not cultivate them were not directly sold to those who could. Yet it is possible that even on the Glastonbury estates a surrender on the ground of incapacity may have been nothing else than a pre-arranged preliminary to a sale of land by men incapable of cultivating it.[19] And whatever was the practice at Glastonbury there is no doubt that on most other estates the connexion between sales and the incapacity of the sellers was very real. There is no reason for doubting it in the Crowland instances already cited. That the connexion was equally real elsewhere is shown by the frequent decisions of manorial courts to remit the fines for illegal sales on account of the sellers' or lessors' poverty.[20]

It is therefore not surprising that women tenants, mostly widows, should figure very frequently among the lessors. Such were, for instance, Matilda, a widow in the St Albans manor of Cashio, or Edith Blanche, of Halesowen, or Alice of Middleton on the Ely estates, or Genilda on the Ramsey manor of Cranfield, or other widows or unmarried women on occasions too numerous to list.[21] It is indeed apparent that unless and until a widow inheriting the husband's property remarried (as so many did), sub-letting was her most obvious way of turning the inheritance to account.

Mutatis mutandis, the persons buying land or taking it on lease were sometimes landholders of substance. Such was apparently Richard de la Grene, a villein of Wakefield who in the last decade of the thirteenth century acquired, in addition to his holding in Wakefield, a messuage with buildings in Pontefract, a bovate with buildings in Barnsley, and an annual rent elswhere, or indeed several men whose purchases are

19 Glastonbury Court Rolls, Longleat MSS. 11250 (Walton: John Cole; Buckland: Adam Cockerel); 11254/3 (Baltonsborough: John le Graa; Damerham: Robert le Crokere); 10654 (Pilton: John Rois; Batcombe: John Saber; Kingston: William Pistor), and many others. The typical entry is that N. 'senex et debilis est et non potest pro paupertate iura etc. sustinere', or 'non potest iura tenere nec domum sustinere' (e.g. ibid., 11254/3, Baltonsborough), though sometimes poverty alone is alleged. A striking case in which the lessee is the prior of Southwark and the lessor is too poor to plead, is in D. M. Stenton (ed.), *Pleas before the King or his Justices, 1198–1202*, I, Selden Soc. 67 (1953), p. 362 (no. 3487).

20 That poverty could be due not to the insufficiency of the holding, but to personal circumstances is illustrated by a late thirteenth century case in D. M. Stenton (ed.), loc. cit.: Sewell son of Robert, lessor of two virgates, unable to prosecute his claim against the lessee because of his poverty.

21 The Court Rolls of St Albans, *passim*, in A. E. Levett, op. cit., esp. p. 310; the Ramsey *Cartularium*, I. 439; *The Court Baron*, p. 104; R. A. Wilson (ed.), *Court Rolls of the Manor of Hales*, III (Worcs. Hist. Soc., 1933), 43, 71, 96, 103, 107; *Curia Regis Rolls*, *passim*, e.g. VIII (1219–20), 187.

recorded in the *Carte Nativorum* and who will be mentioned again later.[22]

I doubt, however, whether rich peasants predominated among the buyers to the same extent to which poor ones predominated among the sellers. Among the buyers whose economic position we know, we find numerous men of humble rank, smallholders, or wholly landless persons who presumably disposed of idle hands, but were under-provided with land. Thus, a list of sub-tenants, to whom some time before 1281 one William Attehulle, a villein of Chalgrave, had let out a large part of his holding, appears to consist of village labourers and cottagers. A similar list of men who took land from Edith Blanche also appears to be made up of members of the 'labouring classes', such as Agnes la Seriant, or Henricus Tinctor.[23] In addition, the Court Rolls contain a great deal of indirect evidence pointing the same way. Thus, relatively few of the buyers or lessees of land were substantial enough to figure among the men who serve regularly on juries or inquests or acted as pledges. In general the little we know about the 'undersettles', i.e. the tenants' tenants, suggests that they were as a rule small men. More, however, will be said about them presently.[24]

There were thus two countervailing pressures at work. On the one side there may have been the desire of the lords and perhaps that of the village community to maintain the virgated tenancies intact; on the other hand there was the pull of the villagers as individuals away from the stable pattern of customary holdings. On the one hand the land market was bound to be to some extent restricted or at least controlled by authority, and the controls could not be expected to disappear altogether until the manorial demesne and the related system of peasant dues faded away in the late fourteenth and fifteenth centuries. But on the other hand the restrictions were not as a rule so severe, and the lord's opposition

22 W. P. Baildon (ed.), *Court Rolls of the Manor of Wakefield*, I (Yorks. Arch. Soc., Record Ser. XXIX, 1901), 242. Other evidence containing instances of large holdings, assembled by piecemeal purchases in Douglas, *Social Structure of Medieval East Anglia*, pp. 63–4; Levett, op. cit., p. 187; J. Booth (ed.), *Halmota Prioratus Dunelmensis*, Surtees Soc., 1886, pp. 14–16 (this last a remarkable case of a holding of several hundred acres assembled mostly by purchase, largely unlicensed, between 1315 and 1345), and elsewhere.

23 M. K. Dale (ed.), *Court Rolls of Chalgrave Manor, 1278–1313* (Beds. Historical Rec. Soc., 28, 1950), pp. 14–15; *Court Rolls of Hales*, III. 107.

24 Below, pp. 121–2, Professor Kosminsky is one of the very few medievalists not only to acknowledge the fact of 'informal' inter-peasant transactions in the thirteenth century, but to work it into his analysis of rural society. He has, however, assumed that the buyers and lessees of peasant land were mostly richer men (op. cit., pp. 225–6). Cf. W. G. Hoskins, *The Midland Peasant: the economic and social history of a Leicestershire village* (London, 1957), pp. 49–52.

not so consistent as to impede regular transfers of land from villein to villein all through the period for which evidence is available.

The evidence is not of course available in equal profusion for all the centuries in the Middle Ages. Direct evidence bearing on the economic management of the estate and the social relations in the village seldom reaches back beyond the middle of the thirteenth century. The documents best capable of revealing the functioning economy of the manor, the so-called bailiffs' accounts, do not become at all common until the second half of the thirteenth century, and, moreover, tell us little about private dealings of villagers. Most of our information about these dealings comes from the rolls of manorial courts recording litigation among tenants and the more important transactions among lords and tenants. But no court rolls have survived from the twelfth or the beginning of the thirteenth centuries; and although a few rolls of the second quarter of the century have come to light, most of those available to historians date from the end of the thirteenth century and later. This being the distribution of evidence, it is not surprising that historians should have found the existence of the village land market in the earlier period screened from their view.

The screen, however, is not wholly impenetrable. To begin with, some evidence of the land market will be found in non-manorial sources and especially in the records of the King's Court. The surviving enrolments of the proceedings of the king's justices at the turn of the twelfth and thirteenth centuries are very few and summary, and villein business in them is very rare. It is therefore highly significant that a large proportion of these early cases of peasant land and inheritance should be concerned with land, both free and unfree, acquired by villeins by purchase or lease. Some of these acquisitions may have been made with the permission of the lord, as in the case in the *Curia Regis Roll* for 1214 concerned with a holder in villeinage in Peterborough who had, some one or two generations previously, sold his land to another local man.[25] But there is no indication of the lord's consent in some other cases, such as that in 1219 in which a villein in the Dorset manor of Pimperne is described as having purchased a holding in villeinage in the lifetime of his landlord's predecessor.[26]

These references in the records of royal courts do not stand alone. A closer attention to other sources will reveal the operations of the land market long before the time when the manorial or even royal court rolls are able to display them in full. Thus, the earliest of the enrolled bailiffs' accounts, those for the estates of the bishops of Winchester for 1209–25, also contain, in addition to indirect reflections of the land market, direct evidence of transactions among villeins. The sections of the accounts

[25] *Curia Regis Rolls*, VII. 62.

[26] Ibid. VIII. 98–9; IX. 92–3.

devoted to the profits of courts record numerous payments by tenants for permission to demise their land: *pro licentia dimittendi*. The entries occur on the two earliest of the Winchester Rolls – those of 1209 and 1210 – and there is nothing in the form of entry to suggest that transactions were at that time in any way unusual or novel. In fact the wording of the entries is so laconic and so devoid of the explanatory matter which commonly prefaces references to new sources of revenue in the bishop's accounts, as to leave a clear impression of a stereotyped entry recording a well-established practice.[27]

Other indications in our records hint at the practice of unlicensed as well as licensed alienations at very early dates. Thus the rolls of manorial courts, though somewhat later than 1209, often deal with land transfers going back to the opening decades of the century and even earlier. I have already indicated that many of the charters in the *Carte Nativorum*, roughly contemporaneous with the cartulary itself, merely wind up series of transactions stretching over a number of generations. In one case the *Carte Nativorum* record an inquest into the history of a villein holding going very far back into the past. The history and the genealogy on which it is based begin with the purchase of 18 acres of land by a William Gressop, a villein with family connexions in Ingthorpe. The parties contesting the succession at the time of the inquest (1292) were William Gressop's grandchildren, and great-great grandchildren, who at one and possibly two stages descended from William through younger children. Allowing for medieval expectations of life, the interval between the original purchase and the inquest was at least seventy-five years long and probably longer, and the purchase must have taken place at the turn of the twelfth and thirteenth centuries.[28] A descent of a purchased villein holding through a number of generations almost equally long is recorded in the Court Rolls of Wakefield. We read there of a piece of villein land which one Gerard le Double had bought from a villein and subsequently gave or bequeathed to one Ellen, possibly his daughter. The land then passed through the hands of several people, some of whom obtained it by purchase, until it came to be claimed by Ellen's son. If Ellen was Gerard's daughter, three generations would have separated the purchase from the date of the hearing.[29] In that case the purchase must have taken place very early in the thirteenth century, if not earlier.

Early thirteenth-century purchases can also be detected in numerous other cases of later date. Thus, the list of villein purchases by charter recorded in 1239 on the Ramsey Abbey court rolls consist almost wholly

27 There are at least fourteen references to *licentia dimittendi* in the bishop's roll for 1210–11 (P.R.O. Ecc. Comm. 2/159270/B) and at least four in the Roll for the preceding year (ibid., A).

28 *C.N.* 390.

29 *Court Rolls of Wakefield*, II (1906), 81.

of transactions now legitimized by the payment of fines. The purpose and significance of this legitimization will be discussed later, but it is worth noting that some of these purchases must have taken place many years before 1239. Thus we are told that William Marshall, a well-established tenant of mature years, frequently serving on juries, resigned to the abbot the land that his father had bought from a villein; that a number of villeins had bought land by charter from Simon fitz Ulph, a deceased father of one of the abbot's villeins, and that at least one of the purchasers, Ralph Trigolf, had also passed away since the date of the purchase; that one Gilbert, a villein, had some time previously sold 1½ acres of villein land which he had still earlier bought by charter from one Herbert also a villein.

Most of the early rolls of the King's courts and Bracton's notes from them record similar brief histories of peasant dealings reaching back to dates much earlier than the rolls themselves. Thus when we read of a case in 1233 of a holding sold or let by its two owners, Alexander and Robert, to one Adam Crane, who, in his turn, sold it to a man called Gilbert, who two years before his death had leased it to his son Martin for a term of years which expired some time before 1233, we are compelled to conclude that the sale to Adam Crane by which the series was initiated must have taken place many years before the date of the case, probably at the end of the twelfth century. Similar instances will be found on most of the rolls, and in combination they build up a strong case for the view that the habit of selling land (and, as I shall argue later, also of leasing it) had been fully formed before the date of the earliest *Curia Regis* rolls or that of the earliest bailiff's account: certainly by the turn of the twelfth and the thirteenth centuries.[30]

This view finds support in what we know about certain developments in the villages of the twelfth and thirteenth centuries which could not have occurred except through villein sales and sub-lettings. One of these developments was the proliferation of free and quasi-free appendages to customary holdings frequently listed in the surveys of the early thirteenth century. I shall have more to say about this matter later, but it is relevant to mention here that while some of the free lands in the hands of villeins must have come to them by grants from their lords, others they must have acquired by purchase. It will be remembered that many of the holdings in the *Carte Nativorum* had been bought by villeins from sokemen and freeholders.

Another development was the subdivision of customary holdings on some (by no means all) manors in the twelfth and thirteenth centuries. For this subdivision the growing village population was obviously respon-

[30] *Cartularium de Rameseia*, I. 423 ff.; F. W. Maitland (ed.), *Bracton's Note Book* (Cambridge, 1887), II, no. 783, no. 1837; see also nos. 1203, 1256.

sible, and there is some evidence to suggest that the lords responded to the pressure of population and to its promise of profits by splitting the larger tenements at the death or the resignation of sitting tenants. But there is also much evidence to suggest that some of the subdivisions resulted from the alienation of portions of customary holdings.[31]

An even more significant, though heavily disguised, manifestation of the village land market will be found in the existence of the so-called undersettles. Most historians are now agreed that the villages in the twelfth and thirteenth centuries contained a category of men who were tenants of the lords' tenants. Unless they also held land of the lords they would not as a rule be listed in the manorial surveys. But now and again the existence of the sub-tenants is revealed in the manorial documents, as in cases when the manorial administrators tried to obtain some services from the undersettles. Thus, we find the inquisition into the bishop of Ely's estates in 1251 extending some labour dues to the peasants' servants (*anlepemen*) and to cottars whether residents on the bishop's land or that of his villeins: *cotterellus manens super terram alicuius custumariorum suorum*.[32] But the commonest of all references to them will be found in the portions of manorial custumals and surveys defining the labour services of tenants. These services frequently imply an obligation on the part of the tenants to bring their sub-tenants with them on boon-days.[33] On the manor of Meon, belonging to the bishop of Winchester, we find a tenant who presents himself at the great harvest boon works with as many as twenty-five sub-tenants. This land holding, though listed among customary tenancies, and held by a customary title of some sort was, by all appearances, not a peasant unit but an entire sub-manor. But it is easy to find in the returns of boon works on the bishop's estates, as on all other estates, numerous tenants bringing with them on harvest days other men in numbers much less than twenty-five yet large enough to suggest that sub-tenants were included among them.[34]

Needless to say we could not expect this class of sub-tenants to be equally represented everywhere. But a curious and significant feature of the class closely linking it with the land market is that while it was

[31] This was obviously the manner in which some customary holdings in Bishop's Waltham were subdivided: below, Additional Note 1 on *Subtenants on Some Manors of the Bishops of Winchester*.

[32] Brit. Mus. Cotton MS. Claudius C XI, f. 312v; also *Chertsey Abbey Court Rolls*, p. 41, no. 431 and pp. 46, 58 (nos. 481 and 583–6): subtenants mostly cottagers on holdings of other villagers; also W. O. Ault (ed.), *Court Rolls of the Abbey of Ramsey and of the Honor of Clare* (New Haven, 1928), p. 186.

[33] E.g. W. D. Peckham (ed.), *Thirteen Custumals of the Sussex Manors of the Bishops of Chichester* (Sussex Rec. Soc. XXXI, 1925), pp. 33–4. For general discussion of undersettles see G. C. Homans, *English Villagers*, pp. 211–12; E. A. Kosminsky, op. cit., p. 79.

[34] E.g. Nicholas de Lanrishe, Martinus de Barlye, and Johannes Clericus in the Meon Custumal of *c.* 1250. B.M. MS. Egerton 2418.

obviously present on some estates it left no trace on others. The contrast can sometimes be explained by the local variations of village economy and geography. Thus sub-tenancies may in fact have been infrequent on manors surrounded with large colonizable reserves from which new holdings could easily be carved out. But elsewhere the difference could be most plausibly explained by the working of the village land market and by the lords' attitude towards it.

The attitude of the lords to peasant sub-tenancies was bound to vary from estate to estate; and as I shall presently argue, it also changed from epoch to epoch. Wherever and whenever a landlord demanded that all men acquiring land from his tenants should hold directly from him, and was able to enforce his demands, the effect of the land market was to accelerate the turnover of the customary tenancies and generally to disrupt the apparent symmetry and stability of customary tenures. Such was apparently the position on the estates of the abbot of Glastonbury. But where the landlord did not try or found it impossible to enforce the surrender of land by sellers previous to its sale, the conventional pattern of customary holdings might persist in the extents while a class of sub-tenants would grow up concealed from our view. This may have been the position on some estates of the bishops of Winchester in the thirteenth century.[35]

We must therefore have it both ways. While the subdivision of customary holdings betrays the action of the village land market, the stability of the virgated pattern of villein holdings need not signify its absence. This it may signify on manors on which the demand for land could be met by newly reclaimed holdings. But elsewhere the persistence of the virgated pattern must be taken as an indication that it was left to the unofficial land market to reconcile the ancient tenurial pattern to the changing fortunes of individuals.

3

What with the deductions from backward-looking entries in thirteenth-century judicial records and the evidence of under-tenants and that of subdivision of customary lands and the free appendages to villein holdings, the presumption of an active village land market in the twelfth and early thirteenth centuries is well supported. How is it, then, to be reconciled with what we are told of the villeins' inability to lease, buy, or sell land, especially villein land, and more especially by charter? And how are we to define and to explain the lords' attitude to villein transactions as they appear in the records of the late thirteenth century?

[35] This by itself may be too summary a distinction, for there were differences in the functioning of the land market even within the two estates contrasted here. See below, Additional Note 1.

In theory the purchase of a villein holding – indeed of any tenant's holding – was possible only by 'surrender and admittance'. The seller had to surrender his holding to the lord, while the buyer had to take it from the lord as his tenant. But in fact this was not the form which all land transfers went through; and least of all in the earlier centuries. 'In this region', says Maitland, 'there seems to have been but little custom', which is another way of saying that rules were uncertain and unequally applied.[36] The manorial rules may have been stricter towards villeins' sales than they were towards their purchases and leases. In general, however, there is no doubt that such rules as there were could frequently be evaded.

The evasions could be more or less complete. Complete evasions were surprisingly frequent. At the end of the twelfth and in the early thirteenth centuries land was frequently bought, sold, and leased by villeins without any recorded licence from the lord. This is at any rate the impression which the earliest crop of presentations in manorial courts must leave on the student; and is also the impression he will derive from the very circumstances in which villein sales came before royal courts. Many, perhaps most, of the cases hark back to transactions for which the lord's consent had not been invoked or was not claimed in the pleadings. In many of these cases the buyers might have continued to hold their lands undisturbed, had not a death, a conflict of claims, or even a crime intervened to bring the history of the holding before the courts. Thus, in a Dorset case before the king's justices in 1219, cited above, the defendant denied that he was a villein, but admitted that he held in villeinage land which he had bought (*quam emerat*) some time previously. In the end his villein status was affirmed, but his purchase went unchallenged, even though he did not claim the lord's sanction for it. An even more striking case, going still further back, concerned the abbot of St Albans. In the course of the hearings it transpired that the defendant, one Busseye, whose land the abbot claimed as his villeinage, had bought it of Alexander Waterletere, who had bought of James La Weyte, who held of Richard Burdun, who held of James, who held of the abbot. According to the abbot's plea, Alexander, the last seller, was of his villeinage; according to the latter's account, he had sold his land for 4 marks in order to raise ransom money after he had been captured at war. Here, in other words, was a whole series of alienations and sub-lettings of a holding which the lord regarded as his villeinage, but which apparently changed hands without his cognizance.[37]

[36] Pollock and Maitland, I. 382.

[37] *Curia Regis Rolls*, XII. 91 (no. 465). Also ibid. VII. 108, Osbert of Norbroc who claims to be holding the villeinage of the Bishop of London is sued for a holding which the plaintiff's father is alleged to have leased to him.

The very frequency with which landlords enacted and re-enacted their prohibitions is perhaps in itself evidence of widespread evasions. Miss Levett has shown how unavailing for a very long time – probably until the middle of the fourteenth century – were these injunctions on the estates of St Albans; and how until 1355 the manorial administrators of St Albans did not control, or had given up the attempts to control, leases for less than two years.[38]

The by-passing of the landlord was sometimes revealed by the issue of charters. There is little doubt that the villeins of Peterborough were not alone in acquiring lands by the same process by which freemen acquired free land, i.e. by charter. Indeed, a very large proportion of the earliest references to unlicensed alienations which came up before manorial courts relate to lands thus sold. That these were, almost by definition, illegitimate transactions, goes without saying. In theory the villeins had no right to a seal, and could not sell, and most probably could not buy, land by a sealed instrument.[39] Yet the earliest pocket of direct references to land sales in manorial courts – that on the Ramsey estates in 1239 – relates to at least eleven and possibly as many as nineteen charters mostly involving villein land. So do also a number of other batches of similar cases occurring in the other surviving court rolls.[40] So common and so familiar was the use of personal seals by villeins in the thirteenth century, that the Statute of Exeter, in dealing with Grand Inquests, could permit that, when a sufficient number of freemen could not be found, substantial villeins could serve, provided they possessed seals.[41]

The villeins obviously required charters and treasured their possession even though the land was unmistakably villein and the seller of the land was himself a serf. The reasons for this are not far to seek. A villein's charter might not, as a rule, be worth producing in court, but it still remained an incontestable record of purchase, and could be cited in the informal disputes before neighbours or arbitrators which undoubtedly

38 A. E. Levett, *Studies in Manorial History*, p. 188.

39 Maitland's version of the official doctrine excludes the villein by implication: 'before the end of the thirteenth century the free and lawful man usually had a seal': Pollock and Maitland, II. 224. An early case in the King's Courts relating to the villein's right to seal documents will be found in *Curia Regis Rolls*, IV (1205–6), 19: '*non potest cirographum fieri, quia non est certum utrum sint villani necne*'; a similar case 21 years later in ibid., XII. 354 (no. 1734). Yet there is no doubt that villein charters in our cartulary and elsewhere were sealed. For a description of villein seals see Hilton, *Univ. of Birmingham Hist. Journ.* IV (1953–4), 13 ff.

40 *Cartularium de Rameseia*, I. 423–8; *Court Rolls of Wakefield*, I. 88. W. O. Massingberd (ed.), *Court Rolls of the Manor of Ingoldmells* (London, 1902), pp. 100–2, and elsewhere.

41 'E si defaute seit en les avauntdite viles . . . ke il ny eyent taunt de francs houmes, seient ajoyntz de meillors et des plus sages e leals bundes e ke checun eyt seal.' *Statutes of the Realm*, I. 211. I owe this reference to the courtesy of Professor V. H. Galbraith.

occurred in medieval villages as they have done in villages and communities of other times and countries. Besides, the charter might not be altogether useless even before the manorial or royal judges. When the villein's own status was called into question, the possession of a charter might be a useful bit of ancillary evidence. The records of royal courts have preserved several cases in which the villein defendants claimed free status on no other ground than the possession of a charter, even though the land had been sold and the charter issued by someone who was not the villein's lord.[42]

Needless to say the use of charters by villeins was opposed by manorial lords. The very reasons why purchase by charter commended itself to the villein must have condemned it in the eyes of the landlord; and at first sight the condemnation might appear uncompromising. Most of the manorial injunctions against the alienation of villein land specify transfer by charter. Similarly, proceedings against unlawful acquisitions of land by villeins in the early court rolls seldom fail to mention the charter as an aggravating circumstance. In some entries it is the charter rather than the alienation of land itself that appears to have drawn the fire of the landlord's jurisdiction. In Chalgrave in 1302, where a tenant is accused of having acquired two acres of villein land, the main burden of the accusation is that he did so by vicious charter: *per scriptum viciosum.*[43] And it is apparently the right to alienate land by charter rather than the right of alienation itself that ranged the cellarer of St Albans against the abbey's tenants in Barnet and elsewhere in a struggle which Miss Levett tells us was as long drawn out and as persistent as the friction about suit at the abbey's mills, famous in the social history of the fourteenth century.[44]

The frequent use of charters by villeins in unauthorized deals in the first half of the thirteenth century or even earlier betrays a general laxity of manorial controls. This laxity revealed itself in other ways as well: not only in the lord's failure to prevent such complete breaches of the law as the use of villein charters, but also in permitting partial evasions by recourse to informal manorial record. It appears that very often landlords did not require their tenants wishing to sell or let their lands to go through the formalities of surrender and admission. A licence and a fee appeared to suffice.

This use of licences may have had a connexion with the early appearance of undersettles. For whereas in transfers of land by surrender and admission buyers held of the lord himself, transfers by licence, like

42 *Curia Regis Rolls*, II (1201–3), 13–14. For an early twelfth-century grant of land by a landlord to a villein in free title upheld by the courts see ibid. v. 94.
43 *Court Rolls of Chalgrave*, p. 43.
44 A. E. Levett, op. cit., p. 192; cf. p. 149, n. 5.

transfers without the lord's knowledge and agreement, created sub-tenancies of existing tenants. The difference was similar to that which we find in the more exalted sphere of holdings in fee simple between lands transferred by substitution and those transferred by subinfeudation. If so, I might stretch the parallel a little further by likening the situation in the twelfth and the early thirteenth centuries to that which prevailed on free lands before the days of the Statute of *Quia Emptores* (1290), when in Maitland's words 'subinfeudation was certainly much commoner than substitution'.[45]

The laxity of manorial controls thus revealed itself in several ways: in the issue of peasant charters, in other wholly unlicensed alienations, in transactions under informal licence. It would also be, so to speak, selective, i.e. more effective in some transactions than in others. It is possible that most of the evasions occurred not when villeins sold their holdings but when they acquired land, more especially free land; for when it came to the purchase of free land by villeins, the lords could well afford to be indulgent. The possession of a free holding did not impair the villein's ability to discharge the obligations of his customary holdings; it did not threaten to withdraw any property from the sway of manorial authority. On the contrary, under feudal law and local custom some of the lord's authority over villeins' property could extend also to the free land acquired by them. It is therefore not surprising that the manorial documents contain so few, if any, proceedings or injunctions against villeins acquiring free land. Nor were there any objections in common law. The common law view apparently was that the villein could acquire and hold free land freely from anybody who was not the landlord himself or his villein. The doctrine, as it was formulated in the thirteenth century, was that a serf could be enfeoffed with land by someone other than his lord, and would have recovery by the same action of *novel disseisin* which gave recovery to all free holdings. At the same time a villein owning free land had some advantages over sokemen and freeholders. By pleading that his property was legally his lord's, a villein owner of free land could bar all attempts to lay execution on his land for debt, or to disseise him on other legal pretexts.[46]

[45] Pollock and Maitland, I. 345.

[46] G. E. Woodbine (ed.), *Bracton de legibus et consuetudinibus Angliae*, III (New Haven, 1940), 33, 91. *Curia Regis Rolls*, IV. 169: a typical case in 1206 in which the claim to inheritance under the assize of *mort d'ancestor* is successfully rebutted by a sitting tenant on a plea that he holds in villeinage. For other cases in which villeinage is invoked to bar pleas of debt, broken covenant, or inheritance, see ibid. I. 98 (1199), III. 273 (1205), IV. 172 (1206), VI. 117 (1211), VII. 108 (1214), &c.; also G. H. Fowler (ed.), *Cal. of the Roll of the Justices on Eyre, 1247* (Beds. Hist. Rec. Soc. XXI, 1939), no. 205. The records have preserved several cases of men who held or had acquired land freely, converting it into villein tenancies for security against creditors. Thus, *Curia*

The lords' indulgence could not, however, have stopped at this point. The protection which the law gave to the villein dealing in free land and the tolerance which the lord showed towards alienation of free land to villeins must also have offered a loophole to villein dealings in villein land. The distinction between free land and customary land, so clear in theory, was often blurred in practice. There was a great deal of land in the villages of the second half of the twelfth and the thirteenth centuries the status of which was open to question. As a result of wholesale commutations in the twelfth century, or by virtue of agreement more ancient still, much villein land was held for rent only. When land such as this was sold or let, it was possible for the parties to believe or at least to pretend that the land was free. There are numerous cases before the royal courts, mostly those of inheritance, in which one of the parties claimed free titles to the holdings on the ground they were held for rent. In these cases other evidence before the royal courts frequently established the villein condition of the holding, but the very fact that for holdings of uncertain status, free tenure could be claimed in courts must have encouraged many more transactions than the local supplies of saleable freeholds could alone support.[47]

Whether the loopholes in the doctrine and practice of villein tenure were the sole cause for the apparent laxity of the manorial controls is difficult to say. But whatever the causes of the apparent liberality, they seem to have had a greater effect in the late twelfth and the early thirteenth centuries than in the late thirteenth and the early fourteenth centuries. For there is some evidence for the view that by the turn of the thirteenth and fourteenth centuries evasions had become less frequent, transfers by surrender more common. The attitude of the manorial administrator showed signs of stiffening.

How is that stiffening to be explained? Certainly not by the lord's growing concern for the integrity of the villein holdings or for the effective collection of labour services. Elsewhere in this essay I invoked these

Regis Rolls, VI (1210–12), 117: the plaintiff alleges that his creditors unlawfully seized his crops after he 'deposuit se de libero servicio terre sue in Akeburne et posuit se in servicio vilenagii'.

[47] The best-documented cases are those relating to the complaints of thirteenth-century communities of rent-paying villagers – 'molmen', '*censuarii*', and villein-sokemen of ancient demesne – against being treated as villeins. But references in our records to individuals claiming free holding or even free status because they held for rent, are also very numerous: e.g. *Curia Regis Rolls*, XI. 320 (no. 1600); cf. ibid. XII. 208. For free land held by villeins or vice versa, see ibid. II (1201–3), 13–14: a man of alleged villein status holding land freely by a grant from a third person. Ibid. VIII. 114–15 is a case of a large holding of 100 acres held in villeinage at the end of the twelfth century by a man whose personal status the jury in 1219 could not decide for lack of evidence. For other similar cases see ibid. VII. 108, and VIII. 98–9; F. W. Maitland (ed.), *Select Pleas in Manorial Courts*, I, Selden Soc. 2, 1888, p. 22.

conventional explanations of the lord's attitude; but in doing so I warned the reader that this attitude did not appear to dominate the manorial practice of the late twelfth and the early thirteenth centuries. It certainly did not dominate it in the following hundred years. By 1300 the integrity of the customary virgate was on many manors a thing of the past, and so was also the lord's dependence on the full discharge of labour services. Indeed had his main preoccupation been with the virgate and its labour dues he would have confined his prosecutions to the men who alienated their holdings piecemeal and would have spared the sellers of entire virgates or semi-virgates, or of non-virgated land. But this was not what the landlords and their officers in fact did. When they called the sellers and buyers and leasers of land to account – as many of them did in the thirteenth and early fourteenth centuries – they were as hard on the sellers of whole virgates as they were on the men selling or leasing odd acres or roods. And when and where the routine of recording peasant sales was finally established, the manorial courts sanctioned and enrolled sales of odd pieces of customary land by the score.

This fact Maitland noticed and found somewhat inexplicable. In his introduction to the *Select Pleas in Manorial Courts* he drew attention to the very large numbers of entries in the thirteenth-century court rolls of Ramsey Abbey, by which men surrendered small pieces of land in the hands of the lord *ad opus* of third persons. These he rightly concluded were sales of land. But in that case, he observed, 'how this traffic in roods was compatible with the system of virgate holding that we see in the extent of the manor is not very clear'.[48] The truth of the matter is that the lords who administered the system of sales and registrations, as we find it in the late thirteenth century, were not primarily concerned with the defence of the virgated pattern of village lands and obligations.

It is difficult to avoid the impression that behind the wholesale prosecutions of villein sellers, lessors, and lessees in the court rolls in the second half of the thirteenth and fourteenth centuries, and also behind the well-organized routine established by that time, were considerations which were mainly fiscal. One important fiscal motive could be the wish to safeguard the revenues from death duties (heriots), for these could be avoided by timely alienation or gift of a holding.[49] This motive, however, could not have grown stronger in the late thirteenth century than it was earlier and could not by itself have produced a marked change in the manorial proceedings. On the other hand the growing shortage of land in

[48] F. W. Maitland (ed.), *Select Pleas in Manorial Courts*, I, Selden Soc. 2, 1888, pp. 105–6.

[49] M. M. Postan and J. Titow, 'Heriots and Prices on Winchester Manors', *Econ. Hist. Rev.*, 2nd ser., XI (1958–9), 392 ff., esp. pp. 394 ff. (reprinted as Chapter 9 below).

the thirteenth century, the greater opportunities for raising rents whenever holdings changed hands, the chance of levying an entrance fine (or in other words in sharing with the sellers some of the proceeds of the sales): all these would come naturally to an acquisitive landlord at the time when land values were on the rise. That the values were on the rise is a fact I have argued elsewhere and am proposing to take for granted here;[50] the acquisitive attitude of the landlords could also be taken for granted. It was part and parcel of the new-found efficiency which we associate with the progressive landlords of the time: men like Michael of Amesbury and Roger Ford at Glastonbury, Henry Eastry at Canterbury, Richard of London at Peterborough, Henry de Lacy on what were to become the Lancaster estates. Most of these reforming administrators tried and were able to squeeze out of their estates higher profits than ever before. And it was in the spirit of the times that they should have also tried to lay their hands on the rising values of the land transactions of their villeins.

This 'laying of hands' may in some cases have been a gradual process, a piecemeal tightening of the procedure whereby the lord could assert his concern in the transactions of his villeins. In many places, however, the landlords imposed their control over the transactions by a single act of administrative innovation. This may sometimes have been preceded by a general inquiry into past sales of customary land, as on the manor of Chalgrave in 1294.[51] But whether any such inquisitions took place or not, the time came in a number of manors when the landlord issued orders or invitations to the villagers to bring their charters into the court and offered to have them recognized and recorded on the payment of a fee. This was certainly the procedure in a case before the court of King's Bench in 1296, when the jurors gave evidence that one Robert of Barnham in Norfolk, the plaintiff's father, whom his lord claimed to be his villein, had some years previously (probably in the 1260s or 1270s) acquired land by charter and held the charter in his own custody until the steward 'summoned all the tenants of the aforesaid manor on a certain day, and held the court . . . and enjoined upon all that, if they had acquired any lands by charters, they should give him their charters. Among them it happened that the aforesaid Robert de Eastgate gave him his charters, and all these charters he afterwards returned to the aforesaid Robert for a fine of half a mark . . .' The context makes it clear that before the bailiff issued his order the tenants of this manor had been in the habit of

[50] This will, I hope, be discussed at greater length elsewhere, but cf. M. M. Postan's 'Chronology of Labour Services', *Trans. Royal Hist. Soc.*, 4th ser., xx 1937), 185 ff. (reprinted as Chapter 7 above).

[51] *Court Roll of Chalgrave*, pp. 33–8. In 1294 the jury of customary tenants present the names of unlicensed buyers or lessors of land among villeins. This is apparently the first such presentation in the surviving rolls, and is followed by others in the subsequent two or three years.

acquiring land by unrecorded charters; and the context also suggests that the steward's order was something of an innovation.[52]

I know of no other equally plain story of the change; but that some such story was hidden behind many a dry record of the court rolls appears highly probable. Its outline, however shadowy, can be discerned in nearly all the court rolls containing numerous entries. Thus, when we find that at two courts held in the Ramsey manor of Brancaster on 22 February 1239, a large batch, perhaps as many as seventeen or eighteen villein transactions in land were recorded, we could safely assume that something had been done in that manor to net in not only the transactions of that year but all the past transactions still outstanding. As I have already mentioned, some of the entries refer to an event or a date which places the transaction well before 1239.[53] It is therefore significant that although transfers of land by charter continue to be recorded on the rolls of this and other Ramsey manors after 1239, they no longer occur in large batches of half a score or a score, but in small driblets and at wide intervals commensurate with the sizes of the villages.

The 'reform' on the Ramsey manors occurred at an unusually early date. But, date apart, the evidence of bunched entries reveals the introduction of similar 'reforms' in many other manors, mostly taking place late in the thirteenth century. Thus, when we find on the manor of Chalgrave in Bedfordshire in the three years between 1294 and 1297 at least ten villein sales recorded in the court rolls we must bear in mind that no comparable numbers will be found in the earlier rolls (these are available from 1278 onwards) and that both before 1294 and after 1297 entries of peasant sales occur in ones and twos. And indeed it is implied that in 1294 or shortly before, the customary tenants were instructed or persuaded to return all the known cases of land in the hands of men who had bought it from other villeins.[54] Unfortunately the court rolls of Halesowen and Wakefield are too late to reveal the events of the thirteenth century. The rolls of Wakefield for 1315 and 1316 contain licences to take up other tenants' land in very large numbers, possibly as many as 190. They may, however, be nothing more than applications to occupy newly asserted land, and would in that case be due not to a change in manorial procedure but to an important advance in the internal colonization of

[52] G. O. Sayles (ed.), *Select Cases in the Court of King's Bench under Edward I*, III (Selden Soc. 58, 1939), 47 ff. The court did not pronounce on the plaintiff's personal status, but the fact that both he and his father paid *chevagium* gives some substance to the lord's claim on him as his villein. The court did, however, think it relevant that he did not owe any other servile dues.

[53] *Cartularium de Rameseia*, I. 423 ff.; however, we find on the Ramsey Manor of Stukeley in 1294 a small batch of three orders to men who had bought land some time previously, to come and show their charters: W. O. Ault (ed.), *Court Rolls of Ramsey*, p. 214.

[54] *Court Roll of Chalgrave, passim*, esp. pp. 33–8.

Yorkshire.[55] On the other hand the bunched returns of peasant sales in the late forties of the fourteenth century on the court rolls of some of the St Albans manors can be taken as evidence of a mass surrender of charters which I believe followed an inquisition and a bargain between the cellarer and the abbot's villeins in 1345.[56]

An implied bargain probably lies behind the 'reform' on most estates. The sellers and the buyers of villein land by charter had all broken the law. The legal penalty for the breach was the cancellation of the contract and even the forfeiture of the land. Yet the manorial administrators offered in exchange for the delivery of the charters what amounted to an amnesty and the recognition of the sales both past and future, as in the Barnham case cited above. From now on the greater regularity of registered sales in manorial records would make the lord's control more effective. But this very regularity shows that it was not the purpose of control to restrict, still less to destroy the village market, and that the lord's object was to profit from his villein's transactions. Transfers by surrender and admission may have become more general, though even now not universal.[57] Provided he obtained a fee, sometimes an increase in the rent, and commonly an undertaking by the new owner to perform all due services, the lord gave the buyer and the seller not only his consent, but also the security of official enrolment.

These at any rate were the terms on which the charters in the *Carte Nativorum* appear to have been legitimized and enrolled by the administrators of the Peterborough estates. I have also shown that the collection must have been made up of charters which were brought into court quite late in the thirteenth and early in the fourteenth century together with the earlier, mostly undated and unlicensed, charters relating to previous tranfers of the same holdings. It is for these reasons that I am inclined to consider the compilation of the cartulary as evidence not of a suddenly emerging land market but of a new attitude towards it on the part of the abbot of Peterborough and his servants.

[55] J. Lister (ed.), *Court Rolls of the Manor of Wakefield*, IV (1930), *passim*.

[56] St Albans Court Rolls, *passim*, in B.M. MSS. Stowe 849 (Codicote), ff. 1–85, Add. 40625 (Park), ff. 1–119; Add. 40626 (Cassio), ff. 1–92; Add. 6057 (Croxley), ff. 6–16; Levett, *Studies in Manorial History*, p. 149, n. 5.

[57] Cases of tenants surrendering land *ad opus* of buyers will be found on a number of estates. This may always have been the practice on the estates of the abbey of Ramsey. In the later thirteenth century we find it on the estates of Glastonbury and Bury St Edmunds: Longleat MSS. 10654, 11254/3, 11250, 10654, 10655, 10656, *passim* (Glastonbury); Bacon MSS. in the University of Chicago, Court Rolls of Redgrave and Hinderclay, *passim*. On the latter, however, this was not the universal procedure, and the more informal procedure of fees for licensed sales will also be found, e.g. Hinderclay Court Roll of 4 Edward I: 'fecit finem ad vendendam terram'. For the estates of St Albans see below, Additional Note 2.

4

The conclusion that the village land market was much older than the documents like the *Carte Nativorum* and may have been as old as the village itself, does not necessarily mean that transfers of land did not become more frequent as the Middle Ages drew to their close. Students of the later Middle Ages have been inclined to represent that period as specially favourable to traffic in land. In doing so they can draw upon a number of well-established presuppositions about the later Middle Ages. If we are right in assuming that the manorial bias against alienation of villein holdings was strongest when and where labour services were exacted, then we must be allowed to conclude that the bias lost its strength with the final commutation of labour services in the fourteenth and fifteenth centuries. Similarly if we are right in believing that the land which lent itself best to buying and selling was 'free' land or generally land held for rent, then we must also conclude that sales became easier in the later Middle Ages, when supplies of easily saleable land were more plentiful. If to these general presuppositions we add the documentary evidence of very frequent land sales in the late fourteenth and fifteenth centuries, we may find it easy to understand why historians generally believe that in the closing century and a half of the Middle Ages the village land market was much more active than in the early periods.

This contrast between the later and earlier centuries must not, however, be driven too far: certainly not to the extent of assuming that all the impediments to the land market were in the twelfth and the thirteenth centuries and all the facilities in the fifteenth. Historians are now agreed that commutation of labour services was by no means a new phenomenon in the late fourteenth century. There was widespread, and on some estates, wholesale, commutation of labour services in the middle of the twelfth century, as a result of which, by the end of the century, large areas of customary land were no longer burdened by heavy labour dues. Professor Kosminsky has recently reminded us that by 1279 – the date of the Hundred Rolls – labour dues no longer were the main source of the lord's income from his peasant tenants. I believe that further examination of manorial evidence will reveal that the Hundred Rolls if anything minimize the extent to which the labour services had been commuted, and that the commutation had in all probability gone very far – perhaps near to its 1279 position – by the first quarter of the thirteenth century. But even if this belief were not borne out by researches now in progress, it would still remain true that in the thirteenth century customary tenancies held wholly or mainly for rent were very numerous and thus more than sufficient to sustain an active land market.

The same holds true of 'free', i.e. non-customary lands held for rent by customary tenants. These could come from three main sources. One source was the demesne lands let out by the lords, another was land recently reclaimed from the waste, and the third was land sold or let by freeholders other than the tenants' landlord, mostly petty landlords of the neighbourhood. Of the three sources the last is the one least explored by historians, and until more is known about it we are not in a position to tell whether more freeholders' land was on offer in the fifteenth than in the thirteenth century. Of the other two sources, one, that of demesne lands, may have grown more abundantly in the second half of the fourteenth century than before, for as we all know, much demesne arable was at that time let out to tenants. Yet the extent of demesne lettings of the earlier periods was also quite considerable. Much demesne land had been farmed out to villagers in the middle and the second half of the twelfth century; and although on a number of estates the process was arrested for a time in the thirteenth century, it did not cease altogether everywhere. As for the remaining source – that of newly reclaimed land – it may in most places have been more important in the twelfth and the early thirteenth centuries than in the later Middle Ages. It is enough to cast a glance at the evidence of thirteenth century surveys of estates in regions where reclamation was active – those of St Paul's in Essex, or those of the bishops of Worcester in the West Midlands, those of Glastonbury Abbey in west Somerset, or those of the bishops of Winchester in the east Cotswolds or the Hampshire Downs – to realize what a large proportion of land in the hands of villeins in the twelfth and the early thirteenth centuries consisted of rent-paying holdings recently reclaimed from the waste. What happened to this land in later centuries, how much of it remained in cultivation and for how long, is a subject as yet insufficiently studied by historians and cannot be discussed here. It is, however, fairly certain that in England taken as a whole the process of reclamation petered out in the later Middle Ages, and that in many places it had begun petering out in the late thirteenth century.[58]

So taking all in all, supplies of 'non-customary' land which, by definition, lent themselves best to free transfer, did not necessarily grow, or at any rate did not grow fast or continuously throughout the Middle Ages. In so far as the development of the village land market was dependent upon them, the advantages it enjoyed in the fifteenth century compared with, say, the twelfth century may not have been so great as to justify a striking historical contrast.

[58] The chronology of medieval reclamation has, I believe, been accurately indicated in H. E. Hallam, *The New Lands of Elloe* (Leicester, 1954) and M. Clough, 'The Estates of the Pelham Family in East Sussex before 1500' (an unpublished thesis in the University of Cambridge), ch. 9.

Easier to observe, though even less obvious, were the variations in space, i.e. between different parts of England and more still between different villages. Professor Homans in his discussion of alienation of land has suggested that in this respect East Anglia and south-east England differed from other parts of the country and especially the west. His argument is that the land transfers were more common in East Anglia or Kent where the manorial influences were not as all-pervading or as rigid as elsewhere, and where partible inheritance prevailed. The evidence which Professor Homans cites fits well into his territorial contrast, though I doubt whether the fit would have been quite so close had Professor Homans been able to use some of the evidence of the Midlands and the West Country which was not available to him at the time when he wrote his book.[59] On general grounds, however, the distinction he draws appears plausible and is probably true. The fragmentation of free holdings by partible inheritance in regions like Lincolnshire or much of Norfolk may have created a multitude of holdings too small to sustain a family without recourse to wages or to the land market. What was equally important was that in some eastern counties free land and soke land were prevalent, and as we have seen, it is possible to argue that free lands were easier to draw into a land market than holdings held on villein tenure.

Yet the very connection between freeholds, fragmentation and land market must warn us against an over-simplified regional demarcation. Freemen and sokemen probably were more numerous in Kent or in the Danelaw than elsewhere, but this does not mean that they were absent or unimportant in other parts of England. If the evidence of the Hundred Rolls is to be trusted, there were whole Hundreds in Oxfordshire, Bedfordshire, Warwickshire, and probably in Buckinghamshire with a very large proportion of freemen or sokemen.[60] There were also large pockets of freeholders and sokemen in Yorkshire, Derbyshire, the counties on the Welsh and the Northern border, to say nothing of the counties on the fringes of the Danelaw such as Leicestershire and Northamptonshire. Above all, some of the free holdings of villeins, including probably much of the new land in the waste, were not everywhere subject to the manorial or feudal rules of succession to a single heir. So while the principle underlying the territorial distinctions is doubtless right, the frontiers separating areas favourable to alienation from those unfavourable to it formed a network more confused than the lines suggested by Professor Homans.

What also confused the lines was the lack of uniformity in the manorial control of sales on different manors within regions of broadly similar social structures. Some of these differences may be more apparent than real. As I have repeatedly stressed elsewhere, our documents and par-

59 G. C. Homans, *English Villagers*, ch. xiv, esp. p. 204.
60 E. A. Kosminsky, *Studies*, pp. 116–42.

ticularly manorial extents, do not all exhibit the same degree of change in the distribution of customary holdings. Some present the pattern of holdings as remarkably stable, others record continuous changes by subdivision and proliferation. I have also suggested that these differences sometimes reflected the attitudes of the landlord to the land market; but sometimes it is possible to detect real economic differences behind the contrasts in our documentation.[61]

Equally significant, though even more difficult to trace, may have been the difference in relative frequency of leases, on the one hand, and of outright sales, on the other. If I have so far treated leases and sales as if they had the same history, I did this partly for convenience of exposition and partly in mimicry of our records. In most of our sources illegal transfers are frequently lumped under the verb *tradit* or *dimittit*; as a rule the student will not discover whether sale or lease is in question except by going behind the terminology of the records and by exploring the circumstances of each case. Leases and sales are also frequently lumped together in manorial injunctions against transfers of land.[62]

This indiscriminate treatment of sales and leases may in part have been due to the fiscal preoccupations of the manorial administrators. But what may also have influenced the manorial administration is that the titles conferred on a villein by purchase and by long lease were very similar, indeed almost identical. In medieval law, both royal and manorial, the villein's right in the customary holding he purchased, and perhaps even in the holding he received from the lord, was nothing more than a life tenure. In practice the custom recognized succession to rightful heirs, and it was very unusual for a customary holder or his successors to be disturbed in the continuous occupation of the holding. Yet the doctrine of life tenure was invariably invoked in all changes of customary title in manorial courts. Every time a customary holding fell vacant by death, lapse, or sale, the lord and the new tenant went through the form of a new re-letting. It is this form that the lords tried to enforce by the registration of land transfers in manorial courts, and it is probably this doctrine

[61] Above, p. 132.

[62] A variety of terms were used in the late twelfth and thirteenth centuries to designate leases. *Dimittit* occurs very frequently, but can also relate to alienations as when the Bishop of Winchester's bailiff referred to customary tenants holding *ex dimissione* of N. The terms most frequently employed in royal courts are *inuadiauit* or *inuadiauit ad terminum* (below, p. 142 n.). *Ceperunt ad firmam* occurs frequently especially in Glastonbury records, as in Longleat MS. 11250 (Middlezoy, Thomas Gydye); so does also *tradidit ad terminum*: ibid. 11254 (East Brent, Richard Robyn). On the estates of Durham Priory short-term leases are described as 'ploughings': 'Walterus Stirleling pro licencia . . . arandi terram Conani ad medietatem'; J. Booth (ed.), *Halmota Prioratus Dunelmensis*, Surtees Soc. 1886, p. 3, also pp. 1–11, *passim*; see also W. O. Ault (ed.), *Court Rolls of Ramsey*, p. 194. For *conduxerat* see *Select Pleas in Manorial Courts*, I. 21.

that prompted their opposition to sales by charter. For a typical charter almost invariably conferred property rights in perpetuity.

It is thus easy to understand why in so many transfers of customary land by licensed sale the new title was deemed valid only for the life of either the seller or the buyer. This condition certainly attached to all the transfers made under what I suggested was the procedure of later years. The case from Wakefield already cited elsewhere is in this respect especially interesting because it concerns a villein holding which changed hands six times in the period of fifty years. The alienations which took place there with the lord's permission, described as if they were purchases, were in fact valid only for the lives of the buyers.[63] Professor Homans quotes a case in the records of Halton in Buckinghamshire, which lays down that no tenant of the lord could demise his land except for his lifetime: *nisi ad vitam suam*. And similar cases could be cited from almost every estate for which court rolls have survived.[64]

Thus, in legal appearances, purchases and life leases were sufficiently alike to justify the refusal of medieval clerks to differentiate between them. Yet some differences of legal position there doubtless were. And when it came to short leases, the difference between them and sales was of course very profound. Outright sale finally broke the ties between the owner and his land and could therefore result in the permanent break up of some holdings and the building up of others. Students of medieval sources will have no difficulty in citing numerous cases of old holdings and families fading out in this way and new ones emerging to take their place. Several instances of some such transformation by sale will be found in the *Carte Nativorum*.[65] On the other hand, leases, especially short leases, were passing events not intended to make irrevocable changes in the owner's property. They were, so to speak, current adjustments to the fluctuating circumstances of individuals. And in so far as the purpose of the land market was to provide a mechanism whereby the rigorous system of customary virgates could be fitted to the unstable fortunes of

[63] *Court Rolls of the Manor of Wakefield*, II. 81, see above pp. 130–1.

[64] G. C. Homans, *English Villagers*, p. 196. However, the distinction between inherited villein tenancies held in perpetuity and purchased holdings tenable only for lives may be too categorical; cf. p. 147 below for the St Albans practice. A more plausible distinction is that of tenure for the life of the tenant in cases of holdings received from the lord, and tenures for the life of the lessor in the case of life leases by persons other than the lord.

[65] The most striking examples are noted in *C.N.*, p. xiv. Large holdings could of course be also assembled by a series of short leases: e.g. a tenant in Middlezoy (Thomas) who in the same year covenanted to have half the profits of 18 acres which he leased for three years from Thomas Gydye and also leased 4 acres for three years from another villager, and 5 acres for four years from yet another man; or altogether 27 acres. We do not know whether these leases were renewed three years later, but in the nature of things this could not be an enduring tenancy: Longleat MS. 11250 (Middlezoy).

peasant families, a lease was obviously the instrument by which that fitting could best be done.

'Could best be done': the conditional is here employed because the evidence is not sufficient for an indicative categorical. It is, however, sufficient to suggest that among individual customary holders leases may have been the commoner form of transfer. The records, especially the earlier ones, give the impression that villagers did not resort to outright sales except as extreme expedients whereby uneconomic holdings were finally reduced or wound up. I have already cited several instances from Miss Page's study of the Crowland estates in which a series of leases preceded the final liquidation of holdings by sale.[66] Similar cases will also be found in the court rolls of other estates; and if these cases are truly typical, they would make it highly probable that in the history of individual holdings in the twelfth and the thirteenth centuries leases were more frequent and often preceded outright sales.

The possibility that on peasant holdings, considered individually, leases often preceded sales, suggests the yet further hypothesis that some such chronological sequence marked the history of land transactions considered in the aggregate. This particular hypothesis is, of course, of the very vaguest; it may be even more difficult to prove or to disprove than most other hypotheses about private affairs of villagers. Yet if proved it could illuminate so many recesses of social history now dark and forbidding, that it would be well worth exploring as far as our scanty records will take us.

This exploration is still a task awaiting an historian. All it is possible to do here is to indicate very briefly the nature of the argument, and in doing so, to remove some of the presuppositions which have so far inhibited the discussion of the subject. The evidence is of course both scanty and opaque, but it is not altogether absent. To begin with, there is the general impression that the use of short leases for land transfers among villagers (as distinct from the lord's leases to his tenants) is not as common in the records of the late fourteenth and fifteenth centuries as we might expect in view of what historians have told us of the spread of leaseholds in the later Middle Ages. Yet transfers of land by sale were very frequent. If so, it may well be that as the Middle Ages drew to their close, outright sales were becoming more common and leases relatively less so than they had been in the earlier centuries.

This possibility is of course consistent with the other features of the time, and more especially with the general 'upgrading' of smallholders in the fifteenth century. In all the villages for which evidence is available, the numbers of landless men drastically fell and the average holdings of smallholders became considerably larger than they had been in the thirteenth century. Professor Kosminsky has described this transformation in

[66] Above, p. 115.

the village of Brampton in Huntingdonshire, and I believe that all other studies of the fifteenth-century countryside will bear Professor Kosminsky out.[67] Some of this upgrading doubtless resulted from occasional amalgamation of vacant holdings and from new opportunities for the enlargement of holdings opened up by the break-up of the demesne. But many a smallholder was able to enlarge his holding not by acquiring portions of erstwhile demesne or by receiving from the lord a larger customary holding, but by buying land from other villagers. These enlargements must not, however, be confused with the action of the land market so far discussed here. Land transfers capable of achieving a permanent reshuffle in the social structure of the countryside and of altering the entire pattern of tenures in custumals and surveys were not the current and temporary adjustment to changing individual circumstances which I have treated as a permanent phenomenon of village life. And if leases were the appropriate instrument for the latter, sales were an equally appropriate instrument for the former.

Historians may indeed find it only too easy to accept the hypothesis of wholesale land transfers by sale at the end of the Middle Ages: what they may find more difficult to accept is the countervailing proposition that leases were common in the earlier centuries. For this proposition may appear to run counter to some of our current notions of the antiquity of the leasehold contract. In so far as historians have thought or written about leases – and this they have done very seldom or very briefly – they have been inclined to treat the land lease, and especially the peasant land lease, as a phenomenon characteristic of the period after the Black Death. This inclination colours the whole of Maitland's approach to the problem, and he happens to be one of the few English historians who have approached the problem at all. According to him, tenancies for terms of years (presumably both free and unfree) were rare. 'No doubt in the year 1150 they were still uncommon, and it is not until 1200 that we begin to read much about them.'[68] The logic behind this chronology will not perhaps carry as much weight nowadays as it did in Maitland's time. 'The man who was in quest of land was looking out, not for a profitable investment, but for a home and the means of livelihood.' Were there homes on the innumerable roods and acres whose sales and leases Maitland himself noted in the early court rolls of Ramsey? Are we sure that a husbandman with a home but insufficient livelihood would not wish to supplement the latter by leasing land?

However, the main difficulty is not about the logic but about the facts. When it comes to facts Maitland may be right in reminding us that we

[67] E. A. Kosminsky, 'The Manor of Brampton from the XI to XVI centuries' (Russian), *Srednie Veka*, II, 1946; cf. also M. Clough, op. cit., ch. 14.
[68] Pollock and Maitland, II. 106 ff., esp. p. 111.

do not read much about leases before 1200. But do we read less about them than we do about other dealings of humbler folk in the twelfth century? Indeed, if the distribution of available evidence is taken into account, the dates of 1150 and 1200 are more likely to appear as landmarks in the volume of surviving documentation than as turning-points in the history of the lease.

In the history of the lease as an institution no such turning-points need be assumed. Abroad the landlord's lease has a continuous and well-documented history. The Roman *locatio* or *conductio*, the Italian *libellus*, the Merovingian and Carolingian *precaria*, the land leases for terms of years in the twelfth, thirteenth, and fourteenth centuries, all range themselves in an almost unbroken sequence.[69] In this century the students of Anglo-Saxon England are also familiar with leases in charters and codes of law. Yet the prevailing tendency is to regard the 200 or 250 years of the Norman and Angevin era until almost as late as the end of the thirteenth century as something of a hiatus and to treat the lease of the fourteenth and fifteenth centuries as a new departure.

In reality no such hiatus existed. The manorial 'farms' – and in the twelfth century most manors were farmed away – were leases, and some twelfth-century collections of documents, notably those of St Paul's and Bury St Edmunds, contain numerous examples of stock and lease contracts between the landlord and the persons to whom the demesnes were sublet. When and where the 'farmer' happened to be not an individual entrepreneur, but villagers, collectively or individually, the portions of the demesne they took over were presumably held under contracts of the same kind as those of the ordinary demesne farmer. Many villagers holding portions of the demesne frequently appear in records under the name of *firmarii*; and though some of them may have acquired their demesne fields in perpetuity, others obviously held them for a limited period and were nothing else but leaseholders for a term of years or for lives.[70]

69 Maitland's notions about *precaria* and their general conversion into *beneficia* and fiefs are mostly derived from that standby of English legal historians, Brunner's *Deutsche Rechtsgeschichte*; yet Brunner discusses *precaria* for terms of years (vol. I, 2nd ed., Leipzig, 1906, pp. 304 ff.). For *precaria* in general see below, Additional Note 3.

70 W. H. Hale (ed.), *Domesday of St Paul's*, Camden Soc. LXIX (1858), 122–39; Bury St Edmund's register in Cambridge University Library MS. Mm. 4. 19, ff. 80, 80v, 144v, 168, 223, etc. The best-known cases of villein *firmarii* will be found on the estates of the bishops of Durham (see references in M. Postan, *Trans. Royal Hist. Soc.*, 4th ser. XX (1937), 177–8) and Worcester Priory (H. R. Luard (ed.), *Annales Prioratus de Wigornia, Annales Monastici* (Rolls Series), IV (1869), 419). In this case the farming of Shipston by the villagers probably goes back many years beyond 1227. Cf. also ibid., p. 425. Another well-known instance, however, will be found in the little cited case of three manors of St Swythun's Priory in Hampshire, farmed by villagers for at least forty years in the twelfth and very early thirteenth centuries, *Bracton's Note Book*, III, no. 1237.

This type of contract may have become less rather than more frequent in the thirteenth century, for at that time most landlords resumed the direct management of their demesnes wherever this could still be done. But the landlord leases did not as a result drop out of use. We still find landlords leasing to the villagers pieces of assarted land and portions of desmesne fields; above all, we find everywhere short leases of meadows and pastures.[71] Now and again the records mention leases of customary land which the lords relet to villeins at money rent for lives or a term of years. A sudden outcrop of such lettings might appear all of a sudden on any estate in which the landlords happened to be badly in need of cash and were prepared to convert customary tenures into leases in consideration of lump sums down. Recently one or two historians, more especially Mr R. H. Hilton, have drawn our attention to the thirteenth-century documents recording these contracts between lords and villeins in the second half of the thirteenth century.[72]

These are not of course the leases in which we are interested. They are landlord's leases, contracts between the lords and their tenants, whereas we are concerned with the 'inter-peasant' transactions between one villager and another. Yet the prevalence of lord's leases of every kind is evidence that the leasehold itself had a continuous history; that it was well known to the medieval villagers; and that from this point of view, there would be nothing unusual or strange in their frequent employment by villagers in the twelfth and early thirteenth centuries, which I have assumed throughout this essay.

On this point the evidence though unambiguous is not, of course, voluminous, since the documents of that date which could be expected to refer to inter-peasant leases are very few. But such documents as we possess abound with relevant references; and among them we find leases, both long and short, for terms of years, or for one year only, mainly for rent but sometimes on *champart: per campi partem*.[73] In the early pro-

71 These are too numerous to cite. There is hardly a thirteenth-century bailiff's account without some landlord leases. In early years these are most frequently annual leases of meadow or pastures, though leases of arable or colonisable waste also occur.

72 R. H. Hilton, *Univ. of Birmingham Hist. Journ.* IV (1953–4), 8 ff.

73 A mid-twelfth century reference to a possible lease will be found in an Abingdon charter: M. M. Bigelow (ed.), *Placita Anglo-Normannica* (London, 1879), p. 111 (lands 'quas Modbertus dedit vel praestitit'). The largest extant collection of early leases will be found in Bracton's Note-Book, where at least forty cases of leases for terms of years are noted. Nearly all these cases came before the courts in the 20s and early 30s of the thirteenth century, but many related or claimed to relate to leases granted in the previous generation and even earlier, e.g. *Bracton's Note Book*, II, nos. 57, 663, III, nos. 1224, 1470, 1490, 1619, 1735, 1750, also II, nos. 183, 451, 607, 658; III, nos. 1258, 1304, 1419, 1768, 1769, 1869. In the first eight instances cited here a late twelfth-century lease is either alleged, or can be deduced with reasonable probability from the circumstances. For other instances of leases, which are mainly inter-peasant, see

ceedings in the king's courts at the very beginning of the thirteenth century, leases are frequently invoked to bar tenants' claims to ownership or are brought up when they happen to be involved with the claims of heirs and widows. But countless other leases could have been taken up, renewed, or allowed to run out without coming into conflict with other men's titles and thus failing to leave a trace in our records. Some leases were not recorded in manorial court rolls because they had been removed from the lord's control. I have already mentioned that on the estates of the abbot of St Albans the lord conceded that leases for two years and less could be granted without his licence; and this presumably also covered leases renewable at two-yearly intervals.[74]

Yet in spite of all the reasons why peasant leases should have bypassed our records, references to them are very numerous. Perhaps one of the reasons why they escaped the notice of historians is that in terminology, and sometimes in substance, they can be confused with other transactions and especially with mortgages. Under the so-called beneficiary leases accompanying a loan of money the creditor became a lessee and thereby obtained not only the security for his loan but also payment of principal and interest out of the land's income. The records have also preserved cases of leases, which though not beneficiary in the strict sense of the term, were nevertheless accompanied by loans, as in the case before the royal justices in 1201 concerning a lease for thirty-five years for an annual rent of 6*d* per annum as well as a loan of 15 marks.[75]

An insight into the circumstances of these transactions is often required before loan and mortgage could be differentiated from a contract of real or 'husbandman's' lease. Unfortunately, a learned editor of some of the earliest rolls has not made this differentiation any easier by having

Court Rolls of Hales, III. 11, 52–3, 75, 77, 101, 103, 105, 109, 138, 140–1, 145; *Court Roll of Chalgrave Manor*, pp. 14–15; Court Rolls of St Albans in Levett, *Studies*, pp. 301, 312 and in B.M. MSS. listed above, p. 131; *Glastonbury Court Rolls*, *passim*, e.g. Longleat MSS. 11254/3 (Brent); *Select Pleas in Manorial Courts*, I. 21, 28, 36; W. O. Ault (ed.), *Court Rolls of Ramsey*, pp. 189, 194; *Curia Regis Rolls*, I, 86, 103, 109, 403; II. 14; III. 299–300; IV. 65, 221–2; V. 258; VII. 108; VIII. 187, 338; IX. 109; *Halmota Prioratus Dunelmensis*, pp. 1–11. Among these leases, *metayage* and other forms of *champart* are more frequent than the rarity of *champart* leases in later ages would lead us to expect. Leases *ad campi partem*, *ad seminandum*, *ad medietatem*, or *pro media vestura* are to be found on all manors cited here: e.g. *Halmota Prioratus Dunelmensis*, pp. 1–5; St Albans Court Rolls in Levett, op. cit., p. 312; and *The Court Baron*, p. 104.

74 Above, p. 124. Miss Levett's reference to this rule may give the impression that the concession came later than it did: the rule appeared to be well established by the last quarter of the thirteenth century. B. M. Stowe MS. 849, f. 12v. *Quare dimisit terram suam ad terminum ultra spatium duorum annorum.*

75 *Curia Regis Rolls*, II. 88–9. A similar case occurred in 1204, when the land was held 'at farm', but the farm was secured by a loan, ibid. III. 166; cf. also VIII. 376.

decided, perhaps justifiably, to adhere to the literal sense of the judicial terminology, and to render as 'gage' the term 'baille', which Anglo-Norman lawyers frequently employed to designate leases for terms of years, and which still is the modern French term for leasehold.[76] That in most of these cases leases were in fact meant is shown not only by the context but also by the discussion of leases and the terms employed in legal manuals and treatises, including Bracton's *Note Book*. The attention which these books give to the problems of leases is, of course, in itself evidence of the great part leases played in the English countryside of the twelfth and thirteenth centuries.[77] And it may perhaps be argued, *pace* Maitland, that the leases would not have been employed as a cloak for interest had they not been a familiar arrangement commonly employed for purposes unconnected with loans and usury.

So much for the evidence of judicial records. Evidence of short leases at an early period can also be read into references to 'agreements' in the earliest surviving bailiff's accounts and manorial court rolls. These references will often be found among entries of 'licence to agree', *licentia concordandi*: a familiar entry in manorial documents. Licensed agreements did not of course refer to leases only. They were as a rule related to amicable settlements of disputes which had come before the courts and were, so to speak, a manorial counterpart of the 'final concords' in the

[76] D. M. Stenton (ed.), *Pleas before the King or his Justices, 1198–1202*, I, Selden Soc. 67, pp. 362 (no. 3487), 380–1 (no. 3506), 406 (no. 3538). The editor of the *Pleas*, etc. herself occasionally translates *invadio* as lease: ibid., p. 363. There is little doubt that in a large number of these cases *invadiamentum* referred to leases unaccompanied by loan, or in Maitland's terminology, 'husbandmen's leases'. Sometimes the clerks responsible for the Rolls used the term *invadiavit* and the more unambiguous terms, such as *tradidit ad firmam*, interchangeably in the same entries, e.g. *Curia Regis Rolls*, VIII. 376. Cases in which *invadiavit* apparently describes leases will be found in *Curia Regis Rolls*, II. 14, 88, 184, III. 299–300; VII. 108, VIII. 63, 97. For the medieval use of the term *baille* to designate leases see W. H. Dunham (ed.), *Casus Placitorum*, Selden Soc. LXIX (1952), pp. 28 (no. 81), 32 (no. 6). In the latter cases the clerk uses the expressions *baille a un autre*, and *luy lessa a terme* interchangeably.

[77] Bracton's twelfth-century predecessors, represented by Glanvill, treated the lease as a loan regulated by private agreements in which the king was not concerned: G. E. Woodbine (ed.), *Glanvil de legibus et consuetudinibus regni Angliae* (New Haven, 1932), pp. 137–9, 145. The existence of leases is, however, clearly implied in all references to *locatio-conductio* and *commodatio*. Thus 'sed quid si conductor censum suum statuto termino non solverit?' (ibid., p. 145); or '... sed per ipsum tenentem vel per aliquem antecessorum eius, veluti in vadium vel ex commodatione ...' (ibid., p. 162), also ibid., pp. 142–3. Bracton's references to leases for terms of years or for lives are too numerous to be listed, especially in the books *De Assisa Novae Disseisinae* and *De adquirendo Rerum Dominio*, e.g. pp. 183–4 (*De locato et conducto*) and p. 161 ('*Si firmarius* ...') in vol. II of G. E. Woodbine's edition, p. 69 in vol. III, and especially pp. 21–30 and 42–3 in vol. IV. See also *Casus Placitorum*, pp. 28 (no. 81), 41 (no. 83), LXXXIII (no. 73), LXXIX–LXXX (no. 39), LXXXI (no. 50), LXXXII (no. 67); W. H. Dunham (ed.), *Radulphi de Hengham Summae* (Cambridge, 1932), pp. 63–5.

records of royal courts. But in those cases in which the manorial record happens to reveal the contents of the licensed agreements, their subject frequently turns out to be the lease of land.[78]

Historians must thus assume that the leasehold contract was familiar to the villagers of the thirteenth and the late twelfth centuries, and was commonly employed in their dealings with each other. If so, the chronological sequence of leases and sales which I have suggested here does not run against any fundamental obstacle of fact or principle. All we need is a further study of the evidence; and this let us hope will not be long in coming.

5

Some of these changes and variations – the expansion in the village land market in the late fourteenth and fifteenth centuries, regional and local variations in the turnover in peasant land, the prevalence of leases – all these are propositions well supported by evidence. Others, and above all that of the chronological relation between leases and sales, are hypothetical in the extreme. But whether they are borne out by subsequent researches or not, they will not affect our main conclusion that the village land market functioned throughout the centuries for which evidence is available: certainly during the thirteenth and the late twelfth centuries, possibly earlier. If this conclusion is accepted, historians will have to draw a number of conclusions. The conclusions may prove uncomfortable because they make it more difficult to take some of our most important sources at their face value, and may compel us to modify some of the distinctions both regional and chronological which have become part and parcel of

[78] For *Licentia concordandi* in Glastonbury Court Rolls, see Longleat MSS. 10654 (Middlezoy), 11254/3 (Badbury), etc. For covenants relating to inter-peasant transfers on St Albans estates, see Additional Note 2 below. Personal contracts to sell doubtless preceded more formal stages of transfer, e.g. Longleat 1155, 10654, Glastonbury: Henry Herring surrenders his land to the lord *ad opus* of William Sannery 'per quandam convencionem inter eos factam'. These 'covenants', when legitimized by fine, would not, however, be as a rule recorded as *licentia concordandi*. For cases in which the records happen to disclose the lease implied in the licensed agreement, see: Longleat MSS. 11254/3 (Middlezoy: Alexander Clericus), ibid. (Baltonsborough); ibid. 10654 (Middlezoy: William Thomyn), etc.; and above all in the remarkable chain of licensed agreements covering two generations of tenants in ibid. 11254/3 (Badbury: Thos. Seriaunt and others). Cases in which the substance of the agreements is disclosed as concerned with land will also be found elsewhere. Thus '. . . in misericordia pro eo quod fecerunt conventionem de tenemento extra curiam quia sunt nativi': J. Amphlett and S. G. Hamilton (ed.), *Court Rolls of the Manor of Hales, 1272–1307*, II (Worcs. Hist. Soc., 1912), 407–8. In another case a villager is found by the jury 'quod convenit cum Matilda filia Nicholai de una dimidia acra terre sibi ad terminum annorum dimittenda. Ideo preceptum est quod teneat hujusmodi convencionem inter eos factam . . .': *Select Pleas in Manorial Courts*, I. 36.

the accepted version of medieval social history. A detailed discussion of these rearrangements would be out of place here, but as a warning and as an anticipation I must permit myself to indicate, however briefly, the points at which the existence of a village land market impinges upon the problems of rural England in the Middle Ages.

In the first place, historians, looking for evidence of population or of actual occupation of land, cannot use for these purposes the lists of tenants and tenancies in manorial extents unless and until they have satisfied themselves that the local practice of the manorial administrators enabled the extents accurately to reflect the economic and demographic changes. This they by no means always did. To repeat what has already been said here more than once, the extents were concerned with the lord's rights and entitlements; they confined their lists to the lord's tenants and were therefore inclined to pass over in silence the villagers who held of other men. In places and in periods in which the lord did not require formal surrenders, the pattern of actual economic occupation of land might diverge very widely from that of official tenancies. If so, the extents are not as a rule a reliable guide to population; and even when admissible as evidence of population (as they may be when they happen to record sales of land and mention tenants by name) they must be ruled out as evidence for the number of acres which each household in fact cultivated in any given year.[79]

If this limitation of the evidence is borne in mind the picture of the medieval village as largely made up of virgates and semi-virgates will have to be greatly modified, if not given up altogether. The virgated patterns of holdings, stable, regular, and symmetrical, have already suffered greatly at the hands of historians who have noticed in the extents and surveys the non-virgated bits of land in the hands of villeins and also discovered places and whole regions in which the regular pattern of holdings had altogether disappeared if it ever existed. We may now have to go a step farther and admit that even in places for which surveys and extents still exhibit the virgated pattern in all its stability and symmetry, the actual occupation of land by families may have been both unstable and unsymmetrical. If it does not look like that in some of our extents, this may be merely because on some estates short leases and unrecorded sales were not able to influence official appearances.

From this it would naturally follow that the two best-known deviations

[79] Professor Kosminsky, though aware of the inability of the extents and the extent-like Hundred Rolls to record leases and informal sales, justifies his reliance on this evidence by the argument that the informal transactions merely accentuated the process of 'social differentiation' which the extents exhibit: op. cit., pp. 212–13, etc. The evidence available to us suggests that the effect of the land market was much more variable and irregular. It was able to level off the differences in official tenures as well as to accentuate them.

from the conventional pattern of village society – that of the non-manorialized parts of England all through the Middle Ages and that of the fourteenth and fifteenth centuries all over England – may in fact have been not as great as they appear in our documents. For it is quite possible that at least some of the differences in the composition of the villages in, say, the non-manorialized parts of the Danelaw on the one hand, and the manorialized parts of the midlands on the other, loom greater in our documents than they may have done in life. Where sokemen and free-holders predominated and the manorial hand lay lightly on the land, the transfer of property and its effect upon the occupation of the soil could be, so to speak, patent, i.e. it could find expression in tenurial titles and in documents recording them. On the other hand, in parts of England where holdings were mainly customary, but where, nevertheless, the rules of transfer by surrender were not strictly enforced, the effects of the land market remained hidden and were unable to disturb the visible pattern of tenurial relations. In these parts of England – to use an expression familiar to modern historians in an entirely different context – the *pays réel* was not always or necessarily the *pays légal*; and we must guard ourselves from contrasting the 'real' England of the Danelaw with the 'legal' England of Somerset.

The same may apply also, *pari passu*, to the contrast between the later Middle Ages and the twelfth and thirteenth centuries. Social history never ceased; fundamental economic transformations were taking place all the time, and to some of the changes I have drawn attention here. Yet the same reason for which the real changes in the occupation of land were visible best in the non-manorialized regions may also have been the reason why in the fifteenth century, when manorial restraints had nearly all gone, the documents were better able to reveal changes in ownership and in patterns of tenure than they would have done in the earlier centuries. If so, much of what historians have reported as signs of social transformation may to some extent be an optical illusion: a mere change in the ability of our sources to reflect the facts of life.

ADDITIONAL NOTES

1. *Subtenants on some manors of the bishops of Winchester*

In general, transfers of land among the bishop's tenants were by sub-letting under informal licence, or to use the terminology of feudal studies, by subinfeudation, rather by substitution. On this, as on other estates, the latter method, involving surrender of land by the seller and its regrant by the lord, becomes more prominent in the records of the fourteenth century. Throughout the thirteenth century, and even the early fourteenth, the visible pattern of customary tenancies remained remarkably stable, and the student is left with the clear impression that real changes were taking place, so to speak, under the surface, by means of informal sales and leases. How stable the virgated pattern was is revealed by the comparison of the customary holdings in the surviving mid-thirteenth-century set of surveys (B.M. MS. Egerton 2418) with the lists of customary tenants liable to service in the bailiffs' accounts of the late thirteenth and fourteenth centuries. On a few manors the stability is probably real. Thus on the 'colonizing' manors of the bishop – such as Witney in the Oxfordshire fringe of the Cotswolds, or Wargrave, with its large woodlands above the Thames valley – much new arable was being carved out of the waste throughout the century, and it is probable that out of this arable the demand for new holdings was met. The absence of any sign of sub-letting on these manors need not therefore cause any surprise. But on the other manors in the anciently settled regions on which reclaimable lands had nearly all been taken up – e.g. Fareham or Bishop's Waltham – the signs of sub-letting in bailiffs' accounts and in surveys are more abundant; in some of these manors the process left its mark even on the surveys, presumably because some of the transfers went through the formality of 'surrender', or were otherwise supervised by the officials. This appears to apply especially to Bishop's Waltham, which, in addition to being an anciently and fully settled village, was also a 'headquarters' manor and a place of residence of the bishop's officials. It would not be too unreal to suppose that the failure to go through the formality of 'surrender' was due to laxity of manorial control, and the control would be less lax at Waltham than elsewhere.

Whatever the explanation, a large number of sub-let or subdivided holdings appear in the survey of Bishop's Waltham in the B.M. collection of 1260. At that date we find signs of alienation on fourteen customary holdings – those of Richard Coldusk de Caldecote, Richard le Cornmonger, Richard Everard, William Frogge, Walter de Combe, Henry Cok, Robert Strong, William Seylde, Henry Parmentier, Germanus de Waltham, Thomas Fysace, Henry Cupere, Adam Cutte, Walter Frankelain. It appears that in a few of these cases the holders of alienated portions held directly of the lord. Presumably the alienations had gone through the hands of the lord, probably by surrender. On most of the holdings, however, it had been carried out by a more informal process and created sub-tenancies. The difference is probably reflected by the form of words used, and also in the amount of rent paid. Thus, a new holding established on Walter de la Combe's land pays a substatial rent to the lord (5*s*), and the holder is described as holding land 'ex terra Walteri de Combe etc.'; or as in a similar case, that of Thomas Fysace, as land 'que fuit Roberti Curtis'. In the third case, which may also be one of surrender, we are told that the tenant, Henry Parmentier, now pays for his holding 2*s* 9½*d*, and no more, because the other men pay to the lord 4*s* 10½*d* for portions of the holding.

These cases, however, are very few – not more than three out of the fifteen. In the remaining twelve cases the rents payable to the lord are very small – a few pennies – and are out of proportion to the areas of the holdings. Some are described as no more than 'increments' of the rent; the substantive rent is still payable by the main tenant. In nearly all of them the holders of portions of the land are said to hold 'of' (de) the main holder. In at least three instances the sub-tenants are not even mentioned by name. Thus in the case of Richard Everard's virgate holdings we are merely told that 'tenentes de eadem terra debent pannagium si habeant porcos'; in the case of Henry Cox's half-virgate we are merely told that his *socius* performs no services to the lord; and in the case of Robert Strong's holding, we are told that he owed *auxilium* for one Scutt, 'qui est suus landymake'.

2. *Land transfers on the estates of the abbey of St Albans*

The land traffic on the St Albans estates has been briefly described and documented by Miss Levett. The evidence must be used with caution as the fifteenth-century text available to us is not a full transcript of the court rolls, but a selection of what presumably were from the compiler's point of view the more important cases. This, however, makes the absence or rarity of certain types of entry in the earlier folios, and their appearance or proliferation in the later, all the more interesting. Judging from the late appearance of entries recording transfers by formal process, it would seem that on most St Albans estates the transfers in the earlier part of the thirteenth century, i.e. until the beginning of Edward I's reign, were by informal licence. This as a rule takes the form not only of the *licentia dimittendi* to the seller, but also the *licentia accipiendi* to the buyer; and the presumption is that when a transaction is accompanied by two licences, both the seller and the buyer were the abbot's tenants: e.g. B.M. Stowe 849 (Codicote), ff. 1, 1v, 2, etc. up to f. 15; or Add. 6057 (Croxley), all folios. Some of these informal transfers – certainly most of the leases – are transacted by covenants between the parties, and the court rolls merely recorded the fine '*pro conuentione affirmandi*' (Stowe 849, f. 3 – John de Ravensack and others; f. 3v). Fines for illegal transfer are nearly all for alienation without licences (ibid., f. 3, etc.); fines for alienation contrary to prohibition (*contra defensionem*) begin to appear much later. One of the earliest is dated 51 Henry III (ibid., f. 9v: Eleanora filia Walteri). In Codicote the surrenders of land *ad opus* of buyers appear some eight years after the commencement of the series, i.e. in 1245 (ibid., ff. 2v and 3), but do not become regular until the late 1260s and 1270s. The first clear case of substitution is dated 42 Henry III ('Henry de Cokeheath positus est in seisina de duabus acris terre et dimidia de uenditione Thome Whitelock': ibid.). In Croxley surrenders do not become at all general until the 1280s.

Two further points may be worth noting. Firstly, on St Albans estates inter-tenant sales of land did not necessarily limit the title of the buyer to one life (e.g. Stowe 849, f. 2: *licentia accipiendi* of the holding sold in perpetuity: '*sibi et heredibus suis*'). Secondly, a number of licences are accompanied by a clause obliging the buyer not to assign the land to the Church or to the Jews, and sometimes also add that he should not alienate the lord's right in the land ('nec aliquo modo alienabit iura domini abbatis'; e.g. ibid., f. 3).

3. *Leases abroad*

Abroad the study of leases is made difficult by the almost total absence of evidence on inter-peasant dealings, and by the exclusive dependence of scholars on the monastic cartularies, and especially the collections of *traditiones*. The discussion is thus confined to 'landlord tenancies' on monastic estates. Even so, the existence of leases, i.e. non-perpetual tenancies in usufruct for rent throughout the Middle Ages does not appear in doubt and is generally accepted. Doubt attaches only to the history of the short lease (*Zeitpacht, baille à terme*). In Italy, both the short lease in the form of *libellus* and the lease for life or lives in the form of *precaria* appear to have had an uninterrupted history throughout the early Middle Ages, i.e. from the sixth century to the thirteenth.[80] This is apparently how Brunner in his all-too-brief references to leases represented the position in the early centuries, i.e. before the tenth, all over Europe. He lists contracts of *precaria* at will, for terms of years and for lives, and mentions monastic *precaria* renewable at intervals of five, ten, or fifteen years.[81] This, however, is not quite the unanimous view of the German lease. Inama-Sternegg, the most authoritative codifier of orthodox notions, saw the germs of *champart* lease in certain practices of the Carolingian age, but in general appeared to be certain that neither *champart* nor any comparable form of short lease made its appearance until considerably later, i.e. until the twelfth and thirteenth centuries, when they began to spread rapidly.[82] A. Dopsch showed that various types of *champart* were a well-established form of rent in Carolingian times,[83] but this by itself cannot be taken as clear evidence of short leases. The view which appears to prevail, as expressed by von Below,[84] is that although *Zeitpacht* did not become common until the twelfth and thirteenth centuries, it was to be found even in the Merovingian and Carolingian ages.

A chronology of the short lease similar to Inama-Sternegg's was proposed for France by Sée.[85] More recently L. Genicot has emphasized that in the Namurois the lease (*bail*) for a term of years was little developed until the end of the Middle Ages; and A. Déléage has similarly argued the absence in Burgundy in the ninth and tenth centuries of the *contrât à termes* analogous to the Italian *libellus*.[86]

In considering this chronology it is important to bear in mind the intentional neglect of short-term contracts by the compilers of monastic cartularies.[87] Among the long-term contracts recorded in them, life leases are very common. In the Merovingian and Carolingian epoch these were represented by the various contracts of *precaria* or *prestancia*. The form of *precaria* which the monastic documents preserved very fully are the *precaria remuneratoria* and other similar arrangements by which tenants rented for a term of life or lives from the lord the

80 L. Hartmann, *Zur Wirtschaftsgeschichte Italiens im frühen Mittelalter* (1904); F. Schupfer, 'Precarie e livelli nei documenti e nelle leggi dell'alto medio evo', *Riv. italiana per le scienze giuridiche*, XL (1905).

81 H. Brunner, *Deutsche Rechtsgeschichte*, I (2nd ed., 1906), 304 ff.

82 *Deutsche Wirthschaftsgeschichte*, I (Leipzig, 1879), p. 366, and II (1891), 350; and K. Lamprecht, *Deutsches Wirtschaftsleben im Mittelalter*, II, pt. 2 (1885), 750; but cf. G. v. Below, *Probleme der Wirtschaftsgeschichte* (1926), pp. 46–7.

83 *Wirtschaftsentwicklung der Karolingerzeit*, I (1912), 276 ff.

84 Loc. cit.

85 *Les Classes rurales et le régime domanial en France au moyen âge* (Paris, 1901), pp. 221 ff.

86 L. Genicot, *L'Économie rurale Namuroise au bas moyen âge* (Louvain, 1943), p. 277; A. Déléage, *La Vie économique et sociale de la Bourgogne dans le haut moyen âge* (Mâcon, 1941), pp. 598 ff.

87 A. Dopsch, *Verfassungs- und Wirtschaftsgeschichte des Mittelalters* (Vienna, 1928), p. 535.

land they themselves had previously 'donated' to the monastery and to which sometimes the monastery attached an additional holding.[88] There is clear evidence of such life leases created by the contract of *precaria* in the ninth-century estates of St Germain des Prés.[89] For Burgundy in the ninth, tenth, and eleventh centuries Déléage has listed leases for lives instituted by contract of *precaria*, including *champart* leases.[90] The same has been done for Germany by most historians, including the editors and students of the main monastic collections.[91]

It is possible that many of the erstwhile *precaria* had by the twelfth and the thirteenth centuries developed into heritable tenements, and thereby swelled the ranks of the numerous class of rent-paying customary tenancies (*censuarii*, etc.).[92] By this time, however, the recorded instances of the temporary lease (*Zeitpacht*) begin to accumulate. If the distribution of evidence justifies any conclusion about the history of the lease itself, it might justify the view that as *precaria* were developing into heritable customary tenancies, the landlords were beginning to make wider use of the lease for a term of years. This at any rate is the conclusion which appears to emerge from S. Rietschel's historical survey of the hereditary lease.[93] But this view may not allow sufficiently for the possibility that the short lease was employed, more commonly in the earlier centuries than may appear at first sight. In the first place, the records of *precaria* are confined almost entirely to transactions between monastic landlords and the freeholders who had donated their land. Where, as in Italy, the dealings with unfree tenants are also recorded, the latter appear to hold by the short-term *libellus*.[94] In the second place, the early documents occasionally refer to *conductores*; and, in spite of some disagreement about the meaning of the term, it appears highly probable that 'farmers' in the English sense are meant. This was the Roman use of the term and this is what is obviously meant by it in the injunction of the Council of Paris of 829: 'ut presbiteri nullo modo fiant uilici et conductores.'[95] This sense of the term is confirmed by its use in other injunctions against the employment of clerics as farmers or collectors of taxes: e.g. 'conductores uel procuratores siue exactores fiscalium rerum'.[96] In view of these uses Inama-Sternegg may have overdone his scepticism about the sense in which the term *conductores* is used in a well-known Freising document.[97]

88 'donation restituée en usufruit': Déléage, I. 599 ff., esp. p. 601.

89 B. Guérard, *Polyptyque de l'Abbé Irminon*, I (Paris, 1845), 575–7 (2 ed., 1895, ed. Lognon, I, 82–5).

90 Op. cit. pp. 603 ff.

91 G. Caro, 'Studien zu den älteren St. Gallener Urkunden', *Jahrb. f. Schweizerische Geschichte*, XXVII (1902), 300–4; Hermann Bikel, *Die Wirtschaftsverhältnisse des Klosters St. Gallen* (1914), pp. 136 f.; Th. Bitterhauf, *Traditionen des Hochstifts Freising* (1905), pp. LXII–LXXIII.

92 Déléage, op. cit., p. 602.

93 'Die Entstehung der freien Erbleihe', *Zeitschr. d. Savigny Stiftung für Rechtsgeschichte*, XXII (1901), Germ. Abt., 181–244, 455–6. But see H. Wopfner, *Beiträge zur Geschichte der freien bäuerlichen Erbleihe Deutschlands im Mittelalter* (Breslau, 1903).

94 L. Hartmann, F. Schupfer, loc. cit.

95 *Mon. Germ. Hist., Leg., Concilia*, II. i. 630.

96 Ibid., *Leg., Capitularia*, II. 122, A.D. 850, ch. 18.

97 Bitterhauf, op. cit., no. 238; Inama-Sternegg, op. cit. I. 366; cf. Dopsch, *Wirtschaftsentwicklung*, p. 277.

9

HERIOTS AND PRICES ON WINCHESTER MANORS*

(With J. Titow)

1

The present essay is the product of a co-operative enterprise. Several years ago, while working on the records of the Bishops' of Winchester estates, one of the authors, Mr Postan, was struck by the apparent fluctuations in the numbers of recorded heriots. Several possible explanations occurred to him then, including of course variations in harvests. Such evidence of crops as he then collected appeared to support that hypothesis and to suggest a striking parallel with some well-known trends abroad.[1] He nevertheless decided not to pursue the enquiry until he or somebody else had been able to investigate the history of the Winchester estates in greater detail. Subsequently, he noticed similar fluctuations on some other estates, especially on those of Glastonbury.[2] When, two years ago, Mr Titow, then a research student in the University of Cambridge, embarked on the history of the Winchester estates in the thirteenth century, Mr Postan suggested to him that an enquiry into heriots might be one of his tasks. Mr Titow accordingly extracted from the Winchester bailiff's accounts of five manors all the evidence of heriots and prices, and the present essay is the result of his and Mr Postan's combined efforts to deal with the evidence thus assembled.

The division of labour has been as follows. The main table (Table 9.1) and the graphs are the work of Mr Titow, although the eventual shape of both is the result of protracted consultations between the authors. The text of the essay itself is the work of Mr Postan, who bears the entire responsibility for the way in which the argument has been presented. Mr Titow, however, was consulted at every stage in composition and helped

* This paper first appeared in *Economic History Review*, 2nd ser., XI, 1959.

1 The most obvious foreign parallel was that of Swedish death rates in the eighteenth century, as summarized in G. Sundbärg's *Bevölkerungsstatistik Schwedens, 1750–1900* (Stockholm, 1907), and commented on in E. Heckscher's article on the same subject in *Economic History Review*, 2nd ser. II (1950), 'Swedish Population Trends before the Industrial Revolution'.

2 These and some other demographic data of Glastonbury estates will be discussed elsewhere.

to elucidate a number of problems, especially those arising out of the Waltham surveys.

In the concluding stages of the work a third participant joined the enterprise. As the enquiry and the writing of the essay involved the authors in complicated statistical and demographical argument, they had to draw heavily upon the assistance of Mr Longden, a statistician with the Faculty of Economics in Cambridge. Mr Longden has tested the reliability and the relevance of the data, has calculated the correlations between heriots and prices and subjected the final draft of the essay to statistical criticism, as a result of which several sections of the essay have been modified. In addition Mr Longden has compiled tables of correlations of heriots and prices, of expectations of life, and of grain prices. These tables, and notes on their contents and significance, are published here under Mr Longden's own name.

2

References to heriots, i.e. death duties levied on holdings of customary tenants, will be found in large numbers in all the bailiff's accounts of the Bishops' of Winchester manors. This evidence, needless to say, is beset with obvious pitfalls. In the first place the entries in our accounts do not apparently provide a complete record of the deaths among tenants liable to heriot. The accounts of some manors record only the heriots paid by delivery of animals and do not record heriots in the form of small money payments levied on holdings too small to deliver animals. This omission does not of course mean that on these manors all the customary holders possessed animals, but that for some reason or another small-holdings were not subjected to death duties. However, at some time in the middle of the thirteenth century the authorities of a number of manors began to levy money payments, usually sixpence but sometimes as much as one shilling, on property of deceased small-holders and on certain transactions between living persons involving small parcels of land. In the accounts of the fifties and sixties these money heriots are still few, but on at least five of these manors – Taunton, Meon, Waltham, Wargrave and Fareham – they become well-established, possibly by 1255, and certainly by 1270.[3] We therefore propose to confine our study to these manors.

The evidence of heriots raises a number of questions which must be answered before it can be used for the study of mortality on the Bishops' of Winchester estates. Do they record all the deaths in that section of the manorial population to which they relate? Do they record deaths only, or also other changes within the group?

The answer to the first question is obviously in the negative. It is easy

[3] See below pp. 153–5.

enough to discover the group of persons to whom the evidence relates. The manorial tenants liable to the payment of heriots were the Bishops' customary tenants, a group which, as we shall soon see, is not very difficult to define or to measure. Within that group, however, by no means all the deaths left behind evidence of heriot payment. Heriots were levied not on persons but on holdings; they were not a personal tax but an estate duty. They were, therefore, payable only by heads of households and can be used only as evidence for the mortality of adults. Unfortunately it is difficult to determine the precise age groups to which the term 'adult' should apply. The manorial custom in general and that of the Winchester estates in particular did not appear to lay down a hard and fast age qualification for accession to property. Minors could succeed, though in all the records of court fines and litigations available to us we have encountered clear evidence of minors in legal possession of customary holdings only in isolated cases, except in the year of the Black Death, when, in the absence of adult heirs, children frequently succeeded to the holdings of parents or relatives.[4] But, even if, contrary to our impressions, minors acquired legal title to customary holdings, the likelihood of their figuring among customary holders in proportions anywhere near their proportion in the population is very remote. We must therefore assume that the overwhelming bulk of villagers succeeding to customary land were adults.

However, our uncertainties on this point do not end here. The term 'adults' is used here in the general sense of 'grown up' and does not imply that 'adult' holders of customary land were all legally 'of age', i.e. older than twenty. All we can assume is that in general the group contained very few children or very young persons and no, or almost no, infants, but we cannot be absolutely certain that it did not include men and women in their 'teens.

Our answer to the first question thus is that the evidence of heriots excludes the deaths of infants and children but may include a few instances of deaths among boys and girls in their 'teens. The bulk of the evidence relates to male adults and is therefore comparable, not with general mortality of other periods and societies, but only with that of their adult populations.

The answer to the second question, i.e. whether heriots included transactions *inter vivos*, can be formulated more definitely, but the formulation requires a close and a somewhat delicate analysis of the evidence. In general there is no doubt that by definition and in actual operation the heriot was a death duty pure and simple, and that the overwhelming proportion of heriots recorded in our documents were levied on holdings of deceased tenants. There is certainly no reason for doubting that when-

[4] See below pp. 170–1.

ever animals were taken in payment of heriots the tenants must have died some time previously. Such accidental information about these cases as our records contain, leaves us little doubt on this point. But we have seen that not all heriots took the form of delivery of animals. Some of the heriots were paid in money, and very occasionally in goods, and although many of these heriots were collected from holdings of deceased men (presumably men too poor to possess a taxable animal), some were apparently paid by men selling portions of their holdings. The payments of heriot were in these cases additional to the entry fines payable by the buyers of land.

This complication may appear to invalidate the evidence of money heriots and reduce our sample to the tenancies charged with animal heriots, i.e. to the more substantial holdings. Fortunately a closer attention to the circumstances in which money heriots were levied may dissipate some of the difficulties which they at first sight appear to raise. In the first place many of the money heriots on transfers of property *inter vivos* appear to be connected with the tenants' deaths, even though the connexion is not immediate. That some connexion must have existed is suggested by the curious incidence of money heriots. The collateral evidence of the Bishop's entry fines in the manorial courts makes it quite clear that in the great majority of land transfers the only payment extracted by the lord was the entry fine payable by the buyer. Why then should the lord have imposed additional payment of heriots on some transfers and not on others?

We believe that the answer to this question will be found in the ages of the sellers. In a great majority of cases in which money heriots are levied on transfers of property, the sellers appear to be advanced in years and could presumably be expected to die within a few years of the transactions. What probably happened was that when the seller was an old or elderly man the lord refused to allow him to sell the holdings except on the payment of a heriot. This practice was obviously adopted in order to prevent the avoidance of heriots by previous transfers of property to younger men, and is therefore comparable to the rules which the Inland Revenue apply to gifts *inter vivos* in our own day.

If this explanation is correct we should expect the lords to allow their tenants to sell land without heriots while they were still young and to impose heriots as they were getting older. Numerous examples of this discrimination between younger and older sellers of land will be found on all our manors, more especially on manors like Waltham, for which we happen to possess both accounts and custumals.[5] Thus we find Henry

[5] Waltham happens to be one of the very few Winchester manors to have been surveyed both in the middle of the thirteenth century and in the early fourteenth. MS. Eccl. Com. Various, 159512, 1/9: B.M. MSS. Egerton 2418.

Marshall, a substantial tenant holding several pieces of land in Waltham in the 1320s selling some of his land apparently for the first time in 1325. At that date he probably was not older than 35, for his father, Galfridus le Marshall, married in 1289 the woman whom the records later describe as Henry Marshall's mother. This first sale, transacted while he was still in his prime, is not accompanied by a heriot, but in 1338, i.e. thirteen years after his first recorded transaction when Marshall was probably in his late forties, he is recorded as paying a heriot of one shilling on two acres of land sold to another man. We find him paying two further money heriots on similar sales in 1339 and 1340. He must have died soon after the last payment of a money heriot, for in 1342 his wife held his land as a widow. An even clearer case is that of another Waltham tenant, Richard Ude.[6]

That these cases were typical is shown by the low expectations of life of the men recorded as paying heriot on the sales of their land. The death rates on the five manors, as measured by heriots, suggest that the expectations of life of the substantial tenants, i.e. the intervals between their accession at 20 and their death, should have varied from about 24 at the beginning of our period to just under 20 in the period following 1292.[7] The figures, based as they are on uncertain guesses as to the average age of accession to property, are bound to be inexact; yet their inexactitude is not so great as to obliterate the wide difference between these figures and the actual expectations of life of the man who paid money heriots at their first payment. Their average expectation of life on the manor of Waltham, i.e. the average intervals between the first payment of heriot and actual year of death, would be five years. This average is so low because in fact, 25 out of 36 heriot-paying sellers of land died less than five years after their earliest payments of heriot, and only five, i.e. 15 per cent, died more than seven years after the first payment.

But for a few questionable cases, the interval between the first money heriot and the date of death, i.e. the expectations of life of heriot-paying sellers, would have been even shorter than that estimated here. Some of the 'questionable' cases appear to be those of men who happened to survive to ripe old age. Even in the Middle Ages some men lived very much longer than most, and some survived to the Methusalean age of eighty and over. Thus when we are shown Thomas Schogell of Waltham paying heriot in 1339 for a part of his holding transferred to his son, but do not find a clear reference to his death until nearly ten years later, i.e. 1349, we must not forget he was already an established tenant in 1332 when the Waltham survey was compiled and was then already old enough to set up

[6] Eccl. Com. 2/159311, 159458 1/2, 159332, 159337, 159451, 159349, 159350, 159352, 159358. Waltham Rental: Eccl. Com. Various, 159512, 1/9.

[7] See below, Mr Longden's table and notes on Expectations of Life.

a grown-up daughter on a holding of her own. At that time, though father of a grown-up daughter, he was still not deemed old enough to pay heriot on the transfer, but when several years later he made a similar transfer to his son a heriot was levied.[8] Similarly, Richard Ude, whose case we have already cited, died in 1349, i.e. full seven years after the date on which the money heriot was levied on the land he sold. But there is every reason for believing that at this time he was an old man, perhaps a very old man. Not only were his heirs in 1349 his grandchildren, but his holding listed in extent in 1332 contained eleven separate pieces of which at least four he had himself purchased some time before 1332.[9] He must therefore have been an established tenant many years before 1332. Similarly, Lora atte Wynde and Constance Colsweyn who paid heriots while still alive, were old enough to have married daughters at the time of the first payment. Christina atte Hassele, who paid heriot in 1328 for a portion of her land but may still have been active in 1339, was at the time of her first heriot payment a widow with a grown-up son.[10] In all these cases sellers of land apparently lived beyond the spell of life allotted to them both in our demographic schedule of expectations of life and in the workaday expectations of manorial administrators. All these were men and women who happened to live longer than most; their longevity does not therefore belie the general impression that the heriots were levied as a precaution against the evasion of death duties on sales of land by tenants of advanced years.

Moreover, in many of the questionable cases, in which long intervals separated the first payment of money heriot from the date of death, we cannot be certain that the person who paid the heriot did not in fact die earlier than our records indicate. For it so happens that the fog which surrounds the identities of some of the holders is so composed and distributed as to magnify the apparent length of the period of the payment of the heriot *inter vivos* and the death of the seller. In many, perhaps in most of the instances in which we have had to presume that the seller was alive for several years after he had paid heriot on his sale, this presumption is based wholly on the evidence of personal names. When a reference to a John Smith paying heriot in one year is followed by a reference to a John Smith paying a fine or a heriot years later we have as a rule concluded that in both cases the same John Smith was meant. But since Christian names were bound to re-appear over a period of time

[8] P.R.O. Eccl. 2/159344 (grown-up daughter on a holding of her own in 1332); 159349 (first heriot in 1339); 159358 (animal heriot and death in 1349); also Waltham Rental, P.R.O. Eccl. Com. Various 159512, 1/9.

[9] P.R.O. Eccl. 2/159352 (first heriot in 1342); 159358 (death and taking over of his land by grandchildren in 1349); also Waltham Rental, op. cit.

[10] P.R.O. Eccl. 2/159337 (first heriot); 159338 (marries off daughter); 159342 (*do* another daughter). For Christine atte Hassele, see ibid. 159340 and 159349.

within the same family, it is quite possible that the John Smiths paying fines or heriots on different dates were in fact different persons.

Now and again this is borne out by our records. Thus in 1328 we read of a heriot and an entry fine paid in Waltham by Richard atte Downe for land which belonged to Richard his father, but years later in 1349 we read of yet a third Richard atte Downe, *Ricardo filius Ricardii*, paying an entry fine for the same holding. Thus in three generations in the same family the heirs have the same names; and, but for the references to parentage and exceptionally clear indication of holdings and entry fines, we might have been led to assume that all the entries related to the same person and that Ricardus atte Downe was alive for twenty years after he had paid his first heriot.[11] Similarly, in 1297 heriot is paid for the land of Richard Schogell which goes to his son John. But in 1301 Richard Schogell is recorded paying a fine for the holding of his father, John Schogell. He is obviously a grandson of the man with the same name who paid heriot only four years previously. Yet if the name of his father had not appeared in the entry (and the names of fathers frequently do not appear) we would have taken it for granted that Richard Schogell II was the same man as Richard Schogell I.[12] There are several other cases in the Waltham records in which supplementary information enables us to discover that the same names in fact related to different persons.[13] But in many cases no such supplementary information is available, and in these we have had to assume that the same person was meant in all the entries and have computed our average expectations of life accordingly.

These 'questionable' cases greatly swell our sample of heriot-payers who lived longer than five years after the first heriot payment. Yet even thus swollen, the cases represent not more than ten per cent of the total number of money heriots. We must therefore conclude that by imposing money heriots on certain sales of land the Bishops did not divert the heriots from their original function of death duties. This general conclusion emerges very clearly from the analysis of some 2235 instances of heriots and entry fines on the manor of Waltham for the period 1325–51

[11] Ibid. 159340 (1328) and 159358 (1349).

[12] Ibid. 159315 (1297) and 159319 (1301).

[13] Thus in Eccl. 2/159343 for 1331 we find a heriot *post mortem* Roberti de Forde, but in the following year (ibid. 159344) a Robert de Forde pays a fine for a holding. In 1343 (ibid. 159353) a heriot is paid for the land of Adam le Melemongere who we are told *bastardus fuit et obiit sine herede de se*, but in 1350 (ibid. 159359) an Adam le Melemongere pays a fine for a holding. In ibid. 159358 (1349) we find a heriot paid for land of Robertus atte Putte, and also a fine by *Robertus filius Roberti atte Putte pro terra que fuit patris sui*, and in 1350 Robertus atte Putte junior pays a fine for marrying (ibid. 159359). But for the fortunate existence of the record of the fine we should have been unable to distinguish the father from the son and should have classified this case as one of a tenant surviving for a long period after payment of heriot.

collated with the tenancies recorded in the Waltham rental of 1332/33.[14] Of some 400 deaths represented by heriots in Waltham, about 350, i.e. about 88 per cent, were levied on the holdings of deceased tenants soon after their deaths. The remainder were levied on land transactions *inter vivos* in which the sellers were old men or women who might be expected to die within a few years of the transaction.

However, this element of anticipation does not leave our evidence or its meaning wholly unaffected. Though it does not prevent us from treating the figures of heriots as record of death duties, it is bound to affect the use to which they can be put. To the extent to which some of our heriots – 12 to 15 per cent of the total – do not coincide with the actual years of death, the annual fluctuations in the figures of heriots would not reflect with absolute accuracy the fluctuations in the deaths themselves. And as there is no reason for doubting that the distribution of sales *inter vivos* was random, their effect on our figures would be to reduce the sensitivity of our figures to such lethal factors as bad harvests. We shall have to show presently that some other peculiarities in our records also tended to reduce or modify the apparent amplitude of fluctuations in annual deaths. If so, the effect of heriots *inter vivos* would be to make the statistical records of deaths appear smoother than it must have actually been. However, more will be said about this later.

With this correction in mind the figures of the heriots may be used to trace the course of mortality on the five estates of the Bishops of Winchester. But before this can be done, yet another logical and statistical hazard must be surmounted. The most usual procedure for measuring mortality is to express it in the form of death rates, i.e. as annual percentages of the total population alive at the beginning of the year. In our tables and graphs here we propose to deal not with death rates but with absolute numbers of deaths: a procedure which is more convenient for dealing with smaller samples. Yet the main statistical problem of a 'rate' is not thereby avoided. For if the absolute figures of deaths are to have any significance and are to be comparable over the period as a whole they must be assumed to relate to a 'stable population', i.e. to a group which remained the same in size throughout the period. Our assumption must therefore be that the numbers of customary tenants liable to heriot – about 1700 – did not materially change in the 100 to 120 years before 1348.

Is this assumption justified? We believe that it is; and our belief is based both on our assessment of changes which must have occurred in

[14] The entry fines and heriots are derived from the following accounts: Accounts: Eccl. Com. 2/159337 to 159348; Eccl. Com. 2/159451; Eccl. Com. 2/159349 to 159354; Eccl. Com. 2/159361 and Eccl. Com. 2/159355 to 159360. Waltham Rental: Eccl. Com. Various 159512, 1/9.

the size of the group and on those measurements of the group as a whole which we happen to possess.

Changes in the size of the group could have been brought about by several causes. Taking the thirteenth and fourteenth centuries as a whole, the numbers of customary tenants must have suffered a slow erosion, partly by manumission and partly by the lapse of tenancies and the absorption of holdings into demesne. But the difference this makes to our figures, especially over the period between 1270 and 1348, when the figures happen to be most continuous, is very small. On most of the Bishops' manors the customary holdings drawn into demesne appear to have lapsed by 1209 and very few lapsed after that date. The same applies to erosion by manumission. Outright manumissions lifting tenants wholly out of villein condition were very few and far between on most medieval manors. Unfortunately we do not possess for the Bishopric of Winchester any registers of charters containing manumissions, but if manumissions on the episcopal estates were as infrequent as the instances which in fact appear in the records, the accumulated reductions in the numbers of customary tenants by the middle of the fourteenth century could not have exceeded three per cent.

Small and slow changes like these may have slightly reduced the size of our group by the early fourteenth century. The possible reductions were in part compensated by certain small changes working in the opposite direction, i.e. those resulting from subdivision of customary holdings. However, on the Bishops' estates these were also very few. So on the whole we should be quite justified in assuming that even if the numbers of customary tenants declined somewhat during the period, the decline was too small to affect materially our calculations and to prevent us from assuming that our figures of heriots related to a body of customary tenants which remained fairly constant in size throughout the period.

This conclusion is supported by such direct measurements as we possess. Thus on the Manor of Waltham, for which surveys at two points of time are available, the number of customary tenants in the dated survey of 1259 differs very little from the corresponding number in the survey of about 1332. It is *c.* 355 in the former and 349 in the latter.[15]

Similarly, in the other manors for which comparable figures are available the numbers of men liable to boon services (a group almost identical with customary tenants) listed in the bailiff's accounts of the early fourteenth century differ little from the numbers of customary tenants in the surveys of the mid-thirteenth century. Thus for Taunton, the largest manor in the group, the numbers are *c.* 635 in the mid-thirteenth-century survey and *c.* 592 in boon works of 1322. The numbers might be even nearer if we excluded the non-virgated holdings in the surveys, on the

15 MSS. B.M. Egerton 2418.

ground that some of them were held by non-customary tenure. These holdings, however, do not account for more than ten per cent of the total, and moreover contain a number of tenants paying heriot.

It will be noticed that such differences as these figures disclose show some decline in numbers, but small as the decline appears to be, it probably exaggerates the actual reduction in the numbers of customary tenants liable to heriot. For the lists of men charged with boon services in the bailiff's accounts of the mid-fourteenth century do not as a rule include tenants who had permanently commuted their services while continuing to hold by customary tenure subject to heriot.

The total changes in the group as a whole were thus too small and too uncertain to justify an attempt to correct our figures by an assumed or an estimated allowance for error. Such small changes as there were, were mostly in the downward direction, and a statistical allowance for them would merely accentuate the rising trend of death rates towards the end of the period which our figures show in any case. More about this will, however, be said presently.

3

For all these reasons we believe that the series of heriots available to us provide us with a useful indication of the real numbers of deaths among customary tenants. Though not expressed as percentages of the totals of customary tenants in surveys, the series approximately represents the movements of death rates among the adult members of the group. The figures for the manors taken together are summarized in Table 9.1 and are presented graphically in Graph 1. Graph 2 represents the same figures for the manor at Taunton, the largest manor in the group, which accounted for nearly one-third of our heriots. These graphs and tables also include the data of wheat prices as an indication of harvests.

The most obvious feature of the figures, taken as a whole, is their magnitude. The annual average of deaths is 70 for the period as a whole and about 90 for the last 55 years, i.e. the years between 1292 and 1347, for which the data are most continuous and reliable. As our total group of customary tenants numbered just over 1700 in 1321 our figures of heriots are equivalent to death rates of 40 and 52 per thousand. This is an exceptionally high rate. The crude death rate in post-war England and Wales is about 12 per thousand. At first glance the rate at its higher variant appears to be nearly twice as high as the death rate of the English population in 1801, and even higher than the death rates in other pre-industrial societies of Europe and Asia. An approximate estimate of European death rates in the early nineteenth century (Sundbärg's) puts them at 32 per thousand, even though at that time it was only 26–8 per thousand in Sweden.[16] In India the lower estimates of death rates of the total population puts them at over 25 per thousand in the 1930s, and over 35 between 1890 and 1930. A higher and more recent estimate is that the Indian death rates were over 41 per thousand between 1881 and 1901, and 40 to 50 between 1901 and 1921. In Russia the rates were over 38 per thousand in the 1860s and about 30 per thousand in the second half of the nineteenth century taken as a whole.[17]

However, these are very rough juxtapositions which cannot be taken and are not offered here as an accurate comparison of the relative levels of mortality in medieval England and in other pre-industrial societies. The differences were wider than the superficial comparison of figures would suggest. Our figures, are of course, 'crude' rates, i.e. rates not corrected for differences in age structure. To this extent they may at first sight appear to exaggerate the real incidence of deaths in medieval England compared with nineteenth-century India or eighteenth-century England. Whereas the Indian population grew fairly fast, the English population of the late thirteenth and early fourteenth centuries probably grew relatively slowly. In our own day, the high proportion of children and young persons in fast-growing populations will reduce the 'crude' death rate well below the real rate; on the other hand in slowly-growing populations crude mortalities may be relatively high merely as a result of greater proportions of persons in older age groups.

However, this tendency of our figures to exaggerate the moralities in medieval England, when populations grew very slowly, in comparison with those of nineteenth-century Russia or India, when population grew much faster, is more than offset by the fact that the Winchester figures are confined to adults and leave out altogether the deaths of infants and small children whose mortality in pre-industrial societies is invariably much higher than that of adults. Indeed infant and child mortalities in backward societies are, as a rule, so high as to lift the average death rates of persons under 20 well above those of persons over 20; and that in spite of the fact that adolescents and young adults in the ages between 15 and 20 as a rule suffer fewer deaths than other age groups in the population, except of course the very aged.[18] In eighteenth-

[16] Sundbärg, op. cit.; H. Gille, 'Demographic History of the North European Continent', *Population Studies*, III (1949–50), 33 seq.

[17] Kingsley Davis, *The Population of India and Pakistan* (Princeton, 1951), p. 36. The Russian figure for the 1860s is an average of the ten years from 1861 to 1871 (the figures for 1866 missing) in A. G. Rashin, *Naselenie Rossii zu 100 liet* (Moscow, 1956), p. 186.

[18] Indeed the remarkable feature of the 'age specific' mortalities of pre-industrial societies (and on this point their similarity is remarkable) is the exceptionally high death rates of children other than infants, and mostly of those between 1 and 5 years of age: Gille, op. cit. p. 47; Octavio Caballo, 'The Demography of Chile', *Pop. Studies*, IX (1956), 249; G. W. Roberts, *The Population of Jamaica*

century Sweden the death rate of males under 20 was between 55 and 60 per thousand compared with about 30 per thousand for the population as a whole. In Russia between 1908 and 1910, out of every thousand deaths of males, 682, or rather more than two-thirds, were accounted for by the deaths of males 20 years old and under, and mainly by those of infants and children under five. With the overall Russian death rate in these years standing at about 30, the death rate of males over 20 must have approximately equalled 20 per thousand. If these differential death rates of the Russian adult population were used to convert the Winchester death rates of adults in those of the population as a whole, a crude rate as high as 70–5 per thousand would result.[19] Somewhat similar results would emerge from the comparison of Winchester rates with the adult death rates of Indian population between 1890 to 1920. There is thus very little doubt that the mortality on the Winchester manors in the second half of the thirteenth and the first half of the fourteenth centuries was at least as high, and probably much higher, than the mortality in any other pre-industrial society whose evidence is available to us.

4

The other feature of the graph is the apparent rise in the secular trend. Over the period as a whole the apparent rise appears to be most spectacular. For whereas the average number of deaths in the first forty years was about 40, the corresponding average for the last fifty years was at least 52. Needless to say, this contrast is in some respects more apparent than real. It conceals important differences between the mortalities of different sections of village population (more will be said about this later) and to this extent masks the real trend. As we have already stressed elsewhere, the manorial administrators before 1240 did not apparently collect money heriots from poor tenants with any regularity. The records of heriots in these years certainly underestimate and sometimes completely leave out the deaths among the poorer tenants. Judging from manorial accounts and returns of the manorial courts, the collection of money heriots became regular in the second half of the century, and was for all we know complete after 1270. From that time onwards our statistics show a pronounced rise in the numbers of poor men's heriots which became

(1957) (for 1881); Sigismund Peller, 'Mortality Past and Future', *Pop. Studies*, I (1947), 424–9.

19 Gille, op. cit., table on p. 47; Rashin, op. cit., p. 202; according to the available data of the age structure of Russian population in 1897, persons of 20 and over formed in that year 51·3 per cent of the total population, or little more than half. The vital statistics of Russian population, and its age-structure did not alter sufficiently between 1897 and 1908 to prevent our fitting the generation tables of the latter year to the mortality figures of the earlier period.

very steep after 1290. Indeed so clear and so rapid is the rise in the trend, especially in the 1290s, as to suggest the possibility that the series between 1270 and the 1290s was also influenced by an administrative change. But although this possibility must not altogether be excluded, the evidence at present available makes it appear very remote. Our documents bear no trace of a change in the administration of the heriots, and the record of heriots is well matched by that of entrance fines and thus appears complete.[20]

Moreover, the rise continues beyond 1290. There is no statistical reason for suspecting any change in the basis of assessment and collection of heriots between 1290 and 1347; and the figures in our possession are not only full and comprehensive, but also appear to be statistically consistent when arranged in a series. Yet at a first glance the deaths in this period also exhibit an upward tendency. The graph of deaths rises to a hump during the years of disastrous harvests at the end of the second and the beginning of the third decades of the century. With the passing of this bad patch the hump levels out and death rates decline below the summit of 1317–18, but they still keep above the level at which they stood in the early 1290s.

However, the figures are open to yet another objection which must be considered before any definite conclusion about the trend is drawn from them. This objection, like another objection already dealt with, relates to the 'crude' character of our death rates. As long as the death rates remain unadjusted to changes in the age composition of the population, such trend as they may exhibit can be suspected to represent not greater or smaller ravages of death but changes in the age structure of the group. In our case the rise in the 'crude' rates might signify nothing more than a gradual increase in the proportions of older men.

This objection does not find much support in the purely statistical feature of our series. The fact that the minimum numbers of animal heriots in the four quarter centuries were so consistent – 24, 24, 28, 24 – strongly indicates that the group remained essentially comparable in numbers and in age structure. This purely statistical conclusion is supported by the general balance of historical probabilities. If it could be shown that mortality among children and youths was rising throughout the period, the probability that the average age of the population was also rising would be very great. But in a social group in which mortality of infants and children was always very high, a rising trend of deaths was not necessarily characterised by still higher proportions of infants and children among the dead. Indeed, in so far as the increased deaths were due to greater frequency and severity of famines and diseases following from them, the evidence of other countries, such as Russia and India,

20 See below pp. 180 *seq.*, Mr Longden's note.

suggests that the victims were the old and the infirm as well as infants and children, and that the highest rate of survival was among the older children and the younger adults.

The main reason, however, why high mortality among the young might not have affected the age structure in our group is the nature of the group itself. For our group is not a self-reproducing demographic entity but a purely tenurial assortment of people. It was recruited not by natural increases within its own ranks but by succession to holdings. If our evidence is to be trusted a surprisingly large number of successors were men who married the dead men's widows and who very frequently had come from outside our group. Some of the incumbents, especially those who acquired holdings by purchase and were parties to anticipatory money heriots, were complete outsiders and might even have come from other villages. If so, the rising mortality of the young in the population as a whole, even if it were rising, need not have altered the average age of incumbents to new holdings, or at any rate need not have altered it to a significant extent.

The true causes of changes in the age composition of our group, if changes there were, were probably economic, i.e. the prevailing land hunger and the plethora of would-be tenants. The growing difficulties of hiring, buying or inheriting a holding must have greatly increased the numbers of 'unplaced' men in those age groups from which came most of the men who in more spacious times acquired holdings, married, and settled down. It is only in so far as the reservoir of would-be successors to the dead tenants contained an ever-growing number of older 'expectants' that we could expect it to influence the age composition of our group.

These arguments, both statistical and historical, cannot of course be decisive. As long as direct evidence of age structure of medieval populations is not available, we must not altogether exclude the possibility, however remote, that the age composition of our group rose sufficiently to account for some of the apparent rise in deaths during the period. However, even if this demographic ambiguity attached to our trend, it would not deprive it of economic significance. From the economic point of view, the rising death rates – if they were really rising – and the changing age composition of the group – if it was changing – would be merely different manifestations of the same economic malaise: the shortage of land in the thirteenth and early fourteenth centuries and the relative over-population of the countryside with its adverse effects both on the standards of life and on the age composition of incumbents to holdings. This conclusion anticipates the next and more purely economic stage in our argument.

5

This purely economic argument is suggested by the rather striking feature of our Table 9.1 and Graph 1, i.e. the violent short-term year-to-year fluctuations. What makes these fluctuations all the more remarkable is that the main statistical bias of our figures is to smooth out such fluctuations as there were. One such feature has already been discussed. Those heriots which were by nature 'anticipatory', i.e. were paid not on holdings of deceased tenants but on those of aged tenants selling their land, could be expected to be distributed at random. And a random dispersion of these heriots would tend to blur the actual record of fluctuating death rates, in so far as the fluctuations were due to the visitations of plague or famine.

This, however, is not the only levelling bias in our statistics. The whole distribution of heriots, their collection and their recording, were such as to carry some of the entries over into one or two years following the actual years of death. In the first place there was the accounting convention of manorial documents. Bailiffs' accounts almost invariably ran from Michaelmas to Michaelmas. A death occurring in the late summer and producing its heriot in the following autumn would thus be recorded not in the accounting year in which it occurred but in the accounts of the following year. For this reason higher records of heriots sometimes occur not in the year of the famine or epidemic which probably caused them, or at any rate not only in that year but also in the year following.[21]

In so far as deaths were caused by bad harvests and famine a further interval was bound to intervene between our figures of deaths and the events which caused them. Starvation, unlike an epidemic, does not kill men outright. It may debilitate them and thus condemn them to an earlier death than the one to which they would otherwise have succumbed, but this would not necessarily result in immediate demise. In any case, in years of bad harvest, shortages were sometimes at their worst in the late summer, i.e. on the eve of the new harvest. The worst effects of a famine would therefore be felt in that tail end of the accounting year which, as we have already seen, would not produce its crop of recorded deaths until the following accounting year.

Yet further discordances between the fluctuations in the records of deaths in our sources on the one hand and the incidence of the factors causing the deaths on the other will be found in the periods in which 'bad years' succeeded each other without appreciable intervals. Generally speaking we might expect that, short of a total failure of crops, a

[21] Yet this tendency is not sufficiently consistent to allow us to plot our figures with a one year lag, as in Gille's study of Scandinavian mortalities, op. cit. p. 45.

moderately bad harvest would not necessarily cause numerous deaths from starvation, but that a succession of such years would so enfeeble the village population as to send the death rates sharply upwards, and keep them high even in the intervening years of relatively low prices. On the other hand a year of severe epidemic or a really disastrous famine, in the course of which most of the old, infirm, or poor starvelings perished, would 'purge' the population of its weaker element and be succeeded by a year of lower death rates, even if it also happened to be a year of famine or disease.

For these reasons we might expect our figures to be not only less liable to fluctuate from year to year than actual deaths must have done, but also to be somewhat irresponsive to the immediate impact of bad harvests and famines. It is therefore all the more remarkable to find how much our figures in fact fluctuate and how nearly the fluctuations coincide with harvests or other catastrophic mortality factors. In some years, to be mentioned later, the figures of heriots appear to reflect the deaths of preceding years while in others the high numbers of deaths follow not a dearth or famine in the year in which they occur, but a whole sequence of bad years. But in general the figures fluctuate sharply, and most of the sharper fluctuations appear to synchronise with the events which could be expected to cause deaths in thirteenth-century villages.

We believe that the fluctuations, or at least a large number of them, can be correlated with the main causes of deaths. But while tracing this correlation, and especially while drawing evidence of prices and harvests into our discussion, we must bear in mind not only the warnings already uttered, but some other warnings more strictly relevant to our search for underlying causes. In the first place, only wide fluctuations in numbers of deaths and in prices need be considered. It is only when deaths rise well above the average, i.e. above 45 for animal heriots, and 85 for total heriots after 1290, that the action of severe lethal factors such as famine or epidemic, can be suspected. Similarly, with the average secular price of wheat averaging somewhere around five shillings per quarter, prices only a little higher than that could not be taken to denote failures of harvest and severe privation for the cultivators. On the whole it would be reasonable to consider the effects of only those rises which carry the price above say, seven shillings a quarter, and not to speak of real famine until the price exceeded, say, eight shillings. But in applying this principle we must also bear in mind that prices frequently changed in the course of a year, and that a moderate annual price often conceals a steep rise from low prices at the beginning of the year to really high prices at its end, or else a fall of prices from a high maximum. It will therefore be sometimes advisable to take into account not only the average prices listed and traced in our Table 9.1 and Graph 1 but also the maximum prices.

Finally, while accepting the relevance of wheat prices it is important to remember that the villagers' 'daily bread' was as a rule not wheat but rye or mixed grains containing barley and oats. In general it is safe to assume that in years in which wheat failed the rye crops also failed badly. It is, however, possible that in years in which winter crops, i.e. wheat and rye, failed, spring crops, i.e. barley, oats and legumes, did well, and *vice versa*. We must not, therefore, exclude the possibility that in some years in which prices of wheat were high the villagers were nevertheless sufficiently provided with other food grains. The extent to which this possibility may disturb or cancel the correlation between prices and deaths will have to be subjected to separate statistical tests, but in general the evidence at our disposal makes it clear that the years in which famine prices prevailed were those of general failure of crops.[22]

With these warnings and complications in mind we can now proceed to survey the fluctuations of deaths from year to year and to attempt to suggest the causes of high deaths in years in which they happen to be discoverable.

For convenience of exposition we must begin with the discussion of total heriots even though it will be shown further that the fluctuations in total heriots may be consistent with the absence of significant fluctuations in the heriots of more substantial tenants. Our series opens with four years, 1245–9, in which heriots synchronized with the movements of prices in two years, notably in 1247–8 and 1248–9, and may or may not have synchronized in the other two. The fluctuations may not, however, be of much importance; while prices were on the rise and stood at a relatively high level and the deaths were also somewhat above the average, neither the rises nor the subsequent falls diverged far enough from the average to lend them special significance. For the following two years, 1249–51, we have no evidence, but between 1252–3 prices and deaths rose simultaneously. The rise in prices may not appear to be very high, but this is one of the years in which average prices are probably misleading. The chroniclers report heavy rains in the early autumn of 1251 followed by bad drought in summer and a failure of crops in 1252. As a result, the prices which had been low at the beginning of the year rose considerably higher in the late summer and early autumn of the same year, reaching a level of eight shillings and above, denoting a real scarcity.[23]

After a year's gap in our series, we find in 1254–5 prices and heriots at a low level; in 1257 and 1258, after another gap, heriots were above

22 See below, Mr Longden's note on grain prices; also D. L. Farmer, 'Some Grain Price Movements in Thirteenth-Century England' in *Economic History Review*, 2nd ser. x, no. 2 (1957).

23 Eccl. Com. 2/159291A; *Matthaei Parisiensis monachi sancti Albani Chronica Majora*, Rolls Series (1872–84), x, 279.

average and prices high: the chroniclers again report wet weather, failures of crops and great dearth.[24] After yet another gap in our records we find that in 1263 both figures are lower again; and both are still level between 1265–6. An uncertain interval due to insufficient evidence follows; and when the series resumes both prices and deaths rise to the high peak of 1271–2, which was apparently preceded and prepared by a year of very high prices in 1270.[25] The chroniclers in fact tell us that 1270–1 was a wet year followed by the exceptionally wet spring of 1271 in which crops were ruined. The following autumn was apparently also wet and inclement and was followed in the summer of 1272 by a punishing drought which brought famine and death to the whole of Western Europe.[26] The peak of deaths and prices was reached late in 1272 (probably late in the year) and thereafter both indices appear to fall sharply to 1274. The interval between 1275–83 is badly served by evidence.[27]

When in 1283 our run of evidence is resumed, the opening period – up to 1287 – is marked by fluctuations, mostly small and perhaps for that reason not very significant. In 1283 there occurred the first apparent divergence between our indices, for whereas prices for 1283–4 fell to four shillings and eightpence, the deaths rose somewhat. The rise in deaths may perhaps have been too small to correlate with prices, but in any case our record of low prices in this year may be misleading. Though the average prices were low, the maximum prices were high. They had been very high in 1282–3, reaching ten shillings and twopence in Taunton,[28] and stayed high in the early months of the following year, when they reached nine shillings and fourpence a quarter in Oxfordshire; on Winchester manors they stood round eight shillings in Meon, Wargrave and Taunton, and only a little less elsewhere. The chroniclers indeed report that the spring and summer of that year were very wet. Spring-sown grains must have fared badly and prices of oats and drage were in fact quite high.[29] In the following year, 1284–5 prices and deaths moved downwards together, but the movements are again too small to be very significant. In 1285–6 – a year which according to the chroniclers was

[24] Thorold Rogers reports abundant evidence of very high prices in that year all over the country, wheat having sold in July for 9*s*. His evidence of high prices comes largely from Hampshire, i.e. from one of the Winchester manors. Rogers believes the high prices were due 'to the unfavourable prospects of the coming harvest rather than to the scantiness of the actual crop, prices rising rapidly towards the summer of 1271'. J. E. Thorold Rogers, *A History of Agriculture and Prices in England*, I, 188–9. However, see below footnote 25; Matthew of Paris, op. cit. V, 728.

[25] Eccl. Com. 2/159299; 159300.

[26] Gervase of Canterbury, *Opera Historica*, Rolls Series (1879–80), II, 272.

[27] There are no Account Rolls for the years 1275/6 and 1278/9 to 1281/2.

[28] Eccl. Com. 2/159305.

[29] J. E. Thorold Rogers, op. cit. I, 191; *Florentii Wigorniensis Chronicon*. Eng. Trans. Bohn (1854), p. 369.

one of drought followed by a wet autumn – both prices and deaths rise. Then in 1286–7 there occurs a divergence between the two movements which may be too slight to be of any importance; but after a year of falling indices we come to the year of 1288 which is marked by divergences between prices and deaths which appear to be both wide and significant. Whereas prices in 1287–8 and 1288–9 were among the lowest in the century, death rates in the later year soared to the yet unprecedented level of seventy-six. This divergence is indeed sufficiently important to deserve a more detailed consideration.

High death rates of 1288–9 were clearly due to causes other than bad harvests. The chroniclers tell us that in the dry year of 1288 harvest was abundant and bread was cheap; and the Winchester prices fully bear out the account of the chroniclers.[30] But most chroniclers also report that in the summer of that year drought was so continuous and the heat was so intense that a multitude of people died. The presumption of course is that what caused the deaths were the epidemics characteristic of prolonged drought and heat in an era of poor water supplies and primitive sanitation. Wells and streams must have dried up, people must have drunk brackish and infected water, and refuse was not washed down to the sea. According to some chroniclers the drought continued into 1289 until it was broken by violent thunderstorms and followed by a failure of crops.[31]

That death rates should have fallen as they did after the high peak of 1289 is something to be expected. We must not, however, conclude that the fall occurred despite the high prices, for prices were apparently average through the greater part of 1290 and did not begin to rise until the summer in anticipation of the next year's bad harvest. Having risen to over eight shillings (9*s* 2*d* in Taunton), they stood high during 1291–2, a year which the chroniclers describe as cold and wet.

Prices continued to move somewhat irregularly until 1303. These years marked the beginning of a period during which the secular trend of deaths rose markedly above the level of the previous half-century. As we have already suggested, it is possible to argue on purely statistical grounds that the apparent rise in the trend at the end of the thirteenth century may have resulted from an unknown change in accounting methods. But we have also noted there is nothing in the records themselves to indicate an accounting change, and that we cannot therefore dismiss the evidence of the rising trend on the ground that it reflects a fuller collection of the heriots. It is however, permissible to conclude that

30 *Annales Prioratus de Dunstaplia*, Rolls Series (1866), p. 341; *Annales Prioratus de Wigornia*, Rolls Series (1869), p. 495.

31 *Wilhelmi Rishanger Chronica et Annales regnantibus Henrico Tertio et Edwardo Primo*, Rolls Series (1856), p. 119.

where the year-to-year oscillations do not carry the numbers of deaths much below or much above the heightened secular average, the annual movements may be of little account. Prices in their turn do not fluctuate to any great extent during this period.

When after a short gap in our evidence the record becomes continuous again in 1306 both prices and deaths enter into a clearly marked phase covering the first two decades of the fourteenth century, when frequent and disastrous failures of harvests were accompanied by exceptionally high death rates. Prices were high in 1308 and had been rising in the latter part of 1307 in anticipation of a bad harvest. Deaths also rose to a high level. But whereas in the following years – 1309 – the deaths fell somewhat (though they still stood above eighty), perhaps in reaction to the high deaths of the previous year, the prices entered into the first of the headlong rises which characterised the period as a whole. As our table and graph show, deaths during this period reached the exceptional height of 100 and above. The years of 1312 and 1313 saw a return to more moderate prices and a pronounced reaction in deaths. But the years 1315, 16, 17 witnessed a heightened crisis in agriculture and a rise of mortality to unprecedented heights. The disastrous sequence begins with the wet winter and failure of crops and high prices of 1314–15. The prices were not only generally high but were apparently mounting in expectation of the truly disastrous crops of the following year. In that year (1316) failure was complete, and the price of wheat at some places approached the giddy level of 24 shillings per quarter, and over great parts of southern England stood at over three times the secular average. The chroniclers tell us that the mortality was great and our table and graph show the deaths rising to over 170, a level very much higher than any other year before the Black Death. So high it was that, but for the Black Death itself, these years might well have left their mark in historical records and popular memory as the years of highest mortality in the Middle Ages.

When death rates stood at so high a level and bad years occurred at such frequent intervals it would perhaps be unwise to analyse annual fluctuations too closely, since years of heavy mortality were bound to be followed by years of reaction when death rates plunged even if conditions continued to be hard. Yet the general effect of bad years is unmistakable, and prices and deaths continued to move together for at least another three years after 1317 and possibly for six years till 1325.[32]

32 Our records unfortunately do not provide us with data of the next disastrous year – that of 1322. Our tables show prices in 1321 fairly high – over 8*s* per quarter, but in fact prices had been much lower and rose at the end of the year in anticipation of the disastrous harvest of 1322. There is thus nothing surprising in the deaths of 1321 being as yet fairly low. In 1322 the rise continues to a level very nearly as high as that of 1316. Rogers's Sussex prices are as high as 21*s* 6*d* per quarter; elsewhere they are only a few shillings lower; and chronicles

During an interval of about five years till 1332 the two series appear to be moving without any recognizable relation. Indeed, at two points in 1328 and 1332 the divergences between the two indices are nearly as wide as we have noticed them to be in 1288–9. The heriots of 1328 may have reflected the high mortalities of the previous summer. The chroniclers tell us that 1326–7 was a year of unprecedented drought, 'brooks and streams, wells and marshes which previously had never dried up became dry everywhere'.[33] It is therefore probable that the conditions were the same as those of 1288–9, and the drought of late summer was accompanied by an epidemic which left a deposit of heriots in the accounts of the year beginning in the following Michaelmas. More difficult to account for is the divergence between prices and deaths in 1332. In that year and to some extent in the preceding year (1330–1) deaths slumped though prices were high and rising. A possible explanation is the very high mortality of the previous years, after which a reaction was to be expected. That the high mortalities had indeed carried away a large proportion of the population is shown by the complaints of Winchester bailiffs of the shortage of men for harvest work – the same complaint which we saw in the records of the great epidemic of 1288–9. There are several references in the bailiff's account of 1332 to the *nimia caristia falcatorum, caristia metencium, caristia messorum*.[34] However, both prices and deaths rose to a high level in the following year.

After a gap of a year, the series resumes in 1335. The figures of the first two years, 1335–6, appear to suggest that deaths and prices synchronized: the prices rose slightly and so did the deaths, but the increase in deaths does not carry the rate above its average for the period and may be fortuitous. The prices and deaths for 1337–8 again appear to diverge, but the deaths in that year, though high, were not much higher than the average level in this period of high deaths. On the other hand, in 1342, the divergence is very marked. This may again have been a year of pestilence. Direct evidence of pestilence in that year is not, however, to be found in our records. Between 1343–8, the eve of the Black Death, both heriots and prices appear to be interrelated. But as we shall see presently the interrelation was not equally close for the different

report high mortalities. Prices apparently continued very high in 1323 and 1324, though in some places they fall somewhat during the summer. Unfortunately we have no evidence of heriots for these years, but it would be surprising if deaths were not high.

33 *Annales Paulini*, Rolls Series (1882), p. 312.

34 P.R.O. Eccl. 2/159344, Suttona, Expensa Autumpnalia: *In 2 acris vescarum et 4 acris pisarum falcandis ad tascham 3s. 6d. pro acra 7d. et tantum hoc anno propter nimiam caristiam falcatorum*; Eccl. 2/159344 Farnham, Expensa Autumpnalia: *In blad(is) metend(is) . . . pro acra 7d. hoc anno propter magnam caristiam messorum*; Eccl. 2/159344 Alresford, Expensa Autumpnalia: . . . *et hoc anno tantum propter caristiam metent(ium) et allec(um).*

groups of tenants. The general level of mortality was above average, but the correspondence with prices appears only in 1346, when both deaths and prices were low, and in 1348 when deaths were high and prices had stayed high for two years.

Little need be said about the Black Death itself. In order not to affect our averages and trends unduly, the catastrophic events of 1348–9 have been left out of all our computations. The reader must, however, be warned against at least one unwarranted conclusion about the Black Death. Our tables and our graph suggest a death rate somewhere near 500 per 1000. The actual death rates during the epidemic may in fact have been higher than is commonly assumed, but our data must not be employed to measure them. In a group like ours which, to repeat, was not a demographic entity but a tenurial one and which was renewed not by births but by accession to tenures, it was possible in catastrophes such as 1348–9 for the same holding to be re-let to successive tenants several times in the course of the same year. Indeed we read of cases in which customary tenants succeeded each other three or four times. Mortalities in a group like ours obviously cannot be used as a sample of mortalities in the population as a whole during years in which death could cause successive changes of tenures in the same year. Fortunately, for our statistics and our arguments, the years of 1348–50 were the only ones in which this appeared to be probable.

To sum up. Our records provide figures of heriots for some 83 years over a period of about 110 years. In the last 19 of these, i.e. 1245–6, 46–7, 83–4, 84–5, 86–7, 1292–1303 and 1327–32, and perhaps also in 1335–6 and 1344–5, the fluctuations in deaths and prices were not of such magnitude as to be significant even if on several occasions the movements happen to synchronise. In one of these years – 1283–4 – a possible association between deaths and prices may have been obscured by the artificial price average of the year as a whole.

However, in most of the remaining years – at least some 40 and possibly some 60 – the underlying causes of fluctuations in deaths can be surmised with some degree of confidence. The years of 1288–9, 1328–9 and possibly 1331–2 were years of summer epidemics. Epidemics may also have raged in other years but their effects are masked by those of bad harvests occurring in the same years. In one year, 1342, high deaths may have been due either to an epidemic or to famine conditions created by currency disturbances or to some other cause unknown to us. All the other spectacular rises in mortality coincide with or follow bad harvests and conversely all the high peaks of prices (except that of 1332) are accompanied by corresponding peaks of mortalities.

6

The heriots and their correlations have an obvious bearing on the economic and demographic problem of the medieval countryside. A society in which every appreciable failure of harvests could result in large increases in deaths is a society balanced on the margin of subsistence. A balance so precarious and so frequently upset implies either or both of two inter-related possibilities. One is that cultivation was pushed to the point at which land could sustain its cultivators only in years of favourable harvests such as could be expected to occur in only about two years out of three; the other is that individual holdings were so small as to be unable to support their cultivators except in years of good yields. Both possibilities indicate an extreme degree of rural over-population. Whether in absolute numbers the population of the English countryside in the thirteenth century was greater than in other periods is immaterial. What is material is that given the productive powers of their soil, their technical knowledge, their capital resources and the burden of their rents and taxes, the numbers of peasants on the land were greater than its produce could support.

Put in this form the conclusion is of course too general and too much concerned with averages to mean much to historians. Historians could always find in their documents people who obviously did not starve every time the harvests failed. In a well-stratified society, such as medieval rural society certainly was, there must have been men more prone to succumb to failure of harvests than others. And it does not require much imagination to realize that the social group most likely to suffer from failures of crops was that worst provided with land and capital. The fact that the village as a whole, measured and judged by its averages, appears to have been poised on the verge of subsistence may mean nothing more than that a large proportion of the village population belonged to a class specially sensitive to failures of crops. Historians of medieval England need not be told that the thirteenth-century villages in fact contained large numbers of people thus placed. They were the smallholders and the cottagers whose holdings barely sufficed to maintain them and who often had to supplement their livelihood by work for wages. These people would suffer from the failure of harvests twice over – through the failure of their own produce and through the high prices they had to pay for the food they bought.

This general argument finds corroboration in our figures of heriots. Throughout this essay references have been made to money heriots levied on holdings too small and too poor to yield a heriot animal. The evidence of these heriots enables us to differentiate the deaths among the poor peasants from those among the more substantial villagers. The distinction can only be a very crude one. It is possible to find in most manorial documents references to holders of substantial tenements who did not possess any animals. They were probably men who, while figuring in our records as substantial tenants, in fact sub-let the whole or a portion of their holdings. On the other side of the dividing line it would be possible to find small holdings and cottages well provided with animals, more especially in pastoral regions or in villages with large commons. But in general there is little doubt that the bulk of holders who could not deliver a heriot animal were poor men. Our documents frequently imply this by explaining that a heriot animal could not be levied because the man had no animals.

The other shortcoming of money heriots has been mentioned elsewhere. Among the money heriots a proportion, perhaps as large as 20 per cent, and certainly not less than 10 per cent, is represented by what we have described as anticipatory death duties levied on sales of land *inter vivos*. The anticipatory element in the money heriots introduces a twofold complication. It may reduce the apparent responsiveness of money heriots to the underlying lethal factors; and it may blur the social distinctions as between money heriots and animal heriots. For even though most money heriots were levied on holdings of poor men, some were paid by substantial tenants selling portions of their holdings.

These crudities in our record must be expected to reduce somewhat the difference between respective price–death correlations of animal heriots and money heriots. It is therefore significant to find that the evidence, in spite of its indefinite lines of demarcation, shows money heriots responding much more immediately and sensitively to harvest failures than the animal heriots. Indeed our figures suggest that over the greater part of our period animal heriots show no correlation with prices, and that it is only in the first quarter of the fourteenth century – the time of the great famines – that animal heriots respond at all clearly to variations in crops.

The logic of these figures is further underlined by what we can observe from the behaviour of heriots in the years in which high mortality was due to epidemics. Whereas failures of harvests could be expected to hit first and worst the poor villagers, epidemics would presumably decimate the poor and the rich alike. And indeed in 1288–9 and 1328–9, the two years which were probably years of epidemics, the heriots of the poor and those of the rich rose simultaneously and approximately to the same extent.

The village smallholders and labourers were thus the harvest-sensitive element in rural society. It is through them that the effects of bad crops and high prices were transmitted to the village society as a whole. And it is their mortality that largely accounts both for the height and for the fluctuations of overall mortality. If the secular trend was rising it was at least in part because the proportions of smallholders in village population was also rising. The catastrophic failures of crops in the first half of the fourteenth century may of course have been due to unprecedented rainfalls, or to the progressive impoverishment of the soil, or to the spread of cultivation to marginal lands, or to all these factors in combination. But the sharp response of mortalities to crop failures undoubtedly reflected the high and rising numbers of tenants whose holdings were too small to enable them to sustain themselves in years of bad harvest.

To students of rural society in England these conclusions may appear familiar and indeed self-evident. They certainly agree with what we know of the incidence of deaths in other over-populated and backward agricultural societies. In Poland, in Russia, in China – in fact in all the pre-industrial societies for which evidence is available – the size of the holdings greatly influenced the demographic record, births as well as deaths, of peasant families.[35] But though not unexpected, the conclusions of our study may help historians to fill yet another gap in the puzzle of medieval population and to disclose some of the underlying social and economic facts.

NOTES TO TABLES AND GRAPHS

1. On both graphs the broken black line represents the average annual price for the five manors calculated from average annual prices of individual manors. The solid red line represents total heriots. The broken red line represents animal heriots. The solid black line represents money heriots.
2. A circle round the figures of total heriots on Graph 1 indicates that for that year evidence for one of the manors is lacking. The gap in the figures has been filled by assuming that the deaths on that manor were equal to the average mortality for a number of years – usually 8 – preceding and following the gap.
3. The total figure given for each manor disregards (a) all heriots in excess of one whenever collected from one and the same person, (b) all cases of suicide or accidental death and (c) a few cases (about four) in which the death of a tenant appears to be in doubt.
4. The breaking of the total figure into 'animal' and 'money' heriots follows the Account Rolls, but in a very few, mostly early, cases the sums levied are so large as to imply money equivalents of animals. Since the purpose of the breakdown was to differentiate between the poor and the not-so-poor peasants these few cases have been excluded from 'money' heriots. These instances are in general so few as not to affect our statistics. That they occur mostly before 1245 may perhaps point to the fact that the origin of the later small 'money' heriots is to be sought in an earlier practice of commutation.
5. All dates are those of Michaelmas *at the end* of the accounting year to which the figures relate.

[35] Rashin, op. cit. p. 207 (table 159); A. Tshajanow, *Die Lehre von der bäuerlichen Wirtschaft* (Berlin 1923), p. 73; W. Stys, 'Influence of Economic Conditions on the Fertility of Peasant Women', *Pop. Studies*, XI (1957), 136 et seq.; R. H. Tawney, *Land and Labour in China*, p. 72; F. Burgdörfer, *Bevölkerungsentwicklung im Dritten Reich* (Berlin 1937), pp. 46 and 78.

TABLE 9.1 *Heriots and prices on five Winchester manors*

	1245	1246	1247	1248	1249	1252	1253	1254	1255	1257	1258	1263	1265	1266	1268	1269
COMBINED TOTAL																
Total	41	52	41	58	43	49	58		40	34	58	44	28	28	29	31
Price	2·9	3·10	6·8	6·7	3·6	3·6	5·7		3·2	6·9	8·2	4·3	4·6	4·6	3·7	5·6
Animals	30	44	29	47	39	43	42		34	24	46	41	27	27	29	27
Non-animal	11	8	12	11	4	6	16		6	10	12	3	1	1	0	4
FAREHAM																
Total	8	9	7	8	6	8	3	6	2	4	4	4	4	3	1	–
Price	2·9	4·0	6·1	6·4	3·5	4·0	6·0	3·4	3·8	8·0	9·0	4·3	4·6	3·8	3·6	5·6
Animals	6	5	6	8	5	7	3	6	2	3	3	3	4	3	1	–
Non-animal	2	4	1	–	1	1	–	–	–	1	1	1	–	–	–	–
WALTHAM																
Total	9	16	8	9	11	3	10	8	7	11	11	9	12	4	4	7
Price	3·3	4·1	5·9	5·6	3·5	3·9	5·1	–	3·0	8·0	8·0	4·1	5·0	4·7	3·6	4·9
Animals	8	13	6	8	11	2	8	6	6	6	9	9	12	4	4	7
Non-animal	1	3	2	1	–	1	2	2	1	5	2	–	–	–	–	–
MEON																
Total	7	5	7	13	14	4	8		4	1	5	6	2	3	–	5
Price	1·8	2·8	6·3	5·4	2·11	3·5	5·2		2·7	6·3	7·5	4·6	5·0	3·8	4·0	5·9
Animals	4	5	2	9	11	4	5		4	1	4	6	2	3	–	4
Non-animal	3	–	5	4	3	–	3		–	–	1	–	–	–	–	1
WARGRAVE																
Total	6	7	7	12	1	5	9	11	9	3	8	9	5	6	5	8
Price	2·1	3·6	5·5	6·5	3·6	3·0	5·6	3·4	3·4	7·4	9·2	4·2	3·8	4·10	3·1	5·0
Animals	3	7	4	11	1	5	7	7	9	3	8	8	4	5	5	6
Non-animal	3	–	3	1	–	–	2	4	–	–	–	1	1	1	–	2
TAUNTON																
Total	11	15	12	16	11	29	28	20	18	15	30	16	5	12	19	11
Price	3·11	4·9	10·0	9·2	4·2	3·6	6·4	3·3	3·3	4·1	7·5	4·1	4·4	5·9	4·0	6·4
Animals	9	14	11	11	11	25	19	17	13	11	22	15	5	12	19	10
Non-animal	2	1	1	5	–	4	9	3	5	4	8	1	–	–	–	1

N.B. All prices are expressed in shillings and pence and *not* in shillings and decimals of shillings.

TABLE 9.1— *cont.*

	1271	2	3	4	1275	6	7	8	9	1280	1	2
COMBINED TOTAL												
Total			43		40		51	50				
Price	8·0	8·7	5·7		7·6		7·10	5·5				
Animals			36		26		35	33				
Non-animal			7		14		16	17				
FAREHAM												
Total	4	5	5	3	5		7	7				
Price	8·4	9·0	5·8	5·6	8·2		7·3	6·0				
Animals	4	4	3	1	2		4	5				
Non-animal	–	1	2	2	3		3	2				
WALTHAM												
Total		14	9	6	8		15	19				
Price	7·8	8·2	5·10	6·8	7·6		7·11	5·2				
Animals		13	7	5	6		8	10				
Non-animal		1	2	1	2		7	9				
MEON												
Total	1	17	10	3	3		7	6				
Price	8·2	9·0	5·6	6·11	7·7		7·6	5·0				
Animals	1	8	7	3	1		2	5				
Non-animal	–	9	3	–	2		5	1				
WARGRAVE												
Total	8		3		8		7	4				
Price	6·11	5·6	5·4		7·6		7·4	5·2				
Animals	7		3		8		7	3				
Non-animal	1		–		–		–	1				
TAUNTON												
Total	4	27	16	6	16		15	14				
Price	8·10	8·8	5·9	8·7	6·9		9·1	5·9				
Animals	4	23	16	5	9		14	10				
Non-animal	–	4	–	1	7		1	4				

	3	4	1285	6	7	8	9	1290	1	2	3	4	1295	6	7
COMBINED TOTAL															
Total	38	45	36	49	53	45	76	48		58					70
Price	7·8	6·10	(4·10)	6·5	4·8	3·3	3·11	6·1	7·7	6·7	6·8				6·5
Animals	32	35	24	43	39	33	54	28		42					29
Non-animal	6	10	12	6	14	12	22	20		16					41
FAREHAM															
Total	4	6	8	3	1	3	8	4	8	4					5
Price	7·3	6·7	4·8	5·7	4·8	3·4	4·0	6·0	7·9	6·8	7·0				6·8
Animals	4	2	3	2	–	3	5	1	4	3					1
Non-animal	–	4	5	1	1	–	3	3	4	1					4
WALTHAM															
Total	6	6	1	9	6	6	8	17	11	4	3				15
Price	7·6	7·1	4·9	6·4	5·0	3·4	3·11	6·0	8·0	6·8	7·0				6·8
Animals	6	5	1	9	6	6	8	10	7	3	1				6
Non-animal	–	1	–	–	–	–	–	7	4	1	2				9
MEON															
Total	7	13	4	7	13	6	9	1	8	9	5				16
Price	7·6	6·8	4·2	5·10	4·9	3·2	3·8	6·0	6·0	6·4	6·4				7·0
Animals	3	11	4	4	8	3	6	1	3	7	2				4
Non-animal	4	2	–	3	5	3	3	–	5	2	3				12
WARGRAVE															
Total	9	7	11	5	4	10	13	10		16	12				15
Price	8·0	6·5		7·0	4·7	3·6	4·0	6·0	8·0	6·10	7·6				7·0
Animals	8	7	8	5	3	7	8	5		11	8				4
Non-animal	1	–	3	–	1	3	5	5		5	4				11
TAUNTON															
Total	12	13	12	25	29	20	38	16	21	25					19
Price	8·3	7·7	6·2	7·5	4·6	2·9	4·1	6·6	8·1	7·5	5·7				4·8
Animals	11	10	8	23	22	14	27	11	14	18					14
Non-animal	1	3	4	2	7	6	11	5	7	7					5

COMBINED TOTAL																					
Total	64	64	58		61	63	78	73	98	86	96	102	84	69	94	76	121	171	135		67
Price	7·5	5·9	6·5	5·11	(5·7)	4·6	6·0	5·1	6·5	8·2	8·4	9·1	6·1	5·9	6·3	7·5	16·11	16·7	9·2	4·9	(6·8)
Animals	34	33	39		38	40	45	42	57	46	47	56	46	37	54	40	42	69	48		28
Non-animal	30	31	19		23	23	33	31	41	40	49	46	38	32	40	36	79	102	87		39
FAREHAM																					
Total	7	4	6	6	9	8	8	7	6	12	11	11	3	11	6	3	12	21	10	16	4
Price	8·0	6·8	6·0	6·0	–	4·0	6·4	5·8	6·2	8·0	8·8	9·4	5·4	5·6	5·11	7·4	19·11	17·0	9·6	4·6	6·11
Animals	2	1	4	2	6	5	2	7	1	4	3	5	–	5	3	2	5	3	3	4	–
Non-animal	5	3	2	4	3	3	6	–	5	8	8	6	3	6	3	1	7	18	7	12	4
WALTHAM																					
Total	16	18	11	7	15	14	16	21	24	26	28	18	7	15	20	16	25	22	35	23	13
Price	6·8	5·2	6·8	5·10	5·10	4·8	6·8	5·3	6·10	8·6	8·4	9·0	6·0	6·0	6·0	8·0	16·1	17·0	9·5	5·5	6·11
Animals	10	9	6	5	10	12	9	6	12	9	13	9	4	7	12	11	6	9	10	10	5
Non-animal	6	9	5	2	5	2	7	15	12	17	15	9	3	8	8	5	19	13	25	13	8
MEON																					
Total	7	5	9	8	8	–	6	6	11	12	16	22	12	8	13	13	25	33	13	11	7
Price	7·4	6·4	8·0	5·5	5·5	4·6	6·0	5·3	6·7	8·6	8·0	8·10	7·10	5·7	5·11	7·0	17·5	16·0	9·6	4·9	6·11
Animals	2	3	6	3	5	–	5	–	6	6	6	9	6	3	6	6	3	9	8	4	3
Non-animal	5	2	3	5	3	–	1	6	5	6	10	13	6	5	7	7	22	24	5	7	4
WARGRAVE																					
Total	13	14	11	14	8	12	6	17	14	10	14	10	19	13	11	13	20	7	13		7
Price	8·2	5·1	5·4	6·0	5·4	5·0	5·0	4·10	6·0	8·0	6·8	8·0	5·0	5·0	6·8	8·0	17·0	16·0	8·5	3·8	6·0
Animals	8	7	6	9	5	3	5	17	9	8	7	9	10	9	8	5	8	7	5		4
Non-animal	5	7	5	5	3	9	1	–	5	2	7	1	9	4	3	8	12	–	8		3
TAUNTON																					
Total	21	23	21		21	29	42	22	43	26	27	41	43	22	44	31	39	88	64	48	36
Price	6·9	5·7	5·11	6·5	5·6	4·5	5·10	4·5	6·5	7·8	9·10	10·2	6·3	6·7	6·8	6·11	14·4	16·11	9·0	5·6	–
Animals	12	13	17		12	20	24	12	29	19	18	24	26	13	25	16	20	41	22	15	16
Non-animal	9	10	4		9	9	18	10	14	7	9	17	17	9	19	15	19	47	42	33	20

1298 9 1300 1 2 3 4 1305 6 7 8 9 1310 11 12 13 14 1315 16 17 18 19 1320 1 2 3 4

TABLE 9.1—*cont.*

	1325	6	7	8	9	1330	1	2	3	4	1335	6	7	8	9	1340	1	2	3	4	1345	6	7	8	9	1350
COMBINED TOTAL																										
Total	81	77		109		96	83	61	96		61	95	79	101	97	92	91	115	96	101	103	63	98	101	1429	138
Price	7·10	5·8	4·9	5·9	7·3	7·2	8·9	9·2	6·0		5·3	5·11	4·10	4·5	4·7	7·2	4·9	5·4	4·10	7·4	4·5	4·10	8·1	7·9	4·7	7·1
Animals	43	40		60		42	35	35	38		24	44	33	57	37	41	46	41	34	38	42	30	48	33	754	20
Non-animal	38	37		49		54	48	26	58		37	51	46	44	60	51	45	74	62	63	61	33	50	68	675	118
FAREHAM																										
Total	6	10	9	9	11	5	2	2	9		8	9	3	8	6	4	7	9	11	6	7	4	5	2	100	5
Price	8·7	5·10	5·2	5·8	7·0	8·1	8·7	9·0	6·8		5·6	6·8	5·4	4·8	3·11	6·8	4·6	5·4	4·8	8·0	5·0	5·4	8·0	8·4	5·0	6·8
Animals	5	4	3	8	4	3	1	2	6		2	5	2	5	5	3	4	5	6	2	3	2	4	1	63	2
Non-animal	1	6	6	1	7	2	1	–	3		6	4	1	3	1	1	3	4	5	4	4	2	1	1	37	3
WALTHAM																										
Total	17	14	10	29	25	22	21	17	16		16	24	17	31	23	20	14	31	29	17	21	13	17	23	242	3
Price	6·8	6·0	5·0	5·10	6·8	7·4	10·0	8·6	5·6		5·5	6·0	4·9	[4·2]	4·8	8·0	4·7	5·4	5·0	7·4	5·0	5·0	7·8	8·8	4·6	8·0
Animals	6	8	6	17	11	8	10	9	10		9	8	7	15	8	2	5	7	7	6	9	6	7	8	159	3
Non-animal	11	6	4	12	14	14	11	8	6		7	16	10	16	15	18	9	24	22	11	12	7	10	15	83	–
MEON																										
Total	16	7	5	10	8	13	7	14	14		3	9	10	5	18	9	8	15	11	14	11	11	5	12	156	13
Price	9·9	5·8	5·2	6·0	7·1	7·8	9·1	9·1	5·9		5·5	6·5	5·2	5·0	5·4	7·4	5·2	6·0	5·4	8·0	4·3	4·9	8·9	8·4	4·0	6·8
Animals	6	2	3	4	5	7	3	10	3		1	4	2	–	8	3	3	5	4	4	1	2	2	3	69	1
Non-animal	10	5	2	6	3	6	4	4	11		2	5	8	5	10	6	5	10	7	10	10	9	3	9	87	12
WARGRAVE																										
Total	6	18		17		4	6	4	11		2	9	17	9	11	12	13	19	12	23	23	12	17	10	224	14
Price	8·4	5·0	3·8	4·5	8·0	6·2	6·11	8·0	3·2		4·0	4·11	4·4	3·8	3·8	6·0	4·4	4·4	4·6	6·6	3·8	3·11	6·10	7·0	4·2	6·4
Animals	5	10		10		4	6	3	6		2	9	12	7	4	9	9	5	7	9	12	7	9	4	155	3
Non-animal	1	8		7		–	–	1	5		–	–	5	2	7	3	4	14	5	14	11	5	8	6	69	11
TAUNTON																										
Total	36	28	41	44	34	52	47	24	46		32	44	32	48	39	47	49	41	33	41	41	23	54	54	707	103
Price	5·10	5·10	4·7	6·11	7·4	6·9	9·1	11·1	8·11		6·1	5·9	4·5	4·7	5·3	7·10	5·1	5·8	4·7	6·11	4·0	5·3	9·0	6·6	5·1	7·10
Animals	21	16	15	21	12	20	15	11	13		10	18	10	30	12	24	25	19	10	17	17	13	26	17	308	11
Non-animal	15	12	26	23	22	32	32	13	33		22	26	22	18	27	23	24	22	23	24	24	10	28	37	399	92

STATISTICAL NOTES ON WINCHESTER HERIOTS

By J. Longden

I must thank Professor Postan for introducing me to this very interesting material and for his counsel and guidance in interpreting it. For the methods used and errors in what can only be a tentative analysis of the data, the responsibility is my own.

1. Animal heriots – see Table 9.2

The average number was 38. This was the level in the middle decades of the thirteenth century. During the rest of the century heriots were below average (30–3) except for the 1280s which included the presumptive pestilence year, 1289. In the first three decades of the fourteenth century heriots were well above average (44–9) rising to a maximum in the famine years of the second decade. The average for the 1320s was raised by the high mortality of 1328 which may also have been a year of plague; between 1330 and the year of the Black Death the average was once more about 38 – as it had been a century earlier.

Did the number of tenants effectively liable to pay an animal heriot remain about the same? The consistency of the minima at 24–8 in each quarter-century suggests this. If so, there was a complete 'cycle' in the numbers of animal heriots, as the tide of mortality ebbed and flowed and began to ebb again. But there is documentary evidence that the proportion and numbers of substantial tenants declined in the century before the Black Death. Therefore mortality in this group may have been higher in the 1340s than in the 1240s – in which case the cycle represents a long-term fluctuation, not about a consistent level, but about a rising trend.

2. Non-animal or 'money' heriots – see Table 9.2

The data for the earliest years are known to be incomplete. Subsequently, at about 1260, 1270 and 1295, there are abrupt, and as yet unexplained downward or upward shifts in the level of money heriots. This is very unfortunate, as after 1295 changes in money heriots are far more instructive than the changes in animal heriots. We can say only that the recorded figures of money heriots before 1295 are much lower than they were thereafter, and that until more fully investigated these earlier figures are mainly useful for short-term comparisons.

The average number of money heriots in the first half of the fourteenth century was 46: animal heriots averaged 43 in the same period. In the first decade of the century it was only 30, and there may have been another unexplained upward shift after this. The average rose to 56 in the following decade of famine, fell to 41 in the third decade and rose progressively to 47 and 56 in the two decades before the Black Death. In these years money heriots became as high as they had been in the decade of famine thirty years earlier.

The apparent increase in the number of smallholders – who form the population at risk – may account for part, but not all, of the rise in money heriots: the figures imply a real and substantial rise in mortality for this group.

TABLE 9.2 *Heriots and wheat prices on five Winchester manors, 1245 to 1348*

	Number of heriots			
Period (1)	Animal (2)	Money (3)	Wheat prices per quarter (4)	Number of years covered out of total possible (5)
			Shillings and pence	
1245–9	38	9	4 8	5/5
1250–9	38	10	5 5	5/10
1260–9	30	2	4 6	5/10
1270–9	32	14	6 7	4/10
1280–9	37	12	5 4	7/10
1290–9	33	28	6 5	5/10
1300–9	44	30	6 0	7/10
1310–19	49	57	9 6	9/10
1320–9	44	41	6 6	4/10
1330–9	38	47	6 3	9/10
1340–8	39	56	6 1	9/9
1245–99	35	12	5 6	6 decades
1300–48	43	46	6 10	5 decades
1245–1348	38	28	6 1	11 decades

(1) Excluding years when records for any of the manors were missing or incomplete. It is possible, but not necessary, to include the partial data as well, the effect on the figures even for the 1270s and 1320s, when only 4 years out of 10 are fully covered being small.

(2) Long-term averages of the decade averages, not of the annual figures. They differ because the number of years missing varies.

3. *Comparison of animal and money heriots*

The impact of the famine decade on mortality among animal-paying tenants was, at most, half as severe as the impact on money-paying tenants; in the period which followed money heriots again rose while animal heriots fell and became stationary. The divergence of the two series may reflect changes in the relative numbers of substantial tenants and smallholders, as well as divergent mortality rates.

TABLE 9.3 *Correlations, and partial correlations, between animal heriots, money heriots, and wheat prices on five Winchester manors, 1245 to 1348*

Period and no. of years data (1)		Animal and money heriots (2)	Correlation (r^2) between animal heriots and wheat prices (3)	Money heriots and wheat prices (4)
			Direct correlations	
1245–59	(10)	0·00	0·01	0·37
1263–9	(5)	0·11	0·07	0·64
1273–92	(12)	0·07	0·00	0·00
1297–1321	(20)	0·32	0·23	0·75
1325–41	(13)	0·03	0·04	0·12
1342–8	(7)	0·05	0·09	0·02
			Partial correlations	
1245–59	(10)	0·00	0·01	0·37
1263–9	(5)	0·04	–0·00	0·62
1273–92	(12)	0·07	0·00	0·00
1297–1321	(20)	0·12	–0·00	0·67
1325–41	(13)	0·01	0·03	0·10
1342–8	(7)	0·04	0·08	0·00

(1) The division into periods conforms to the phases apparent in the data.
(2) There were two years when we can assume there was epidemic mortality – 1289 and 1328 – and these have been excluded in computing the correlations.
(3) A minus sign denotes a negative correlation.
(4) Correlations of less than ±0·10 may not be significant.

4. 'Expectations' of life – see Table 9.4

Table 9.4 shows the total numbers of heriots recorded in each decade. From 1300 onwards overall 'expectations' of life on assuming the tenancy are included. The overall expectations are got by dividing average annual heriots into 1725, the total number of heriot-paying tenancies in 1321. The average for the five decades is 20 years.

The shifts of the money heriots before 1295 decided me not to begin the overall series before 1300. On internal evidence, the animal heriots seem to be a statistically consistent series, but the number of the tenancies liable to pay them is not certain. The expectations for animal-paying tenancies are therefore worked out to yield the same average expectation of 20 years over the five decades 1300–48. This is equivalent to assuming that 48 per cent of the tenancies paid animal heriots as 48 per cent of the recorded heriots were animals. The difference in trend between the numbers of animals and money heriots referred to above is reflected in the figures of expectations, and is illustrated by the expectations for money-paying tenancies, which have been made consistent with those for animal-paying tenancies.

TABLE 9.4 *'Expectation' of life on entry into tenancies on five Winchester manors 1245 to 1348*

	Number of heriots recorded in period		Expectation of life (years)		
Period (1)	Overall (2)	Animal (3)	Overall (4)	Animal-paying (5)	Money-paying (6)
1245–9	235	189	...	22	...
1250–9	239	189	...	22	...
1260–9	160	151	...	28	...
1270–9	184	130	...	26	...
1280–9	342	160	...	23	...
1290–9	304	166	...	25	...
1300–9	517	307	23	19	30
1310–9	948	439	16	17	16
1320–9	334	171	20*	19	22
1330–9	769	345	20	22	19
1340–8	860	353	18	21	16
1245–69	634	529	...	24	...
1270–99	830	556	...	24	...
1300–19	1465	746	20	18	23
1320–48	1963	869	19	21	19
1245–99	1464	1085	...	24	...
1300–48	3428	1615	20	20	20
1245–1348	4892	2700	...	22	...

This table must be read in the light of section 4 of the Statistical Notes.

* Only this figure can be regarded as an 'expectation' of life in the ordinary sense. The others assume equal numbers at risk throughout, and equal expectations of life on entry among animal-paying and money-paying tenants.

Because of these differences in trend the expectations depend partly on the period used to equate the average expectations. Based on the period 1320 to 1348 the expectancies for animal-paying tenancies would be 2 per cent less, those for money-paying tenancies 2 per cent more – and the proportion of tenancies paying animal heriots 46 per cent instead of 48 per cent.

The assumption of equal expectations in the two groups of tenancies is probably false, even allowing for the possibility that money-paying tenants usually took over their plots at an earlier age than animal-paying tenants. Presumably the expectations for animal-paying tenants should all be increased by some unknown factor representing a greater-than-average longevity, and the expectations for money-paying tenancies decreased by a factor of similar magnitude. Almost certainly the factor would be more than 5 per cent.

Other evidence has suggested that the absolute and relative numbers of tenants liable to different types of heriot were changing during the period, and that animal-paying tenancies diminished while money-paying tenancies, and total tenancies, increased. This would affect the real 'expectations' systematically, those for animal-payers being tilted up at the beginning and down at the end; and conversely for money-payers, and overall. As the extent of the change is still conjectural, and the adjustment needed is straightforward, I have left this to the reader.

5. *Grain prices – see Tables 9.2 and 9.5*

The recorded wheat prices often differed from manor to manor. At the beginning of the period the highest average may be double the lowest. In the middle years the greatest differences amount to half the minimum; and at the end to one third. The differences may be caused by sales at different seasons in different manors as well as by local differences in harvests and price levels.

The average price of wheat before 1270 was just under five shillings. Thereafter the normal price seems to have been just over six shillings – i.e. about 25 per cent more. During the second decade of the fourteenth century wheat prices rose much higher, reaching seventeen shillings, and the average was nine shillings.

Local prices of different varieties of food-grains are apt to be correlated because they grow in like weather conditions, and because they are partial substitutes. Wheat prices are here used to indicate the level of the grain harvest in general, and it is of interest to consider these prices in relationship to the prices of other grains, as exemplified in Thorold Rogers' data. His figures for the period from 1260 show that wheat prices were more variable than barley, drage, or oats – oats prices being the least variable of the four. Barley prices are the most strongly correlated with those for wheat; suggesting that it was a close substitute (and also reflecting failures of both wheat and barley in cold wet seasons). The correlations between wheat prices and the price of drage, and oats, which does better in cold or wet years, were generally only about half as good.[36] During the first quarter of the fourteenth century, marked as it was by a series of disastrous harvests, all grain prices are highly correlated with those of wheat; drage and oats evidently serving as substitutes

[36] 'Half as good' in the sense that twice as much of the total variation in recorded prices is left unexplained.

for both wheat and barley. Thereafter the prices of drage and oats fell less than those of wheat and barley.

The correlations are high; but the level of local wheat prices must often be a very misleading indicator of the level of prices for other grains, having moved divergently from other grain prices. Substantial discrepancies of up to two shillings a quarter are likely to have occurred during two or three years in each decade. This limits the value of wheat prices for the present study; but enhances the significance of any correlation between wheat prices and heriots that analysis may disclose.

TABLE 9.5 *Correlations – direct, partial, and multiple – between prices of selected food and grains, 1260 to 1348, based on Thorold Rogers's data*

Type of correlation and kind of grain (1)	1260–70* (2)	1271–1300 (3)	1301–25 (4)	1326–48 (5)
Direct correlations r^2_{ab}				
Wheat and barley	0·02	0·81	0·86	0·84
Wheat and drage	0·00	0·60	0·87	0·72
Wheat and oats	0·01	0·66	0·89	0·69
Barley and drage	0·00	0·62	0·94	0·87
Barley and oats	0·09	0·78	0·80	0·85
Drage and oats	0·32	0·73	0·78	0·74
Partial correlations $r^2_{ab.cd}$.				
Wheat and barley	0·02	0·44	0·00	0·34
Wheat and drage	0·56	0·06	0·11	0·00
Wheat and oats	0·27	0·00	0·49	0·01
Barley and drage	0·03	0·00	0·64	0·38
Barley and oats	0·12	0·29	0·03	0·31
Drage and oats	0·33	0·30	0·02	0·00
Multiple correlations $R^2_{a(bc.)}$.				
Wheat with barley, drage and oats	0·57	0·83	0·94	0·84
Barley with drage and oats	0·12	0·79	0·95	0·93
Drage with barley and oats	0·34	0·73	0·95	0·87
Oats with barley and drage	0·40	0·85	0·80	0·85

In Thorold Rogers the dates appear as 1259 to 1347.
* Data generally scanty: those on drage prices relate to only six of the years before 1271.

6. *Heriots and wheat prices – see Table 9.3*

Part of the annual variation in the number of heriots must be accidental; and where the averages are small this accidental variation must be rather large in proportion to the annual totals. Moreover the payment of a money heriot was often delayed until after the harvest, and recorded in the next year. Many factors independently reduce correlations between the recorded numbers of heriots and the average recorded prices of wheat.

Nevertheless there is a clear correlation between wheat prices and money heriots, except between 1273 and 1292 and between 1342 and 1348. For the earlier period the money heriot figures are low and subject to sudden shifts: the later period was followed by the Black Death, which seems to have caused exceptionally high mortality among heriot-paying tenants on these manors: 50 per cent at least.

Only in the first quarter of the fourteenth century is there any apparent correlation between wheat prices and the number of animal heriots. This suggests that although the wealthier tenant was immune from the effects of ordinary fluctuations in harvests, failures of harvests as extreme as those of the first quarter of the fourteenth century led to higher deaths even among the more substantial villagers.[37] Apart from this quarter century, variation in the number of animal heriots seems to have been merely accidental.

The variation in the numbers of money heriots is much too great to be discounted in this way, and – in so far as the series can be regarded as statistically comparable – strongly confirms the view that this group was living near the margin of subsistence. The two reapers normally occupied the opposite ends of a demographic see-saw; when the harvest of corn fell the harvest of heriots rose.

7. Conclusion

The foregoing notes deal only with data so far extracted from the original rolls. From discussion with Professor Postan it is clear that there is still a great deal of information of potential demographic value to be gleaned from this source. It may later be possible to estimate the mortality on these manors with greater confidence and rigor than one can now.[38]

[37] (The partial correlations on) the data suggest that this enhanced mortality may have been due to increased disease in a generation of famines rather than to the direct effect of famine.

[38] *Reference*: J. E. Thorold Rogers, *A History of Agriculture and Prices in England* (Oxford, 1866).

10

SOME AGRARIAN EVIDENCE OF DECLINING POPULATION IN THE LATER MIDDLE AGES*

1

In recent years a number of economic historians, writing about England in the later Middle Ages, have tried to project their studies against a background of a relatively low or falling population. The projection has an obvious convenience. The alternating phases in the history of population – its rise in the earlier centuries, and its fall in the fourteenth and fifteenth centuries – fit well with what is becoming the accepted chronology of medieval development, and may indeed supply the most plausible explanation of the economic ebb and flow. Yet, in spite of its convenience, the projection is still very much of an hypothesis and is still apt to be questioned.[1]

Most historians may be prepared to accept as proven the high mortality of the Black Death and perhaps also the high mortality of the two or three lesser plagues which occurred within a generation of 1348. But they continue to differ about the exact rates of mortality during the plague and still more about the length of time medieval population took to recover. In general they are inclined to treat the period of pestilences as a temporary interlude in the continuous progression of English history. Thorold Rogers who knew his medieval facts (none of his contemporaries and very few of his successors knew them equally well), went furthest in trying to accommodate the assumption of growing population to the facts of the Black Death. This he did by presenting the years of the plague as a revolutionary interlude in English development. Population fell suddenly

* This article is based on a paper read at the Annual General Meeting of the Economic History Society on 27 May 1949 and appeared in *Econ. Hist. Rev.*, 2nd ser., II, 1950.

[1] M. Postan, 'Chronology of Labour Services' in *Trans. Roy. Hist. Rev.* (1937), vol. XX, and 'The Fifteenth Century' in *Econ. Hist. Rev.* (1939), vol. IX, no. 2, and see above Chapters 3 and 7; J. Saltmarsh, 'Plague and Economic Decline in England in the later Middle Ages', *Cambridge Historical Journal* (1941), no. 1; R. A. L. Smith, *Canterbury Cathedral Priory: A Study in Monastic Administration* (Cambridge, 1943); Marjorie Morgan, *The English Lands of the Abbey of Bec* (Oxford, 1946).

and steeply, and as a result, the whole economic and social structure of the medieval countryside tumbled down. Yet the population trends were not thereby upset. Whereas the manorial system of agriculture succumbed to the indirect effects of the Black Death and finally broke down, the direct effects of the Black Death on population were soon made good. By the fifteenth century population had recovered from the plagues, and by the time the first Tudor came to the throne England was again overflowing with Englishmen and Englishwomen.[2]

Other historians, and above all Miss Levett, were not prepared to allow a break even that short. In her view the mortality from the plague was not high enough to make a deep impression on either the society or the economy of the fourteenth century; in the parts of England she knew recovery was rapid and complete.[3] Allowing for Miss Levett's correction, the accepted view of the demographic trends has remained more or less in the shape Rogers gave it – rising throughout the Middle Ages, though broken for an interval of uncertain duration after the Black Death.

In this version the assumption of a rising trend has entered almost all the economic histories written before 1936 and 1937, and into some histories written since. Quite recently Clapham reproduced it in a manner characteristically both downright and cautious.

> An opinion often expressed, which is perhaps near the truth, is that the population of England and Wales doubled between 1100 and 1300; fell sharply with the Pestilence; and rose again to about its former maximum by 1500.

Still more recently Professor Kosminsky, in one of his infrequent sorties outside the bounds of the thirteenth century, has invoked the most telling arguments in the Russian armoury in defence of a largely similar position. A relatively low or a declining population would in his view be not only difficult to account for, but would also run counter to other facts of the later Middle Ages. In accordance with the inner logic of the dialectic process, the late fourteenth and fifteenth centuries must necessarily have been

[2] J. E. Thorold Rogers, *Six Centuries of Work and Wages* (1909), pp. 222 seq. Rogers expounded the same view with a greater emphasis in his controversy with Seebohm, *Fortnightly Review* (1865 and 1866).

[3] While Miss Levett was inclined to minimize the effects of the Black Death, she was apparently prepared to assume that medieval population in general was slowly declining in the later Middle Ages. This assumption of Miss Levett has, however, been overlooked and only her views upon the Black Death have made an impression. A. Levett, *Black Death on the Estates of the Bishopric of Winchester*, Oxford Studies in Legal and Social History, vol. v (Oxford, 1916), *passim*, especially p. 152. 'A clear distinction is drawn in the accounts of some manors between works which had been definitely 'relaxed', and those which were 'defects'. The 'defects' are generally not balanced by any increase of the rents of assize, nor, in many cases, of the leases; they speak rather of a gradual process of rural depopulation, which generally does not date back as far as 1349.' See also pp. 86 and 151.

an age of growth. Feudal forms of economic organization were doubtless breaking down, but manorial documents, being manorial, were bound to exaggerate the extent of the decline and to neglect new growth outside the manorial villages. And new growths – the cloth industry, the expanding towns, the rising number of free peasantry and proletariat – all belied the theory of a falling or a stable population.[4]

An opinion so virile as still to be avowed in 1948 and so plausible as to be held simultaneously by a Clapham and a Kosminsky obviously deserves serious examination, and some such examination will be attempted here.

2

The most orthodox and, from every point of view, the most satisfactory method of displaying population trends is by direct demographic measurement. Nothing short of frequent census or census-like enumerations would make it possible to reveal the long-term changes in population levels and also to measure the rates of change. Unfortunately, no such consecutive series is available for the Middle Ages. English medieval records abound with evidence capable of yielding demographic measurements to an extent undreamed of abroad, and since Matthew Hale's day repeated attempts have been made to wring from English medieval sources a complete enumeration of medieval population. Yet none of the demographers have so far succeeded in extracting from the records more than at most two independently based estimates of the total population; one for the end of the eleventh century, based on the Domesday Book, and another for the last quarter of the fourteenth century, based on the poll-tax of 1377. The estimates derived from these two sources have, of course, differed very widely, but even if historians agreed about them, there would still be no more than two figures separated by nearly 300 years of English history. There is no direct evidence on which to build estimates of total population in the intervening period; and what from the point of view of this paper is worse, there is no way of directly estimating the total population after 1377.[5]

[4] A. Levett, op. cit.; F. M. Page, *The Estates of Crowland Abbey: A Study in Manorial Organisation* (Cambridge, 1934); J. H. Clapham, *A Concise Economic History of Britain* (Cambridge, 1949), pp. 77–8; E. Kosminsky, 'Problems of English Agrarian History in the XVth Century' (Russian), *Voprosi Istorii* (1948), no. 3.

[5] The estimate for 1377 until recently accepted by most writers has been David MacPherson's (*Annals of Commerce* (1805), I, 584), who put the number at 2,500,000. The estimates for 1086 have been attempted by most students of Domesday statistics, but historians are most familiar with Maitland's 1,375,000 (*Domesday Book and Beyond* (Cambridge, 1897), p. 437). For a summary of these and other estimates, see J. C. Russell, *British Medieval Population* (Albuquerque, 1948), pp. 6–14.

In the absence of 'global' enumerations the demographer is thrown back on other statistical methods. There is enough evidence about the ages of medieval men participating in testamentary acts of various kinds or referred to in Inquisitions Post-mortem to enable an expert demographer to compute the changing expectations of life at different points in the Middle Ages and to compile from them the changing proportions of different age groups. In this way it is also possible to form some idea about the size of the average family or household and thus to discover 'multipliers' by means of which the lists of tenements and households in extents and elsewhere can be converted into numbers of individuals.

A study of this kind has in fact now been done. Professor J. C. Russell, an American historian, well equipped with the techniques of the demographer and acquainted with a wide range of medieval sources, has recently published a circumstantial and ingenious study, which carries the statistical discussion of medieval population problems to a point much further than any of his predecessors were able to reach. Using a rather low 'multiplier' he has re-calculated the population in the Domesday Book, re-computed the figures for 1377 and compiled a number of demographic devices for measuring population changes. In addition, he has compared the evidence of the thirteenth- and fourteenth-century extents, suitably treated by his 'multiplier', with the evidence of the Domesday Book, and has thereby demonstrated the expansion of population between the eleventh century and the middle of the thirteenth, and the decline of population for some time thereafter.[6]

Very little now remains to be added to what Mr Russell has been able to achieve by the methods he has chosen. It is not that his book contains all that can be said about the magnitude of medieval population and about its trends, or that all things he says will be accepted as established facts of medieval demography. Some of his conclusions will inevitably carry less conviction than others. Thus, students of agrarian history will be left with the impression that his chief evidence for the trend – surveys and extents – deserve a somewhat more discriminating treatment than he was able to give them, and that there was more in Miss Levett's argument against simple statistical use of extents than Mr Russell is prepared to concede. Similarly, his highly plausible discussion of the average family and household, by means of which he seeks to justify his 3.5 'multiplier' for the Domesday Book and the extents, still appears to overlook certain well-known fictions and silences of medieval tenurial accountancy, and moreover breaks down in periods of rapidly changing population. Above all, the quantity of material which Mr Russell has had to employ is so vast, and from his point of view so new, that he has not been

[6] J. C. Russell, op. cit. Professor Russell's figures for 1086 and 1377 are 1,110,000 and 2,250,000 respectively.

able to analyse it as carefully as the needs and the habits of medieval study demand. Minor transgressions of scholarship and faults of interpretation therefore abound. Yet, in spite of its imperfections, Mr Russell's study makes it unnecessary and impossible for anybody at the present moment to follow in his footsteps in the hope of putting him right. In the present state of medieval agrarian studies other students will find it no easier than Mr Russell to see through the statistical opacities of the sources, and, until this has been done, exploration by demographic methods will have to rest at the point to which Mr Russell has brought it.

Fortunately, the method of demographic statistics is not the only one whereby the problem of population trends can be attacked. So important must have been, and were, the effects of population changes on economic life that it is impossible to imagine them unreflected in the general body of economic evidence. The reflections will in fact be found everywhere. They will, of course, be too indirect to enable the student to measure the magnitude of the population changes, let alone to count up the population itself; yet they can be found in series sufficiently consecutive and sufficiently comparable to enable us to do what direct demographic methods cannot do, i.e. to form a judgement of the continuity and the duration of the trend.

3

Of the various categories of economic evidence capable of reflecting population trends the fullest and the clearest, as well as the most neglected, is that of wages. Payments to workers of every kind are recorded in vast numbers of medieval documents, and there is hardly a manorial account without them. And although the portion of the data so far studied is very small, and the portion published is smaller still, what has already been unearthed reveals an unmistakable tendency. Wages were rising throughout the greater part of the fourteenth and fifteenth centuries in a manner too uniform and too continuous to be wholly fortuitous. Thorold Rogers, who was the first to assemble English wage data and to view them with the eye of the economist, was greatly impressed by the high and rising level in the later Middle Ages. A record of rising wage rates equally suggestive has been built up by Lord Beveridge and others from the evidence of the estates of the Bishops of Winchester.[7] The present writer has also been able to assemble similar wage figures from the estates of Glastonbury Abbey, Peterborough Abbey and the Duchy of Lancaster, and from a large number of smaller estates all over England, as well as some disjointed figures of industrial wages from the accounts of the royal wardrobe and exchequer. When published they will bear out in full the

[7] J. E. Thorold Rogers, op. cit. I, 232–7; W. Beveridge, 'Wages in the Winchester Manors', *Econ. Hist. Rev.* (1936), vol. VII, no. I.

Rogers-Beveridge impressions of constantly rising wages. The trend can be fully seen in Table 10.1.

TABLE 10.1 *Daily wages of agricultural labour on the estates of Bishops of Winchester*

	Wheat prices				Wages		
	(1)	(2)	(3)	(4)	(5)†	(6)	(7)‡
Years	In silver pence	%	In grains of silver	%	Wages in silver pence	%	Wheat equivalents %
1300–19	7·00	100	1734	100	3·85	100	1·00
1320–39	6·27	89	1547	90	4·78	124	1·40
1340–59	6·30	90	1372	79	5·12	133	1·48
1360–79	7·56	106	1508	89	6·55	169	1·54
1380–99	5·58	80	1113	65	7·22	188	2·35
1400–19	6·35	90	1188	68	7·33	189	2·10
1420–39	6·55	93	1107	64	7·32	189	2·00
1440–59	5·65	80	926	53	7·29	189	2·36
1460–79	6·02	86	812	47	7·22	188	2·20

* The wheat prices are based on the data of Bishops of Winchester's estates, both those which Lord Beveridge kindly placed at my disposal and those independently collected by myself and 'worked up' in the same manner. The figures of wages are derived from Beveridge's 'Wages in the Winchester Manors', *Econ. Hist. Rev.* (1936), vol. VII, no. 1. A tabular and graphic representation of Thorold Rogers's figures will be found in G. F. Steffen, *Geschichte der Englischen Lohnarbeiter* (Stuttgart, 1901), vol. 1.

† Piece-rates per quarter of grain, threshed and winnowed.

‡ Product of columns 6 and 2.

The figures are clear enough. Expressed in the current silver coin of the realm agricultural wages rose without a break from the beginning of the century to the end of the first decade of the fifteenth and at that point they remained more or less stable for another fifty years. The real rise, however, must have been greater – both steeper and more continuous than the figures of wages in silver shillings reveal. For while wages were rising the price of wheat was gently falling, and the fall in prices continued beyond the point at which wage rates expressed in silver shillings were stabilized. As a result, the purchasing power of wages in terms of wheat rose between 1300 and 1480 by 220 per cent. The purchasing power of wages in terms of commodities other than wheat may or may not have risen in the same degree, for our knowledge of non-agricultural prices is as yet very imperfect.[8]

In detail the movements of wages require little more comment. The

[8] The figures probably underestimate the rise of wages in the years immediately following the passing of the Statutes of Labourers, for now and again the Bishop made a show of conforming to the law while in fact evading it. Beveridge, op. cit. p. 37.

spectacular rise in money wages occurred in the years immediately following the Black Death. The real wages in the same period did not increase to the same degree owing to a brief spell of very high agricultural prices on the morrow of the Pestilence. It is also possible that in the middle years of the fifteenth century the relatively smooth curve of rising wages conceals a number of short and divergent fluctuations reflecting the disturbed conditions in various parts of England during that period. In general, however, the main trend of real wages is one of continuous and uninterrupted progression.

An upward movement thus real and continuous, and yet largely confined to wages, must be accounted for by some 'real' changes in economy and society and not by monetary phenomena alone. Silver content of the English coinage was lowered by several stages, but wages rose and wheat prices fell even when measured in grains of silver. Nor is there any evidence, or any probability, of other monetary changes capable of raising the price of labour. It will be stressed again that the total volume of investment did not expand in the later Middle Ages, but most probably contracted; the proportion of bullion hoarded could not have declined; the velocity of circulation could not have risen. And even if monetary changes of this kind occurred, why should they have raised the price of labour and failed to raise all other prices? Can, then, historians point to an economic process outside the range of monetary phenomena to explain the continuous trend of rising wages?

The question will perhaps be easier to answer by eliminating the processes which, in theory, are capable of causing long-term changes in wage levels, but which in fact could not be expected to operate in the later Middle Ages. One such process easily suggests itself to modern economists. Economic historians of modern Europe take it for granted that the rise in the income of individuals in the last century and a half was due to the constantly rising total income of society. Would it then be similarly possible to account for rising wages by a concomitant rise in England's national product, or to be more exact (since the real wages are calculated in terms of wheat) by a constantly growing agricultural output?

This, indeed, might have been a plausible explanation in Cunningham's day; it will not carry conviction in our own. The tendency among economic historians now is to assume that national product and economic activity in general did not increase in the fourteenth and fifteenth centuries. What happened to English industry and trade in that period may still be open to argument and will again be referred to later. But by far the most important activity in England was agriculture; and about agriculture there is now little doubt. Output per acre may or may not have declined but it certainly did not grow. The evidence of manorial accounts shows that in the country as a whole average returns from lands under plough did not change much. And this, in its turn, suggests that real yields per acre may have been falling, since marginal lands were going out of arable cultivation.[9] But whether yields were declining or not, acreage under cultivation was shrinking at the very time when the wage rise was at its steepest. Manorial documents thus bear witness to the decline of agricultural output, and their testimony is supported by other facts. Exports of agricultural products apparently dwindled, and it is also probable that the internal market in foodstuffs contracted. If so, the rise of real wages is not to be accounted for by the pleasant possibility that there was more to go round.[10]

If the rise of real wages was not due to expanding real product, could it have been due to the changed distribution of such product as there was? Is it possible that a smaller proportion was now taken in taxation, or was received by independent cultivators, or was appropriated by merchants and landowners as rents and profits; and that a larger amount was therefore left to be distributed among the same, or perhaps even a rising, number of labourers? No one would of course dare to answer any of these questions with certainty. Distribution of income is still a subject on which medievalists prefer to discourse without much reference to facts and figures. One thing, however, is certain: such facts and figures as are available are sufficient to put out of court all notions of declining taxation. The king's share in the cake grew very fast in the early years of Edward III's reign, and, though it appeared to decline somewhat after the first phase of the Hundred Years War, it stayed throughout the late fourteenth and fifteenth centuries on roughly the same high level which it reached by the end of Richard II's reign.[11]

[9] Agricultural yields have formed a subject of a learned disputation between Sir William Beveridge, Mr M. K. Bennett and Mr Reginald Lennard. (See W. Beveridge, 'Yield and Price of Corn in the Middle Ages', *Economic History Supplement*, no. 2 (1927); M. K. Bennett, 'British Wheat Yield per Acre for Seven Centuries', ibid., vol. III, no. 10 (1935); R. Lennard, 'Statistics of Corn Yields in Medieval England', ibid. (February, 1936). See also idem, 'The Alleged Exhaustion of the Soil in Medieval England', *Economic Journal* (1922).) Allowing for Mr Lennard's warning against manorial evidence of yields, the conclusion of the discussion appears to be that the average yields reported in manorial accounts did not change much during the later Middle Ages.

[10] These and subsequent statements about the fortunes of English agriculture, where not supported by specific references, are based on the author's unpublished researches, but see N. S. B. Gras, *The Evolution of the English Corn Market from the Twelfth to the Eighteenth Century* (Cambridge, Mass., 1915), pp. 44, 64 and 111. Exports of foodstuffs from this country cannot be discussed with any certainty until more is known about foreign trade in the thirteenth century. The impression left by evidence of the customs of the fifteenth century is that the exports of foodstuffs were by then fitful and relatively unimportant, but cf. Thorold Rogers's references to exports of malt from East Anglia, op. cit. I, 289.

[11] Sir J. H. Ramsey's *A History of the Revenues of the Kings of England* (Oxford, 1925), vols. I and II, is a very imperfect guide to the budgetary problems of

Less is known but much can be guessed about the other sharers. Independent peasant producers had apparently improved their position. The main bulk of peasant produce did not go to the market and a very small part of their outlay took the form of wage payments. They were thus more or less insulated from the effects of both the low prices and the high wages. On the other hand, they were bound to benefit from fallings rents and land values in general, and the average sizes of their holdings apparently increased. Whether the total share of production falling to the class as a whole grew by as great an increment as the economic well-being of individual peasants, or whether it grew at all, depends of course on what happened to their total numbers, and this particular conundrum cannot at this point be discussed without begging the whole question of population. But there are grounds for thinking that the numbers of independent peasant producers did not greatly decline.

The one section of society who, as a group, may have received a lower income was the landlords. What with the fall in rents and in other payments for land and with the decline in the profits of demesne agriculture, the individual feudal landowner must have become poorer. So much poorer must some of them have grown that the class as a whole may have suffered a cut in aggregate income proportionally greater than the decline in national production. Yet great as was their impoverishment it could not possibly have resulted in transfers of income to other classes large enough to provide in, say, 1400 a body of labourers as numerous as they had been in 1300 with wages twice as high. The presumption, therefore, is that the number of labourers themselves was smaller; in other words, that the rise in wages was due not to there being more to go round, but to the shrinking numbers of men making up the 'round'.

4

This indeed is the conclusion to which the wage data inevitably lead. Labour became dear because, relatively to other factors of production, it had become scarce, and a growing labour scarcity argues for a declining population.[12] Yet before this argument can be clinched, another intermediate possibility must be cleared away. How far was the scarcity of

medieval England, but his main facts of royal taxation are sufficiently simple and straightforward. A full account of the rising exactions of the Crown in the early years of Edward III's reign will be found in the forthcoming study by E. B. Fryde. For Richard II's financial impositions see A. B. Steel's *Richard II* (Cambridge, 1941), *passim*. For the Lancastrian Kings, see J. H. Wylie's *History of England under Henry the Fourth* (1884–98), vols.. I–IV, *passim*. For Henry V, see idem, *The Reign of Henry V*, vols. I and II, continued as Wylie and Waugh, vol. III (Cambridge, 1929), *passim*.

12 Supplies of labour could of course decline in greater proportions than population as a whole. See pp. 210–11 below.

man-power in the later middle ages 'general'? Could it not have been confined to the one occupation to which our wage data mostly refer, i.e. to agriculture? Was it not in fact possible that whereas labour in villages and agriculture was getting scarcer, labour supplies in industry and towns were getting more abundant; that in other words labour supplies were being re-distributed? This in fact is the economic essence of Kosminsky's argument about the new growth outside the bounds of the feudal system. In accordance with this argument, towns and urban occupations were developing at a pace sufficient to absorb not only their proportional share of the country's total increment, but also an additional influx of rural labour large enough to create conditions of scarcity in agricultural villages.

The argument has a familiar ring, but its familiarity should not blind us to its, to say the least, hypothetical nature. One of the hypotheses on which it rests is that medieval labour became more mobile in the later middle ages than it had been in the twelfth or thirteenth centuries. No doubt the mobility of medieval labour was much greater than it once appeared to the German historians and economists responsible for the view of the Middle Ages as a period when economy was uniformly 'natural' and society uniformly servile. Historians nowadays realize that neither the continued settlement of the European interior nor the growth of the towns before the fourteenth century would have been possible without a great deal of wandering and migration. Yet the ease and the extent of the movements can easily be exaggerated. The range of migrations in medieval England, like that of migrations during the Industrial Revolution, was as a rule very short, and cross-country movements were few. They were certainly too few to prevent great regional differences in wage levels both in villages and in towns. What is more, such mobility as there was did not necessarily grow more perfect in the later Middle Ages. Serfdom and other legal obstacles to free movement may have declined, but what kept peasants at home was not only, and not so much, the legal tie of status, but the economic tie of property and occupation. And the proportion of men with property large enough to act as a tie grew in the fourteenth and fifteenth centuries, just as the proportion of landless proletariat declined. There is, therefore, nothing surprising in Lord Beveridge's discovery that the differences between the wages of artisans in London (or rather Southwark) and elsewhere grew wider in the later Middle Ages.[13]

The other assumption behind the arguments of 'new growth' is that

[13] Sir William Beveridge, op. cit. pp. 33–4; Thorold Rogers, ibid. pp. 171–2; D. Knoop and G. P. Jones, *Economic History* (1933), vol. II, no. 8, pp. 474–8. Rogers draws attention to the high wage rates in East Anglia, but accounts for it by greater industrial opportunities there. Were they any greater than in Hampshire or Wiltshire?

trade and industry in fact grew in the fourteenth and fifteenth centuries. Put boldly, the argument may sound plausible. Yet it is surprising how little it owes to established historical facts and how much it derives from ancient pre-suppositions of Victorian historiography. Medieval trade, like all things medieval, was expected to grow through centuries of history; and the general impression that England had been poor and small in 1086 and became great and famous in the modern era, lent conviction to the doctrine of growth. Things had to grow bigger and better from generation to generation if they were to end as big and as good as historians knew them to have been in Queen Elizabeth's time. This pre-supposition is, however, no longer tenable. The course of English trade and industry in the later Middle Ages may perhaps have been too uneven to be represented by a simple and smooth curve: some of its branches developed, while others decayed, and spurts of activity were followed by depressions. Yet, if generalize we must, a falling curve would fit into facts of English industry between 1350 and 1470 much better than a rising one. The broad outline is one of very slow decline frequently arrested but seldom reversed.

On a closer view it is of course possible to discern local oscillations, much sharper and more irregular than the main trend. Thus, trade in agricultural surpluses most probably dwindled in the late fourteenth century, but we do not know whether it continued to decline in the fifteenth. On the other hand, foreign trade in general, including the wool trade, while still buoyant in the fourteenth century, declined in the fifteenth. Similarly the cloth industry and cloth exports, having passed through some forty or fifty years of boisterous growth, entered in the fifteenth century a period of fifty or sixty years during which depression alternated with recovery. The course of other industries was apparently equally irregular. Thus building in stone never stopped, but there is no evidence that the level of activity in the building industry between 1350 and 1425 was any greater than in the late thirteenth and the early fourteenth centuries; and there is some evidence to suggest that it slumped after the Black Death and did not fully recover until the seventies of the fifteenth century.[14]

The notions of towns and town trade being able to compensate for the decline of agriculture fails to fit the general picture of English economy in the later Middle Ages. Nor does it fit such specific evidence of urban areas and populations as there is. Abroad, historians have been able to assemble a great deal of topographical data showing how in the later Middle Ages

[14] H. L. Gray, 'The Production and Exportation of English Woollens in the Fourteenth Century', *English Hist. Rev.* (1924), vol. XXXIX; idem, 'English Foreign Trade from 1446 to 1482' in Eileen Power and M. M. Postan, ***Studies in English Trade in the Fifteenth Century*** (1933).

settlement failed to fill the outer belts of urban territory and sometimes even retreated into the most ancient and narrowest lines of city walls. On the strength of this and other evidence a German historian has computed that the population of north German cities fell in the course of the fourteenth and fifteenth centuries by at least 25 per cent.[15] No such computation has been possible in this country, for the study of urban settlements and topography is still in its infancy. The English evidence of declining towns largely comes from somewhat suspect sources, and the most suspect of all are perhaps the facts alleged by the municipalities themselves. In the late fourteenth and fifteenth centuries most of the old corporate towns filled the air with protestations of poverty and with claims for reduction of royal taxes on grounds of depopulation. Unfortunately, the documents in which these plaints are most frequently recorded are parliamentary petitions, and it has become a convention among historians to disbelieve and disregard arguments alleged in medieval petitions to the Crown or to Parliament. In this case, however, scepticism may have been a little overdone, for grievances which were convincing enough to wrest from the Crown fiscal concessions (as many did) must be sufficiently real to command some respect even from historians. And if real, they must reinforce that impression of falling urban population which is also suggested by other miscellaneous evidence.

The actual movement of population in towns was of course a complex process, mostly discontinuous and sometimes compensated by local advances; and some of the local advances were so boisterous that in the absence of quantitative data they might well give the impression of a balance successfully redressed. Thus, while the population of most English towns fell after 1350, it may have grown, or at least remained more or less stationary, in London; and it may for a time have increased in the cloth-making centres of East Anglia, Yorkshire and the West Country.[16]

In general, the cloth industry must have compensated in some measure for decline elsewhere. The measure must not, however, be exaggerated. However generously estimated, the numbers engaged in the English cloth industry at its height could not possibly have accounted for more than an insignificant proportion of the rural population in the country. There are several ways of computing the numbers, but the simplest is to deduce them

[15] W. Abel, *Die Wüstungen des ausgehenden Mittelalters* (Jena, 1943), pp. 24–30.

[16] If Professor Russell is right in thinking that the rate of increase in urban population since 1086 was the same as in the country as a whole, the case for large-scale migration into towns in the earlier period would rest on the assumption that mortality in towns was much higher than in the countryside. Such evidence of urban increase after 1377 as he is able to assemble mostly rests on the evidence of 1545. Yet even that evidence does not support the impression of increased migration into towns. Indeed, Professor Russell is compelled to conclude that 'it is doubtful if as large a percentage lived in the boroughs in 1545 as in 1377' (Russell, op. cit. pp. 303–6).

from costs of production. The average price of broadcloth to the wholesaler in 1400 is reckoned at £3, though the average may have been not more than £1 15*s* if we are to believe H. L. Gray. At eight cloths per sack the cost of wool is reckoned at 15 shillings, though it was often much more than that; some good quality wool sometimes cost £8 per sack, and some cloths may have contained as much as 3 tods of wool or nearly ¼ of a sack. Nothing is reckoned for cost of other materials. Profits are reckoned at 5*s* or less than 10 per cent of the wholesale price, though they too were probably higher than that. All these exceedingly small allowances would leave for wages not more than about £1 15*s* per cloth, or rather less than the equivalent of fifteen weeks' earnings of a rural artisan. At the beginning of the fifteenth century, not more and probably less than 50,000 broadcloths were made per annum. Their equivalent in man-power therefore represented the work of not more than 15,000 fully employed persons, or little more than 0·65 per cent of the lowest of all the recent estimates of English population at the time of the 1377 poll-tax. And this computation in all probability errs on the side of generosity.[17]

Total employment in the cloth industry was thus small; additional employment, over and above the man-power of the cloth industry in the beginning of the fourteenth century, must have been smaller still, since some cloth industry had always been in existence. Moreover, the English cloth industry did not stay at its height throughout the fourteenth and fifteenth centuries. It expanded very rapidly in the second half of the fourteenth century and then entered into a long-drawn-out period, during which times of depression and recovery succeeded each other at frequent intervals. It was not until the late sixties or seventies of the fifteenth century that the late fourteenth-century levels of production were decisively overtaken and the industry resumed its uninterrupted progress. Thus, throughout the greater part of the fifteenth century the industry's ability to absorb the successive waves of migrants from other industries must have been very small. It would indeed be much more sensible to assume

[17] For prices of wool and cloth and equivalents of wool per cloth, see H. L. Gray, 'English Foreign Trade from 1446 to 1482' in Power and Postan, op. cit. pp. 7–13 and footnotes 27 and 33. Further allowances should be made for dyeing and chemical treatment after dyeing. In a piece of cloth of high quality the cost of the various finishing processes could amount to as much as 40% of the total costs. On the other hand, the labour costs of producing undyed and unfinished cloth were considerably lower. If it is true that English exports to the Continent in the fifteenth century were to an increasing extent made up of unfinished cloth, the fifteenth-century totals would represent even smaller equivalents of labour than computation in the text may suggest. See M. Postan, 'The Economic and Political Relations of England and the Hanse from 1400 to 1475' in Power and Postan, op. cit. p. 153 (and reprinted in M. M. Postan *Medieval trade and finance* (1973)). For another computation based on eight cloths per sack see H. L. Gray, 'The Production and Exportation of English Woollens in the Fourteenth Century', *English Hist. Rev.* (1924), XXXIX, 25.

that in some years reduced activity led to reduced employment, and the industry shed some of its man-power.

The main burden of the economic evidence is thus strongly against the hypothesis of new growths. The rise of wages in agriculture could not have been caused by the migration of labour to industrial centres, and by the resulting 'local' scarcity of labour in the countryside. This general conclusion is supported by what we know of the movement of industrial

TABLE 10.2* *Daily wages of artisans (pence)*

Years	(1) Carpenters	(2) Tilers	(3) Thatchers	(4) Masons	(5) Masons	(6) Average	(7) %
1300–9	2·82	3·11	2·20	2·93	2·75	2·76	100
1310–19	3·41	2·93	1·95	3·13	4·00	3·08	112
1320–9	3·39	3·01	2·08	3·27	3·75	3·08	112
1330–9	3·18	2·80	2·09	3·10	3·87	3·01	109
1340–9	2·96	2·87	2·21	2·89	3·50	2·89	105
1350–9	3·92	3·39	2·98	3·80	4·87	3·79	138
1360–9	4·29	3·88	3·00	4·13	5·37	4·13	150
1370–9	4·32	4·00	3·50	4·04	6·12	4·39	159
1380–9	4·40	4·00	3·11	4·00	6·00	4·30	156
1390–9	4·13	4·00	3·07	4·00	5·62	4·16	150
1400–9	4·64	4·00	3·67	4·29	6·00	4·92	178
1410–19	4·51	4·07	4·00	4·30	6·00	4·58	165
1420–9	4·52	4·00	4·00	4·31	5·50	4·47	162
1430–9	4·75	4·50	4·28	4·75	6·00	4·87	176
1440–9	5·18	5·00	4·50	5·15	6·25	5·22	189
1450–9	5·23	5·00	5·00	5·26	6·25	5·35	196

* The figures in this table with the exception of those for masons' wages are derived from figures published by Beveridge, see 'Wages in the Winchester Manors', *Econ. Hist. Rev.* (1936), vol. VII. The figures in column 4 relate to the Manor of Taunton alone. The figures in column 5 are Thorold Rogers's as tabulated by G. F. Steffen, op. cit. The figures of masons' wages, analysed by Knoop and Jones in *Economic History*, loc. cit., broadly agree with Steffen's index, even though they emphasize wide local variations.

TABLE 10.3 *Comparative indices of wages*

Years	Wages of artisans: In pence	Wages of artisans: In wheat	Agricultural wages in wheat
1300–9	100	100	100
1310–19	106	109	121
1320–39	110	121	140
1340–59	122	136	148
1360–79	155	147	159
1380–99	153	190	235
1400–19	173	192	210
1420–39	169	182	200
1440–59	193	241	236

wages. Tables 10.2 and 10.3 show that wages of artisans also rose in proportions and at a pace little different from wages of agricultural labour.

The tables show that on the estates of the Bishopric of Winchester and in those scattered places which supplied Thorold Rogers with his examples of payments the general level of artisans' wages was moving upward throughout the period. The process was of course less continuous and less uniform than summary tables can reveal. Here and there the rising trend may have been broken by lengthy recessions. Expressed in terms of wheat, wages appeared to be rising almost everywhere throughout the fourteenth century, but wages in current coinage slumped somewhat on the Bishop's estates in Hampshire and Wiltshire during the twenty or thirty years preceding the Black Death. On the other hand there is some evidence for the view that in certain regions not represented in the table, and more especially in the Home Counties, the slump may never have taken place and the money wages may have been rising more or less continuously since the second decade of the fourteenth century. There were also differences between occupations. On the manor of Taunton the wages of carpenters did not rise in the first half of the century at all, while the wages of masons did more or less without interruption.

Yet on a broad view the local and temporary variations are not such as to obscure the general outlines of a trend similar to that of agricultural wages. In the course of some 160 years wages in terms of wheat rose by some 250 per cent above their level in 1300. The corresponding rise of agricultural wages in the same period was 236 per cent. There is thus very little reflection in the wage statistics to substantiate the theory of a wholesale movement from agriculture to industry or from the country to the towns. At the risk of appearing excessively obvious it is worth stressing that a redistribution of labour capable of causing a relative scarcity in agricultural occupations would have assumed an initial level of industrial wages higher than those in agriculture, but rising thereafter more slowly than the wages of agricultural labour.[18]

This argument would not of course apply if it could be shown that investments mounted – and, what is more, continued to mount – to such

[18] At first sight the relevance of these tables to the movements from villages to towns may be questioned since the bulk of the evidence comes from the rural estates of the Bishops of Winchester. But on a closer view it will be noted that the most continuous of the series is that of Thorold Rogers's figures for the wages of masons, which are largely based on London and Oxford evidence. The masons' wages listed in Knoop and Jones, op. cit., are also urban in the main, or are derived from accounts of royal works. There is also a great deal of similar evidence about wages paid by the Bishop in Southwark. We do not unfortunately possess any study of cloth-workers' wages, but in so far as the amounts under the Statute of Labourers reflected real economic trends (and this they probably did) they reveal a rising trend of wages in the industry throughout the late fourteenth and fifteenth centuries.

an extent that carpenters, masons and tilers were becoming increasingly scarce in spite of all the influx of labour from agriculture. This is, however, highly improbable. Enough has already been said about economic activity in the later Middle Ages to indicate that the course of investment was the very opposite of inflationary. So also was the effect of changing investment on wages. Although the direct reflections of investment on wage rates cannot be clearly and separately distinguished, it is just possible to discern in the slump in the wages of carpenters and tilers on the eve of the Black Death the effects of falling agricultural investment. For that was a time when prices were low and manorial profits depressed. Yet on the whole the evidence of falling profits and investments in agriculture during that period is much more abundant and more unanimous than that of the slump in wages. Unmistakable signs of agricultural depression in the first half of the fourteenth century can be seen in a number of places such as the Duchy of Lancaster estates in the north and the east, the Peterborough estates in the east midlands, and various smaller estates in the Home Counties. Yet in none of these places is there any clear evidence of wages of artisans in the thirties and the forties receding to the same extent as on some of the Winchester estates. The presumption

TABLE 10.4* *Wages for skilled and unskilled artisans on some manors of the Bishops of Winchester*

Decades in fourteenth century	Tiler on the manor of Farnham	Tiler's helper on the manor of Farnham	Tiler as percentage of helper	Carpenter (on 8 manors) as percentage of labourer (on 7 manors)
00–9	—	—	—	188
10–19	4·69	2·19	214	183
20–9	4·00	2·05	195	179
30–9	3·84	1·90	102	179
40–8	2·71	1·56	174	159
49–59	4·24	2·84	149	138
60–9	4·00	3·00	133	132
70–9	4·06	3·00	135	136
80–9	4·58	3·08	149	131
90–9	4·81	3·03	159	125
Decades in fifteenth century				
00–9	4·95	3·00	165	131
10–19	5·09	3·54	144	122
20–9	5·22	3·78	138	118
30–9	5·00	3·83	131	123
40–9	5·07	4·00	127	126
50–9	5·17	4·00	129	130

* The data are Beveridge's. Ibid.

therefore is that the fall in investment, such as there may have been, was insufficient to counterbalance the effects of growing scarcity of man-power.

In this way the available series of artisans' wages strengthen the hypothesis of a 'general' rise, i.e. a rise not confined to agricultural labour alone. Indeed they may do more than that. Further analysis will disclose in our wage series at least one further symptom of what would now be described as overfull employment and of what in the context of this paper could only be considered as a result of declining population. In analysing his Winchester wage series Lord Beveridge drew attention to remarkable discrepancies between the movement of skilled wages and that of unskilled. Both rose, but the latter rose much more steeply: indeed so much more that by the end of the period the 'differential' between the two rates was in some places and occupations reduced by as much as three-quarters.

Writing as he did in 1936 Lord Beveridge could not do much more than suggest a number of likely causes, such as great diffusion of skill or improvements in training. But English observers in 1949, will not fail to recognise in the contracting differential between skilled and unskilled rates the symptoms of labour shortage. In modern conditions the phenomenon is sometimes accounted for by the tendency to 'dilute and upgrade' the learners and the semi-skilled when skilled labour is scarce. In general, when labour is scarce labourers find it easier to qualify for skilled rates of payment. In a manner still more general it can be argued that in times of full employment and of labour scarcity the 'hierarchy' of wage scales, established in times of 'unemployment' and abundant labour, is apt to be turned upside down. When supplies of labour are 'easy', the less eligible (i.e. the heavier, the dirtier, the less respected, and more open to direct recruitment from the countryside) is the occupation, the lower is the wage it commands. But when labour is scarce the less eligible the occupation the more difficult it is to recruit and the more likely it is to be depleted by promotion.

To what extent can the logic of a theory of wages in the post-war world be applied to facts of fourteenth and fifteenth centuries still remains to be seen. Even in England of 1949 its full rigour is apt to be moderated by lingering custom, collective agreement, legislation and what not; and obstacles to free labour contract were far more insuperable in the Middle Ages than they are now. Nevertheless, in some measure the logic must have applied; and in so far as it did, it helps to account for at least one significant symptom of labour shortage.

5

Another group of evidence, next in the order of clarity – though not necessarily in that of importance – is that of land values. In a society so predominantly agricultural and in an agricultural system so predominantly 'peasant' as those of medieval England, changes in population must *ex hypothesi* have had a direct effect on demands for land. It is now a generally accepted view among economic historians that the rising rents of the thirteenth century denote a growing population. Under the pressure of greater numbers internal colonisation made great headway. Not the whole of the pressure, however, found an escape-valve in new settlement, and the demand for land anciently settled and cultivated also grew and led to increases in rents and in other payments for land and its use.

So obvious was the connexion between population and rents in the earlier period that rising rents have themselves been used as evidence of growing population. On the same grounds a fall in rents and payments for land would justify a presumption of a falling population. For a number of foreign countries, in which a fall of this kind has been observed, such presumptions have in fact been made. Payments for land, both capital values and annual rents, appear to have been falling during long periods in the fourteenth and fifteenth centuries throughout Europe. Thus on the estates of St Germain-des-Prés, near Paris, rents fell without a break from 84*d* per *arpent* in the second half of the fourteenth century to 55*d* in the middle decades of the fifteenth and to about 30*d* in the seventies and eighties; and that in spite of the headlong fall in the value of the French pence itself. The proportions were not the same, but the process was equally clear and continuous in Sweden, Denmark, Norway and western Germany.[19]

The process emerges almost equally clearly from the evidence in this country. The fall in English land values shows most clearly in the payments which came nearest to economic rent, i.e. in payments for free leases or for freely negotiated 'farms' of demesne lands. A later study will, it is hoped, show that on the estates of the Duchy of Lancaster the terms on which farms were let, already on the decline in 1400, fell by another 20 per cent between 1400 and 1475; and the Duchy was, if anything, better off than the other great landlords. On the Bigod manor of Forncett in Norfolk, farms and leases fell from $10\frac{3}{4}d$ per acre in the seventies of the fourteenth century to 8*d* in the first half of the fifteenth century and to 7*d* in the second half of the fifteenth century. On the

[19] For a general summary of the evidence for falling land values abroad, see Johan Schreiner, *Pest og Prisfall i Senmiddelalteren* (Oslo, 1948).

Glastonbury estates in Somerset and Wiltshire leases declined in the course of the fifteenth century by at least 30 per cent.[20]

The corresponding decline, or indeed any decline at all, will not at first sight be noticed in the evidence of customary rents. Being customary, they were protected by the law of the manor and therefore appeared immobile. The immobility, however, was largely one of appearance, for a fall in customary payments, however disguised or delayed, came in the end to most estates. It could take two forms. In the first place, the entry fines payable at the beginning of each customary tenancy could be used by landlords to compensate for their inability to vary the annual dues. On estates at the Abbey of Glastonbury, the entry fines, having risen from less than a pound per virgate in the early thirteenth century to £5 and more in 1345, began to fall again after that date and were reduced to small nominal payments by 1450.[21]

In the absence of records it is difficult to trace the same movement with equal clarity everywhere, and it is possible that on some estates entry fines were not used for the same purpose. But one of the reasons why the fall in the values of customary holdings did not always express itself in lower entry fines is that it almost always led to another and a very familiar change in customary terms. This change is sometimes described as commutation of services, but from the economic point of view commutation was merely one of the many ways of lightening the terms on which customary lands were being re-let. The general impression is that in the second half of the fourteenth and the first half of the fifteenth centuries tenements burdened with heavy dues could not as a rule be re-let except by altering, i.e. by improving, the terms of the contract other than the money rent itself. Agreement to commute was one such improvement; more liberal redefinition of services was another. Sometimes even these alleviations were insufficient, and customary holdings stood vacant.

6

The mention of vacancies brings us to the best known but also to the most difficult and ambiguous group of evidence. The shrinkage in the area effectively occupied is one of the best established and most frequently described features of the later Middle Ages, and is the exact counterpart

[20] F. G. Davenport, *The Economic Development of a Norfolk Manor, 1086–1565* (Cambridge, 1906), pp. 60 and 71.

[21] Miss Levett finds it difficult to discover whether on the Winchester estates the fines were raised or lowered, because 'the pre-pestilence fines were so disproportionate', op. cit. p. 122. A more detailed comparison with thirteenth-century fines would nevertheless have revealed a general decline of entry fines. On the St Albans estates studied by her the fall is indicated by the tabulated evidence. At least 36 out of 330 new tenants were admitted without any fines. A. E. Levett, *Studies in Manorial History* (Oxford, 1938), pp. 256–85.

of the evidence commonly adduced to prove the rise of population in the earlier Middle Ages. It has already been mentioned that historians of continental countries have connected the known facts of internal colonization with increasing populations. *Mutatis mutandis* the picture of declining population which the historians abroad are apt to draw is, as a rule, derived from the facts of what perhaps should be described as 'de-colonization'; migration to distant lands arrested, fields and holdings in countries both old and new abandoned, villages depopulated, towns shrinking. The study of abandoned holdings, or, to use the German term, *Wüstungen*, has gone furthest in Germany, and most of what is known about it has recently been summarized in a well-argued essay by a German economic historian. But a great deal is also known about the vacant or waste lands and tenancies in various parts of France in the late fourteenth and fifteenth centuries, and more recently a great deal has been done to bring together similar evidence for Denmark, Sweden and Norway. In general it appears that the lands described as deserted or abandoned formed by the middle of the fifteenth century a very large proportion of the total area once in occupation – as much as 50 or 60 per cent in parts of western and southern Germany. Historians of course realize now that these crude figures cannot be taken at their face value and that they are subject to a number of corrections; but, however discounted, they form a formidable corpus of evidence of the declining rural and urban population.[22]

English evidence of 'de-colonization' is not quite equal to the continental. It is not that direct and simple references to lapsed tenancies and abandoned land are lacking. The contemporaries obviously believed that they were living in an age of contracting settlement, and there is no reason why we should not accept their belief at its face value. Yet when it comes to measuring the extent of the vacancies or to estimating their economic and social effects, the data at once become too difficult even for the shrewdest of students.

The easiest to interpret is the urban evidence, such as there is. The difficulties are mostly those of darkness, not those of confusion, and are due to the poverty of the evidence so far assembled and not to its ambiguity. It will bear repeating that in this country the historical topography of medieval towns is still a very youthful subject, and its achievements are still very meagre. But such evidence that has been brought to light, e.g. that of Lincoln or Northampton, corresponds very closely to continental examples, and does not present any difficulties of interpretation.

Not so the evidence of contracting settlement in the countryside. Most of it comes from entries in bailiff's accounts recording the so-called *decasus*

[22] Abel, op. cit. pp. 18–22.

redite, i.e. the deductions from their liability to the landlords which the bailiffs claimed for the rents no longer due from holdings no longer in the hands of their tenants. The entries are very common in the manorial accounts of the late fourteenth and fifteenth centuries and should leave no doubt about the contracting area of medieval settlement and cultivation. They cannot, however, be added together to form an estimate of the decline. To begin with, some decays of rent, especially the earlier ones, did not result from contracting cultivation. In the earlier period the *decasus redite* could sometimes be a sign of rising demand for land. At the very height of the agricultural boom of the thirteenth century manorial lords occasionally tried to enlarge their demesnes at the expense of their tenants; when they succeeded, the transactions would as often as not be described in the accounts by an entry of the *decasus redite*. Thus, when in 1314, an account of Rolleston, a Staffordshire manor of the Earls of Lancaster, records that out of the £23 due for free leases £6 was 'decayed' because a number of tenements had been drawn into the demesne and its park, the situation is exactly the opposite of what was to happen on some Lancaster manors fifty years later when the lords were unable to let their lands on old terms, and rents 'decayed' in consequence.

TABLE 10.5 *Decayed rents on some Glastonbury manors*

	1353 £ *s* *d*	1366 £ *s* *d*	1368 £ *s* *d*	1381 £ *s* *d*
Walton	—	—	3 14 5	3 15 0
Street	0 9 3	2 13 4	—	—

	1395 £ *s* *d*	1405 £ *s* *d*	1448 £ *s* *d*	1452 £ *s* *d*
Walton	6 7 4	4 1 4	—	9 7 9
Street	—	5 5 4	12 9 2	—

This distinction must be borne in mind in dating the beginning of rural depopulation, though it need not complicate the study of the process in its later stages. From 1350 onwards transactions like that of Rolleston occurred very seldom, if ever at all, while the *decasus redite* signifying true decay mounted with a consistency truly remarkable. Very clear statistical examples, for reasons presently to be mentioned, are not perhaps easy to find, but Table 10.5 gives the figures for the Glastonbury manors of Walton and Street for which the figures happen to mean more or less exactly what they purport to represent.

If the corresponding entries in the accounts of other manors are not cited here wholesale and not presented in aggregate, it is because most of them, unlike the figures for Walton and Street, cannot be taken at their face values. In the first place they were apt to be recorded on a basis too inconstant to permit the construction of a single statistical series. In a typical manorial account, the accounting officer – reeve, or bailiff – was 'charged', i.e. held responsible for rents and labour services as listed and defined in an earlier survey or rental. This meant that at any given point of time the *decasus redite* represented not the accumulated decline in the yield of rents, but only the difference between the actual yield and the amounts which happened to be recorded as due in the most recent rental. And as surveys and rentals were periodically adjusted to keep pace with falling yields (and in the late fourteenth and fifteenth centuries rental and surveys were as a rule adjusted downwards), the bailiff's liability for rent declined from revision to revision. To this extent therefore the figures of decays recorded in manorial accounts in any given year are apt to underestimate the decay which had taken place over a longer period.

On the other hand, the decay of rents as given in manorial accounts at times also contains an element of exaggeration, and it is of this feature that historians like Miss Levett have been most conscious. The figures of decay are *gross*, i.e. they do not allow for countervailing revenues, i.e. for revenue from holdings which were being added to the settled area at the same time as other holdings were being abandoned or for such revenue as the 'vacant' holdings could still be made to yield. At no time, not even within a few years of the Black Death, was agricultural stagnation so utter and the decline so universal as to prevent a landlord or a tenant here and there from adding odd pieces of reclaimed land to the areas previously under cultivation. What is even more important is that some of the lapsed lands were sooner or later re-let or put to other economic use capable of bringing in some revenue. For all these reasons only a close study of the areas of lands in the hands of the lord with the areas re-let, and of the uses to which lands newly re-let had been put, can reveal the true extent of declining occupation. And unfortunately very few manorial accounts contained the data for reliable comparisons of areas and uses.

The chief difficulty of interpreting the evidence is that very little land – none but the poorest – need have remained vacant as long as the landlord was prepared to let it on lower terms. The true measurement of the decline must therefore be sought in the figures of the lord's total revenues and in the figures of the average sizes of peasant holdings. The former have already been discussed; the latter cannot be finally settled until more has been done about the economy of peasant landholding in the later Middle Ages. The overwhelming balance of probability, however, is that in the later fourteenth and fifteenth centuries the average size of peasant holdings increased, and more will be said about this presently.

7

Where evidence is so ambiguous and so complex, historians often find it difficult to interpret it without misunderstanding the very nature of the economic and social facts to which it relates. A misunderstanding of this kind is largely responsible for Miss Levett's story of the Black Death on the estates of the Bishops of Winchester. Her study of the manorial accounts of a group of the Bishops' manors revealed that holdings left vacant after the Black Death were re-let within a few years and that there could not be any question of decline in either settlements or population. This particular conclusion has been repeatedly re-echoed in historical writing, and moreover typifies a method of argument common in medieval scholarship. It may therefore call for a more detailed examination even at the cost of a slight digression.

An unfortunate feature of much current writing on medieval history is that writers are often apt to see the economic and social problems of the Middle Ages with a vision unencumbered with theoretical concepts, whether economic, sociological or demographic. This has undoubtedly saved their books from aridities and technicalities similar to those which legally trained historians have imported into some recent writings on constitutional and legal history; it may above all have saved them from the dreadful sin of looking for modern phenomena in medieval situations. But this freedom from the vices of technicality and anachronism may well have been bought at too high a price, for it has been responsible for the air of inconsequence which pervades some of the studies reputedly economic.

Miss Levett's study – otherwise a masterpiece of detailed history – shows some inconsequence in the very choice of its manorial sample. Miss Levett confined her investigations to the group of highly profitable manors situated on the wealthy agricultural areas of Hampshire, Wiltshire and Somerset, and deliberately excluded the less profitable estates further north which had provided one of her predecessors, Miss Shillington, with the bulk of her evidence. It is not therefore surprising that Miss Levett's manors, unlike Miss Shillington's, still earned profits high enough to maintain them through the crisis more or less intact, or that on her manors relatively little land appears to have remained vacant for any length of time. What is surprising is to find that Miss Levett herself and the historians who used her work should for some reason have decided that her sample was more relevant to the problems of England's settlement and population than Miss Shillington's. Had they been mindful of the order in which lands could be expected to go out of occupation, they might perhaps have reversed Miss Levett's choice and paid greater attention to what happened on Miss Shillington's marginal, and, for that very reason, more significant sample.[23]

This does not of course mean that even within Miss Levett's sample her facts prove all that has been read into them. To conclude that, with all holdings re-let, population must have returned to its pre-pestilence level assumes without much justification at least two important conditions. It assumes that before the Black Death the reservoir of all-but-landless would-be tenants was not large enough to fill the gaps in the ranks of customary landholders. It also assumes a so-to-speak *postquam* condition that at the end of the period of adjustment, i.e. after the lapsed holdings had been re-let, land was distributed as before; that holdings were of the same size; that the number of men without holdings was the same; that the lapsed holdings were re-let on old terms. In other words, it entails the assumption that demand for land had not changed.[24]

In order to make these assumptions or to examine them, a far more perfect series of surveys and rentals is necessary than has in fact survived from Miss Levett's estates. But there is sufficient general evidence both there and elsewhere to suggest that the conditions cannot and must not be assumed. If the state of the Bishop's manors at the end of the thirteenth century was anything like that of the contemporary Wiltshire and Hampshire estates of the Abbots of Glastonbury or of the Duchy of Lancaster, or in areas described in the Hundred Rolls of 1273, then the smallholders and cottagers of every type must have equalled and even outnumbered the core of full-fledged customary tenants, i.e. holders of whole virgates or half-virgates. The corresponding figures for the six main manors of Glastonbury Abbey in the Isle of Avalon were: 260 for full-fledged customary tenants and 350 for holders of 5 acres and less of whom 150 and perhaps more were cottagers. As for the regions covered by the Hundred Rolls, Professor Kosminsky has shown that out of some 13,500 peasant holdings listed by him, more than 6450 or 46 per cent were of quarter-virgate and less, and to this number the landless labourers who did not figure as holders must be added.[25] On estates thus made up

[23] *V.C.H. Hampshire*, vol. v. Miss Levett, op. cit. p. 146.

[24] There is a curious arithmetical omission in Miss Levett's treatment of the lord's revenue from vacant holdings. In trying to estimate the loss to the lord she compares only the rents of the holdings before the vacancy with the rents they produced on re-letting and makes no allowance in the computation (though she does in the text) for loss of labour services and other similar dues. When the value of labour services at their rather low customary valuation is included, the fall in value on new re-lets becomes very drastic indeed. On the Manor of Taunton it may at times have been as high as 75%. A similar computation by Miss Davenport suggests that on the Manor of Forncett the fall was about 60%, i.e. from about 2*s* per virgate to about 10½*d*. Levett, op. cit. p. 83; Davenport, op. cit. pp. 60 and 71.

[25] E. A. Kosminsky, *Studies in English Agrarian History of the Thirteenth Century* (Russian) (Moscow, 1947), chap. v, especially p. 286. Elsewhere Professor

a mortality of 50% and even a permanent diminution of the population to that extent would still have left enough men in the queue for tenancies to fill all gaps among the virgators and semi-virgators. Only in places where mortality was as great as it appeared to have been on the Eynsham manor of Wood Eaton, where only two customary tenants of virgates appear to have survived, would the local reservoir of population fail to supply tenants for the lapsed holdings. But on manors as badly hit and as sparsely settled as these, Miss Levett would not have found the other signs of recovery she discovered on the richer manors of the Bishopric of Winchester.[26]

There is even less reason for assuming the second – the *postquam* – condition. The main group of customary holdings on the Winchester manors may all have been taken up by 1360 (they were not all taken up on most other estates), but there is no reason for supposing that the average customary holdings were now the same size as before. On the Eynsham manor of Wood Eaton, already referred to, the survey of 1360 describes a holding of a semi-virgator which had lapsed into the hands of the lord. The tenement was now re-let, but in the process of re-letting was merged with another tenement to form a virgate (*adjunguntur tenemento Dolle et sic efficiebatur virgatarius, nam ante fuit semi-virgatarius*).[27]

Entries equally explicit were not, however, very frequent, and on the whole it was not among customary virgators that the most conspicuous changes in the size of holdings were to be found. The elements of village population whose numbers and whose holdings were affected most were outside the main body of customary tenants. They were mainly the small-holders who had previously supplied wage labour for the lord and for his more substantial tenants. The evidence of their numbers sinking will be found in nearly every manor for which comparable evidence for both the early fourteenth and the fifteenth centuries is available. It will be found even in areas like those of Sussex Weald, as represented by the Pelham estates, in the uplands of Lancashire as represented by the manors of the De Lacys and the Earls of Lancaster, or in the woodlands of Essex and Herts: all of them places where agricultural expansion continued well after it had ceased elsewhere. Altogether on 130 manors spread over sixteen counties tenements of less than five acres declined in the later Middle Ages to the extent of nearly 35% whereas the number of other holdings declined by not more than 10%.

Kosminsky has pointed out the still greater preponderance of smallholders on the East Anglian Manor of Brampton, where he has also noted an increase in the relative proportion of more substantial tenancies in the later Middle Ages. E. A. Kosminsky, 'Manor of Brampton from the 11th to the 16th Century' in *Srednie Vieka* (The Middle Ages) (Moscow, 1946), vol. II.

26 H. E. Salter (ed.), *Eynsham Cartulary* (Oxford Historical Society Pub.) (Oxford, 1908), II, 19.

27 Ibid., p. 20.

The reason why the numbers of smallholders and all but landless cottagers fell more than the numbers of other customary tenements should not be difficult to discover. Vacant holdings of larger sizes were now available in larger numbers; payments were now smaller; entry fines often declined. The whole village population was thus given the opportunity for a general 'upgrading', and, as a result, the lower ranks were depleted twice over – through a fall in the population as a whole and through absorption into the ranks above them.

If this interpretation of the evidence proves to be correct, it may in part account for the remarkable rise in wages, and it may also warn the student from too simple a use of wage statistics as a measure of the population trend. They do much to prove that a trend there was, but they probably exaggerate its magnitude. For, as a result of twofold depletion, the numbers of men available for wage-labour must have fallen much faster and more steeply than population as a whole; and their wages soared higher than they would otherwise have done. But by the same token the numbers of customary virgators and semi-virgators could not possibly have declined with the rest of the village population. In the conditions of the later fourteenth and fifteenth centuries stable numbers of customary tenants merely denote a combination of a falling population with an upward movement in the social scale. No wonder students like Miss Levett who aproached the problem from the point of view of lord's villeins found the decline of population masked by the promotion of lower ranks into those of full-fledged villeins.[28]

8

The digression about the Black Death on the estates of the Bishops of Winchester brings this survey of evidence to a close. Other economic evidence can no doubt be found, and further study is also bound to reveal more pitfalls and perhaps more meaning in the evidence so far surveyed. Yet it can be doubted whether future discovery will do much to shake off the general impression of a declining population.

[28] The evidence in the Bishopric of Winchester records is not sufficient for a comprehensive summary of what happened to the smaller tenancies. Hence the ambiguities in Miss Levett's treatment of the post-pestilence numbers of smallholders. On the whole she notes that the numbers of smaller tenancies declined in greater proportion than those of the larger ones (op. cit. p. 82), but she does not appear to bring this fact into her argument. She might have done so had she lived to complete her study of the estates of St Albans Abbey. There the peasant holdings were also taken up, but the lists of successors are most revealing. Out of the 491 new lettings after the Pestilence at least 130 and possibly more went to 'strangers' and collateral heirs (sisters, brothers, etc.) and 168 to minors. A. E. Levett, ***Studies in Manorial History***, pp. 256–85. The minors' land was, of course, let to others, or went to swell the effective holdings of their guardians.

This impression in some respects agrees with the conclusion of recent demographic study. It differs from Professor Russell's account mainly in the broad limits of its chronology. In his book Professor Russell carefully avoids too clear a demarcation of the period during which medieval population fell or stagnated. On the whole he appears to date the beginning of the decline with the Black Death and its end somewhere very early in the fifteenth century though he is sufficiently careful and well-informed not to exclude the possibility of a population fall beginning much earlier and ending much later. Professor Russell's chronology, however, is not an essential part of his argument, for the simple reason that his evidence cannot be easily made to yield any recognizable chronological landmarks. It has already been pointed out that the only firm dates in his evidence are those of 1086 and 1377. The rest are statistical constructions showing some growth after 1086 and some decline by 1377, but revealing very little about the dates by which the growth broke and decline began, and less still about the direction of the change between 1377 and the middle of the sixteenth century.

It is at this point that the agrarian evidence, however indirect, can offer something which direct demographic study has so far been unable to do. Although none of our figures – not even those of wages – can give a true measure of demographic changes, they are sufficiently well dated to provide us with a number of fixed points on the time scale.

In the first place, the data of wages and those of rents and vacancies agree in placing the beginning of the decline somewhere in the first twenty years of the fourteenth century. What makes the data all the more certain is the continental evidence, for there too the turning point in employment and occupation of land comes in the first quarter of the fourteenth century. Much less certain are the dates, and indeed the entire nature of the trend, in the fifteenth century. The low or falling wages and the low or falling rents persist until the later sixties or the early seventies, but in some fields, mainly commercial and urban, the turning-point may have arrived earlier than in rural society. The evidence of wages and of land values makes it impossible to say whether the relatively high levels of *c.* 1540 resulted from a steep rise in population after 1470 or whether they were the product of a cumulatively slow growth reaching back into the middle of the fifteenth century. It is even difficult to tell from our evidence whether the indices of 1400–50 reflected the continued fall in population or merely a growth so slow as to be unable to influence the volume of employment, level of wages and the area under cultivation. What is most probable is that the main trend in the first sixty years of the fifteenth century, whether falling or rising, was not a very pronounced one, and was moreover broken by a number of sharp oscillations.

When it comes to oscillations, the difference between the fifteenth century and the fourteenth is merely one of degree. To judge from wages alone the decline of population in the first two decades of the fourteenth century was in some parts of the country arrested in the thirties and forties. Then came the great drop of 1348–9, succeeded by slow recovery of values and numbers and a slight check on wages in the fifties. The sixties, with their successive pestilences in 1361 and 1369, brought the population down again. The eighties and nineties saw some recovery in industry and agriculture and so did also the early years of the fifteenth century, but whether they were also years of rising population seems very uncertain. Judging from the evidence of cultivated areas and that of wages, the second and third decades of the fifteenth century were years of general recovery and the succeeding three decades were years of declining economic activity and population.

This chronology, if true, will make it difficult to hold on to some of the more obvious explanations. Hitherto, historians who believed in the fall in population after the Black Death were able to account for it by the known facts of the Black Death itself. Professor Russell and others have extended the explanation by calling in the smaller epidemics of 1361 and 1369. But a tendency which began some thirty years before the Black Death and continued to be felt for another hundred years cannot be accounted for by pestilence alone. Other causes, hidden in the very foundations of medieval existence, may have to be drawn upon to explain what pestilences cannot. Historians may be called upon to lay bare the essential processes of a society held in by physical or, if the term is used in a broad sense, Malthusian checks. As in all studies of this kind they may be able to find explanations of later decline in the conditions of previous growth. Both the prizes and the penalties of rapid expansion in the social and technical conditions of the thirteenth century may have to be appraised. Thus appraised, they may show how the honeymoon of high yields was succeeded by long periods of reckoning when the marginal lands, no longer new, punished the men who tilled them with recurrent inundations, desiccations and dust storms. Further study may reveal other causes, even more significant, springing from the revolutionary and irreversible changes in the constitution of the family in times of agricultural expansion. Other possibilities will also suggest themselves to questing minds. It is not the object of this paper to enumerate them, still less to answer them; its object is merely to put the problems on the agenda of economic history.

11

VILLAGE LIVESTOCK IN THE THIRTEENTH CENTURY*

1

Much less is known about animal husbandry of medieval England than about its arable agriculture, and what is known is mostly confined to the sheep flocks and vaccaries on the lords' demesnes. Current ideas about the village animals and about the contribution they made to peasant budgets are little more than inferences from what historians happen to know about demesne livestock or about farming practices of the seventeenth or eighteenth century. They bear no relation to medieval facts for the simple reason that no facts or figures have so far been established.

Needless to say our sources are to blame. Being predominantly manorial they do not touch upon the possessions of the villagers except at points at which they affect the lord's rights or income. We may be told about dues for herbage or agistment; about pannage of pigs; about the villagers' payments for the right to fold animals on their own land; or about fines imposed upon them for transgressions on lords' pastures. Some of these payments are often customary and conventionalized, but even where they happen to represent real and fluctuating annual impositions they invariably relate to some, but by no means all, the animals in a village, and leave us in the dark about the size or distribution of village flocks and herds in their entirety.

The darkness, however, is not wholly impenetrable. A student of medieval economic history on the look-out for sheep and oxen will in the end be able to assemble a collection of documents capable of yielding some tangible facts about the village livestock. One such small collection is presented here. Its *pièces de resistance* are three or four surviving assessments for royal taxes, but it also contains certain exceptional documents of manorial origin, and in the first place the returns of tithes for Meon Church in Hampshire. However, the very mention of royal assessments will be sufficient to indicate how selective the collection must be and how important it is to make sure of its trustworthiness before setting out to extract from it the relevant facts and figures. Of the very considerable number of taxation records containing evidence of villagers' possessions

* This paper first appeared in *Economic History Review*, 2nd ser., xv, 1962.

I have chosen three assessments: that of the Hundred of Blackbourne for 1283, that of parts of South Wiltshire for 1225, and that for the *banlieu* of Ramsey for 1291. These are the only three assessments the veracity of which I have been able to establish. They have been tested by their internal evidence as well as by that of the contemporary manorial documents, and the relevant argument has been set out in detail in the remainder of this section. The reader not wishing to be delayed by this preliminary argument, and prepared to take the evidence of the assessment on trust, will be advised to proceed straight to section 2.

The first and the most important of the assessments to be tested here is the return of the collectors of the 'thirteenth' of 1283 for the double Hundred of Blackbourne in Suffolk. The circumstances of this tax are well known and do not require recapitulating in detail. The collectors for the county of Suffolk were appointed in 1283 and were apparently expected to deliver the proceeds to the Constable of the Tower by 13 October, though in fact they may not have completed their operations until the early months of 1284. The L.T.R. Enrolled Accounts contain the full statement of the proceeds of the tax by counties which have been published by Mr Edward Powell in 1910.[1] The detailed assessments, however, have not survived except for the Hundred of Blackbourne and the town of Ipswich. The Blackbourne returns, with some other associated documents, have been published by Mr Powell.[2]

The tax was on moveable goods above the limit of half a mark, excluding treasure, riding horses, bedding, clothes, vessels, capons, hens, bread, wine, beer and cider, and all kinds of food ready for use. In the event the tax was levied almost entirely on the villager's livestock and on the grain found in their possession or sown on their land, but not yet gathered as a crop.

Even a superficial comparison with other tax assessments of the same area will be sufficient to show that the assessment of 1283 was much more comprehensive, i.e. netted in more households and persons, than almost any other pre-nineteenth century assessment for tax known to historians. The total number of taxpayers assessed in 1283 was 1393. The assessment for the subsidy of 1327, one of the most complete assessments extant, lists in the same villages not more than 803 taxpayers, even though the exemption limit for that tax, at 5*s*, was well below the exemption limit of 1283. The surviving assessment for the subsidy of 1560–8 lists in the same area only 368 taxpayers, but in this case the exemption limit – £3 in goods or £1 in annual value of land – was higher than in 1283

[1] E. Powell, *A Suffolk Hundred in the Year 1283* (Cambridge, 1910), p. xiv.

[2] P.R.O. Lay Subsidies 242/41. As reference to the original MS. was made necessary by the need to have the transliteration of names verified, I also decided to re-transcribe the figures as well. Hence the discrepancies – very slight – between some of my totals and those computed by Mr Powell.

even allowing for the intervening rise in prices. For the Hearth Tax of 1674 the assessors listed all the houses in the Hundred. The returns bear every superficial sign of being complete, since they include some uninhabited and ruined houses. Some of the houses – about 15 per cent – were shared by more than one family; on the other hand the assessment of 1674, unlike that of 1283, purported to include every family, however poor, and in fact lists a number of pauper families in receipt of poor rate ('the poor that receive collection'). Yet the total number of houses is 1077, or some 30 per cent less than the number of households assessed in 1283: a margin more than sufficient to allow for the houses sheltering several households. Strange as this may seem to the orthodox or to the uninitiated, the excess of 1283 figures over later ones may in part be accounted for by the fact that population in 1283 may have been denser than in the sixteenth and seventeenth centuries; but the same explanation will not apply to the assessment of 1327. We must therefore conclude that the 'coverage' of 1283 was better, i.e. fuller, than that of any other surviving taxation document of the Hundred.[3]

The administrators of the assessment tried to make it not only comprehensive but also accurate, for the returns bear the marks of careful supervision. The original assessment was revised at least once, and 'increments' were added to some of them after auditing, with the result that the text of the assessment is scored with repeated erasures, corrections and emendations. We learn, for instance, that the tax list for the village of Walsham le Willows had been returned from the Exchequer in order that the grain sown in the autumn should be included, as it should have been if the instructions had been faithfully observed.

The assessment also contains other internal evidence of its verisimilitude. One such piece of evidence is the assessment of the juries. The returns for some of the villages give names of the local jurors and collectors (*tassatores*). These appear to have been composed of representatives of the wealthy, the poor and the middling sections of the village population, who were taxed accordingly. In Wattisfield one of the jurors, Robert le Grop, had his goods valued at £4 14*s*, one of the highest in the village; two others, Ric. Aylmer and Adam Mercion, were valued at the near average sums of £1 5*s* 8*d* and £1 18*s* 1½*d*, while the fourth, Walter del Pot, was valued at the very low sum of 11*s* 4½*d*. The assessments of the jurors were similarly distributed in the two other villages for which we possess evidence, i.e. Market Weston and Hopton.[4] An-

[3] The assessment of 1327 has been published in *Suffolk Green Book, no.* IX, vol. 11 (1906); that of 1568 in ibid. no. XII (1909); that of 1674 in ibid. no. XI, vol. 13 (1905).

[4] It appears that this was the usual way of making up the local bodies of assessors for taxes on moveables, e.g. in the 1313 assessment for Minety (Glos.), where the four taxers are valued at £8. 14*s*, £4. 11*s*. £2. 4*s* and 12*s*, and elsewhere.

other sign of verisimilitude is that manorial lords, including the most powerful landlord in the area, the Abbot of Bury St Edmunds, were heavily taxed. The manorial reeves, where they happened to be wealthy, were also heavily taxed and so were some of the men who, to judge from near-contemporary inquests, could be expected to sit on juries and help in the assessment.

The most important confirmation of the reliability of the assessments will, however, be found in some contemporary manorial documents. We possess several such documents (mostly accounts) for Hinderclay, an important possession of the Abbot of Bury St Edmunds, which passed with other manors into the hands of the Bacon family after the Dissolution and are now in the possession of the University of Chicago. A careful check of names in the Hinderclay documents reveals very few discrepancies. Little less than three-quarters of the names of tenants in the near-contemporary records of Hinderclay will be found amongst the 41 taxpayers in that village in 1283, and the return of the moveables on the demesne at 62 *li* is fully consistent with what we learn from the grange accounts about the demesne grain and livestock.

A somewhat vaguer check is provided by the evidence of the two surviving surveys of the abbey's estates printed by Powell. One of them is that of the *Iter* of 1286 of which copies have been preserved in the Pinchbeck register in the Cambridge University Library and in the British Museum.[5] The other survey is that of the estates of the Abbot of Bury St Edmunds made in 1302 and containing summary evaluations of four of the Abbot's manors in the Abbey Hundred (Coney Weston, Culford, Elmswell, Rickinghall).[6] Of the surveys, the former is too fragmentary to provide a full list of villagers and, if uncritically used, can be misleading. The second survey is very brief and does not list the customary tenants by name. However, it lists the free tenants and, together with the *Iter* survey, enables us to trace and locate some of the taxpayers. The second survey is also useful in so far as it gives full particulars of the juries. The majority of the jurors can in fact be found among the taxpayers in spite of an interval of nearly nineteen years between the two documents, and in spite of the lack of system and consistency in medieval use of surnames.

However, the most relevant of all the corroborating records of the Abbey is a somewhat unusual register listing the *Recognitiones* imposed by Thomas the Abbot in 1302 upon his manorial tenants. These payments were apparently levied on tenants' moveables including their livestock, but some payments were apparently also exacted from men who had no livestock and almost no moveable goods, and occasionally even the names

[5] B.M. MSS. Harl. 743.

[6] B.M. MSS. Harl. 230.

of beggars were recorded.[7] The basis of the assessment is different, and the date is nineteen years later than that of the 'thirteenth' of 1283; yet the concordance of the two documents is very close wherever they happen to cover the same ground. The villages thus covered are those of Culford and Rickinghall Inferior. The comparison of names in Culford will reveal that out of 14 taxpayers who were or could have been the Abbot's tenants, 12 were also recorded in the *Recognitiones*. Inversely, of the 20 names in the *Recognitiones*, at least 12 are also to be found among the taxpayers. Of the remaining eight or ten names in *Recognitiones*, five are of men we are told had no animals and consequently could be expected to fall below the half-mark exemption limit of the tax. There thus remain three, or at most five, names in the *Recognitiones* which cannot be found in the tax-list – not a significant number considering the irregularities in the use of medieval family names and the lapse of time between the two documents.

Even more significant are the numbers of animals. Culford happens to be one of the manors for which not only the money equivalent of the *Recognitiones*, but also the livestock of the tenants were recorded. The total number of sheep in the Culford assessment of 1283 is 599, but of these 146 belong to taxpayers who were apparently not the Abbot's manorial tenants. This leaves 453 to be compared with 573 sheep with which the Abbot's tenants are credited in the *Recognitiones* of 1302. The difference, however, is no greater than one we may find at two points of time in manorial stock accounts, and may in any case be due to the fact that whereas lambs were included in the assessment of 1283 it is not certain that they were subject to the *Recognitiones* of 1302.

Nor is there any sign of bias in individual returns. Roger Curtys is credited with 27 sheep in 1302, but had been taxed only on 12 in 1283. On the other hand Adam Blavant was taxed on 9 sheep in 1283, but apparently had no sheep by the time of the 1302 record. As for one John Goodman, we find him first as a wealthy taxpayer in 1283, but discover that by 1302 the Abbot's officials had to relieve him of all *recognitio* as a *mendicans*.

The check of the Rickinghall Inferior has produced similar results.[8] The tax returns record 59 taxpayers while the *Recognitiones* list 51 names of tenants called upon to pay the levy. Of the 58 taxpayers, 24 are certainly identical with the Abbot's tenants in the *Recognitiones*, and a further 9 are probably aliases or predecessors of 1302 tenants: they are mostly men with unusual surnames (Othyn, Schet, Iote) which are recorded nineteen years later with other Christian names. In view of the

[7] B.M. MSS. Harl. 230. The document has also been published and analysed by Mr Powell, but, owing to the doubts about some of the names, I have used a transcript made at my request by Mr J. Z. Titow.

[8] E. Powell, op. cit. table 24. B.M. MSS. Harl. 230, fo. 57.

time lapse a probable discrepancy of 27 names out of 58 is not excessive, especially as the numbers of the taxpayers are actually larger than the names of tenants recorded by the Abbot's officials nineteen years later.

These multiple checks are in my opinion sufficient to permit the use of the Blackbourne survey as a reliable record of the livestock of the villagers in the Hundred. But even if reliable, how complete is it? The answer to this query depends largely on what we expect the document to yield. Paradoxically enough the document will probably be more useful for estimating the total animal population of the Hundred than for assessing the size of average individual holdings.

The fact that men with possessions under 6*s* 8*d* were exempt from tax would at first sight prevent us from using the figures as a measure of total flocks and herds of the area. I do not, however, believe that the animals which escaped the attention of the assessors could have been at all numerous. In theory 6*s* 8*d* would, at the assessors' valuation, buy either an ox (average price in the assessment 5*s* 8*d*), or an inferior horse (average price 7*s* 6*d*), or a cow (prices varying from 4*s* to 5*s*), or six sheep (average price 1*s*). But would a villager, be he never so poor, hold all his moveables in the form of livestock and have so soon after Michaelmas no grain to eat and no seed in the ground? In the total value of moveables for the Hundred as a whole (3400 *li*), the value of livestock (*c.* 140 *li* represents only 40 per cent as compared with 60 per cent (*c.* 2000 *li*) for grain and other produce. Even if the poor villagers held as little as half their moveables in grain or seed or fodder or wool, that would leave them only 3*s* 4*d* for investment in livestock, which was less than the value of a cow or an ox and would buy no more than three or four sheep. In other words, the exemption limit was set so low – I presume intentionally – as to include the bulk of the villagers with animals. We shall in fact see that, even among the taxpayers, there were large numbers of men who had no cattle. Some of them possessed no more than one or two of the smaller animals.

The conclusion is corroborated by the evidence of the Abbot's *Recognitiones*. The latter were obviously highly comprehensive, for they included tenants too poor to pay anything. Yet the total numbers of livestock recorded in them were not greatly in excess and were sometimes even below those in the comparable taxpayers' lists. I therefore propose to accept the Blackbourne totals as being not only reliable, but also fairly complete. If the margin by which the numbers of tenants in the *Recognitiones* or in the Abbot's surveys exceeded the totals of names in the tax returns are any guide, I doubt whether the underestimate of livestock in the assessment could be greater, or even as great, as 5 per cent.[9]

[9] A simple arithmetical exercise will be sufficient to show that the animals owned by villages below the exemption limit could not have made a great difference to

On the other hand, if we use the assessment to compute the average possessions of individual villagers the margin of error is bound to be much larger. The tax was levied only on villagers of substance sufficient to be taxed. Whether the terms of tax provided for an exemption limit or not, there were always to be found villagers too poor to possess taxable goods, and especially taxable animals. Manorial documents leave no doubt on this score. Thus, the surviving records of heriots – essentially death duties levied on tenants' animals – abound with instances of heriots forgiven or converted into small money payments for the simple reason that deceased tenants did not possess animals on which the duty could be levied. On Winchester manors the average numbers of such heriots fluctuated from year to year, but was frequently more than one-third of the total. In 1348–9 – the year of the Black Death – the tenants without animals formed about 40 per cent of the total and on some places such as the thickly populated manors of Taunton, or the two Meons, deceased tenants on whom animal heriot could not be levied formed 60 per cent of the total.[10] The proportions on the Glastonbury estates were not quite so high since they contained two large cattle-raising manors in Sedgmoor. Moreover on Glastonbury manors heriots of tenants without animals sometimes left no trace in the records. Yet the aggregate amount of such heriots recorded in the manorial accounts and court rolls of the thirteenth century appears to exceed 20 per cent of the total. It is therefore significant that the Blackbourne assessment contained hardly any men without animals. Out of 1339 persons assessed for tax, only 114, or rather less than 10 per cent, possessed no major animals, i.e. neither plough beasts nor cows, and only 49, or rather less than 3 per cent, possessed no animals at all.[11] Obviously the exemption limit for the tax (6*s* 8*d*) was low enough to include nearly all the owners of animals, and yet sufficiently high to exclude the bulk of the poorer villagers without livestock. If so, the averages we can strike by dividing the total numbers of animals by the numbers of taxpayers will relate not to the whole body of villagers, but only to the villagers who possessed animals. These averages will still be useful, indeed indispensable, in enabling us to identify villages apparently pastoral and those apparently arable. The averages may also enable us to reconstruct the distribution of animals among the men who possessed them. But they will not justify any con-

the totals. Even if we make the most unlikely assumption that men who escaped the tax because they had less than the equivalent of three sheep units were as numerous as all the categories of taxpayers put together, the total of livestock in sheep units could not have exceeded that in the assessment by more than about 2000 to 4000, or 5 per cent to 10 per cent. And even this computation assumes that there were no villagers without any animals. See below, Table 11.7.

10 M. Postan and J. Titow, 'Heriots and Prices on Winchester Manors', *Econ. Hist. Rev.* 2nd ser. XI (1959) and reprinted as Chapter 9 above.

11 See below, Table 11.7.

clusions as to what proportion of the villagers did or did not possess any livestock.

The inquiry into the Blackbourne assessment has I hope been sufficiently circumstantial to absolve me from the necessity of explaining in equal detail the checks to be applied to the other assessments in our sample. The assessment I propose to consider next is that of the subsidy of one-fifteenth of 1225 for south Wiltshire.[12] This, one of the earliest of the assessments, has been chosen partly because it relates to an economic area different in character from that of the Blackbourne Hundred, but mainly because its evidence can at some points be collated with that of near-contemporary manorial documents. It contains the assessment of the villages of Damerham and Martin, which formed the Abbot of Glastonbury's composite manor of Damerham. Together with most other Glastonbury manors, it was surveyed during the abbacy of Michael of Amesbury (1235–52), i.e. within one generation of the assessment, and the comparison of the numbers and names in the two documents can provide a valuable test of the reliability of the tax return.[13]

First, numbers. The assessment lists in Damerham and Martin 209 taxpayers; the survey lists 181 tenants: the number of taxpayers is thus in excess of that of tenants. There were doubtless villagers who were not the Abbot's tenants – men who leased land not directly from the Abbot, but from his tenants. The excess of taxpayers over the number of tenants may therefore mean that this hidden population was drawn into the assessors' net; or it may mean that the population had grown by some 15 per cent between 1225 and the time of Michael of Amesbury. Whatever the explanation, it does not detract from the reliability of the record. It was obviously an assessment as comprehensive as we can expect a tax assessment to be.

The impression of reliability is further reinforced by the figures of the demesne flock. The assessment gives the number as 570, whereas the thirteenth-century Minister's Accounts of Damerham (all later than the survey) show the demesne flocks fluctuating around 600.[14]

Yet another check is provided by a detailed comparison of individual entries. Most of the surnames in both documents are, of course, the same,

12 P.R.O. E.179/242/47. The assessment has recently been cited and used in Mrs R. Scott's chapter on medieval agriculture in the *Victoria County History of Wiltshire*, IV (1959). For some villages Mrs Scott's figures differ slightly from mine.

13 The surveys are published in *Glastonbury Rentalia et Custumaria* (Somerset Rec. Soc. 1891), pp. 108 et seq.

14 Longleat MSS. *passim*. Henry of Soliaco's Survey of 1189, *An Inquisition of the Manors of Glastonbury Abbey in the Year 1189* (Roxborough Club, 1882), reports 617 sheep on the manor, but states that a further 500 draft ewes could be kept, but presumably were not kept, in Martin. There was, of course, a great deal of sub-letting in Damerham both before and after 1189.

even though some men may have been recorded under more than one surname, and even though a whole generation may have separated the two records. It is not therefore surprising that not all the taxpayers and tenants with the same family names should have occurred in both documents under the same Christian names. But what is important is that most of the men whom the survey places among the top rank of the tenants, or could be identified as their descendants, are to be found among the most heavily assessed taxpayers (e.g. Roger de Stapleham). The survey also makes it clear that most of the Abbot's full virgaters, 52 out of 66, resided in Martin; and the assessment accordingly places in Martin 51 of the men assessed for more than £1 on their goods.[15]

A further, less precise, but generally convincing correlation will be found in the returns for some of the other villages in the area. Among the latter there were at least six manors belonging to the nuns of Shaftesbury: Berwick St James, Sedghill, Tisbury with Hatch, Donhead, Dinton and Teffont. For some of these estates we possess two twelfth-century surveys, one of which probably dates from the end of the century.[16] It is, thus, of some importance that whereas the number of tenants in Sedghill in the first half of the twelfth century was only ten, the number of taxpayers in 1225 was 17. In Tisbury with Hatch there were 106 tenants in the early survey, while the 1225 assessment contains 108 names.[17] In two other manors the numbers in the assessments were higher than in the survey. In Berwick there were 7 tenants in the early twelfth century and 15 taxpayers in 1225. In Dinton there were 45 tenants in the late twelfth century, but 73 taxpayers in 1225. In the latter case, however, the excess of taxpayers can probably be accounted for by the existence of a group of sub-tenants who held land from three substantial tenants holding 17 virgates, as against 34 virgates held directly of the Abbot. If the distribution of holdings among these sub-tenants was the same as among the direct tenants of the Abbot, we could expect at least 21 households additional to those listed in the survey, which should bring the total probably to 63.

I therefore propose to accept the south Wiltshire figures for the total livestock of the area, though not necessarily for its distribution among villagers. On the other hand, the assessment of grain in the possession of the villages is almost certainly too low to permit useful comparison with other areas. It will be remembered that the Blackbourne assessment was carried out in the autumn and early winter, i.e. soon after the harvest,

15 The total assessment in Martin is 85 as against 124 in Damerham.

16 Harl. MS. 61. Unfortunately Tisbury with Hatch and Dinton are the only ones which happen to be surveyed in the late twelfth-century documents and our knowledge of the others derives from a survey of the first half of the century.

17 The late twelfth-century survey contains only 65 names, i.e. little more than half of the names in the assessment, but the survey is apparently incomplete.

and the assessors were also instructed to include the seed in the ground. On the other hand, south Wiltshire of 1225 was assessed in the spring, i.e. the time when peasant stocks of grain could be expected to have run down. Nor is there any evidence to show that seed in the ground was taxed.[18] We must therefore assume that in comparison with the Blackbourne evidence the grain figures of the south Wiltshire document undervalue, perhaps greatly, the villagers' corn-growing activities.

To these two assessments we may also add a third which, though much smaller, is probably equally reliable, that of the *banlieu* of Ramsey for the subsidy of one-fifteenth of 1291.[19] The assessment relates to five manors of the Ramsey Abbey in addition to that of the vill of Ramsey itself. Here again the returns appear to agree with the evidence of corresponding Ramsey surveys and accounts. Thus, on the manor of Upwood the number of plough animals of the demesne is given as 35; their corresponding numbers in surviving accounts of 1247–57 and 1252 are 38, 31 and 35 respectively, though only 28 in the account of 1316.[20] Similarly, the 380 quarters of grain which the assessors found in the demesne granges of Upwood, if anything, exceeded the amount of grain reported by the bailiffs in most years. The demesne evidence of other manors is equally consistent with the assessment; but an additional check, here as elsewhere, will be found in the names of tenants listed in manorial courts.

By a fortunate coincidence some of the surviving records of manorial courts of Ramsey estates fall within ten or twelve years of the assessment of 1291. The areas covered by them do not always coincide with those of the villages assessed for tax,[21] but at least one series of court rolls, that for Upwood and Raveley Magna for 1280 and 1294, matches the assessment of the same two villages in 1291 and makes it possible for us to collate the names of taxpayers with those of the Abbott's tenants appearing in the courts.

The results of the collation are unambiguous. To begin with, nearly all the taxpayers can be traced to the court rolls: out of 91 names of the assessment only 16 do not appear in the rolls, and of these 16 at least two (Isabella Waryn and John Wyte) may be identical with villagers of the same names, who appear in the court rolls of the neighbouring manor of Wistow. This remarkable correspondence bears out what many historians have suspected for a long time, i.e. that appearance at the lord's court and a fine of one sort or another were regular incidents of customary tenure from which no tenant went free for any length of time. But considered as a proof of the reliability of the assessment this check

[18] P.R.O. E.179/242/47. [19] B.M. MSS. Add. Ch. 34759.

[20] J. Raftis, *The Estates of Ramsey Abbey* (Toronto, 1951), p. 132.

[21] E.g. the court roll for Wistow also includes the cases of Little Raveley, whereas for tax Wistow is assessed by itself.

from the tax record to the court rolls cannot be as conclusive as the reverse check, i.e. that from the court rolls to the tax.

This reverse check is not of course very easy or simple. Here as elsewhere the uncertainty of medieval family names frequently defeats us. A man can be described by his profession in one place and by his descent or his residence in another; a man described in one place as John Tanner can reappear in another place as John son of Nicholas, and a third as John at the Green. A further difficulty is that of time – since at least eleven years separate the court roll of 1280 from the assessment. Furthermore, people appearing in court rolls were by no means all heads of families; on at least 28 occasions members of families other than their heads are expressly named in court rolls. Thus, most of the women fined by courts were tenants' wives prosecuted for unlicensed brewing of ale. Some of the men in the court rolls were resident elsewhere; a whole batch of men mentioned in the court roll of 1294 were members of a tithing fined to appear at court, and for all we know they may also have been absent from the village. Finally, some of the men in the courts were paupers described as such, and were thus not liable to tax.

Wide disparities between the two sets of names are thus to be expected. It is therefore very significant to find that most of the households recorded in the court rolls should also have been assessed for tax. If we allow for the persons in the court roll of 1280 who were not heads of households, i.e. were wives or sisters or servants, and if we also make the necessary allowance for non-residents, paupers and other men not liable to tax, we shall find that of the remaining 105 names in the court rolls at least 82 can be matched in the assessment by the names of the same men or their widows or their descendants. Of the remaining 20 or 25 names some were probably aliases of the men in the court rolls. Could not Johannes Eldman be the same as Johannes le Man or de Man, or Johannes le Longe of 1280 be one of the three or four unidentified Johns of 1291 and 1294? However, even without these 25 names the agreement between the two lists is most impressive. Added to the other corroborative evidence, it should be sufficient to justify our accepting the Ramsey assessments as worthy of trust.

So much for the assessments. Further detailed researches may enable us to cull some more reliable records out of the vast volume of surviving taxation returns. Some direct evidence of peasant flocks may also be found in manorial accounts, though so far I have found very few manorial documents capable of yielding an estimate of totals of peasant flocks and herds. One such record has, however, come to light. The records of Meon Church which belonged to the Bishops of Winchester are included among the manorial accounts of the bishopric. From about 1211 to 1317 these records contained a regular return of the tithes of the

Bishop's composite manor of East Meon and Meon Church. These are, so to speak, private accounts of the Bishop and his officials, and are no less reliable than the main body of manorial accounts. They enable us to estimate, however roughly, the total animal population of the Meon manors, though they will not enable us to measure the distribution of livestock among individual parishioners.[22]

2

Of the three assessments we have so far discussed, two, i.e. that of the Blackbourne Hundred of West Suffolk and that of the Ramsey estates in Huntingdonshire, relate to what were mainly arable regions, while the third, that of south Wiltshire, relates to an area which has always been regarded as a sheep-farming one. Our sample does not unfortunately contain any place exclusively engaged in animal husbandry to the total, or almost total, exclusion of arable farming. Such regions were of course very rare at all times, and rarest of all in the thirteenth century. They were mostly to be found in England's 'highland zones' in the barren and inaccessible outposts of Anglo-Saxon settlement, i.e. in the Northern Pennines, the High Peak of Derbyshire, the moorlands of north-west Staffordshire, the fringes of the 'deep' fens in the eastern counties, in the marshes of Sedgmoor, or on the higher reaches of Exmoor and Dartmoor. Whereas some of these areas, e.g. the High Peak, may have carried flocks of sheep, most of the others were regions of cattle ranches, the great medieval vaccaries. The accounts of the Earl de Lacy's possessions in the Pennines, the accounts of the Earls of Cornwall for the forest of Dartmoor, as well as the Inquisitions Post Mortem of other landowners in the Pennines, bear witness to the local importance of the vaccaries.[23] The accounts of the Glastonbury manors of Brent and Zowy in the Sedgmoor allow us a glimpse of a similar cattle-grazing economy in the West Country. But all this information relates to the lords' herds and provides

[22] Bishop of Winchester's Enrolled Manorial Accounts, Eccl. 2/159270 et seq. A similar record is also available for Fifield Verdon in Wiltshire (R. Scott, *V.C.H.* op. cit. p. 27).

[23] For the vaccaries of Wyresdale, Lonsdale and Amundenesse in the mid-thirteenth century see *Lancashire Inquisitions* (Lancs. and Cheshire Rec. Soc.), XLVIII (1903), 169 seq., and *Pipe Rolls*, 31 Hen. III, m. 14, and 42 Hen. III, m. 14 *dorso*. For the vaccaries of Trawden, Penhill, Rossendale and Accrington, see *Three Lancashire Surveys* (Cheetham Soc.), LXXIV (1868), and G. H. Tupling, *The Economic History of Rossendale* (Manchester, 1927), ch. I. For the vaccaries of Yorkshire, see P. A. Lyons, 'Compoti of the Yorkshire Estates of Henry de Lacy', *Yorkshire Arch. and Topographical Journal*, VIII (1884).

For the pastoral activities of the High Peak and in the forests of North Staffs, see the enrolled accounts of the duchy of Lancaster, P.R.O. DL/29 *passim*. For the horse-herds of Dartmoor, see *Ministers' Accounts of the Earldom of Cornwall 1296–1297* (ed. L. M. Midgeley), II (Camden Soc. Third Ser. LXVII).

little data for estimating the peasants' livestock.[24] We must therefore confine our inquiry to pastoral regions for which we have some evidence of peasants' livestock, and these are best exemplified by south Wiltshire: an area in which animal husbandry was always combined with corn-growing, and where the animals grazed were mostly sheep.

The south Wiltshire survey covers an area of chalk uplands, partly exposed and partly overlaid with clay and flint, where sheep-farming always played an important part in the rural economy and where both the manorial demesnes and the villagers could be expected to possess large sheep flocks. Two sheep-farming areas *par excellence* were represented in the assessment. The first contained the Wilton Abbey manors on the downlands above the Ebble, south-west of Wilton – Bower Chalke, 'Apch' (Broad Chalke?), Homington, Alvediston, Berwick St Johns, and 'Wakefont' – most of which were probably surveyed in the Domesday Book as parts of the great manor of Chalke.[25] The second, and geographically the most remote, group consisted of the combined Glastonbury villages of Damerham and Martin, with the hamlets of Tidpit and Fifhyde. The headquarters manor, Damerham, was in the Avon valley, but all its members stretched into the uplands grazed by the flocks of the Wilton manors to the north. The sheepwalks of Martin must actually have marched with those of Wilton Abbey's Bower Chalke. The third group which possessed downland pastures, but nevertheless did not maintain sheep flocks as large as those of the Chalke and Damerham groups, comprised the Shaftesbury Abbey manors and villages on the Downs above the upper Nadder to the north and north-east of Shaftesbury itself: Tisbury with Hatch, Donhead, Berwick St James, and Dinton with Teffont, as well as two Abbey of Wilton manors, Barford and Chilmark. The fourth and last group was made up of manors of which some (Sedghill, Semley and Little Cheverell) were valley villages in which dairying formed the basis of such animal husbandry as there was; but also of two or three manors (Burcombe, Uggford and Baverstock) which, judging by their position, could have engaged in sheep-farming, but did not.

The animal population of these villages is shown in columns 1, 2, 3 and 4 of Table 11.1. It will be seen that the village flocks varied greatly in size, but from the point of view of our inquiry the most relevant figures

24 For a late thirteenth-century assessment of what may have been a 'highland' area see W. Brown, 'Yorkshire Lay Subsidy, etc.', *Yorks. Arch. Soc.* Record Series, XVI. This, like several other similar assessments, could not as yet be checked for reliability.

25 R. R. Darlington, 'Introduction to Wiltshire Domesday', *Victoria County History of Wiltshire*, II, 91. 'Apch' was probably Broad Chalke. 'Wakefont' probably comprised the whole or most of the area of the modern village of Ebbesborne Wake and perhaps also Fifield Bavant.

TABLE 11.1 *Assessment for the Fifteenth of 1225 in South Wiltshire*

Village	Sheep	Av.	Horses and Oxen	Av.	Cows and Calves	Av.	Pigs	Av.	Grain qrs.	Grain bus.	Av.	Tax-payers
	(1)		(2)		(3)		(4)					
Group I												
'Apch' (Broad Chalke?)	997	*21·2*	64	*1·4*	99	*2·1*	28	*0·6*	48	4	*8·3*	47
Bower Chalke	1008	*25·2*	137	*3·7*	140	*3·5*	26	*0·65*	50	2	*10·1*	40
Homington	238	*23·8*	17	*1·7*	19	*1·9*	4	*0·4*	10	2	*8·2*	10
Alvediston	931	*33·25*	55	*2·0*	54	*1·9*	11	*0·4*	18	4	*5·3*	28
Berwick St John's	786	*31·4*	56	*2·2*	58	*2·3*	8	*0·3*	16		*5·1*	25
Bridmore	534	*35·6*	41	*2·6*	55	*3·4*	10	*0·6*	39	2	*19·6*	14
'Wakefont'	1053	*21·5*	124	*2·5*	90	*1·8*	15	*0·3*	34	2	*5·6*	49
	5547	*26·0*	494	*2·3*	515	*2·4*	102	*0·5*	215		*8·1*	213
Group II												
Damerham	1283	*10·3*	177	*1·4*	339	*2·7*	54	*0·4*	106		*6·8*	124
Martin	2691	*31·7*	190	*2·2*	243	*2·9*	59	*0·7*	138	4	*13·0*	85
	3974	*19·0*	367	*1·8*	582	*2·8*	113	*0·5*	244	4	*9·2*	209
Group III												
Barford	68	*13·6*	16	*3·2*	11	*2·2*	5	*1·0*	10	6	*17·2*	5
Chilmark	896	*16·6*	106	*2·0*	144	*2·7*	14	*0·3*	2	4	*0·4*	54
Tisbury with Hatch	1087	*10·0*	225	*2·1*	342	*3·1*	32	*0·3*	53	4	*3·9*	109
Donhead	1551	*11·3*	288	*2·1*	375	*2·8*	51	*0·4*	23	2	*1·4*	137
Berwick St Leonard	100	*12·5*	5	*0·6*	7	*0·9*	1	*0·1*				8
Dinton	388	*9·2*	49	*1·2*	118	*2·8*	27	*0·6*	35	2	*6·7*	42
Teffont	419	*11·3*	68	*1·8*	82	*2·2*	13	*0·4*	16	2	*3·5*	37
	4509	*11·5*	757	*1·9*	1079	*2·8*	143	*0·5*	139	4	*3·1*	392
Group IV												
Baverstock	4	*0·4*	7	*0·8*	17	*1·9*			1	4	*1·3*	9
Burcombe	156	*7·8*	17	*0·85*	39	*1·95*	1	*0·5*	1		*0·4*	20
Uggford	59	*4·0*	19	*1·3*	25	*1·7*				4	*0·3*	15
Sedghill	10	*0·6*	46	*2·7*	58	*3·4*	7	*0·4*				17
Semley	108	*2·8*	98	*2·6*	188	*4·9*	9	*0·2*	2		*0·4*	38
Little Cheverell	185	*8·4*	28	*1·3*	80	*3·6*	7	*0·3*				22
	522	*4·3*	215	*1·8*	407	*3·5*	24	*0·2*	7		*0·5*	121
'Stych'	435	*17·4*	26	*1·0*	62	*2·5*			17		*5·4*	25
Grand Total	14988	*15·6*	1859	*1·8*	2645	*2·8*	382	*0·3*	626		*5·3*	960

are not the totals of animals in the villages, but the average holding of animals per taxpayer. The latter for the area as a whole was just over 15 for sheep and about 2·5 for horses and cattle. In the two groups of villages in which the average ownership of animals was largest, i.e. in groups I and II, it was well over 20 for sheep and about 2·5 for cattle. However, not all the larger animals, i.e. cattle and horses, should be taken into account in measuring the taxpayers' involvement in pastoral pursuits. Oxen and horses were an essential component of arable husbandry and their numbers varied directly with the acreage possessed and ploughed. I have therefore separated the figures of oxen and horses from those of other cattle and propose to count the latter with the sheep in measuring individual holdings of livestock. Furthermore, the two sets of figures, those for sheep and those for cows and calves, must be reduced to a common denominator if they are to be aggregated into a single index of pastoral activity. This can most conveniently be done by reducing all the livestock into its equivalent in sheep. The reduction can best be done on the basis of the relative valuations of different animals in our records. In the Suffolk valuation of 1283 and the Wiltshire assessment under consideration the average prices of bovine animals of all ages (other than oxen) are equal to about three times the price of sheep of all ages, while prices of pigs and sheep are nearly the same. Thus re-computed the average holding of animals in the south Wiltshire assessment as a whole appears to be equivalent to 24·3 sheep units. In the first two groups best provided with animals the average holding was 30·8 sheep units, while in the third and fourth groups it was 20·4 and 15.

Even if the south Wiltshire figures could, for the time being, be taken to represent a sheep-farming area, those of the Blackbourne Hundred of Suffolk could at first sight be regarded as representative of regions of mixed farming in which the admixture of animal husbandry was relatively small.

The average sheep holdings per taxpayer in the 33 villages assessed worked out at about 10·5 sheep, and the number of cows and young bovines at little more than three. The total holding of animals per villager was equivalent to about 21·5 sheep units compared to 24·3 sheep units in south Wiltshire. This general impression of an economy little dependent on sheep must not, however, be allowed to conceal from view a seemingly sheep-farming territory within it. Some 10–13 villages out of the total of 33 (Barnham, Culford, Euston, Fakenham Magna, Ingham, Rushford, Sapiston, Troston, West Stowe, and Wordwell, and perhaps also Ashfield Magna, Livermere Parva and Knettishall) possessed many more animals per villager than the rest of the Hundred. Their total holding of cows and calves (1169) worked out at rather less than four (in fact *c.* 3·5) per taxpayer, which is only fractionally higher than the average holding per

TABLE 11.2 *Assessment of Blackbourne Hundred of South Suffolk*

Village	Sheep	Av.	Horses and oxen	Av.	Cows and calves	Av.	Pigs	Av.	Grain (qrs.)	Av.	Tax-payers
Ashfield	380+ 3D	*12·7*	34+32D	*1·1*	116+27D	*3·9*	62+ 40D	*2·1*	236+137D	*8*	30
Ashfield Parva	192	*5·8*	26+ 5D	*0·8*	124+19D	*3·8*	73+ 5D	*2·2*	247	*7*	33
Bardwell	1080+ 233D*	*8·5*	96+19D	*0·8*	409+21D	*3·2*	174+ 28D	*1·4*	843+100D	*7*	127
Barnham	1842+ 683D†	*46*	72+ 6D	*1·8*	174+10D	*4·4*	226	*5·6*	311+146D	*7*	40
Barningham	250+ 4D	*4·8*	28+ 8D	*0·6*	162+16D	*3·1*	87+ 14D		331+ 31D	*6*	52
Culford	519+ 80D	*26*	24+ 6D	*1·2*	61+ 2D	*3·1*			159+ 45D	*8*	20
Elmswell	207	*8·1*	23+15D	*0·9*	97	*3·9*	85	*2·5*	245	*9*	25
Euston	931+ 162D	*29*	48+ 7D	*1·5*	127	*4*	4	*0·1*	323+ 33D	*10*	32
Fakenham Magna	412+ 520D	*22·9*	20+ 4D	*1·1*	45+11D	*2·5*	20	*1·1*	76+ 10D	*5*	18
Hepworth	232+ 24D	*4·6*	67+21D	*1·3*	179+25D	*3·6*	210+ 24D	*4·2*	252+ 35D	*5*	50
Hinderclay	232	*5·8*	47+26D	*1·2*	122+39D	*3·1*	100	*2·5*	473	*11*	40
Honington	197	*5·5*	42	*1·1*	95	*2·5*	25	*0·7*	184	*5*	38
Hopton	305	*4*	72	*0·9*	243	*3·2*	45	*0·6*	340	*5*	75
Hunston	50+ 49D	*3·1*	19+17D	*1·2*	17+30D	*1·7*	3+ 42D	*0·2*	67+ 97D	*4*	16
Ingham	707+ 311D	*22·5*	30+13D	*1·1*	102+24D	*3·8*			134+160D	*5*	27
Ixworth	324+ 16D	*6·1*	50+10D	*0·9*	150	*2·8*	2		273+136D	*5*	53
Knettishall	345	*12·3*	35	*1·3*	151	*5·4*	40	*1·4*	194	*7*	28
Langham	121	*5·5*	38+17D	*1·7*	76+23D	*3·5*	36+ 38D	*1·6*	117+102D	*5*	22
Livermere Parva	289+ 360D	*12*	13+ 4D	*0·5*	42+ 9D	*1·8*	9+ 8D	*0·4*	80+ 40D	*3*	24
Market Weston	215	*5·5*	54+24D	*1·4*	140+ 2D	*3·6*	121	*3·1*	222	*6*	39
Norton	383	*11*	33+35D	*0·9*	155+22D	*4·4*	82+ 40D	*2·3*	248+143D	*7*	35
Rickinghall Inferior	430+ 16D	*7·4*	46+18D	*0·8*	167+12D	*2·9*	37+ 12D	*0·6*	282+195D	*5*	58
Rushford	176+ 15D	*19·5*	8+ 4D	*0·9*	34+ 9D				48	*5*	9
Sapiston	650‡	*22·5*	35	*1·2*	102	*3·5*	74	*2·5*	205	*7*	29
Stanton	395	*4*	102	*1*	214	*2·2*	112	*1·1*	517	*5*	97
Stowlangtoft	227+ 24D	*7·6*	31+15D	*1*	127+26D	*4·2*	7+ 52D	*0·2*	129+ 41D	*4*	30
Thelnetham	129+ 84D	*2·5*	55+22D	*1·1*	155+30D	*3*	29+103D	*0·6*	238+174D	*5*	51
Thorpe	182+ 192D	*4·9*	48+12D	*1·2*	137+23D	*3·5*	64+ 42D	*1·6*	261+111D	*7*	39
Troston	550+ 62D	*18*	30+ 7D	*1*	99+15D	*3·2*	3+ 16D		201+ 29D	*6*	31
Walsham le Willows	287+ 50D	*3·3*	88+35D	*1*	206+ 3D	*2·4*	37+ 15D	*0·4*	302+ 74D	*3*	87
Wattisfield	239	*5·4*	70+ 3D	*1·6*	144	*3·3*	75	*1·7*	255+ 12D	*5*	44
West Stowe	1097+ 130D	*54·8*	21+ 4D	*1*	65+ 9D	*33*			171+ 53D	*8*	20
Wordwell	466	*23·3*	27	*1·3*	51	*2·6*			105	*5*	20
Total	14041+3018D	*10·5*	1432	*1*	4298	*3·2*	1842	*1·4*	8069	*6*	1339

D=Demesne animals.
* Mostly sheep from other villages folded in Bardwell.
† Including 565 sheep from other villages folded in Barnham.
‡ To this should be added at least 35 sheep folded in other places, mostly in Bardwell. This has been allowed in computing the averages.

taxpayer in the Hundred as a whole; but their sheep flocks, about 8364 *in toto*, worked out at about 25 per taxpayer and were thus very much higher than the holding of sheep in the other 20 villages (whose average was between five and six) and fully equal to average sheepflocks in the sheep-farming villages of south Wiltshire.

The geographical position of these villages explains why their sheep flocks should have been so much larger than elsewhere. They all lie on the so-called 'Fielding' area of north-west Suffolk, an empty region which bestrode the borders of Norfolk and Suffolk and comprised such extension of the Norfolk Breckland as Thetford Warren, Wayfore and Lakenheath Warrens and the heaths of Icklingham, Elveden and Euston. All these were stretches of countryside utterly unsuited to arable farming which for the greater part of their history have been devoted to grazing. If, in spite of this enclave, the Hundred as a whole had a somewhat lower average of animals per villager this was obviously due to the predominance within it of a much larger group of 20 to 23 villages lying east of the sheep-farming fringe, i.e. just within the 'Woodland', or arable-farming, area of central Suffolk. In other words, the apparent line of demarcation between pastoral and arable areas in our documents lay not between the chalklands of south Wiltshire and the Blackbourne Hundred of Suffolk, each taken as a whole, but within each of these areas. In both it is possible at first sight to distinguish villages characterized by average holdings of about 30 sheep units and over from predominantly arable ones where the number of sheep units per taxable household seldom exceeded 20 and was most frequently below 10. How far this demarcation represents real differences of husbandry is, however, another question to which I propose to return presently.

The villages in our third assessment, that of the *banlieu* of Ramsey, could reasonably be classified both with the predominantly arable and with the largely pastoral ones. They were well within the borders of the anciently arable area of Huntingdonshire, and the manorial surveys and accounts of the Abbey of Ramsey manors in the *banlieu* and near it abound with evidence of extensive cornfields and well-stocked granges. At the same time, however, the eastern fringes of the fens, both drained and undrained, formed part of the *banlieu* territory or marched with it. Pasture was therefore more abundant and the herds of cattle were larger than those we can expect in regions as fully engaged in corn-growing as this. This apparent participation in both types of husbandry is well reflected in the assessment. The Table 11.3 shows that while the average holding of sheep – 6·2 per taxpayer – was as low as that of the mainly arable villages of Suffolk and Wiltshire, their average holding of cows – 4·5 – was nearly twice that of south Wiltshire and was sufficient to bring up the average stockholding of a taxpayer, measured in sheep units, to

23·5 – a rate above that in the apparently arable villages in the other two assessments. This figure would have been still higher had we included in the totals the unusually large herds of demesne cattle – 111 in Bury and 116 in Upwood with Great Raveley.

TABLE 11.3 *Liberty of Ramsey, assessment of 1291*

	Sheep		Horses and oxen		Cows and young		Pigs		Grain		
	Nos.	Av.	Nos.	Av.	Nos.	Av.	Nos.	Av.	Nos. (qrs.)	Av.*	Tax-payers
Wistow	221	*6·0*	100	*2·6*	127	*3·4*	154	*4·2*	317⅞	*68·7*	37
Great Raveley	208	*4·75*	88	*2·0*	161	*3·7*	159	*3·6*	253⅛	*46·0*	44
Upwood	292	*6·5*	109	*2·4*	182	*4·0*	192	*4·3*	339½	*60·4*	45
Bury by Ramsey	146	*7·3*	68	*3·4*	167	*8·35*	82	*4·1*	124¾	*49·9*	20
Heighmongrove	235	*7·8*	51	*1·7*	153	*5·1*	92	*3·1*	139⅜	*37·2*	31
Total without demesnes	1102	*6·2*	416	*2·35*	790	*4·5*	679	*3·8*	1174⅝	*53·1*	177

* Grain averages are given in bushels.

TABLE 11.4 *Tithes of livestock on East Meon manors*

		Cattle		Sheep	
	No. of years	Amount	Annual average	Amount	Annual average
		£ *s* *d*	£ *s* *d*	£ *s* *d*	£ *s* *d*
1212–49	19	10 17 8	11 5½	15 13 1½	16 6
1250–99	20	10 17 7	10 11	14 12 10	15 6
1300–17	13	6 2 9	9 6	10 16 4	14 6

Finally, there remains the evidence of the Meon tithes. The yields of the tithes were as shown in Table 11.4. These returns require a double conversion before they can tell us anything about the numbers of animals in the two Meons. They must first be converted into their equivalent numbers of lambs, calves and foals, and these numbers must in their turn be converted into their equivalents of livestock of all ages. Neither conversion is very easy or simple, though both are feasible.

The conversion of money returns into numbers of young animals is complicated by some uncertainty as to the tithe valuations. At the beginning of the century the valuations for tithe were probably very close to real values as revealed in the contemporary manorial accounts, but we do not know whether the values remained on that level in the subsequent hundred years or whether they kept up with the secular rise in the prices of livestock. At the beginning of our series the average prices of lambs on Winchester estates appears to be about $2\frac{1}{2}d$, while towards the end of our period they approached $5d$. I therefore propose to compile two alternative estimates of the number of lambs at the end of our period – one on the basis of the lower price and the other one based on the higher one. The numbers at the beginning of the period can of course be compiled on the single assumption of the lower, i.e. the earlier, price. Thus estimated the numbers appear to be as follows:

Years	*No. of lambs per annum*
1212–49	80
1300–17	70 at $2\frac{1}{2}d$ per lamb
1300–17	35 at $5d$ per lamb

In order to estimate the size of flocks of all ages consistent with these numbers of lambs I propose to use the proportions in the Blackbourne Hundred in 1283. Judging from Winchester and Glastonbury evidence, the country as a whole did not suffer that year any unusual murrain of lambs, and the proportions agree well with those we find in the records of demesne flocks in other parts of the country,[26] In the Blackbourne assessment we find 3674 lambs in a flock of 17,127, i.e. a little more than 20 per cent of the total. I accordingly propose to obtain my estimate of the total flock by multiplying the number of Meon lambs five-fold. This multiplication will produce about 4000 in 1212–49, and either 3500 or 1750 in 1317. The total number of tenants in East Meon and Meon Church in the middle of the century was about 320.[27] If this was also the number of tenants at the two poles of our period, the average number of sheep per tenant would be 12 in the earlier period and either 11 or 5·5 in the later one.[28] These averages per tenant are well within the range of the averages per taxpayer in our tax assessments, i.e. below the average in the so-called sheep-farming villages of south Wiltshire, and a little above the average in the arable manors worst provided with sheep. Meon was, of course, a corn-growing manor, which comprised within its border some extensive downland pastures.

3

From these figures it should be possible to derive some very important conclusions about the livestock of medieval villagers. The first and the

26 See p. 248 below.

27 B.M. MSS. Egerton 2418. This figure agrees roughly with that independently computed by Mr J. Z. Titow's unpublished Ph.D. thesis on the Bishop of Winchester's estates in the Cambridge University Library.

28 In all probability, however, the numbers of tenants in the first quarter of the fourteenth century were higher than in the first quarter of the thirteenth and the total amount of land in their hands was also somewhat larger.

most important conclusion, of which all our other conclusions will be mere extensions, is that the numbers of animals in our villages were exceedingly low. They were low in comparison with the corresponding numbers at other dates and they were equally low in relation to the scale and needs of thirteenth-century husbandry.

It is quite possible that the numbers were lower, perhaps much lower, than they might have been some centuries earlier. Direct evidence of village livestock for these earlier periods is totally lacking, but a faint and fleeting reflexion of pre-thirteenth century numbers could perhaps be caught in certain manorial customs, especially in those regulating the villagers' rights of pasture and obligations of fold. These customs frequently lay down the number of animals which the tenants were allowed to graze on manorial pastures, or conversely, the numbers of animals they had to fold on the lord's land. These numbers are as a rule cited in manorial documents of the late fourteenth or fifteenth century, but we must presume that they had been fixed at the time when the custom itself was defined, and that the time when manorial customs were in the process of being defined goes back to the earliest Middle Ages. If these presumptions hold good the numbers of sheep with which individual villagers were credited in the grazing and folding customs may be taken to reflect the early medieval holdings of livestock. In that case it is interesting to note that these numbers are often higher than the corresponding numbers deducible from our assessment. We have seen that in the south Wiltshire assessment an average ration of 30 sheep denoted a village within the predominantly 'pastoral' group. This ration was, however, frequently exceeded in the customs of fold and pasture in those Wiltshire villages on which these customs happen to have been defined. Thus on some important manors of the duchy of Lancaster (Aldbourne, Colingbourne Ducis and Amesbury) situated in the northern parts of the Wiltshire chalk, the fourteenth and fifteenth-century payments for pasture and for the right to withdraw sheep from the lord's fold implied customary quotas of sheep per tenant as high as 50 sheep per virgate, and even higher.[29]

However, too much must not be read into these comparisons with

[29] P.R.O. D.L.29/43/9.25; 682/11058; 683/11061–72; 684/11074–85. Mrs R. Scott, who cites these duchy of Lancaster cases in her study of Wiltshire agriculture (*V.C.H. Wiltshire*, loc. cit. p. 27), also quotes similar figures from other Wiltshire manors in the late fourteenth and fifteenth centuries, which suggests the possibility that the average holdings of sheep rose again after the Black Death. Thus, if the 1359 figures of the total flocks of Durrington represented the *maximum* number which the tenants could graze, it would appear that in 1334, when the total number of tenants was 41, the average holding of sheep was about 18. After the Black Death more than 40 per cent of the tenancies were left vacant, and the average holding in 1359 may have been somewhere between 30 and 50. Ibid.

earlier figures. The figures are too few and their meaning is too uncertain to justify anything more than a highly tentative and speculative guess. On the other hand, the contrast between the figures in our assessments and the corresponding modern totals is clear and unmistakable.

The total numbers of livestock in the Blackbourne Hundred, as listed in the assessments, were 17,059 sheep, 2321 pigs and 6525 cattle and horses.[30] These figures comprise also the demesne animals which I have excluded from my tabulation, and could therefore be taken to represent the total numbers of animals found in the Hundred in 1283. The comparable totals for 1908, which the Board of Agriculture and Fisheries communicated to Mr Powell, were 34,404 sheep (or double the number in 1283), 8274 pigs (or four times the number in 1283) and 6236 cattle (about the same). Reduced to sheep units the totals were 38,767 in 1283 and 61,386 in 1908. Even these figures, however, do not represent the disparity at its widest, for it is quite possible that at some other periods, such as the 1830s, the numbers of animals in the Hundred were higher than in 1908. What is more, the animals of the later period, though not necessarily larger, were fed better and presumably also were more productive in meat, milk, wool and, above all, manure.[31]

A wholly identical set of Ministry of Agriculture figures for the villages in our Wiltshire assessment has not been available for this study. Though for some of the villages the returns would be available at the Ministry, the area as a whole cannot be matched by a corresponding regional subdivision in modern statistics. It is, however, possible without a great strain on our figures to compare the modern and the medieval provision of livestock in the area by collating the available assessments of acreages and of livestock for the country as a whole. In 1867, i.e. at the beginning of the Ministry of Agriculture series of detailed figures of livestock, the total number of sheep in the county was about 700,000. Considered proportionately this number is somewhat smaller than the 500,000 sheep at the close of the eighteenth century in south Wiltshire alone which T. Davis gives in his report.[32] The 1867 figures worked out at 1033 sheep and 107 head of cattle for each 1000 acres of crop and pasture. Allowing for 20 per cent of wholly unproductive land, the 1867 figures would be

[30] These totals, based on Mr Powell's figures, differ very slightly from the totals in my tables.

[31] We must assume a general improvement through selective breeding in the various local breeds since the seventeenth century. There may also have been some substitution of smaller and more economical Southdowns and Crossbreds for the heavy Suffolk sheep, but on the other hand the food rations must have risen, especially in winter feeds.

[32] *General view of Agriculture in Wiltshire* (1794), p. 19. South Wiltshire in this context included the whole of Wiltshire chalklands, and comprised in addition to our region, the whole of Salisbury Plain and the valley and Downs of Wylie, but excluded Damerham with Martin.

equivalent to approximately 1000 sheep and 100 cattle for each 1200 acres of superficial area. From the available modern evidence, such as that given in Ellis's *Topographical Dictionary*, it is possible to compute roughly the superficial areas of the parishes corresponding to the assessed villages of 1291. The computation is, of course, bound to be very approximate, partly because some parish boundaries have changed since 1283, but mainly because the acreages of unproductive land at various times in the nineteenth century can be estimated only very roughly. In all the doubtful cases I have therefore chosen the lowest of all the reasonable estimates so as not to run the risk of overestimating the total area of the villages in our assessment. This minimum estimate (excluding Damerham and Martin) works out at 49,383, say 50,000, acres. On the basis of the 1867 provision of sheep for the county as a whole our area should have possessed at that time at least 45,000 sheep.

This estimate is bound to minimize the actual number of sheep in 1867, for the simple reason that provision of sheep in the chalk of south Wiltshire was bound to be higher than the average for the county as a whole. It is thus all the more significant to find that the aggregate number for the same area in 1225 was 10,798, or about one-quarter of our 1867 estimate. We are not able unfortunately to carry out a similar computation for cattle, but such attempts as I have made suggest that in this case the disparity, though considerable, was probably not as great at that in the numbers of sheep.

A similar confrontation of medieval figures with the modern ones should also be possible for the *banlieu* of Ramsey, and when made, it would almost certainly reveal a wide gap between the thirteenth-century totals and the modern ones. But it can be justly argued that owing to the radical changes in the agriculture of the Fenland since the Middle Ages comparisons of medieval figures with the modern ones would be meaningless. I therefore propose to restrict this stage of my inquiry, i.e. the stage concerned with the total numbers of animals, to the evidence of the Blackbourne Hundred and south Wiltshire.

The testimony is, of course, a very restricted one, and its relevance may at first sight appear to be very local. The students of bailiffs' accounts will, however, notice that it tallies with much of what we can learn of the lords' livestock in corn-growing regions of medieval England. For even the lords, in spite of their preferential rights over pastures, appeared as a rule to keep on their arable demesnes fewer animals than would modern agriculturists on the same scale. We shall thus be justified in interpreting the totals in our table as an indication of a general underprovision of livestock in thirteenth-century villages.

This interpretation of the livestock totals finds support in the other characteristic of thirteenth-century animal husbandry which we can deduce from the figures in the assessment, i.e. its 'functional' insufficiency. Considered as a component of mixed farming, livestock in the thirteenth-century villages of Suffolk and Wiltshire was very small not only by comparison with the livestock in the same villages in other times, but also with what appears to have been the needs of arable farming. According to Davis,[33] the practice on the downland farms of south Wiltshire at the end of the eighteenth century was to allow 1000 sheep to fold every night on one 'tenancy' acre, equal to two-thirds of the statutory acre (the allowance was presumably less on the north Wiltshire plain). In other words, a south Wiltshire downland farm of the same size as the medieval virgate, i.e. one containing about 30 'tenancy' acres of arable, might require the dung of at least 100 sheep throughout the year.[34] This ration was far and away in excess of what our south Wiltshire villages of the thirteenth century disposed of.

On the composite manor of Damerham and Martin the arable land in the hands of villagers amounted to about 6000 acres. We do not know whether the acres were statutory or customary, but as for the purposes of our present inquiry it will be safer to under-estimate the acreage than to over-estimate it, I am going to assume that the Damerham villagers' acre was the small customary one comparable to Davis's 'tenancy' acre. The total amount of livestock belonging to the tenants was about 5800, say 6000, sheep units or about one sheep unit per acre. To manure the Damerham virgate containing 40 acres on the eighteenth-century scale should have required at least 125 sheep units, but the number of sheep units a medieval virgate possessing its proportionate share of the village stock in fact commanded did not exceed 40, or about a third of Davis's standard. The actual shares were not of course proportionate; some tenants had more and others had less than their *pro rata* numbers. Yet even those who had more than their ration fell short of Davis's standard. Only some 67 out of some 215 Damerham and Martin taxpayers owned 40 sheep units or more. If sheep alone were considered, not more than 26 possessed 40 sheep or more, and not more than five possessed 100 sheep and upwards. Yet at the time of Abbot Michael (1235–54) there were in Damerham and Martin about 130 tenants with holdings of 20 acres and more, and some 70 tenancies of full 40-acre virgates, held whole or in combination.[35]

A similar picture emerges from the comparison of arable holdings and livestock in Tisbury and West Hatch, a manor of Shaftesbury Abbey for which we happen to possess both the assessment and the detailed lists of

[33] Davis, ibid. p. 61.

[34] Owing to widespread use of artificial fertilisers the modern requirements of dung in south Wiltshire farms cannot be compared with Davis's figures.

[35] *Glastonbury Rentalia and Custumaria* (Somerset Rec. Soc. 1891), p. 108.

villagers' holdings. In the late twelfth century the total area of tenants' land on this composite manor was equivalent to 106, say 105, virgates (this figure includes free tenants, but excludes military tenants).[36] Unfortunately, there is some doubt about the size of the Tisbury virgate. The internal evidence suggests 16 acres per virgate, but as this is much less than the virgates on most other Shaftesbury manors in the area, I propose to compute the acreage on two alternative assumptions – that of 16 and that of 30 acres per virgate. On these assumptions the approximate arable area in the possession of the villagers works out at either *c.* 1700 acres or 3150 acres. With the total livestock in the two manors equalling some 2820 sheep units we get the ratio of either 1·5 or 0·8 sheep units per arable acre. Neither ratio would provide the villagers with more than a fraction of the eighteenth-century requirement of manure. At the lower ratio a 30-acre holding would have less than a fifth of Davis's 125 sheep; at the higher ratio it would have a little more than one-third.

We cannot of course apply to our Suffolk evidence the folding standards of eighteenth-century Wiltshire. The villages in the Suffolk assessment which I classified as predominantly arable were situated in parts of 'Woodland' Suffolk where the soil was more fertile and certainly heavier and more retentive of nutrients than the chalk-cum-flint soils of south Wiltshire arable. No wonder that even in the eighteenth century the farmers in arable parts of central Suffolk, while maintaining considerable numbers of cattle, kept very few sheep and practised no, or next to no, folding. Arthur Young reported that in these parts of the county farmers kept sheep in proportions not greater than that of 20 per 100 acres. He blamed the neglect of sheep and sheep folds for the poor quality of yields and commended strongly the south Wiltshire example.[37] This ratio, however, may not have been much different from that in the 'stronger loam' villages of Hunston, Hopton, Stanton or Walsham-le-Willows in 1283 when the average sheep-holding per taxpayer was about four, and where the average arable holding per taxpayer may have been a little larger than one 20-acre bovate.[38] In this part of the county the

[36] B.M. MSS. Harl. 61, fos. 38 and 43.

[37] A. Young, *General View of Agriculture in Suffolk* (1794), p. 37 and *passim.* Cf. also his Suffolk examples in his *Northern Tour*. This compares with Young's figures for, say, south Lincolnshire, where the numbers of sheep varied from 250 to about 100 per hundred acres.

[38] This was the average holding of tenants above the cottar level in Hinderclay and Redgrave; Bacon MSS. Univ. of Chicago. This does not, of course, mean that the general provision of animals of all kinds in the 'arable' villages of Suffolk was necessarily the same, or about the same, in the thirteenth century as in the mid-nineteenth. Whereas the aggregate equivalents of horses, oxen and cows were about the same, the pig population was nearly four times as great as in 1283, and represented an addition of 1·5 to 2 sheep units per taxpayer. The interesting feature of these villages, however, is that the average of cows

numbers of sheep also remained low in the nineteenth century. If at that time the total numbers of sheep in the Blackbourne Hundred as a whole, and with them the total number of animals, so greatly exceeded the corresponding totals of 1283, this was almost certainly due to much greater numbers of sheep kept in 'pastoral' parts of the north-west and the extreme east ('High Suffolk'). There, both in Young's time and in the early seventeenth century the economy was almost purely pastoral. Writing at the turn of the sixteenth and seventeenth centuries, Robert Reyce observed how insignificant was arable farming in these sheep-grazing regions, where the villagers 'contented themselves only with so much tillage as will satisfy their own expenses', and where men subsisted 'chiefly upon pasture and feeding'.[39] We must therefore assume that the shortfall of animals, and above all of sheep, in the county as a whole in 1283 by comparison with later periods was due mainly to the inability of villagers in the 'pastoral' parts of Suffolk to keep as many sheep as they kept in the nineteenth century, and presumably also in the eighteenth and the seventeenth.

These various totals, and the impression of wider provision they give, will permit us to ask a number of related questions. One such further question concerns the very distinction between the villages I previously classified as predominantly arable and those I equally provisionally described as mainly pastoral.

It is, of course, obvious that both types of husbandry were merely variants of mixed farming, differing in the relative shares of animals and corn in their economy. In some parts of England and in certain periods of English history these relative shares differed sufficiently clearly to mark off regions predominantly arable, i.e. when corn provided the main source of revenue, from those predominantly pastoral, where the main, or at least a very large, proportion of revenue came from animal products. The historian of eighteenth-century Suffolk had no doubts about the reality of this demarcation as between the arable areas of central Suffolk on the one hand, and the pastoral areas of the 'Fielding' of the north-western and the eastern parts on the other. In Wiltshire the distinction has been somewhat confused by the over-emphatic use by older writers (mostly eighteenth-century ones) of the proverbial juxtaposition of 'chalk' and 'cheese'. In the sense in which this juxtaposition is commonly used it denotes two types of animal husbandry – one based on sheep and the other based on dairy cattle – whereas localities predominantly corn-

was about the same in 'pastoral' and in 'arable' villages. Dairying was obviously not an alternative to sheep-farming. In fact some of the highest averages of cattle per taxpayer will be found in such sheep-farming villages as Barnham.

39 Robert Reyce, *The Breviary of Suffolk* (1618), in F. Hervey, *Suffolk in the Seventeenth Century* (London, 1902), p. 29.

growing and those mainly dependent on animals could at some periods be found in both the chalk areas and in the cheese ones.

Our assessments suggest that the distinction between arable and pastoral villages (and incidentally also the distinction between Wiltshire chalk and Wiltshire cheese), however clearly observable in certain contexts, are well-nigh invisible when regarded from the point of view of thirteenth-century villages. In some villages in the assessments the numbers of animals per taxpayer were markedly larger than in others. As a rule these villages were situated in areas well suited to animal husbandry. I have therefore had no option but to describe and to classify them as 'pastoral'. This description must not, however, be allowed to mislead the reader into thinking that in the thirteenth century in these villages sheep and cattle were necessarily the most important source of livelihood for the villagers, and that tillage and the production of cereals was a mere sideline. On the contrary, corn played an important, perhaps the more important, part in the economy of most villages classifiable as 'pastoral'.

The extent to which the villagers in the 'pastoral' villages were involved in arable farming is revealed clearly, if indirectly, by our assessments. If the value of sheep, pigs and cows with their young were taken to represent the villagers' stake in animal husbandry, while the value of their plough animals and, above all, of their stock of grain and their sown seed were taken to represent their involvement with arable husbandry, the comparison of these two values should enable us to judge the relative importance of the two branches of villagers' activities. This comparison is attempted in Tables 11.5 and 11.6. Table 11.5 summarizes relative values in the 'Fielding' villages of the Blackbourne Hundred, which according to the assessment of 1283 were much better provided with animals than the other Blackbourne villages, and where in the seventeenth and eighteenth centuries tillage was relatively unimportant. Yet in the valuation of 1283 the value of grain stocks, seed and plough animals was only little (some 20 per cent) below the value of sheep, pigs and cows. Our tables, moreover, exaggerate the current, i.e. annual, value of livestock compared with grain. As the average life of livestock was at least three years for sheep and possibly as much as five years for cattle, they should be treated as capital assets or as durable consumption goods. For relevant comparisons with consumption goods such as grain, what we need is not the full valuation of livestock but its annual value, i.e. its valuation divided by its assumed life. Thus adjusted the annual value of livestock would not exceed £200 compared with about £450 representing the value of grain plus one-fifth of the value of horses and oxen. Needless to say the values of sheep and cows compared to that of grain and plough animals were still lower in the more purely arable villages of the 'Woodland', where in gross, i.e. unadjusted, values grain and plough animals were £1315 and

TABLE 11.5 *Values of livestock and grain on 'Fielding' villages of Blackbourn Hundred in 1283 (in shillings)*[40]

Villages	Value of cows, calves sheep and pigs	Value of grain and plough animals
Ashfield Magna	790	1046
Barnham	2602	1328
Culford	1092	1407
Euston	1316	1436
Fakenham Magna	567	364
Ingham	1013	626
Kenttishall	838	881
Rushford	278	216
Sapiston	1030	925
Troston	850	894
West Stowe	1292	586
Wordwell	619	508
Total	12,287	10,217
	or £614 7*s* 0*d*	or £510 17*s* 0*d*

those of sheep, pigs and cows were worth £825.[41] In this respect, however, the difference between the two groups of villages is not such as to prevent us from regarding both as communities engaged in mixed farming, in which corn-growing was the main channel of investment and the main source of income. The clear contrast between the sheep farming 'Fielding' and the corn-growing and dairying 'Woodland' belongs to the later centuries when both population and arable husbandry of 'Fielding' receded, and sheep came back into their own.[42]

Had we possessed complete surveys and manorial accounts of these villages we might have checked these computations by comparing the aggregate annual yields of sown fields and of productive livestock. Unfortunately we possess a suitable collection of manorial evidence for only one of the villages – Hinderclay – and the information it contains lacks details of profits of stock. But such general impression as these records give strongly re-inforces our conclusion that, judged by their sources of income, the pastoral and arable villages in the Blackbourne Hundred differed only in degree, and not in high degree at that.

These findings are well supported by the evidence of the villages in the *banlieu* of Ramsey. I have already shown that in the south Wiltshire

40 Livestock valued at the approximate valuation in 1283 assessment, i.e. sheep and pigs at 1*s* each, other animals at 3*s* each. Grain valued at 4*s* a quarter, which is the average value of grain in the 1283 valuation.

41 The adjusted, i.e. annual, value would be about £950 for grain and plough animals and £200 for sheep, cows and pigs.

42 Prof. M. W. Beresford has, in this connection, drawn my attention to the numerous earthworks of deserted villages and ruined churches in the 'Fielding' of Blackbourne.

assessment, which was an Easter one, the villagers' annual holdings of grain were greatly undervalued and could not therefore be used for comparisons with the Suffolk grain figures. On the other hand, in the *banlieu* of Ramsey the assessment was, as in Suffolk in 1283, a post-Michaelmas one, and its grain data is therefore fully comparable with that I have just analysed. What makes the comparison all the more significant is the intermediate character of the *banlieu*'s economy. I have shown that although predominantly arable the villagers in the *banlieu* had access to meadows and pastures in the near-lying fenlands or erstwhile fens, and could therefore maintain larger herds than the inhabitants of arable villages in most other parts of England. We could therefore expect the investment or the annual value of the villagers' livestock to have been not only considerably higher than in the arable villages of north-west Suffolk, but also high enough to match the value of the grain and plough animals. This, however, was not the case. Table 11.6 shows that the 'gross' value of the grain and plough animals possessed by the peasant taxpayers in the *banlieu* was some 50 per cent higher than the value of their sheep, cows and pigs – an excess greater than the one we have noted in the predominantly arable villages of Suffolk. The excess in the adjusted, i.e. annual, figures would be still greater. Here again the greater involvement in animal husbandry apparently did nothing to modify the predominantly arable character of the economy. This arable bias of village economy also shows through our Wiltshire evidence even if it cannot be exhibited by a series of figures similar to the Suffolk ones. I have already noted that the assessments of the Wiltshire villages possess a number of features which at first sight do not consort well with what we commonly assume to be the characteristics of the rural economy of settlements on the type of land on which our south Wiltshire villages stood. One somewhat unexpected feature of the assessment is that it should have comprised a whole group of downland villages – nearly half

TABLE 11.6 *Values of livestock and grain on banlieu of Ramsey in 1291 valued in prices of Suffolk Assessment of 1283 (in shillings)*[43]

Villages	Cows, calves, sheep and pigs	Grain and plough animals
Wistow	750	1572
Great Raveley	850	1304
Upwood	950	1685
Bury by Ramsey	729	701
Heighmongrove	786	712
Total	4071	6034
	or £203 11*s* 0*d*	or £301 14*s* 0*d*

[43] See Table 11.5.

of the total – in which the average number of sheep per taxpayer (though not the total number of animals) was ten and below: an average so low as to lead me to classify them outright as 'non-pastoral' or predominantly arable. In some of them the average was lower than in the anciently and traditionally arable villages of Suffolk or Huntingdonshire.

For these low sheep quotas in some of the chalk villages we can perhaps find valid geographic excuses. Uggford, with barely four sheep per taxpayer, was situated close to Wilton at the confluence of several river valleys. It comprised some downlands with what could have been, and once must have been, good pasture; but they were relatively low and in part covered with clay-cum-flint deposits which lent themselves well to corn-growing. Burcombe, another manor with a low quota, though surrounded with downs, was situated at the lower end of the Nadder valley. But it is difficult to find geographic reasons why Baverstock, a hamlet well up the valley backed to the north by extensive and high downs, or Teffont-cum-Dinton in the very midst of the Nadder uplands with the high Teffont Down behind it, or the somewhat similarly situated village of Tisbury, should have been assessed at no more than ten sheep per taxpayer (Baverstock was in fact assessed at a mere four). The answer to this conundrum is that in spite of the seemingly abundant facilities for grazing, the sheep-and-corn economy of these villages was heavily weighted in favour of corn and that, even allowing for the dairy-farming practised in them, the villages do not appear to have depended on their livestock for livelihood any more than the more purely arable villages on the corn-growing plains.

The dependence on corn was of course older than the thirteenth century. The downs behind the villages, not only those so ill-provided with sheep as Burcombe and Barford, but villages which still appeared to be deeply involved in sheep-farming, like Alvediston, or Berwick St John's, or Bower Chalke itself, lay within a landscape which is now deeply scarred by marks of ancient tillage. The scars, like those to be seen in downland areas elsewhere, probably relate to medieval, i.e. pre-fourteenth century fields.[44] Throughout its subsequent history the region remained one of corn-and-sheep husbandry. Yet the figures in our assessment are unintelligible except on the assumption that in the thirteenth century men had come to employ a much larger proportion of the chalk lands as arable and a much smaller one as sheep runs than they apparently were to employ in the eighteenth century, and may also have employed at some earlier age.

This surmise is borne out by what we can learn from our assessments about the distribution of animals among the villagers. One thing that

[44] H. C. Bowen, *Ancient Fields*, British Association for Advancement of Science, 1961.

must strike every student about the distribution is that a very large proportion of taxpayers in this traditionally sheep-farming area, 381 out of 961, should have had no sheep. The numbers of villagers without sheep must in fact have been still larger, since among men below the exemption limit the proportion of sheepless men must have been much higher than among the taxpayers. In some villages – mostly those with low average quotas of sheep – the majority of the taxpayers had no sheep, e.g. in Baverstock, Tisbury with West Hatch, Donhead, and of course the valley villages of Sedghill, Semley and Little Cheverell.

The second and even more significant feature of the distribution is that such a disproportionate share of the village flocks should have been owned by a few rich men. The distribution is least unequal in Bower Chalke, but even there the four richest men owned 265 out 913 sheep, or nearly 30 per cent. The inequality is very much greater elsewhere. In Alvediston four out of 28 taxpayers owned nearly 60 per cent of the flock, or 548 out of 931. In Berwick St John's four out of 25 taxpayers owned 71 per cent of the total, or 560 out of 786. In 'Wakefont' seven out of 49 taxpayers owned 560 sheep in a vill flock of 1053, or nearly 53 per cent. In West Hatch the entire flock of 233 sheep was owned by the three richest taxpayers (out of 21). In Homington one wealthy man (apparently not the lord of the manor) owned 127 of the village's 238 sheep, or 54 per cent.

The concentration of sheep ownership would have appeared even greater had the flocks obviously owned by the lords of the manors not been excluded from our reckoning. It may, of course, well be that a few of the rich sheep-owners included by me were in fact landowners or members of the landowning class. This does not, however, affect the significance of our figures. For what is significant about them is that in nearly all the villages which on the strength of their average sheep quotas I have classified as sheep-farming, the mass of the villagers should in fact have possessed so few sheep. If we deduct from the village flocks in these villages the possessions of the few rich men listed here, the remainder of the flock would not provide quotas per head of taxpayers any larger than, or indeed as large as, those we find in villages I have from the very onset classified as predominantly arable.

Thus sheep-farming in our part of south Wiltshire appears to have been to a large extent the rich man's occupation. Needless to say the poor men without sheep did not all go without animals. In general it will be noticed that the total number of cows and their young in our area, equal to about 7750 sheep units, was about half as great as the number of sheep. But it will also be noticed that except in Sedghill and Semley – two small villages with the smallest sheep flocks and the largest herds of cattle – the numbers of cows per taxpayer varied little from village to village and

TABLE 11.7 *Ownership of animals in south Wiltshire*

		No. of taxpayers		
Village	Total	Without cattle	Without sheep	Without any animals
Group I				
'Apch' (Broad Chalke?)	47	3	8	0
Bower Chalke	40	0	9	0
Homington	10	0	3	0
Alvediston	28	0	8	0
Berwick St John's	25	1	6	0
Bridmore	16	0	0	0
'Wakefont'	49	1	10	0
Group II				
Damerham	124	1	44	1
Martin	85	2	6	0
Group III				
Barford	5	0	1	0
Chilmark	54	0	3	0
Tisbury with W. Hatch	109	2	72	0
Donhead	137	0	80	0
Berwick	8	1	0	0
Dinton and Teffont	79	0	44	0
'Stych'	25	0	1	0
Group IV				
Baverstock	9	0	8	0
Burcombe	20	0	4	0
Uggford	15	0	7	0
Sedghill	17	0	16	0
Semley	38	0	34	0
Little Cheverell	22	0	17	0

were not necessarily smaller in villages with large sheep flocks (*vide* Bower Chalke and Bridmore). Above all they were more evenly distributed, i.e. were not as a rule engrossed by a few men, but were owned in small numbers by nearly all the taxpayers. As Table 11.7 shows, there were quite a number of taxpayers without sheep, but hardly any taxpayers without a cow or a calf or a pig. As many of the men with but one cow or calf also had a little grain, it would be reasonable to regard them as humble villagers whose few animals were appendages to their small holdings, or *vice versa*. But this is merely another way of saying that the middling and small man in the reputedly sheep-farming villages of south Wiltshire was the man with 'three acres and a cow'.

A similar demonstration in the case of the Ramsey evidence, though possible, would not be equally profitable. Although there the inequalities in the distribution of animals were well marked, they can do nothing to elucidate the distinction between pastoral and non-pastoral communities,

TABLE 11.8 *Ownership of animals in Blackbourne Hundred and banlieu of Ramsey*

		No. of taxpayers			
Village	Total	Without cattle	Without sheep	Without any animals	Without grain
Blackbourne Hundred					
Barnham	40	8*	2	0	8*
Culford	20	3	4	0	1
Euston	32	1	7	0	0
Fakenham	18	4	6	0	4
Ingham	27	3	10	0	3
Sapiston	29	3	4	0	3
West Stowe	20	2	1	0	5
Wordwell	20	4	6	0	3
Great Ashfield	30	1	4	0	0
Parva Ashfield	33	2	5	0	2
Bardwell	127	21‡	25	2	12†
Barningham	52	3	12	1	0
Elmswell	25	1	5	1	0
Hepworth	50	3	25	2	3
Hinderclay	40	3	12	3	0
Honington	38	6**	15	3	3§
Hopton	75	6	32	6	2
Hunston	16	1	7	1	2
Ixworth	53	7	19	2	3
Knettishall	28	1	5	2	0
Langham	22	0	8	0	0
Livermere Parva	24	5††	12	0	6††
Market Weston	39	1	12	0	4
Norton	35	0	14	0	1
Rickinghall Inferior	58	8	13	2	1
Rushford	9	0	0	0	0
Stanton	97	5	26	2	1
Stowlangtoft	30	5‡‡	9	0	5‡‡
Thelnetham	51	1	28	1	1
Thorpe	39	2	21	2	2
Troston	31	1	19	1	0
Walsham	87	2	35	1	2
Wattisfield	44	1	4	17	3
Ramsey Banlieu					
Wistow	37	3	10	2	3
Great Raveley	44	1	25	1	1
Upwood	45	3	15	1	4
Bury by Ramsey	20	0	11	0	6
Heighmongrove	30	2	15	2	6

* Of these, six inhabitants of other villages keeping sheep in Barnham.
† All inhabitants of other villages (mostly Thetford) keeping sheep in Bardwell.
‡ Of whom 12 inhabitants of other villages (mostly Thetford) keeping sheep in Bardwell. § Inhabitants of other places keeping sheep in Honington.
** Of whom three inhabitants of other places keeping sheep in Honington.
†† Of whom at least three non-resident. ‡‡ Of whom two probably non-resident.

for, as I have shown, that distinction is not to be found in the villages of Ramsey *banlieu*. On the other hand the distribution of flocks in the Blackbourne Hundred of Suffolk will repay some further study since in that area the contrast between the sheep-farming villages in the Fielding and the more purely arable ones in the 'Woodland' appears at first sight as sharp, if not sharper, than in Wiltshire. There, as in south Wiltshire, a large proportion of the taxpayers possessed no sheep, though nearly all possessed some animal or other. As in south Wiltshire, nearly all the taxpayers had cows or calves, and the average holdings of these animals were not higher in arable villages than in the sheep-farming ones. In fact the highest average will be found in the sheep-farming village of Barnham. In other words, in 'pastoral' Suffolk, as in south Wiltshire, dairying was not an alternative to sheep-farming.

Similarly the ownership of sheep among those who possessed them was distributed very unequally, perhaps even more unequally than in south Wiltshire.[45] In each of the six villages with the largest flocks or the largest quota of sheep per taxpayer – Barnham, Culford, Euston, Fakenham Magna, Ingham and West Stowe – a few wealthy sheep-owners possessed the lion's share of the assessed flock. In Barnham 1720 out of 2525, or 65 per cent were owned by 11 taxpayers out of 47. In Euston 735 sheep out of 1103, or 67 per cent, were owned by 6 taxpayers out of 34. In West Stowe 6 out of the 21 taxpayers, of whom one was the Master of the Hospital of St Saviour, owned 623 out of the village's total of 1019 sheep, or 61 per cent. A striking, but also doubtful, case is that of Culford, where out of 599 sheep 356, or 58 per cent, were in the possession of only two villagers, both of whom are described as *prepositi* and may have managed other men's sheep. But the extreme case is that of Fakenham Magna where out of 932 sheep 520 were the Abbot of Tilney's, and out of the remaining 412 not less than 335, or more than 81 per cent, were owned by three richer men, while the remaining 15 taxpayers in this traditionally sheep-farming village had only 75 sheep, or five per head. Even that, however, is more than the common run of villagers appear to have possessed in one or two other sheep-farming villages in the Suffolk 'Fielding'. In general, once the large individual flocks which I have specified are removed, what remains of the village sheep in these six sheep-farming villages will not provide an average quota per taxpayer higher than that which we have found on the anciently arable villages on the heavy corn-growing lands of 'Woodland' Suffolk.

[45] As demesne flocks in the Blackbourne Hundred were few and are difficult to distinguish from other large flocks, I have included them in my calculations here. Their inclusion will not, however, materially affect the averages. Some of the larger flocks, here as in south Wiltshire, may include possession of landowners, but it would be contrary to the purposes of this argument to exclude them even if they could all be identified with any certainty.

The distinction between the pastoral and non-pastoral villages in the regions covered by our assessments thus turns out to be something of a phantom. The line is clearly visible from the viewpoint of later centuries or from that of the manorial lord with his demesne flocks and of the richer peasant with his scores and hundreds of sheep. But it is apt to vanish from view the moment we shift our gaze to the small and middling men working their land in the thirteenth century.

This 'crying down' of pastoral husbandry in the Wiltshire and Suffolk countryside might strike an orthodox reader as a statistical disappearance trick, but a reader forewarned by some other recent studies will not find it surprising. Is it anything more than a restatement in concrete and social terms of the economic and social 'model' of the thirteenth-century economy which is now emerging from our researches? The model is one of a society in which population was abundant and growing, land was scarce and getting scarcer, and men in search of sustenance were forced to till the lands which in other and more spacious periods would and should have been used as pasture, and in fact were so to be used again from the fourteenth century onwards.

Thus viewed, exiguous village flocks and herds and the inability of the humbler villagers to maintain sufficient livestock are inescapable characteristics of an age in which the frontier between corn and hoof had moved very far, indeed too far, cornwards. If so, the importance of the assessments discussed here may perhaps transcend the narrow limits of the three regions which they cover and bear directly on the main working hypothesis on which the historians of the thirteenth-century agriculture must operate.[46]

NOTE I. PRICES OF SHEEP AND CATTLE

The crude price ratios, i.e. those of ewes to oxen or those of lambs to calves, are nearer four than three to one. But in medieval flocks the proportions of lambs to sheep over one year old was much lower than the proportion of young cattle to cows and oxen. On the Bishop of Winchester's 32 demesnes possessing sheep, there were in 1275 (an average year) 23,425 sheep of all ages, of which 4,418, or *c.* 19 per cent, were lambs. On the same manors young cattle (725) formed nearly 35 per cent of the total (2,493): (Eccl. 2/159302). The relative proportions were approximately the same on the Blackbourne Hundred of Suffolk in 1283 and on the sheep-farming manors of the Abbot of Glastonbury, such as

[46] Since this article was written, the *Zeitschrift für Tierzüchtung*, Band 76, Heft 1 (1961), has published W. Abel's study of medieval cattle in which he reminds us of the *Vergetreidung* of pastures in medieval Germany, i.e. their wholesale conversion into arable. At the height of the process the livestock was kept only in so far as it was necessary to corn-growing, and was no more than a 'necessary evil'.

the Deverills or Damerham. This is why when total values of sheep in the assessment are aggregated the average works out at about one-third of the average value of bovines similarly computed.

NOTE 2. SHEEP AND LAMBS

In the Blackbourne assessment there were 3674 lambs in a total flock of 17,128 or 21·5 per cent of the total. On 32 of the Bishop of Winchester's manors (being all the manors on which complete flocks were kept) at Michaelmas of 1275 – an apparently normal year – the aggregate flock was 23,425 and the number of lambs 4,418, or about 19 per cent (Eccl. 2/159302). On Glastonbury estates the ratios are somewhat more difficult to compute owing to inter-manorial movements of sheep, but in the Damerham and Martin group, which from this point of view were self-contained, the lambs in normal years formed about 20 per cent of the total. On the Bec Abbey's Hampshire manors of Combe in 1306–7 there were at the end of the year only 151 lambs in a total flock of 851, but that was a year of bad murrain. In the following year the total flock of 951 contained 227 lambs or 23 per cent. (*Documents of the English Lands of the Abbey of Bec*, ed. M. Chibnall, *Roy. Hist. Soc.* (1951), LXXVI, 155.) In 1296–7, on the duchy of Cornwall manor of Berkhamstead, the numbers at Michaelmas were 344 and 88, or 25 per cent; on its Bedfordshire manor of Sundon they were 88 and 25, or 28 per cent. (*Earldom of Cornwall Accounts*, I, ed. Margaret Midgeley, *Roy. Hist. Soc.* (1942), LXLI, 11–25.) In short, 25 per cent was the maximum, and the Blackbourne, Winchester and Damerham coefficient of *c.* 20 per cent was the statistical mode. This is rather less than the proportion of lambs in modern sheep-flocks, but since the Middle Ages there have been great improvements in the breeding of fertile ewes and in the care of lambs and ewes. If modern ratios were adopted here, the Meon flocks would be about one-third smaller than the ones that emerge from my computation.

12

GLASTONBURY ESTATES IN THE TWELFTH CENTURY*

The estates of Glastonbury Abbey have always figured very prominently among the manorial specimens of the twelfth century familiar to historians. The late twelfth-century survey of Henry de Soliaco published by the Roxburgh Society in 1877 has provided historians with a document at least as full and as reliable as the other well-known surveys of twelfth-century estates, i.e. those of the Bishop of Durham, of the abbey of Peterborough, of Bruton Priory and of the canons of Saint Paul's. And until recently this small group of sources formed the backbone of the economic historiography of the twelfth century. It was much used by Vinogradov and his contemporaries and has also been greatly relied on in some more recent studies.[1]

What made the Henry de Soliaco survey specially attractive was the geographical location of the estates. For, unlike the estates of the Bishop of Durham or those of Bruton Priory, the estates of Glastonbury were situated in parts of the country which happened to be fully covered in the Domesday survey (i.e. in Somerset, Wilts, Dorset, Berkshire), and were at the same time sufficiently manorialised in 1086 to be capable of relevant comparison with similar surveys of later date. More recently its value to historians has been further enhanced by Dom Aelred Watkins's edition of the Great Chartulary of Glastonbury. It is now possible to add to its value still more by making public the contents of a most valuable, even though very brief and somewhat fragmentary, collection of surveys of Glastonbury estates in the Hearne MSS.

This collection is contained in a fourteenth-century compilation which now forms part of the Trinity MS. from which Hearne derived most of his material for his edition of the works of John of Glastonbury.[2] The existence of this MS. was a few years ago pointed out to me by Dom Aelred Watkins, who also placed at my disposal his own transcript of its most important parts. The full results of my subsequent study of this document, and possibly the text of the MS. itself, will, I hope, be

* This paper first appeared in *Economic History Review*, 2nd ser., v, 1953.

1 E.g. the present writer's 'Chronology of Labour Services' in *Trans. Roy. Hist. Soc.* (1937), reprinted as Chapter 7 above.

2 Trinity Manuscript 724 (R. 533), f. 115 seq.

included in a later publication. In the meantime historians working on twelfth-century subjects may be interested in a preliminary survey of its contents, and in an equally preliminary summary of conclusions which its study has suggested.

The most important document, and also the one most useful for purposes of comparison, is that embodying the findings of an inquest into the income of the estates carried out in the last quarter of the century by Hilbert the Precentor. This inquest describes the estate at two points of time – the year 1176 in which Henry of Blois, Bishop of Winchester and Abbot of Glastonbury died, and a year unspecified in the reign of King Henry I, i.e. not later than, and probably earlier than, 1135. In the nature of things, much of its evidence is somewhat indirect, for the compiler must have derived his earlier data from other returns and, possibly, from surveys no longer available. The genuineness of the information is not, however, in doubt. On most manors the figures for 1176 approximate to those of the more fully authenticated surveys which were compiled somewhat later, while the figures for the time of Henry I in many cases agree with what some later surveys tell us the position had been in the first half of the twelfth century.

Next to this inquest in chronological order comes a brief survey, the interpretation of which has been greatly impeded by a clerical error in the date. The survey is introduced by the following heading: *Anno ab incarnacione domini nostri Ihesu Christi MCXXVIII quando Dominus Savaricus gracia divina Bathon: episcopus de novo saisivit abbattiam Glaston. tunc invenit quidam manoria abbattie ad firmam et quidam in dominico.*[3] The fourteenth-century compiler who transcribed this heading obviously made a mistake. Bishop Savaricus was abbot in the last quarter of the twelfth century, i.e. between 1192 and 1203. The words 'de novo' suggest that the date is in the late 1190s, the time when Savaricus was reinstated. The real date may then well be 1198 or 1199. The mistake in transcription could perhaps be explained by the copyist's misreading of the second C in MCXCVIII as X or else by his having mistranscribed the alternative version of 98 which is $^{\text{iiii}}_{\text{xx}}$ XVIII. Internal evidence, such as the comparison of rents – in the twelfth and thirteenth centuries rents of assize changed rather slowly – shows that in point of time the survey stands much nearer to the great surveys of the late twelfth and early thirteenth centuries than it does to the Domesday Book or to Hilbert the Precentor's evidence for Henry I's time.

Slightly later still is yet another inquest, that of Reginald de Fontibus, clerk of Hubert Walter, the Archbishop of Canterbury, dated 1201.[4] Though much briefer than the Soliaco survey of 1189, it occasionally

[3] Ibid. f. 117g. The folio is mistakenly numbered as 116.
[4] Ibid. f. 110d.

deals with matters left out of that document, and can usefully be employed in supplementing it.

Thus, counting Henry de Soliaco's survey, there are now five (six, if Domesday is counted) documents describing the estates of the Abbey between 1086 and 1201: truly a unique record of a century and a quarter of continuous change. The continuity of the change comes out very clearly, though its direction is the same as in most other estates in the twelfth century. The first and clearest impression which the series leaves on the mind of the student is that of a slowly contracting demesne. Traces of recent inroads into the area and economy of the demesne can be seen in the survey of Henry de Soliaco of 1189. Whereas it contains very few signs of recent additions to the demesne, it bears clear testimony of recent withdrawals of land, large and small. It may tell us nothing about land which may have gone out of cultivation altogether, but it abounds with references to other inroads into the demesne and more especially to tenants' holdings carved out of lands previously under direct management of the lord. We find at least nine holdings of about a quarter of a virgate each carved out of the demesne of Glastonbury Manor itself, four similar tenements established on the demesne of Berrow, some twelve smallholdings on the demesne of Street, five virgates on the demesne of Badbury, and miscellaneous holdings, mostly small, on the demesne of Walton, Ashbury, 'Brent', and elsewhere.

The area comprised by these holdings may not be large compared to the total extent of the Glastonbury estate, but there is no doubt that they do not exhaust all the twelfth-century impingements on the demesne. They are all relatively recent, and the evidence of the other twelfth-century documents makes it clear that the withdrawals from the demesne had gone on for a long time. Indeed, a comparative study of the other twelfth-century surveys, from the Domesday Book onwards, will show that the changes recorded in 1189 were little more than concluding instalments of a much longer process.

Needless to say, a comparative study of this kind, based as it must be on a collation with Domesday entries, is beset with many dangers. We cannot be certain that terms, including the commonest measurements, were used in the same sense throughout the hundred years separating the Domesday entries from the late twelfth-century surveys. Still less can we be certain that the basic units, the individual manors themselves, remained throughout the period sufficiently stable to be comparable. Some of them may have been subdivided in the course of the century, others, we know, coalesced with neighbouring manors; from some of them sub-manors had budded off, others on the contrary had absorbed smaller properties.

These vicissitudes of manorial ownership must not be overlooked and must be allowed for. As a result of these allowances whole manors have been left out from calculations wherever the Glastonbury chronicles or charters or internal evidence suggest that in the course of the century they may have lost their identity with the manors of the same name recorded in the Domesday. This has meant sacrificing Glastonbury itself, and frequently leaving out the great Wiltshire manor of Damerham, some of the constituent manors of 'Brent', as well as a number of other smaller units. Yet after all these subtractions, there still remain some twenty to twenty-five manors which can safely be assumed to have been essentially the same at the end of the century as the corresponding manors in the Domesday Book. Changes in their structure and area there doubtless were; in fact this study is based on the assumption that the manors underwent important changes. But they were all in the nature of continuous accretions and diminutions, such as would be produced by the action of economic forces, common to entire regions or even the country as a whole. At any rate they do not appear to have been either so radical or so accidental as to invalidate general comparisons or to make it impossible to apply common measurements.

The first and most obvious measurement is that of the size of the demesne as reflected in plough-teams. For some twenty-one manors for which both the Domesday and twelfth-century surveys give unambiguous evidence of demesne plough-teams, the relevant figures appear as shown in Table 12.1.

The figures in column 2 are those of ploughs on the demesne as given in the Domesday entries, the figures in the other columns are either those of plough-teams in the surveys where they happen to be recorded, or else are deducted from the recorded numbers of oxen on the demesne. This procedure is of course open to criticism. For it is possible that in some places the size of the plough-teams had changed during the twelfth century, thus invalidating the multiple of eight adopted here for converting the later figures of oxen into plough-teams and vice versa. None of these objections, however, is strictly relevant to the table as a whole. Deviations in the sizes of plough-teams could only have been local and exceptional and would not affect the global figures of such a widely dispersed monastic estate as that of Glastonbury. Nevertheless, wherever the figures in the Domesday Book seem too difficult to reconcile with other evidence, especially wherever they appear to be so large as to suggest the possibility that a change in the composition of teams had taken place, the entire manor has been left out of the table. Such are, for instance, the figures for Damerham with sixteen plough-teams recorded in Domesday, or for Grittleton with thirteen. The omission, however, does not weaken the general impression of a decline, for had the returns of these two manors been included, the decline would have appeared even more marked than Table 12.1 shows it to have been.

TABLE 12.1 *Plough-teams*

Manor	1086 Domesday Book (TRW)	c. 1135 Henry I	1176	1201
Ditcheat	3½	3	3	2½
Ham	3	2	2	2
Butleigh	5	4	3	2½
Walton	4	3	2	4
Pilton	10	6	3	2
Wrington	6	2	3	2
East Pennard	5	2	2	2
Buckland	4	5	3	4
Baltonsborough	2	2	1½	1
Winscombe	2	2	1	1
Doulting	2	2	1	1
Shapwick	4	4	2	3
Batcombe	2	2	1½	1
'Sowy' (Middlezoy, etc.)	2	2	1	—
Mells	2	3	1	3
West Monkton	4	3	2	2
Marksbury	2	2	2	2
'Brent'	8	6	6	6
Nettleton	4	3	2	2
Badbury	3	2	2	2
Totals	77½	60	44	45

As it is, the trend is clear enough. In the course of the century the number of plough-teams employed by the lord declined by nearly two-fifths, and the position as reflected in the figures for 'the time of Henry I', was half-way between the high figures in the Domesday and the low ebb of the last quarter of the twelfth century. From these figures it should be possible to conclude that the arable cultivation of the demesne declined in somewhat the same proportion. True enough, few of the Glastonbury demesnes entirely depended for their ploughing on the lord's own teams. On most of the manors customary tenants owed ploughing dues with their own animals which in the first half of the thirteenth century would sometimes be sufficient to provide for the ploughing and the harrowing of a large portion of the demesne. It might therefore appear that had ploughing services remained stationary or increased or had they been exacted in full, a fall in the numbers of the lord's own ploughs would not necessarily have reflected a corresponding decline in the cultivated area of the demesne. A simple calculation will show that on estates on which the tenants ploughed one third of the lord's demesne, a drop in the number of the lord's own ploughs by as much as 50 per cent would have corresponded to a drop in cultivation no greater than 33 per cent. But are we justified in assuming that the ploughing services remained stationary and were exacted in full? In the later centuries a proportion of labour services was invariably sold or remitted and there is no reason to suppose that a proportion, albeit a smaller one, was not commonly remitted in the twelfth century. What is even more certain is that throughout the century labour services were commuted for money, now piecemeal, now wholesale, according as customary villein tenancies were converted into rent-paying holdings. This process was in itself connected with the decline of the demesne, but whatever its cause, it makes it impossible for us to assume that while the lord's own ploughs dwindled the peasant's ploughing services continued to be discharged in the old measure. So unless it can be shown that the ploughing services remained the same and were exacted in full, the most probable deduction from the figures is that the numbers of the lord's ploughs roughly corresponds to the decline in the area of demesne lands he cultivated.

The impression of a dwindling demesne economy is reinforced by what we learn about changes in some of the other activities of the lord's demesne. The figures in the consecutive surveys suggest that pastoral activities of the landlords also suffered a decline and on the estate as a whole the fall in the arable acreage was not, as in the sixteenth century, compensated by an increase in herds and flocks. On the contrary, such figures for cattle and sheep as we possess suggest that live-stock declined even faster than the arable fields.

Needless to say the numbers of cattle were greatly influenced by the changes in the numbers of the plough-teams, for draught oxen formed a very large proportion of manorial cattle herds. It is not therefore surprising to find that in the manors for which the twelfth-century surveys give figures of livestock, the total numbers of cattle declined roughly in the same proportion as the plough-teams. On the twenty manors for which comparable returns are available (roughly the same as those in Table 12.1) the figures are 917 for the 'time of Henry I', 497 for 1176 and 438 for 1201. At first sight, the figures appear somewhat less regular than those of plough-teams. In some manors a recovery in livestock appears to have taken place between 1176 and 1201 and numbers actually rise from 13 to 56 in West Monkton, from 17 to 33 in Wrington, from 9 to 40 at Mells, and from 14 to 18 in Batcombe; and but for the exceptional fall from 96 to 14 in Winscombe the total figures for 1201 might not have shown any decline on those of 1176. The decline, however, is unmistakable in the forty or fifty years between the 'time of Henry I' and 1176.[5]

The decline in sheep flocks was even more marked. There are no figures

[5] The occasional figures for livestock in the 1189 survey suggest that on some estates the decline continued for some time after 1176, e.g. Baltonsborough, 'Brent'.

for sheep in the Domesday, but the later surveys provide us with comparable figures for sheep on some nineteen sheep-farming manors. These moved between Henry I's time and 1201 as shown in Table 12.2.

Even a casual glance will show that the figures for sheep are less regular and more variable than those for livestock; but this need not disturb us unduly. We now know that on large estates like those of Glastonbury sheep flocks were, so to speak, inter-manorial; that they were frequently transferred from manor to manor; and that altogether their numbers on individual manors from year to year were apt to vary a great deal. And irregular as our figures are, they are probably as reliable as any other returns in our surveys. Indeed, returns of 1201 provide a useful check on the entire series. They state not only the number of sheep on the manors in that year, but also the numbers which could be kept had the manors been more fully stocked, and these numbers correspond with those actually returned in one of the earlier surveys or are somewhat higher.[6]

The comparisons in the survey of 1201 of the stock actually kept, with those which could be carried gives us also a fleeting insight into another important branch of livestock economy of the demesne, that of dairy farming. The cow is an important but a somewhat mysterious subject of English economic history in the Middle Ages. Manorial records abound with references to vaccaries and dairy farms, and records of English foreign trade in the early Middle Ages are to a large extent concerned

TABLE 12.2 *Sheep*

Manors	Henry I	1176	1201
Street	200	Nil	Nil
Walton	100	Nil	Nil
Shapwick	400	Nil or 200	Nil
Ham	50	Nil	Nil
West Monkton	100	100	113
'Brent'	400	400	Nil
Winscombe	Nil	104	Nil
Wrington	150	100	Nil
Batchcombe	130	Nil	100
Ditcheat	350	Nil	64
Lympesham	100	30	Nil
Buckland	500	400	264
Sturminster Newton	260	Nil	Nil
Marksbury	200	200	700
Mells	200	42	150
'Cravenmere'	20	Nil	Nil
Doulting	258	74	Nil
Pilton	150	30	61
Totals	3568	1480 or 1680	1452

[6] E.g. in the returns of Winscombe and Wrington.

with exports of dairy produce. But direct evidence of dairy farming in our records, especially in those of the later Middle Ages is very scanty. This may well mean that dairy farming had been important in the earlier centuries and declined as time went on, and the hypothesis will be discussed again elsewhere. Here it will suffice to note that, if the 1201 entries are to be trusted, the cows had been fairly important earlier in the century, but had all but vanished from the demesne of Glastonbury by the end of the century. In the survey of that year returns for cows then to be found are coupled with estimates of the number which could be kept had the manor been fully stocked; and in the sixteen manors for which the figures are available, the situation appears to be as shown in Table 12·3.

The contraction of arable, as reflected in statistics of the lord's plough-teams, and the contraction of pasture, as reflected in statistics of livestock, are both direct economic manifestations of the dissolving demesne and of the growing importance of money rents. They are not, however, the only signs of the change. Other evidence, even if less direct and less purely economic, is provided by the transformation of customary tenures.

In considering the social trends in the medieval countryside it is important to bear in mind that the general historical tendency in the Middle Ages was for servile tenures burdened with predial dues to be gradually replaced by rent-paying tenancies. Left to itself, the system of

TABLE 12.3 *Cows*

Manors	Nos. kept	Nos. which could be kept
Sturminster Newton	3	10
Buckland	—	12
'Sowy' (Middlezoy, etc.)	15	25
Wrington	5	11
Winscombe	8	9
Kington St Michael	2	2
Berrow	8	24
Blackford	—	—
Pucklechurch	9	25
Badbury	—	16
Ashbury	—	12
Ham	—	3
Pilton	17	17
Doulting	—	10
'Cravenmere'	—	6
Mells	14	6
'Brent'	8	12
Marksbury	4	—
Wrington	5	11
Totals	98	211

labour services would have probably dissolved as a result of slowly accumulating relaxations in the conditions of individual tenures. But it can be assumed that the contracting demesne would eventually stimulate and speed up the process. Do we then in fact find the labour services relaxing on the twelfth-century estates of Glastonbury, and are the relaxations fast and general enough to be comparable with the record of the contracting demesne?

The answer is in the affirmative. Instances of commuted services and of villein tenancies made free of labour dues abound in the Henry Soliaco survey of 1189. We read of a customary two-virgater in Winterbourne and Monkton receiving his land by a charter some fifteen years previously; of two customary virgaters and one cottar in Badbury converted into rent-paying tenants at about the same time; of some five tenants of one or two virgates each in Buckland Abbas holding for money since the time of Henry of Blois, i.e. since about the middle of the century; of four tenants of half and a quarter virgate in Batcombe holding for rent by the grant of the same abbot; of some seven rent-paying tenants in Berrow holding some 13½ virgates by a grant similarly dated. In other manors, and in the first place in Glastonbury itself as well as in Ditcheat and Street, we find holdings which, we are told, *solebat operari*, i.e. used to work but no longer do so.

These instances do not, however, exhaust all the evidence of commutation. In 1189 they are all fairly recent and are in almost every case authenticated by individual grants, usually charters. The surveys, however, bear marks of commutation achieved in a manner both less formal and more wholesale and for that reason not identified with the specific charter of manumissions or a grant of freedom from services. The clearest instance is that of Grittleton where in 1189 the whole manor was farmed out to tenants and where, as a result, the demesne ceased to function as such, and labour services as far as we can see lapsed. There are also traces of somewhat similar development in the neighbouring manors of Nettleton and Badbury which in the past have been jointly farmed out with Grittleton. It is therefore difficult to escape the conclusion that twelve 'gavelingmen' (the term is generally accepted to mean rent-paying customary tenants) whom we find in the 1201 survey of Badbury were products of a wholesale but informal commutation like that of Grittleton. And the same survey also records existence of twelve 'gavelingmen' in Marksbury, seven in 'Cravenmere', and numerous rent-paying customary tenants not bearing that name in Wrington, Walton, Street, Ditcheat, Glastonbury and elsewhere.

There is of course no clear evidence to show that these rent-paying tenancies were all created in the course of more or less recent changes. But that many of them were twelfth-century creations is supported by the general tendency of the age as reflected in our documents. Whenever changes in conditions of tenure are recorded, they are all invariably in the same direction – away from labour services. This comes out especially clearly in entries dealing with new tenancies. Thus, when at some time before 1189, twenty-four virgaters in Ashbury received additional holdings over and above their old customary tenements, their additions were all held for rent and could not be subjected to service. As one of the entries puts it, the tenant who had received a cotland in addition to his virgate *dat pro ea tantum gabulum quantum alii dant pro una virgata et quietus sit operi*. The same is true of new holdings elsewhere and especially of innumerable pieces of land which were, during the century, given to customary tenants *ad incrementum terrarum suarum*. In 1189, i.e. at the time when these tenancies were recorded, or a little later, steps were already being taken either to withdraw the additional lands or to make them subject to labour services, but there is no doubt whatsoever that at the time when these holdings were created the tide was running the other way – towards rents and away from labour services.

It is because of that tide that, in spite of a general contraction in the economic activities on the demesne, revenue from rents appeared to grow. Our evidence of rents is of course very scanty. Most of it comes from the Savaricus survey in the 1190s and from Hilbert Precentor's returns for 1176. For the earlier period, i.e. the time of Henry I, our record of rents is confined to Ditcheat, Street and Ashbury. Moreover, figures of rents in Hilbert Precentor's survey are confined to manors which do not happen to be farmed in that year, and of those only eight yield evidence clearly comparable with that of the Savaricus survey. The evidence, such as it is, is set out as shown in Table 12.4.

TABLE 12.4 *Rents*

Manors	Time of Henry I			1176			Savaricus survey (1190s)		
	£	*s*	*d*	£	*s*	*d*	£	*s*	*d*
Pilton		—		13	9	0	13	9	0
Pennard		—		4	6	0	4	8	0
Ditcheat	3	14	0	5	10	0	5	10	9
Ham		—		3	13	4	4	4	1
Butleigh		—		4	0	0	3	14	3
Shapwick		—		3	10	0	4	4	3
Baltonsborough		—		2	13	0	3	4	4
Street	1	0	3	1	14	4	1	16	0
			Total	£38	15	8	£40	10	8
Ashbury	14	0	0	14	5	0		—	

This table suggests that in the last quarter of the century the rents of assize, like all the other economic indices, changed relatively little, but that such changes as could be detected were mostly in the upward direction: in the short period between 1176 and the Savaricus survey the total rent revenue of the eight manors rose from £38. 15*s* 8*d* to £40. 10*s* 8*d*. At the same time the surviving evidence of the earlier survey of the three manors, Ditcheat, Street and Ashbury, suggests that the rents had also been rising in the preceding period and had risen since Henry I's time more steeply than after 1176.

The significance of the rising rents will not escape the student of manorial finances. The customary rents in the narrow sense of the term – *redditus assize* – were the most conservative item in the manorial revenues. In general the custumals of the twelfth and thirteenth centuries, and still more the manorial accounts of later periods, make it clear that of all the payments due to the lord, assized rents, established in custom and rooted in time, were very stubborn and highly resistant to change. Rents of individual holdings hardly ever changed. If the total yield from rents sometimes fell, it was merely because holdings lapsed, were abandoned by tenants or were expropriated by landlords; if they rose, it was mostly when additional land was let out to rent-paying tenants so that *incrementum redditi* could be charged, or else when other customary dues, such as labour services, were commuted for money and the money payments were lumped with the rent. So if we find the customary rents rising, as they appear to have done in the twelfth century, the presumption is that either more land was let out to the tenants or that higher rent was being paid in respect of services commuted, or both. And as we now know, both in fact happened: new holdings were being created out of the demesne, and higher money rents were charged for holdings relet free of services. In the Ashbury instance already quoted (p. 258) a customary cotland let free of services paid in rent as much as a virgate burdened with labour dues; and on this basis practitioners of conjectural arithmetic could easily compute the increase in rents which might result from the new demesne tenements recorded in the surveys.

Thus viewed, the increase in rents was merely a financial counterpart of the changes on the manors which we have already measured in other and more real terms. The rents grew while the demesne was contracting. And it is because the rents grew that the total revenues of the manor did not decline during the period to the same extent as the livestock or the acreage under the direct management of the lord. Our evidence of the total financial yield of Glastonbury manors is fortunately more abundant and continuous than that of rents alone. Hilbert Precentor's returns either give us the valuation of manors or else enable us to arrive at some sort of a minimum estimate by adding together his figures for rents and his estimate of the annual value of the demesne yield. For a still earlier period there are the values given in the Domesday Book. We cannot of course be certain that the Domesday valuations were computed on the same basis as in the twelfth-century surveys, but on the whole, it seems unlikely that the Domesday returns of values contained any items other than the rents and the yields of the demesne, or failed to include either. In places like the manors of Glastonbury which were important centres of feudal administration and justice, some of the purely seignorial revenues may have overspilled into the estimates of manorial values. In a few other places, like Damerham or 'Brent', there may have occurred other changes which made their Domesday values difficult to compare with later returns. But if these manors were excluded, the values should be broadly comparable throughout the period.[7] The data of the fourteen least doubtful manors are as follows:

TABLE 12.5 *Values of manors*

Manors	Domesday Book (TRW)			The 'time of Henry I'			1176		
	£	*s*	*d*	£	*s*	*d*	£	*s*	*d*
Pilton	24	0	0	25	0	0	21	14	0
Pennard	12	0	0	6	16	0	9	5	0
Ditcheat	12	0	0	23	14	0	13	15	0
Batcombe	7	0	0	8	0	0	8	0	0
'Sowy'	24	0	0	15	0	0	15	10	0
Butleigh	10	0	0	8	0	0	7	18	0
Walton	15	0	0	12	0	0	9	0	0
Doulting	14	0	0	10	0	0	8	0	0
Wrington	30	0	0	20	0	0	25	0	0
Marksbury	10	0	0	10	0	0	10	0	0
'Cravenmere'	4	0	0	7	0	0	5	0	0
Mells	10	0	0	10	0	0	10	0	0
Ashbury	20	0	0	27	0	0	34	0	0
Shapwick	12	0	0	9	0	0	8	12	0
Totals	£204	0	0	£191	10	0	£185	14	0

The general picture is thus clear. The revenues were stable, but the curve showed the tendency to sag. Even though the rents rose, they were not sufficient to lift the general level of manorial income, or to counteract

[7] Of the larger manors, in addition to Glastonbury, Damerham, 'Brent', those of Nettleton, Grittleton, Winterbourne and Badbury have been excluded from the table. Their inclusion would not have affected the totals appreciably. Between TRW and Henry I, the revenues of Badbury rose from £10 to £15 and those of Nettleton and Grittleton declined. For the years of Henry I and 1176, we also possess the values of Sturminster Newton, Ham and Baltonsborough. These would also have left the totals unaffected since the values of Newton declined by £5 and those of Ham and Baltonsborough remained roughly stationary.

in full the slump of income from the direct exploitation of the demesne. To that extent, at least, the economic reorganization of the manor was not merely an administrative change but a probable response to an underlying economic pressure. How real and how general that underlying change was, the Glastonbury records alone would not reveal. The evidence of other places and even other times may have to be called in to help us.

GLASTONBURY ESTATES: A REPLY[8]

1

I presented my brief note on the Glastonbury manors in vol. v of this *Journal* as a 'preliminary survey' of the contents of the MS. unearthed in the Trinity College Library by Dom Aelred Watkin. I decided to go into print at that stage and in that form in order to draw comment from other students of Glastonbury evidence and to benefit from the criticisms of what I avowed to be no more than a 'preliminary summary of conclusions' suggested to me by the study of the MS. To this extent Mr Lennard's critical observations have not come wholly uninvited and are not altogether unwelcome. If my welcome is nevertheless not as whole-hearted as I might have wished, the fault is partly mine, but mostly Mr Lennard's. My fault is mainly one of compression. In trying to keep my note as brief and provisional as possible I refrained from expounding in detail all the evidence behind my conclusions. To have done otherwise would have necessitated a full-scale description of Glastonbury economy, and would, I thought, not be needed by commentators familiar with Glastonbury evidence. These expectations have to some extent been borne out, since several students, including Dom Aelred Watkin, have written offering further suggestions and emendations. Mr Lennard's article, however, makes it clear that the brevity of my note caused some misunderstanding and confusion. For this I owe my readers and Mr Lennard my apology.

On the other hand Mr Lennard's fault is to have attempted criticism and emendation on the strength of a narrowly circumscribed study. Whereas my 'preliminary conclusions' related to the whole period up to 1201 and were based on the juxtaposition of all the documents in the collection, i.e. Hilbert's Survey of 1171 and the two surveys which accompany it, Mr Lennard has chosen to confine his scrutiny to Hilbert's

[8] This reply first appeared in *Econ. Hist. Rev.* IX in response to an article by R. Lennard, 'The Demesnes of Glastonbury Abbey in the Eleventh and Twelfth Centuries', *Econ. Hist. Rev.* VIII (1956).

Survey and to one, or at most two, columns in my tables. Nor has he tried to interpret the evidence of this one survey with the help of the large amount of data about Glastonbury now available to scholars in both print and manuscript. It is, therefore, not surprising that while trying to correct my presumed mistakes, omissions and interpretations, he should have piled up a mass of ill-supported and, in my opinion, mistaken conclusions.

Some of Mr Lennard's remarks raise questions of principle, but most of them deal with details; and I hope the readers will forgive me if I deal with the latter first. Knowing Mr Lennard's interest in the Domesday Book and the surveys of the twelfth century, I had every reason to expect from his article a large crop of detailed emendations. It has, therefore, been something of a disappointment to find that out of thirty to forty points of detail he makes, only three, or at most four, represent acceptable corrections. The rest appear to me highly questionable and often wholly wrong.[9]

Most of Mr Lennard's emendations relate to manors which I am supposed to have unnecessarily omitted from my tables of plough-teams, sheep and rent. Mr Lennard is, of course, too courteous a controversialist to accuse me of omitting facts in order to better my argument. Unwary readers may, however, easily get the impression that my omissions were disingenuous or at least arbitrary and may be impressed by Mr Lennard's attempts to restore them. Therefore, at the risk of boring the reader, I shall briefly run over the names of some of the manors which Mr Lennard recommends for inclusion, indicating in each case the reasons for which they were omitted and must stay out.

As I explained in my article, the omissions from Table 9.1 are confined to manors whose demesnes may have undergone radical changes in composition between 1086 and 1201. The manor of Glastonbury itself, being a headquarters manor of the Abbey and a semi-urbanized vill, underwent greater changes in its territory than any other of the Abbot's manors. Most of the additions were through acquisition of property from

9 The corrections are as follows. In my Table 12.2 (Sheep) Cranmore is credited with twenty sheep instead of 200 as a result of a typing error. In my Table 12.1 West Monkton is credited with the figure of four ploughs in 1086 which belong to East Monkton. I dated Hilbert's survey as 1176 or the middle year of the abbacy of Robert of Winchester, with whose reforms I associated it. I subsequently discovered that Hilbert died in 1173, and could not have produced the survey in 1176. Finally, in explaining why the figures of Damerham were not usable, I quoted the figure of plough-lands instead of that of plough-teams: this misquotation however did not affect either my decision not to use the figure nor my totals in tables. The question whether my figure for Sowy is right depends on the proper rendering of *ociosa animalia* (see below, n. 27), and on this point I am still unrepentant. My figure for Nettleton in 1171 is an interpolation from the survey of 1189, but Mr Lennard does not apparently regard it as irrelevant (Lennard, p. 355, n. 3).

free tenants,[10] though the main change in Glastonbury territory probably came through the absorption of much of the territory of West Pennard.[11] The next most important omission is that of South Damerham. Not only did the manor at some times include and at other times exclude the large satellite manor of Martin (or Merton as Mr Lennard describes it) but it also at times comprised the berewicks of Twohyde and Tidpit. At one period it was also obscurely involved with the Bishop of Winchester's possessions in the same vill, and in the early twelfth century it also suffered from arbitrary seizures of land.[12] Indeed so confusing was the situation of the manor in 1086 that the Domesday jurors, in a formula most unusual in that survey, declared themselves to be ignorant of the area of the demesne – 'propter confusionem terrae'. Grittleton was omitted because at some time in the twelfth century the demesne was let out to the villagers, some of it may have been shared out among the lessees.[13] Pucklechurch, a detached possession in Gloucestershire, lost a hide to Hugh Mortimer some time in the twelfth century, and I have not been able to discover yet whether and at what time the hide was restored and whether it did or did not come out of the demesne land.[14] Mere was omitted for various

[10] Of this, thirteenth century evidence will be found in Dom Aelred Watkin (ed.), *The Great Chartulary of Glastonbury* (Som. Rec. Soc.), II, 292–5, 340, but the context makes it clear that acquisitions must have begun much earlier. There is also added uncertainty about the islands which were lumped with Glastonbury in the Domesday Book. Later sources account for one of them (Mere), but not for the other two.

[11] Judging from the names and locations of demesne furlongs in the thirteenth century, the ground between the Isle of Glastonbury and the Pennard heights bordering on and probably forming part of the Domesday vill of Pennardminster was absorbed into Glastonbury in the process of being reclaimed, though the twelfth-century core of West Pennard apparently remained a member of the conjoint manor of West and East Pennards. Longleat MSS. Bailiff's Accts. *passim*, e.g. no. 10,762. William of Malmesbury includes the whole of West Pennard in the 'twelve hydes' of Glastonbury.

[12] Longleat MSS. Bailiff's Accts. *passim*, e.g. nos. 10,655, 10,656: cf. also list of Damerham furlongs in B.M. MSS. Add. 17,450, f. 188. At the time of this survey, i.e. in the mid-thirteenth century 'South Todpule' (Tidpit) alone accounted for 160 acres out of the total of 656 in the demesne of Damerham without Martin. For the Bishop of Winchester's lands see Hilbert's Survey: '*Tunc de hoc manerio subtraxit episcopus Winton. duas hidas quas dedit Ricardo Pictavi*', Trinity Coll. MS. 724, R. 5.33, f. 116d. This survey also records the seizure of 300 acres of meadow and pasture by the Earl of Gloucester. For the Bishop of Winchester, see Professor Darlington in *Victoria County History* (*Wilts.*) (1955) II, 84, 86 and 96.

[13] *Liber Henrici de Soliaco* (Roxburghe Club, 1882), p. 107: '*Homines tenent villam ad firmam sed nullum receperunt instauramentum neque implementum.*'

[14] Hilbert's Survey op. cit. '*Tunc de hoc manerio deforciat Hugo de Mortimer unam hidam.*' This is the only reference of this kind in Hilbert's Survey. Similar seizures in some other manors are recorded elsewhere, but do not present much difficulty: in this case the failure of the subsequent two surveys to mention Mortimer's hide is difficult to interpret. In addition, a reliable estimate of plough-teams is made difficult by the statement that land in common fields was ploughed 'as if there were five plough-teams': '*terra in communi arata est*

reasons but mainly because of the difficulty of deciding whether the park and village of Westhay were included in Mere in the twelfth century as they certainly were in the thirteenth.[15] Ashbury was omitted because of its obscure and badly documented territorial involvement with the fields of Kingston (probably Kingston Lisle), but also because of changes in the demesne which were on a scale too great to be explained by piecemeal transformations such as were occurring elsewhere.[16] Blackford, with its striking decline of teams from three to one between 1086 and the 1130s, was originally omitted for the same reason, though on second thoughts I might have included it in my table.

These were my 'omissions' in the table of plough-teams. I may have erred on the side of over-caution in leaving them out, but I am sure that Mr Lennard errs on the side of over-audacity in including them. Had I included them my deduction that plough-teams declined would have been re-inforced, since these manors, including Grittleton, possessed forty-one plough-teams in 1086 and only thirty-two in Henry I. Mr Lennard himself admits that if all his 'emendations' were accepted, the total with Grittleton, but without Sowy, would still reveal a marked decline, even if a slightly smaller one than that shown by the table, i.e. 20·1 per cent compared with my 24 per cent.[17]

My omissions in the table of rents (Table 12.4) were, I believe, equally justified and Mr Lennard's restorations equally ill-advised. Mr Lennard suggests that I was mistaken in omitting from my table the manor of Baltonsborough. The manor was and must be omitted for the simple reason that throughout the greater part of the period it was not accountable for rent. In Hilbert's Survey the description of this manor, and of this manor only, is accompanied by the statement that it *erat ad elemosinam monachorum* and we learn from another source that, in 1079, Abbot Aglenoth gave it to the convent of Glastonbury.[18] It is therefore not surprising that the money payment in the time of King Henry does not look like rent, and is not described as such. The sum – one hundred

adeo bene sicut ibi essent quinque carrucate bovum'. Hilbert's Survey, op. cit., and *Liber Henrici de Soliaco*, p. 101.

15 Westhay is not mentioned in the Domesday. For later references to the park, fields and probably vaccary of Westhay, see G. Elton (ed.) *Rentualia et Custumaria, etc.* (Som. Rec. Soc. Pub.), pp. 209 et seq.; same survey in B.M. Add. MS. 17,450, fols. 145d et seq.: '*quondam domus cum curtilagio ad vaccariam.*' Bailiff's Accts. indicate that the vaccary was probably attached to Westhay: Longleat MSS. 6,365 and *passim*. For the topographical relation of Westhay to Mere, see Dom A. Watkin, op. cit. II, 124.

16 The fields at Combe-by-Kingston appear in the cropping plans of the thirteenth- and the early fourteenth-century Bailiff's accounts, but I have not been able to find any evidence to show whether they formed part of the manor in the earlier period: cf. Longleat MSS. 10,633.

17 Lennard, p. 356 and n. 3.

18 Hilbert's Survey, op. cit. f. 116d; Bodleian MSS. Wood, I, fols. 253–253d.

shillings – is altogether too round as well as too large a figure to represent the real yield of rents of assize. It was almost certainly a money charge levied on the manor: not an unreasonable or an uncommon procedure in the case of prebendiary or conventional estates. The manor of 'Lym' (whether it be Uplyme or Lympsham) is, and must be, omitted from the table of rents because, in addition to money rents recorded in the survey, it also rendered two weights of fish. Not only are the values of fish not given, but we are also kept in the dark as to whether the render was a weekly one, as in 1086, or an annual one, and whether it formed part of the demesne farm, or represented fish rents from tenants' holdings.[19] Wrington is, and must be, omitted because we are told that at a later period the revenue of the manor included £10 of *auxilium* (also an exceptional statement). Had Mr Lennard consulted the inquest of 1201 he would have noticed that the money yield of the manor at that date included an *auxilium* of £2, which apparently had to be added to the figure of *gabulum assisum* to give a proper estimate of rents for that year. We do not know whether this smaller sum was included in the rents of 1171 or in the £10 of *auxilium*.[20] The case of Damerham has already been accounted for.[21]

So much for the details of rents. But overshadowing the argument for the inclusion of this or that rent is Mr Lennard's admission that the inclusion of all the manors of his choice would have made little difference to the final totals: or to quote Mr Lennard himself, the totals show 'a percentage increase slightly smaller' than mine 'but not appreciably different'. If so, was this particular voyage really necessary?[22]

There remains only one allegation of omission: an allegation of a somewhat wider implication than the others. In criticizing my Table 12.2 (Sheep) Mr Lennard suggests that I had 'overlooked' the statistics for sheep in the Exon. Domesday. On this point Mr Lennard, who must be aware of my connexion with Eileen Power's history of medieval wool, might have guessed that I would not dismiss the Exon. Domesday's sheep without some reason. In fact, the reasons are several; and if some of them may not be familiar to historians, others are.[23] Thus one and a rather

19 Hilbert's Survey, ibid. '*tempore regis Henrici . . . reddebat quaque septimana duas summas piscium. Modo. . . reddit duas summas piscium et valet vij li.*'

20 Ibid. f. 115 records the rent of £9 4*s* 0*d*, and total value of £25, but adds, '*sed non potest tantum reddere sine auxilio de Wynescumbe quod valet melius quam x li.*' The survey of 1201 records the rent of only £8 11*s* 6*d*, and a *donum* of £2. As holdings had apparently been increasing and demesne ploughing declining, the decline in rent is highly implausible. Hence the presumption that a *donum* or *auxilium* had been reckoned with it in the past.

21 See above, p. 263 and n. 12.

22 Lennard, pp. 357–8.

23 Lennard, pp. 356–7. Miss Power's difficulty was that of reconciling the figures in Exon. Domesday with the distribution of pastures and with twelfth-

obvious reason is that in 1086 sheep pastures carried considerable numbers of goats, which were in later generations largely replaced by sheep. There were some 300 goats on the nine or ten Somerset manors of Glastonbury alone, and it is unfortunately impossible to make proper allowance for them without having resort to a purely arbitrary conversion factor. The sale value of a twelfth-century goat was about twice that of a sheep, but, judging from modern parallels, its voracity must have been considerably greater, which is probably why it was displaced in a later or more efficient age.[24]

Another and even more important reason why the Exon. figures of sheep are not usable is that, contrary to the apparent implication of Mr Lennard's remarks, the Exon. Domesday does *not* give the figures of livestock for all, or even for the bulk, of Glastonbury estates. Its figures of livestock are confined to the Somerset manors, and leave out not only the detached sheep-farming manors in Berkshire, Gloucestershire and Dorset, but the whole of the Wiltshire possessions of the Abbey where many, and eventually most, of the Abbey's sheep pastures were to be found.[25] Unfortunately we cannot, in dealing with sheep, treat the manors for which evidence is available in isolation from the manors from which the evidence is lacking. Thirteenth-century bailiffs' accounts make it clear that Glastonbury sheep flocks, like those of many other great estates, were inter-manorial, but Mr Lennard need not have gone to the thirteenth-century bailiffs' accounts to discover this. Do we not read in the 1189 survey that the flocks of Martin were supposed to consist of 500 draft ewes, or that on the manor of Ditcheat sheep were kept only in

century flocks. The probability is that the returns represent the numbers of sheep which the commissioners and the juries found on the days on which they visited the manors, and these were bound to fluctuate very widely from season to season. This is probably why the figures were not included in the final version of Domesday Book.

24 The Somerset manors for which the Exon. Domesday gives numbers of goats include Winscombe, Walton, Ashcot, Pilton, Batcombe, Baltonsborough, Wrington, Ditcheat and Glastonbury and the total is 292; it does not include the goats of sub-tenants. Hilbert's Survey does not mention any goats on Somerset manors for Henry I, and only ten (in Winscombe) for 1171. Outside Somerset there was a large herd of goats in Sturminster Newton in the 1130s which apparently disappeared by 1171. But even converted into sheep at the rate of 2 to 1, the goats listed in the Exon. Domesday would greatly outnumber the 438 'additional' sheep in 1171.

25 According to the Domesday summaries the Somerset manors comprised some 195 hides with seventy-five and a half plough-teams on demesnes; those of Wiltshire 337 hides with forty-two ploughs on demesnes. (The actual assessment in Wiltshire amounted to some 258 hides.) The low hidation of Somerset manors undoubtedly reflected large exemptions from geld, while relatively low figures of Wiltshire plough-teams reflected the pastoral character of these manors. In the mid-thirteenth century the 'outlying' manors provided more than a half of the Abbey's revenues. *Exon. Domesday*, fols. 173 and 527b; cf. Darlington, in *V.C.H. Wilts*, II, 218 n. 2.

the summer?[26] These references do not, as Mr Lennard suggests, throw doubt upon the relevance and significance of the livestock data of the survey, but are merely evidence of the inter-manorial character of sheep farming.[27]

This complication might not matter very much in the case of the Wiltshire Deverills, or of South Damerham in South Wiltshire, or Ashbury in Berkshire, which were probably too remote to pool flocks with the Somerset manors. But it does probably matter in the case of Buckland, of Sturminster Newton, and possibly of Winterbourne Monkton, which, judging from the thirteenth-century evidence, were more closely linked up with Somerset manors. In compiling my table I took care to include the first two of these sheep-farming manors, although what I know now about the Glastonbury estates, and did not know in 1952 leads me to think that the omission of Winterbourne has reduced the value of the table. But for the same reasons a column of figures from the Exon. Domesday, from which all the Wiltshire manors were excluded, would be wholly misleading.

So much for my detailed faults of omission. The main faults of commission, which Mr Lennard imputes to me are by comparison very few and are mostly confined to supposed mistakes in the identification of place-names. Unfortunately, I find it difficult to accept Mr Lennard's alternative identifications. I dare say some uncertainty attaches to the manor of 'Lym' which I identified as Lympsham, but which Mr Lennard thinks was the double Dorset–Devon manor of Lyme (or rather Uplyme and Lyme). The case against Mr Lennard's hypothesis is that in later documents, e.g. in those of 1189 and 1201 which he does not consider, Lympsham is returned separately under that name as an associate manor of the Brent group, whereas Lyme is not returned at all; that Lyme in fact had for some time before then been removed from the body of abbatial manors – one of the two manors may have been assigned to a sub-tenant, the other was allocated to the prebend of the Cellarer. The only strong piece of evidence in favour of Mr Lennard's identification, but which Mr Lennard himself does not invoke, is the annual render of

26 *Liber Henrici de Soliaco*, pp. 39, 129 et seq.

27 Cf. Lennard, p. 362. A jury recording only the stock it found at the time of inquest would not bother to specify that certain stock could be kept only in the summer. The two entries apparently mean that Ditcheat had only summer pastures and that its sheep wintered elsewhere, and that the pastures of Martin were not suited to lambs and lambing ewes. I have translated *oves ociosa* as draft ewes. Mr Lennard suspects me of transcribing *ociosa* as *operosa* (p. 355, n. 2). All I have done is to refuse to take the adjective in its classical meaning of 'idle' or 'leisurely'. Its exact sense is somewhat elusive, but the balance of probability is that it was most frequently applied to non-breeding animals: e.g. Doulting in Hilbert's Survey, where the flocks contained thirty-three *oves lactrices* and forty *oves ociosa* (f. 116); also *Liber Henrici de Soliaco*, p. 133.

fish, suggesting a site by the sea. This being the evidence, I am not prepared to defend my identification *à l'outrance*, but the balance of probabilities still inclines me in its favour.[28] No such uncertainty attaches to Mr Lennard's confident theory that the manor of Street was not surveyed in the Domesday, and that the teams of Street were therefore contained in the returns of either Glastonbury or Walton and to that extent invalidate my totals in my table. Had Mr Lennard consulted the evidence of charters and the bailiff's accounts, he would have realized that the manor of Street was in fact part of a composite manor of Street with Upleigh and Leigh and was surveyed in the Domesday under Leigh (Lega).[29]

This I think accounts for the points of detail raised by Mr Lennard. With them out of the way, we can turn to Mr Lennard's more general observations.

2

Mr Lennard's general argument is that the changes on Glastonbury demesnes cannot be viewed as a general trend of declining cultivation and rising rents. Rents did not rise in the same proportion as the plough-teams declined; the decline in plough-teams denoted not a contraction in demesne arable, but an alteration in the terms of farming leases; and in general, the phenomena noted by me were fortuitous in origin and local in incidence.

Mr Lennard's 'general' contentions are thus three in number, and I propose to discuss them in the ascending order of their generality. The first and lowest in this order comes his contention about the relation, or rather the lack of relation, between declining plough-teams and rising rents. Mr Lennard's attitude on this point appears to be coloured by his impression that the movement of rent did not appreciably diverge from that of plough-teams. This impression is, I am afraid, at variance with facts, and may partly be due to a flaw in Mr Lennard's statistical argument. In the three manors about which reliable evidence for the time of King Henry is available the divergence between the trend of rents

[28] *Exon. Domesday*, p. 148. Assignment to cellarer is specified in *Liber Henrici de Soliaco*, p. 9, but not mentioned in relation to *Lym* in Hilbert's Survey. If these two entries relate to the same manor, the assumption would be that the assignment took place between 1171 and 1189. But if the Domesday Lym and the manor I identified as Lympsham are the same, there would still be the difficulty of reconciling the values, which were £3 in the Domesday Book, £7 in 1171 and £12 in 1189. However, the possible confusion between the Devonshire and the Dorset manors might account for the difference.

[29] *Exon. Domesday*, p. 152 (fo. 164b). For fields and holdings in Leigh see Longleat Bailiff's Accts. *passim*: e.g. no. 11271 (12 John of Kent) with 164 acres recently let in Leigh; cf. Dom R. Watkin, op. cit. p. cxliij.

and that of plough-teams is clearly marked. In all of them rents rose, while plough-teams either declined, as in Street and Ashbury, or failed to expand, as in Ditcheat. The rents did not of course rise to the same extent everywhere. The rise was in the region of 50 per cent in Street and Ditcheat, but in Ashbury the rise appears to be less than 2 per cent, i.e. £14 5*s* compared with £14 at the earlier date.[30] It is, however, not the rise of rents in absolute amounts and taken in isolation that concerned me in my note, but their relation to the numbers of plough-teams. The problem in other words is one of correlation. And, although this is not the right place and I am not the right person to expound the niceties of statistical correlation, I hope I shall not be accused of excessive simplification if I point out that had the rents changed in the same direction and to the same extent as plough-teams, the revenue from rents at Ashbury would have been not £14. 5*s*, but somewhere near £9. 10*s*. The divergence between the two trends and the extent to which income from rents failed to follow the declining trend of demesne agriculture is thus not 5*s* but £4. 15*s*. The same, of course, would have applied to the other apparently small increases in rents in the manors which Mr Lennard cites, had their figures been sufficiently reliable to be used.[31]

However, to do Mr Lennard justice his case does not wholly rest upon mere disparagement of increased revenues from rents, but on a detailed argument against my 'deduction from the figures' that the 'numbers of the lord's ploughs roughly correspond to the decline in the area of the demesne lands he cultivated'. His argument purports to show that new holdings on the demesne were as a rule very few, and he bases this argument largely on his estimate of new holdings on the demesne in the survey of 1189. In doing so, he not only underestimates the probable amount of demesne lettings in that survey,[32] but what is even more important, apparently fails to realize that that survey, which is eighteen years later than his terminal date of 1171, cannot provide any evidence of

[30] See my Table 12.4; cf. also p. 259 'the rents of assize . . . changed relatively little, but . . . such changes as could be detected were mostly in the upward direction'.

[31] The only apparent fall in *gabulum* Mr Lennard is able to muster is in Baltonsborough, but this is because he mistook the annual render of the manor for its rent.

[32] Mr Lennard finds in the survey of 1181 lettings of demesne on a considerable scale only on the manors of Kington and Badbury. I believe that if the various 'free' holdings, especially those on the demesne 'forelands', 'overlands' and 'botland's' were properly analysed, large lettings would be found on many other manors, and most clearly in Blackford (45 to 50 acres), Ashbury (90 to 100 acres), South Brent (*c.* 95 acres). The subject of demesne lettings is too large to be dealt with merely in passing, and I hope to return to it again soon, but I should like to record here my conviction that peasant holdings were created on most demesnes throughout the twelfth century; and that this process, coupled with reclamation of waste, accounts for the striking difference between the demesnes in the late twelfth century and their antecedents ('old demesnes', 'inland') of the eleventh and the early twelfth centuries.

the changes on the demesne which may have occurred in the first seventy years of the century. The main function of a manorial survey or custumal was to register the changes which had occurred since the previous survey. As there obviously had been a survey in 1171 or soon after that date, the survey of 1189 would normally draw attention to changes which may have occurred in the intervening eighteen or twenty years. This simple proposition of manorial diplomatics is clearly reflected in those dates which the survey of 1189 in fact mentions. Some of the changes which had taken place before 1171 are referred to as having taken place in Bishop Henry's time, but many of these changes (e.g. new holdings on 'botland') are listed without dates. In general a large proportion, probably most of the new rents and holdings, are said to have been introduced in the time of Abbot Robert, i.e. 1171 and 1188.[33]

However, what I find most puzzling is not Mr Lennard's excessive reliance on an irrelevant survey, but that he should have thought this evidence in any way pertinent to my argument. Why should he find it necessary to prove that the new rents, the areas of new demesne holdings, and the decline of demesne teams were not always in close or faithful correspondence? Did I or anyone else ever suggest that they were? In case other readers might share Mr Lennard's misapprehensions about what I actually said in my article, I shall allow myself to reproduce the relevant passage. On p. 259 of my note I remind the readers that

> if the total yield from rents sometimes fell, it was merely because holdings lapsed, were abandoned by tenants, or were expropriated by landlords; if they rose this was mostly when additional land was let out to rent-paying tenants so that *incrementum reddite* could be charged or else when other customary dues such as labour services were commuted for money, and money payments were lumped with the rent.

I then proceeded to remind the readers that when 'we find customary rents rising, as they appear to have done in the twelfth century, the presumption is that *either* more land was let out to tenants, *or* that higher rent was being paid in respect of services commuted *or both*'.[34] In these passages a second variable – that of commuted services – accompanies all my references to decline of demesne arable, but had I been able to anticipate misconceptions like Mr Lennard's I might also have added a few words about new lands won from the waste and about the demesne acres and furlongs which could be lost to cultivation altogether, not taken up by peasant tenants, and therefore yield no rent: a circumstance to which I drew attention elsewhere.[35] And it is these and similar circum-

[33] The difficulty of listing the changes which occurred before Bishop Robert's time is that they are entered undated. However cf. n. 32 above.

[34] My note, *Econ. Hist. Rev.* v (1953), p. 336 (italics not in the text).

[35] E.g. my article 'The Fifteenth Century', *Econ. Hist. Rev.* IX (1939), 161 (reprinted as Chapter 3 above).

stances that I had in mind in penning the concluding passage of my note. To quote again: 'though the rents rose, they were not sufficient to lift the general level of manorial income or to counteract in full the slump of income from the direct exploitation of the demesne'. In fact neither I, nor anyone else I know of, ever been so foolish or so ignorant as to argue that changes in demesne plough-teams were the only cause of fluctuating rents and that reduction in teams would therefore result in immediate and proportionate increases in the lord's rents.

So much for Mr Lennard's general argument number one. His argument number two is that the numbers of plough-teams and oxen in the surveys, and presumably in the Domesday Book, represent not a true inventory of stock employed on the demesne, but only a statement of the farmer's responsibility for the stock received from the landlord; and that, consequently, the decline in the numbers of oxen in 1171 reflects not a reduction in the agricultural activities of the demesne, but merely a change in the terms of a farmer's lease or in their employment of stock.[36] I am afraid I find this theory unacceptable and unhelpful. It is unacceptable because it wrongly assumes that most Glastonbury estates were at farm; it is unhelpful because it leaves the important questions unanswered.

Let us begin with the unacceptable. Mr Lennard's argument that the decline in plough-teams must represent changes in stock received by farmers pre-supposes that the bulk of the manors were farmed both in 1130s and in 1171. This pre-supposition is in conflict with facts at two points at least. The first clash is with the proper sense of the Latin text. Mr Lennard does not quote in full the passages in the survey of 1171 dealing with stock. As that survey is not easily available, I may be allowed to repair Mr Lennard's omission by reproducing the relevant formula. In describing the manor of Street, the survey declares that in that manor

> tempore regis Henrici quando fuit ad firman erant ibi iij carruce queque de viij bobus, ij auri' et CC oves, sex sues, de gabulo assiso xx s. et iij d. Cum tali instauro reddebat C s. Modo sunt ibi xv boves, j aur', de gabulo assiso xxxiiij s. et iiij d. ob. et valet xlix s. et vj d.[37]

In my simplicity I took it and still take it to mean what it says, i.e. that in King Henry's time when the manor was held at farm its stock was *x*, but that now there were to be found on the manor the stock *y*. The compiler of the survey was obviously not averse from mentioning the farmer and the stock he took over where he had business to do so, i.e. in relation to the past. He did not do so in relation to the present because he obviously was dealing with the actual stock and not the farmer's responsibility for it. But another and an over-riding reason why the compiler

[36] Lennard, pp. 360–1.

[37] Hilbert's Survey, op. cit., fo. 115.

did not mention the farm at the later date is that on that date in most manors there was no farmer for him to mention; and therein Mr Lennard's second clash with his evidence will be found. For had he been able to give proper attention to other surveys of the late twelfth century, he would not have failed to notice that at that time a very large proportion of the Abbey's manors, including nearly all the manors in my table, *were not at farm*.

This rather crucial fact may be worth elucidating at somewhat greater length. The Savaricus survey of the end of the century begins with the statement that the Abbot found the following manors at farm and the following manors directly managed. The list of the manors directly managed comprises Glastonbury, Pilton, East Pennard, Ditcheat, Batcombe, Newton, Kentlesworth, Weston Zoy, Middle Zoy, Othery, Ham, Butleigh, Shapwick, Ashcot, Walton, Baltonsborough, Street, Brentmarsh, and Doulting: nineteen out of the thirty-eight manors listed. Moreover, the nineteen manors directly managed include most of the home manors, while of the nineteen odd manors not directly managed, several, i.e. at least three and possibly nine, were strictly speaking not at farm, but in the hands of the Bishop of St Davids, and only nine appear to have been unmistakably at farm.[38] This separation of manors farmed and unfarmed will not be found equally clearly in earlier surveys, but in case the readers might be inclined to assume that the change over had occurred in the 1190s, immediately before the election of Bishop Savaricus, they would be advised to pay attention to the distribution in the formulae recording the demesne stocks in the survey of 1189. This distinction is drawn more clearly still in the survey of 1171 and gives added meaning to the *fuit* in its formula *quando fuit ad firmam*. The manors in which this statement occurs have their stock enumerated twice: once when at farm, i.e. in 1130, and once in 1171. But only one enumeration – when at farm – is given for a number of manors, mostly outlying ones, which were still at farm in Bishop Savaricus' time, and presumably also at farm in 1171.[39]

38 Trinity Coll. MS. 724. R. 5.33. fo. 177d. The statement that the *Episcopus Menevensis habuit tunc* may apply only to the manors of Nettleton, Grittleton and Kington immediately following, but on purely etymological grounds could also be taken to apply to the seven manors at the end of the list.

39 In Hilbert's Survey of 1171, the wording of entries of the manors of Glastonbury, Street, Butleigh, Walton, Ashcot, Shapwick, Ham, Sowy, West Monkton, Brent, Wrington, Mells, Doulton, Pilton, East Pennard, Ditcheat, Baltonsborough and Lympsham – altogether a series of eighteen manors almost identical with the list of directly managed manors in the Savaricus survey and comprising most of the manors in my table of plough-teams, is the same as the formula for Street quoted in the text here. The other manors – also a list nearly identical with that of 'farm' manors in the Savaricus survey – say nothing about the stock 'now' (*modo*), and the typical formula is that of Winterbourne: '*tempore regis Henrici quando fuit ad firmam pro xiij li tunc habuit xvj boves et unum averum et de gabulo assiso xj li*'. Nothing is said about rents or stock in

So much for the facts behind Mr Lennard's theory. But as I have just said, the theory would be very unhelpful even if its facts were truer than they are. Mr Lennard's contention is composed of at least two independent propositions both of which appear to me to lead to highly improbable generalizations. Thus at one stage Mr Lennard appears to argue that the apparent decline in the numbers of oxteams may have resulted from more efficient employment of stock by the farmers. That in some places manors were understocked and in others overstocked, and that an overstocked manor might lose some of its stock without curtailing its arable, is something which needs no proof and which I took for granted in my note.[40] But how does this help to account for the fact that the changes were all in one direction and that in the period between the Domesday and Hilbert's Survey nineteen out of twenty manors in my table, and if I am not mistaken, twenty-one out of twenty-seven in Mr Lennard's list, showed a decline, and none, or at most two, manors showed a rise? Are we to conclude that in the hands of farmers the English manorial system in the twelfth century witnessed a general rise in the efficiency of capital? This conclusion would be so obviously at variance with the current views of twelfth-century England and so difficult to reconcile with the universal abolition of farming in the course of the thirteenth-century reforms, that I do not believe that Mr Lennard would be prepared to urge it. But the alternative conclusion would be that there was a real running down of stock by farmers – a conclusion not far removed from mine.

To my mind equally unhelpful is Mr Lennard's second proposition relating to farms. According to him, the figures of livestock represent mainly the lord's share of the farming stock and bear no necessary relation to stock actually employed. An unkind critic might, of course, point out that this argument is difficult to combine with the theory of more efficient utilization; but what worries me is the improbable generalization

1171, presumably because the manor was still at farm. In the survey of 1189 the difference appears to be reflected in references to stock. Whereas on manors like Winscombe, Christian Malford, Kington, Idmiston, Nettleton, Winterbourne, Pucklechurch and Brent, the *firmarii* are mentioned, or else the word '*receperunt*' is used to indicate that the stock was listed as received by farmers, on others the stock is either not mentioned at all, or else introduced without any reference direct or oblique to farms. In this group Brent appears to be the only manor not farmed in 1171.

[40] See n. 42 below. Mr Lennard appears to think that my note 'presupposes that the recorded plough-teams are the total numbers wholly employed on the demesnes and that these . . . were sufficient and no more than sufficient for their cultivation' p. 359. This is a misunderstanding. Nowhere did I assume full and efficient employment of stock, and it was unnecessary for me to do so. I was comparing plough-teams at different points of time, and for this purpose all I had to assume was that the efficiency of employment did not materially change during the period. In making this tacit assumption I weighted the case against myself. In the prevailing conditions of disorder and indirect management, efficiency was more likely to decline than to rise.

which it suggests. For if Mr Lennard's explanation were true, the figures in his and my list would indicate that the general tendency in the twelfth century was to raise the farmer's contribution of agricultural capital and to reduce the landlord's. How can this generalization be related to other features of the twelfth century, and where is the evidence to support it?

3

Much more could be said about some of the other aspects of Mr Lennard's handling of farms – his facts as well as his logic, but I propose to reserve my further comments on Glastonbury farms for a further occasion and pass to Mr Lennard's main and most general notion, i.e. that all the changes on the Glastonbury manors which I listed were local and accidental.[41]

There is no denying that on this question disagreement is to a large extent one of outlook and purpose. There will always be some historians who go to their evidence in the hope of finding general causes, and others who do the same in the hope of losing them. I am nevertheless sure that the difference between Mr Lennard and me is one not merely of temperament and philosophy. It is due partly to a disparity in the range of my and Mr Lennard's evidence and partly to an artificial and, I believe, untenable distinction between local events and general forces.

First of all, the range. To me the fact that the total area of plough-teams recorded in the survey of 1171 showed a decline of over 20 per cent compared with the 1130s, and that the decline was exhibited by an overwhelming majority of manors, whereas a rise occurred only in few, was sufficient to establish a *prima facie* possibility that a general tendency was at work. But what in my opinion turned a mere possibility into a high probability is the consistency of the facts of 1171 with other facts which unfortunately fall outside Mr Lennard's self-inflicted chronological and documentary limits. To begin with I could not dismiss the rest of the Trinity MS., which showed that the fall continued for at least another generation after 1171. This I tried to bring out in those columns of my tables which Mr Lennard has chosen to disregard. In addition I also had to take account of other facts which I discussed or at least mentioned elsewhere. Among these facts were the signs of similar decline on other great twelfth-century estates for which comparable evidence is available, i.e. those of Burton, Durham and Ramsey, and probably also on that of Shaftesbury. Above all, I had to bear in mind that the signs faded out or disappeared altogether in the thirteenth century. Taken all together the changes appeared to me too synchronous to be wholly local and accidental.

41 Lennard, pp. 362–3.

In the language of statisticians their distribution was sufficiently 'non-random' to suggest the probability of a general trend.[42]

Mr Lennard may consider my susceptibility to the logic of numbers excessive and my interpretation wrong. In that case I must be allowed to point out that if I err I do so in very good, indeed the best possible, company – that of the official chronicler of the Abbey. For when John of Glastonbury comes to describe the revival of the monastic estates under the reforming thirteenth-century Abbot, Michael of Amesbury, he appears to have no doubt as to what had happened before Michael had succeeded to the abbacy. For we are told that one of the Abbot's achievements was to restore the plough-teams which had fallen into disuse under his predecessor: *carrucas tempore predecessoris sui prostratas celeriter relevavit.*[43] John was obviously not the only contemporary who shared my error. Indeed the whole of Hilbert's survey, on which Mr Lennard has concentrated, reads as a document designed to draw attention to the decline since Henry I's time. For unless this was its purpose why should it have insisted on comparing at every point the situation in his time with that at the time of King Henry? Overt comparisons of this kind are not the real object of manorial surveys, and even if they were, it would have been strange to find the survey harking back to a period nearly forty years earlier. In fact the whole document is a kind of statistical lament for the good old times.[44]

Contemporary testimony alone would have been sufficient to make Mr Lennard's insistence on local causes appear over-confident. What makes them not only over-confident but also much too general is their underlying juxtaposition of local events to national causes. Needless to say, some local accidents there were, and I should have been the first to cite them had they been discoverable. But to account for all that was

[42] The synchronization of the figures would however come out even clearer had I grouped the manors according to the behaviour of their figures. Thus between the 1130s and 1171 the plough-teams in my Table 12.1 declined on thirteen manors, remained the same on six manors and increased on one. Between 1086 and 1171, plough-teams declined on nineteen manors, remained the same on one and increased on none.

[43] *John of Glastonbury's Chronicle* (Hearne, ed.), p. 215. But even if it were argued that John's reference is only to Bishop Savaricus and to Robert of Bath (1223–34) the fact still remains that he does not think it impossible that some abbacies should witness a decline in plough-teams while others should stage a recovery. A study of Glastonbury estates will not fail to bring out that, apart from the brief attempt at reform in Robert of Winchester's abbacy (1171–8), the low ebb continued almost uninterrupted until Abbot Michael's accession in 1225.

[44] Very occasionally other surveys also harked back to the good times of Bishop Henry, as in the Shapwick survey of 1189 recording that in Bishop Henry's time there were 320 oxen and also fourteen cows, 200 ewes and three pigs, which are no longer to be found on the manor (*ista modo ibi desunt*). *Liber Henrici de Soliaco*, p. 53.

happening on Glastonbury manors by fortuitous combination of local circumstances is to succumb to what is now rapidly becoming the occupational disease of historians. Nothing will nowadays win readier applause from the profession than the championship of local phenomena against the encroachment of historical generalization.[45] But it is my profound conviction that, by insisting on local and accidental character of economic changes in the Middle Ages, historians frequently conjure up an artificial contrast between general trends and local events. Very much of what, viewed from within parochial bounds, may appear to be a mere drip from the parish pump, will on more detached view turn out to be a local response to changing pressures in national water mains. Thus, the behaviour of demesne farmers at the different manors, indeed the very existence of farmers, may appear to Mr Lennard to be accidental; but to others they reflect the peculiar conditions of the twelfth century which made the employment of farmers necessary and the efficient control of them difficult. Similarly, the seizure of land by turbulent neighbours and all other incidents of feudal and civil war may appear to Mr Lennard merely as local incidents; but to others like myself (or for that matter the learned author of the *First Century of English Feudalism*) they appear as local manifestations of a *malaise* which during the greater part of the twelfth century affected England as a whole.

At the time when I wrote my note I did no more than hint at the general conditions and refrained from naming them. I was loth to anticipate the conclusions of my projected publications, and above all I did not want to give them out without the supporting evidence. Mr Lennard may therefore be forgiven for failing to divine my underlying hypotheses; and I should like now to repair the omission, however sketchily and briefly. In my view economic movement of the twelfth century was uneven and discontinuous. On the whole, population and settlement expanded, especially in the first thirty years of the century and in areas where lands could be reclaimed for peasant settlement. But signs of receding cultivation could often be found even on lands occupied by peasants and were very general on the lord's demesnes, especially after 1130. For the period between 1130 and the closing quarter of the century was unpropitious for demesne farming. The disturbed condition of the countryside made it difficult to control from afar the management of detached manors. The unsettlement of the times may also have checked the domestic trade in

45 This complaint is not addressed to historians who form the 'school' of local history and have in recent years made the most important contribution to local study – Mr Hoskins or Mr Finberg. Their 'local' studies appear to be conceived as contributions towards a generalized view of English developments (especially Mr Finberg's recent study of Withington in Gloucestershire: Department of Local History, University College of Leicester, Occasional Paper, no. 8, 1955).

agricultural produce, for prices appeared to stagnate at their different local levels. The lords were led to adopt the system of indirect management through farmers, but the system was everywhere inimical to expansion (its very purpose was to stabilize revenues). In most places rapacious or inefficient farming merely worsened the contraction of demesne areas and the dissipation of demesne capital. It was for these reasons that, with the return of settled times and with the revived buoyancy of markets and prices in the thirteenth century, direct management replaced leases to farmers, and agricultural expansion could be resumed on demesnes as well as on the lands occupied by peasants.

If this interpretation is correct – and it is this interpretation which lay behind my reference to general forces in the concluding paragraph of my note – all Mr Lennard has to say about farmers and disturbances is beside the point, and his insistence on local causes is in itself an unfounded generalization.

13

LEGAL STATUS AND ECONOMIC CONDITION IN MEDIEVAL VILLAGES[1]

1

In drawing the distinction between different layers of medieval village society we must guard ourselves against using the term 'classes' in a sense in which it is commonly employed in sociological discussion and in everyday discourse. Even in these discussions it is now generally admitted that in most periods of European history frontiers between classes have been neither permanent nor impassable, and that in the most class-ridden societies the frontiers have shifted from time to time and have at all times been crossed and recrossed by individuals. More impermanent still, and certainly much fainter than most of the observable class distinctions, were the demarcations between social groupings in the medieval village – indeed so faint were they that historians will justly hesitate to describe them as those of class.

Uncertain as the definition of social class is, it is commonly taken to apply to groups largely self-contained as regards social intercourse and inter-marriage and clearly marked off from each other by enduring differences of wealth or by unequal shares of power in state and society. In these respects English medieval society taken as a whole was far from classless. Few other societies have known such profound differences of status, wealth and authority and such impenetrable barriers to social intercourse as those which divided the top rank of the feudal order from other men and more especially from the great mass of villagers. The feudal landlords possessed the near-monopoly of the ownership of the soil; they commanded the sole access to political power in the state, and a great – sometimes overwhelming – influence in local administration. By contrast, the majority of the villagers held their land by inferior titles and paid heavily, in money or services, for such titles as they possessed. Nearly all of them stood in political and social subordination to their lords. Most

[1] This paper first appeared in *Modernization and Industrialization*, Essays presented to Yoshitaka Komatsu, Tokyo, 1968. The subject is treated similarly but somewhat more briefly by me in the second edition of the *Cambridge Economic History*, vol. I (Cambridge, 1966), pp. 604–17.

of them were their lords' serfs, had no part in the government of the country and but a small part in local administration. Indeed, the contrast between the two Englands – that of the subject mass of villagers on the one hand and that of the omnipotent feudal landlords on the other – was from some points of view the most fundamental feature of medieval society and also one of the main reasons why medieval economy developed, or failed to develop, in the way it did.

By comparison with this cleavage – the great crevasse of the social glacier – the lines which separated the urban bourgeoisie from the feudal top on the one hand and from the rural masses on the other, may not have been very profound or unbridgeable. Yet it also marked off a social group possessing most of the attributes of class in the usual sense of the term. It is only within the two main social divisions – the landlords and the villagers – that the relations of man to man give the general impression of a classless order. Men in the upper ranks of medieval England – from the humblest knights of the shire to the topmost magnates of the realm – were linked to each other by common attitudes and ethical standards, by mutual ties of contract and service and by unobstructed channels of social intercommunication, above all by those of family ties and marriage. In this sense medieval villagers were also a single class: theirs was a 'peasant' society forming, so to speak, a common 'universe of social intercourse'.

The term 'peasant' is used here advisedly. Like all social terms, it is sufficiently vague to mean different things in different contexts and to be often employed in a sense so loose as to be confusing. Yet the term and the concept behind it can be very useful in helping historians and sociologists to identify a distinct social group with attributes all its own. These attributes compose themselves into an 'ideal type' of a peasant which enables us to distinguish in a significant way the true peasantry of pre-industrial Europe or the underdeveloped Afro-Asian lands of our own times from the mere petty agriculturists of the American farm belt in the twentieth century or from their British counterparts, or from sections of medieval society, which though rural, could not be described as 'peasants'.

One of these attributes is that of scale, since a typical peasant could be expected to 'occupy' i.e. to inhabit and to cultivate, a holding of small or moderate size. Another attribute is that of labour: a typical peasant family would itself provide all or some of the labour required for the cultivation of his holding. Yet another attribute would be one of relative self-sufficiency: a typical peasant would consume all or most of his output within his own household. But perhaps the most important, even if intangible, attribute of the peasant would be found in his relation to land. To a typical peasant land is not merely a factor of production to be acquired or got rid of in obedience to his calculations of profitability, but an end in itself, an 'economic good', the possession of which establishes him as a head of a household and as a member of his village society, and measures his worth and standing therein.

These features of the peasantry, and above all the peculiarities of its labour supply, its relations to the market and its attitude to land, largely explain its successful competition for land and for survival with other and seemingly better-provided types of agricultural enterprise. It proved its viability during the agricultural crises of the nineteenth and twentieth centuries in Russia, Germany and elsewhere; a viability which is of course more striking and surprising in modern conditions than it would have been in the Middle Ages. For, as a social phenomenon, peasant agriculture fits more naturally into the economic background of the Middle Ages than it does into that of modern industrial civilization.

Needless to say, even in the Middle Ages, the 'ideal type' of peasants would seldom be found complete and pure. Yet historians will not fail to recognize in the physiognomy of the medieval villager most of the traits of a true peasantry. Some of the medieval villagers may have been landless or all but landless, while others have occupied extensive holdings; yet most villagers possessed family holdings of modest size, while many others occupied holdings not markedly greater or smaller than that. Similarly, even though many villagers employed hired labour, that labour was as a rule additional to the work of the holder himself and his family. A large share of the villagers' crop was of course grown for sale; yet there is no doubt that the average household largely depended on its own output for food and fodder. As for attitudes to land, they seem to have been equally typical. At any rate, this is the impression we get from what we know about the part which possession of land played in men's ability to marry or establish a family, and still more, from our knowledge of the village land market, its responsiveness to demographic factors, and its lack of response to such purely economic considerations as prices of agricultural produce.

This combination of attributes distinguished the medieval villagers from other classes of contemporary society and from rural societies of certain other centuries and epochs. Within the group, thus marked off, there were few barriers to social intercourse, and men freely mingled in those habitual associations which could be expected among members of the same social class. Judging by personal names in documents, villagers differing in wealth or legal condition acted as each other's witnesses to wills, warrantors in court and suitors in marriage. In the course of generations families throve and declined, but they very seldom rose so high or fell so low as to move out of peasant society altogether.

2

Social and economic differences within the village could not therefore be regarded as class distinctions in the strict sense of the term. This does not however make them any the less real or less amenable to historical study. On the contrary, the medieval village society must draw to itself the attention of historians, precisely because its social divisions were so easily crossed and recrossed, because its social grades were so unstable and, for this very reason, highly sensitive to historical influences. This is especially true of the economic demarcations. Broadly speaking social distinctions within peasant society composed themselves into two main patterns – that of legal status and that of economic condition; and naturally, the economic pattern exhibits most clearly and faithfully the action of economic forces in the countryside.

Differences in personal and legal status are of course more familiar to historians than those of economic condition. Every schoolboy now knows that in the country as a whole the majority of medieval villagers were men in semi-servile condition – villeins, serfs, *nativi*. Of late, medievalists have also been made aware of the large numbers of free or very nearly free villagers in most regions of medieval England, and especially in the eastern counties and in Kent. Historians have also been able to bring into view the various subdivisions of status within the main groups of free and unfree. Within the general class of villeins there were villeins holding wholly or mainly for rent (*censuarii*, molmen, *firmarii*), as well as villein-sokemen and customary tenants of royal demesne, whose status carried relatively few insignia of serfdom, especially in the matter of labour dues and arbitrary tallage. Among the free peasants historians have always distinguished between wholly free freeholders or franklains, on the one hand, and sokemen, on the other. Different categories of sokemen varied in their freedom of movement, their title to their land and their liability to labour dues.

All these distinctions, being legal in nature, were capable of being defined and proved by record of court and by other documentary testimony. They are therefore very well served by written evidence, lend themselves easily to historical study and have in fact been more fully studied and are better understood than other and perhaps more significant social differences. They were of course highly important. Free men had much easier access to royal courts than the villeins, especially in matters affecting their relations to their landlords or their titles to property. They had a far greater part to play in the affairs of government and local administration, though it appears that substantial villeins could participate in the most important of the local government functions, i.e. the service as juries and responsibility for the maintenance of order (i.e. view of frankpledge).

The disabilities of villein status, such as the obligation to pay a fine for marriage or for residence outside the manor, must also have influenced their general ranking in the eye of their contemporaries. But the chief disabilities of servile status were directly and indirectly economic. Most frequently, though not always, free holdings were charged with smaller payments than the servile ones. In some parts of the country rents charged on holders of free land were so much lower than the payments of villeins as to give the former an economic position and a social rank altogether superior to villeins holding the same amount of land. Heavier economic burdens often resulted from other disabilities of villeinage. Although marriage and residence outside the manor could be purchased easily and not very dearly, purchased they had to be. Even more burdensome could be the restrictions on the right to dispose freely of land or to enter into contracts. These were also subject to fines, and were thus mainly economic in their effect. Similarly, freedom of testamentary dispositions had also (certainly by the beginning of the thirteenth century) become purchasable by fine, commonly by means of transfers of land to would-be heirs *inter vivos*, but the purchase was an added economic burden on the villeins. On those occasions in the thirteenth century when the lords tried to reimpose labour services on their rent-paying tenants, the latter's villein status greatly prejudiced their chances of resistance and could result in the imposition of new heavy payments. Liability to labour services could in itself be a heavy economic burden, whether they were or were not discharged by hired substitutes; and almost equally heavy could be the lingering uncertainties of villein payments, and especially the liability to tallage.

The freedom of person and property must therefore have been prized not only for the social dignity and personal independence which they conferred but also for their economic benefits. Yet at a risk of a tautology I must stress that the economic demarcations in the countryside and the hierarchy of individuals according to their material condition were largely independent of their legal status. It is true that the topmost layer of village society, a layer in which it is somewhat difficult to distinguish the wealthy peasants from small landowners, was to a large extent composed of freeholders. Yet even in this layer villeins were to be found. Thus, to take but one example, in the Bishop of Worcester's manors, such as Blockley, holdings by military tenure could be as small as one virgate and even smaller, though freeholders for rent could be as large as four or three virgates each.[2] On the same manors, however, some villeins could

[2] M. Hollings (ed.), *The Red Book of Worcester*, parts I–IV, Worcester Hist. Soc., 1937–51, *passim*.

hold three and two virgates each. Similarly, customary tenants, i.e. villeins, may have predominated in the middle ranks of village society, but in some areas, especially in the eastern counties, there were numerous freeholders among the middling villagers. The lowest class of all, that of smallholders and all-but landless labourers, contained a very large number of freemen and sokemen. In some parts of the country wage-earning labourers were largely recruited from among poor freemen.

Thus freedom could not secure for a peasant a standard of life higher than that of most villeins, or prevent him from descending to the bottom of the economic ladder. This is probably why so few of the more substantial peasants went to the trouble of buying their legal freedom. While commutations of labour services were common and in the end became universal, instances of legal manumission, i.e. formal grants of full personal freedom, were comparatively rare. Some landlords granted, or were requested to grant, manumissions more frequently than others. Manumissions were very few on the Glastonbury estates; they were more frequent on the estates of St Swithins Priory, Winchester. Yet even there the numbers of manumissions in any one year seldom exceeded two, and whole years and even decades could pass without a single manumission. More frequent again were the manumissions on the estates of the Bishop of Winchester before 1289 (they cease almost altogether after that date). In the 31 years between 1209 and 1289, for which the evidence is available, the total number of manumissions was 218. This number does not include 22 manumissions in 1220 and 27 in 1245 which represent in the main the creation of burgage tenures in new towns. But it includes the relatively high number of 15, 11 and 14 for 1283, 1284, and 1285, which may also have been due to special causes. Even with these numbers, the total number of manumissions in the Bishop's 25 manors did not exceed 7 persons per annum. If manumissions in the missing years before 1289 were granted at the same rate as in the years for which records are available, the total number of manumissions in the preceding 80 years could not have been greater than 550. The total number of the Bishop's villein tenants exceeded 3400. In computing what proportion of the tenancy was at the end period represented by the cumulative totals of manumitted villeins we must bear in mind that when a manumitted villein moved away from the village or lived away from the manor, as some undoubtedly did, his place could be taken by another villein. We must therefore reckon that by 1289 or, what is the same thing, 1345, the process of manumission had reduced the villein tenancy of the Bishop by about 10 per cent.[3]

Among the very numerous cases before the Royal Courts concerning the

[3] The evidence of the manumission on the Bishop's estates come from the unpublished Cambridge thesis of J. Z. Titow.

status of individual villagers, claims to freedom by manumission are equally rare, though allegations of presumed freedom, i.e. freedom implied in the possession of charters or in land-holding by free title, were very frequently claimed.

The landlords may of course have been reluctant to grant full manumission, but there is no reason for supposing that this reluctance, like other similar reluctances, could not have been overcome at a price, or that the price would have been beyond the reach of the wealthier peasants. Where documents happen to record payments for manumission they are seldom as high as the fines for entry into substantial holdings, or as the purchase money villagers paid to each other for quite small parcels of land. When in 1265 one of the Glastonbury tenants, William Guneman, bought his manumission he paid for it no more than 2½ marks, which was at that time much less than the entry fine for quite a small holding.[4] Payments for manumission on Winchester manors were apparently equally modest and, as a rule, much lower than the average entry fines of virgates. Yet the numbers of villeins who paid entry fines for virgate holdings and remained villeins were many times greater than the numbers of men who paid fines for manumission.

The student of medieval court rolls and charters is thus bound to carry away the impression that although freedom had an economic value and was in itself a desirable attribute, it did not rank in current valuation as high as additional land or as many other purely economic acquisitions, such as additional pasture, or the right to build a house or sublet a tenancy. Hence the frequent occurrence of marriages of free men to serf-women: marriages which sacrificed the personal status of descendants to the immediate economic advantages of a good match. The instances of men voluntarily accepting a servile condition not only for their future children, but also for themselves, are not of course very common, though much commoner than they might have been had freedom ranked more highly in people's estimation than the possession of land. The men who contracted away their freedom for the sake of villein holdings were to be found among the recent immigrants into villages, such as the *liberi et adventitii* on the manors of St Albans, who, on taking on villein land, made a contract with the lord to be 'in scot and lot', to render tallage and services, pay merchet and heriot, and to be subject to him in body and goods. And now and again we find free men or holders of free land who were not *adventitii*, accepting similar conditions.[5]

[4] Numerous similar instances will be found in the Glastonbury Court Rolls, *Longleat MSS., passim.*

[5] Sources contain numerous references to tenants by free title claiming villein status for greater security of tenure, or as a bar to pleas of debt, or to support claims of inheritance; e.g. C. H. Fowler (ed.), *Cal. of the Rolls of the Justices in Eyre*, 1247, Beds. Hist. Soc., vol. XXI (1939), no. 205. In *Curia Regis Rolls*, vol.

3

We must therefore conclude that even though free status and serfdom must have left a powerful imprint on the lives of men, they were not the distinctions to which the villagers themselves attached the greatest importance. It may even be that the value which the villagers attached to the purely economic benefits of freedom were lower than they need have been. The economic historian has the advantage over contemporaries in being able to view the economic consequences of status as it changed through time. And when viewed across centuries, the economic disabilities of serfdom may well turn out to have been greater than they appeared to be to the villagers themselves at any single point of time. For even when at the beginning of our period the economic position of villeins or freeholders occupying holdings of the same size happened to be very similar, the freeholder or a villein holding for free rent would fare better in the subsequent 200 or 250 years than men holding by uncommuted and unreformed villein service.

The effects of twelfth-century changes on the freeholders or the *censuarii* are of course difficult to gauge. In the old and unregenerate days of medieval historiography it was generally believed that it was during the twelfth century that the manorial system finally took shape and villeinage became universal. Even an historian so firmly anchored in documentary evidence as Vinogradoff spoke at times of the twelfth century as the period which added the final instalment to the process whereby freemen and sokemen were reduced to serfdom. This may have happened in legal theory, for in the course of the twelfth century the lawyers gave the concept of villeinage the definition and the conformity it may have previously lacked. This was not, however, the actual course of events in villages. In some places the villagers were for a time oppressed by arbitrary exactions, but taking England as a whole this was the time when the number of men holding by free title or at rent greatly multiplied.

Although reliable statisical comparison between the Domesday Book and thirteenth-century sources is very difficult, it is probably true that, as Kosminsky believed, there are relatively more freeholders in the documents of the thirteenth century, i.e., in the Hundred Rolls and the Surveys, than in the Domesday Book. But it is perhaps unlikely that the increases were very great since most additions to the numbers of wholly

VI (1210–12) a plaintiff alleges that his creditors unlawfully seized his crops after he had '*deposuit se di libero servicio terre sua in Akeburne et posuit se in servicio villenagio*'. Instances of free men marrying bondwomen for the sake of their land abound in our sources: e.g. *Curia Regis Rolls*, vol. IV (Selden Soc. Publications), p. 305 (A.D. 1206). For a twelfth-century case of voluntary submission to villeinage of 3 immigrants, allegedly free, ibid. vol. I, p. 45.

free men would probably come by direct descent from the freeholders of the Domesday. Whether considerable additions could have come from other sources is doubtful. We have seen that manumissions were few and far between. Colonization played a highly important part in spreading free land tenure, though now and again, especially in the twelfth century, servile holdings, as well as free ones, were being established on recently reclaimed land. But however great were the emancipating effects of colonization on tenure, they were not as a rule capable of changing the legal condition of men. In many cases in which we find newly assarted holdings held as free land they were frequently no more than appendages to customary tenancies held by villein title and by villeins.

Another process whereby the numbers of freeholders could be somewhat increased was the widespread conversion of villein holdings into rent tenancies; but it is very doubtful whether many villagers improved their legal status thereby. In thirteenth-century surveys the rent-paying customary tenants were as a rule described and classified as such, i.e. as *censuarii*, as molmen, or *firmarii*, or simply as customary tenants at rent. When at the turn of the twelfth and thirteenth centuries on a number of estates, such as those of Bury St Edmunds, the question of the rights and obligations of molmen was called into question, the manorial juries had no difficulty in defining their legal position for what it was: that of customary tenants, i.e. villeins, who had at some time in the past been able to convert their various obligations into money rent. Similarly when rent-paying tenants and molmen tried on occasions to claim free status before royal courts, they hardly ever succeeded in doing so. Freedom from servile dues did not make a man a freeholder.

So even if here and there squatters on assarted land, *adventitii* and some rent-paying villeins managed to 'pass' as free men, the bulk of free peasants of the thirteenth century must have descended from the free men of the earlier centuries. In other words, if the number of freemen increased, that increase was to a large extent a demographic process, so that the relative proportions of wholly free villagers could not have increased very greatly. On the other hand, if freedom is taken in its broader sense, i.e. that of conditions of tenure, rather than that of personal status, the twelfth century undoubtedly was a time when freedom, though diluted and restricted to rent and services, spread far and wide.[6]

What effect did this have, or could this have had, on the economic conditions of men? Undoubtedly villeins who acquired newly colonized land free from labour services or, still more, succeeded in converting their villein holdings into those of molland or *terra ad censum* must have greatly benefited from the economic climate of the late twelfth or the

[6] *Cambridge Economic History*, vol. I, 2nd ed., pp. 604–10; M. Postan, 'Chronology of Labour Services', *Trans. R. Hist. Soc.*, 1937 (reprinted as Chapter 7 above).

early thirteenth centuries. The spectacular rise in prices which occurred at the turn of the century was bound to reduce the real weight of money rents fixed in the previous two generations. This alone should have made considerable difference to the economic position of villagers. The five shillings rent which a molman on the Bishop of Durham's manor of Newton-juxta-Boldon paid for his two-bovate holding in the 1170s was equivalent to about four quarters of wheat, or the net produce of about four acres, i.e. more than a quarter of his total area under seed, whereas in the first quarter of the fourteenth century the same rent represented not more than about one quarter of wheat or the output of one acre. For this reason, if for no other, men liable to fixed or 'free' rent, i.e. freeholders or sokemen, or customary tenants on the erstwhile royal demesne, found themselves at the thirteenth century paying a mere fraction of what was at that time the full rent of an equivalent servile holding.

The other twelfth-century changes from which villeins undoubtedly suffered, but to which freeholders must have been immune, were those resulting from the lord's arbitrary impositions and especially from his tallage. These impositions could be so heavy, and for all we know, so frequent as to break into patches of light and shadow our whole view of the twelfth century. While the widespread conversion of predial services into *censum*, *mala* and farms appeared to lighten the position of villeins, here and there new burdens, mostly tallage, darkened it.

As far as we know, both the light and the shadow were cast at one and the same time by the same combination of events. The twelfth-century villeins who converted their labour services into rent were able to do so by exploiting their lord's weakness in places where owing to political disorders he happened to be weak. Here and there the villeins, in changing over to rent, may even have taken the law into their own hands. But the same lack of governance and breakdown of centralized supervision may have enabled forceful and unscrupulous landlords, or the landlord's agents or farmers, to wreak their will upon their villeins. The *Rotuli di Domanibus* of *c.* 1185, in recording the measures taken by the King to repair the damages which the estates of widows and wards had suffered during the period of troubles, lists a number of manors where the local administrators greatly enhanced their value by merciless impositions on the villeins. We are told that when the Bishop of York had administration of the manor of Billinghay in Lincolnshire, he succeeded in raising its revenue from £6. 10*s* 8*d* to £16, which in the view of the jury was nearly £5 more than the most of the manor was worth. As a result, the jury tells us, *est villa distracta et homines distracti.*[7]

That the chief instrument of oppression was tallage is indicated by other similar cases, such as that of the manor in Missenden where

[7] J. H. Round (ed.), *Rotuli de Domanibus* (Pipe Rolls Pub.), p. 3.

augmented revenues came *de dono hominum* – the *donum*, or aid, being the current euphemism for tallage. Whether the rent-paying customary tenants were, like other villeins, subjected to the exactions we do not know. Their legal position was ill-defined and highly variable. On the occasions on which the lords levied tallages on the same pretexts as feudal aids, i.e., as help in times of political and military emergency, the liability fell not only on the villeins, but also on the freemen. On most estates, however, tallages were clearly distinguished from feudal aids and were imposed without any pretence of an emergency. From these tallages *censuarii* would not be legally exempt. Judging by the Bury St Edmunds example already cited, molmen and *firmarii* were, like other customary tenants, tallageable at will. It may well be that in the disturbed conditions of the mid-twelfth century the strict letter of the law mattered less than the relative positions of weakness and strength, and that where the villagers had sufficient strength to wring for themselves the right to hold for money rent they would probably also be able to resist attempts to impose heavy tallages. But the contrary is also true. In places in which the over-powerful lord ruled supreme, he could, if he wished, tallage mercilessly and indiscriminately both his villeins and his rent-paying *censuarii*. Only the freemen and perhaps the sokemen (especially the King's sokemen) would be able to resist the pressure.

This, so to speak, 'differential' reaction of free villagers and servile villeins to economic and political influences continued beyond the twelfth century into the thirteenth. To begin with, tallages themselves continued; on some manors they developed into a regular system of payments. In the course of this development the very nature of tallages may have changed. Judging by the few examples available to us, heavy tallages were rare in the twelfth century, and regular tallages were low. On the other hand, in the thirteenth century, tallages on some manors became regular and grew in weight from year to year. On these manors tallages were probably a means whereby the lords recouped themselves for the unyielding nature of customary rent, and in this respect they were substitutes for entry fines. If so, the use of tallages in lieu of entry fines brought yet another 'differential' disadvantage to villeins. For whereas entry fines were paid by all tenants irrespective of status, tallages were exacted only from tallageable men: as a rule villeins.

Free tenants and also probably the *censuarii* enjoyed an immunity from at least one other thirteenth-century development: they were spared the trials of manorial reaction. Where, as on the estates of the Bishops of Worcester and Ely, the landlords succeeded in redefining the labour services to the disadvantage of the tenants, and especially where they reverted to higher quotas of labour dues, the men who suffered were the villeins who were still holding on the old terms of *ad censum vel ad opus*, i.e. for rent or for work at the lord's will. The freeholder was in this respect beyond the landlord's reach, and so was also the *censuarius*. Only when and where the latter's tenurial contract had to be renegotiated – as when he sold his land, or passed it to an heir who was not a direct successor – could the lord insist and obtain additional rent. In general it remains true that the enhanced power over tenants, which landlords acquired as land grew scarcer and dearer, lay lightly on the *censuarii* and lighter still on the freeholders. The chief sufferers from the twin process of growing land shortage and manorial reaction were again the villeins.

So much for the economic consequences of legal status and tenurial title. They overlay the economic demarcations in village society without obscuring them. To the wealthy peasant, free personal status must have been an added economic benefit. But to the smallholders and landless men, the economic effects of status, linked though they were with payments for land, were of relatively small import. Some, or most, of their income came from wages, the income they derived from the cultivation of the holding, and consequently also the payments they owed the lord for them, were to that extent less important than they were to the middling villagers. And among these, freeholders (but not *censuarii*) were very few.

INDEX

Subjects of essays and their inclusive page references are in **bold** type, references to statistical tables are in *italic* type.